SECOND EDITION

# Programming Jakarta Struts

# Other Java™ resources from O'Reilly

**Related titles**
Java™ in a Nutshell
Head First Java™
Head First EJB™
Tomcat: The Definitive Guide
Learning Java™

Java™ Extreme Programming Cookbook
Java™ Servlet and JSP™ Cookbook™
Hardcore Java™
JavaServer™ Pages

**Java Books Resource Center**
*java.oreilly.com* is a complete catalog of O'Reilly's books on Java and related technologies, including sample chapters and code examples.

*OnJava.com* is a one-stop resource for enterprise Java developers, featuring news, code recipes, interviews, weblogs, and more.

**Conferences**
O'Reilly brings diverse innovators together to nurture the ideas that spark revolutionary industries. We specialize in documenting the latest tools and systems, translating the innovator's knowledge into useful skills for those in the trenches. Visit *conferences.oreilly.com* for our upcoming events.

Safari Bookshelf (*safari.oreilly.com*) is the premier online reference library for programmers and IT professionals. Conduct searches across more than 1,000 books. Subscribers can zero in on answers to time-critical questions in a matter of seconds. Read the books on your Bookshelf from cover to cover or simply flip to the page you need. Try it today with a free trial.

**SECOND EDITION**

# Programming Jakarta Struts

*Chuck Cavaness*

## O'REILLY®

Beijing · Cambridge · Farnham · Köln · Paris · Sebastopol · Taipei · Tokyo

**SHROFF PUBLISHERS & DISTRIBUTORS PVT. LTD.**
*Mumbai      Bangalore      Chennai      Kolkata      New Delhi*

**Programming Jakarta Struts, Second Edition**
by Chuck Cavaness

Published by O'Reilly & Associates, Inc., 1005 Gravenstein Highway North, Sebastopol, CA 95472.

O'Reilly & Associates books may be purchased for educational, business, or sales promotional
use. Online editions are also available for most titles (safari.oreilly.com). For more information,
contact our corporate/institutional sales department: (800)998-9938 or corporate@oreilly.com.

**Editor:** Brett McLaughlin

**Production Editor:** Philip Dangler

**Cover Designer:** Emma Colby

**Interior Designer:** Melanie Wang

**Printing History:**

> November 2002: First Edition.

> June 2004: Second Edition.

**Third Indian Reprint:** September 2005

**ISBN:** 81-7366-818-3

Published by **Shroff Publishers and Distributors Pvt. Ltd.** C-103, MIDC, TTC Industrial Area, Pawane,
Navi Mumbai 400 701, Tel: (91 22) 2763 4290, Fax: 2768 3337, e-mail: spdorders@shroffpublishers.com.
Printed at Decora Printer, Andheri, Mumbai.

# Table of Contents

# Preface

Over the last few years, web development has turned a very important corner. Gone are the days when Java™ developers wrestled with a single JSP that contained presentation logic, database access via SQL, and navigational intelligence. Java web developers have learned from their mistakes, paid the price in debugging and maintenance time, and moved on.

The number and variety of readily available web frameworks today is immense. It's hard to point a browser at a Java technical site without finding a newly released web framework that's going to revolutionize the modern world. While some may see this as a bad thing that might divide the Java community, the truth is that the constant emergence of new frameworks is just evolution at work.

The design and construction of today's nontrivial web applications pushes developers to the limit of what's logically and physically possible. Myriad solutions are thrown at the problems these applications present. Some of the solutions stick, and as with human evolution, valuable characteristics are passed on in future generations of software. Other solutions do not—those that fail to serve the needs of users and add value usually fall by the wayside.

Through this evolutionary process, the Jakarta Struts framework (created by Craig R. McClanahan and donated to the Apache Software Foundation in 2000) has emerged as one of the best web frameworks available. This book covers Version 1.1, which contains many major enhancements over the previous Jakarta Struts release. If you are building applications, web-based or not, one of the main things you will learn from this book is that frameworks such as Struts are a great time investment.

## Organization

This book begins with a preliminary discussion that lays the groundwork for the rest of the material. This discussion will be a refresher for some and completely new for others. From there, we explore the components of Struts's MVC implementation, including a look at the JSP custom tags that are part of the framework. Then, to round out your understanding of the value of the Struts framework, we look at several complicated but important topics related to building web-based applications.

Chapter 1, *Introduction*

This chapter discusses some preliminary concepts, such as the MVC pattern, Model 2, and the idea of a software framework. Although many developers may already be familiar with some or all of the ideas presented here, I want to ensure that all readers are starting from the same place. The concepts presented in this chapter help to lay the foundation for the rest of the book.

Chapter 2, *Inside the Web Tier*

The Struts framework is based on the Java Servlet technology and, to a lesser extent, JavaServer Pages, and therefore is tightly coupled to a web container. For Struts developers, understanding how the web container processes client requests is fundamental to understanding the framework itself. This chapter discusses the components of the web container and the responsibilities of each.

Chapter 3, *Overview of the Struts Framework*

This chapter provides an overview of the Struts framework; it does not attempt to cover all of the features or go into significant depth. It emphasizes how all the pieces fit into the MVC and Model 2 architecture presented in Chapter 1.

Chapter 4, *Configuring Struts Applications*

The Struts framework uses two separate but somewhat related types of configuration files, which must be configured properly before an application will function properly. Due to the popularity and flexibility of XML, both types of configuration files are based on XML. This chapter presents the syntax of the files.

Chapter 5, *Struts Controller Components*

The Struts framework uses a servlet to process incoming requests; however, it relies on many other components that are part of the controller domain to help it carry out its responsibilities. This chapter takes in-depth look at the components that are responsible for the controller functionality in the framework.

Chapter 6, *Struts Model Components*

This chapter introduces the components that make up the model portion of a Struts application. The model represents the business data for an application and should closely resemble the real-world entities and business processes for the organization. This chapter explores the roles and responsibilities of the model components within the Struts framework and focuses on building an architecturally correct implementation for the Storefront application. Special attention is given to using a persistence framework that can be integrated into a Struts application easily and effortlessly.

**Chapter 7, *Struts View Components***

This chapter introduces the components that make up the view portion of the Struts framework. The framework uses the view components to render dynamic content for the client. Based primarily on JavaServer Pages, the components provide support for internationalized applications as well as for user-input acceptance, validation, and error handling, all of which make it easier for the developer to focus on business requirements. This chapter concludes the three-part discussion of how the Struts framework implements the MVC pattern.

**Chapter 8, *JSP Custom Tag Libraries***

This chapter looks at the different categories of tags and how they can help make developing applications with the Struts framework even easier. It is not meant to be an exhaustive reference for every tag that's part of the Struts tag libraries—that information can be found within the Struts user guide or JavaDocs. The real purpose of this chapter is to put forth the benefits of using the Struts tag libraries and to provide a few strategies that can help make the switch to using the tags less painful.

**Chapter 9, *Extending the Struts Framework***

One of the biggest advantages of using a framework is the ability to extend and customize it based on the needs of the application. The Struts framework is no exception; it provides several important extension points for developers. This chapter takes a quick glance at several of those extension points and examines the benefits and drawbacks of extending the framework.

**Chapter 10, *Exception Handling***

This chapter looks at how to use the Java exception-handling mechanism within your Struts applications to make them more robust and allow them to respond gracefully when things don't go as expected. Special attention is given to the differences between performing the exception handling programmatically and using the new declarative feature added to the Struts framework in Version 1.1.

**Chapter 11, *The Validator Framework***

This chapter introduces the Validator framework, which was created specifically to work with Struts components. The Validator allows you to declaratively configure validation routines for a Struts application without having to program special validation logic.

**Chapter 12, *Internationalization and Struts***

This chapter focuses on what it takes to make a Struts application available to customers from around the world, regardless of their language or geographical location. As is often the case in software development, planning ahead is the most important thing that you can do to help ensure success. After reading this chapter, you should be able to build Struts applications that can support a broad range of customers.

Chapter 13, *Struts and Enterprise JavaBeans*

This chapter covers the issues you need to consider when developing an interface between your Struts actions and an application tier. It focuses on interfacing to a model built using Enterprise JavaBeans™ (EJB).

Chapter 14, *Using Tiles*

This chapter looks at the Tiles framework, which now is part of the core Struts distribution. The Tiles framework is an advanced templating framework that reduces the amount of redundant code a web application contains and allows developers to better separate content from layout.

Chapter 15, *Logging in a Struts Application*

This chapter examines how the use of logging in your Struts applications can help you identify defects before the applications get into production and, if your software already is being used in production, how logging can help you identify problems and arrive at solutions much more quickly.

Chapter 16, *Packaging Your Struts Application*

This chapter discusses the best practices for packaging and deploying a Struts application and what it takes to automate the build process for your environment. Special coverage is given to Ant, the Java-based build tool available from Jakarta.

Chapter 17, *Addressing Performance*

This chapter explores the performance implications of using the Struts framework and its associated technologies to build web applications and discusses how certain design and programming decisions affect the overall performance of the applications. It covers performance, load, and stress testing, and the steps necessary to carry out each.

Chapter 18, *JavaServer Faces*

This chapter provides an overview of yet another Java technology being birthed from the Java Community. JavaServer Faces provides some promising continuation for the Java web development community. Although some overlap exists between Struts and JSF, there is plenty of room for both and this chapter explores what that integration looks like.

Appendix A, *Changes Since Struts 1.0*

This appendix enumerates the new features within the 1.1 release.

Appendix B, *Downloading and Installing Struts*

This appendix discusses the steps for downloading and installing Struts in your environment.

Appendix C, *Resources*

This appendix lists several resources that can help increase your knowledge once you've mastered the concepts in this book.

# Conventions Used in This Book

The following font conventions are used in this book:

*Italic* is used for:

- Unix pathnames, filenames, and program names
- Internet addresses, such as domain names and URLs
- New terms where they are defined

**Boldface** is used for:

- Names of GUI items (window names, buttons, menu choices, etc.)

Constant width is used for:

- Command lines and options that should be typed verbatim
- Names and keywords in Java programs, including method names, variable names, and class names
- XML element names and tags, attribute names, and other XML constructs that appear as they would within an XML document

 Indicates a tip, suggestion, or general note.

 Indicates a warning or caution.

# Using Code Examples

This book is here to help you get your job done. In general, you may use the code in this book in your programs and documentation. You do not need to contact us for permission unless you're reproducing a significant portion of the code. For example, writing a program that uses several chunks of code from this book does not require permission. Selling or distributing a CD-ROM of examples from O'Reilly books *does* require permission. Answering a question by citing this book and quoting example code does not require permission. Incorporating a significant amount of example code from this book into your product's documentation *does* require permission.

We appreciate, but do not require, attribution. An attribution usually includes the title, author, publisher, and ISBN. For example: "*Programming Jakarta Struts*, Second Edition, by Chuck Cavaness. Copyright 2004 O'Reilly Media, Inc., 0-596-00651-9."

If you feel your use of code examples falls outside fair use or the permission given above, feel free to contact us at *permissions@oreilly.com*.

# Comments and Questions

Please address comments and questions concerning this book to the publisher:

O'Reilly Media, Inc.
1005 Gravenstein Highway North
Sebastopol, CA 95472
800-998-9938 (in the U.S. or Canada)
707-829-0515 (international or local)
707-829-0104 (fax)

There is a web page for this book, which lists errata, examples, and additional information. You can access this page at:

*http://www.oreilly.com/catalog/0596006519*

To comment or ask technical questions about this book, send email to:

*bookquestions@oreilly.com*

For more information about books, conferences, Resource Centers, and the O'Reilly Network, see the O'Reilly web site at:

*http://www.oreilly.com*

# Acknowledgments

Writing a book of this type is never the work of just one person; it literally takes an army of hardened soldiers, and this book is no exception. From the editors to the marketing organization to the reviewers of the manuscript, this book simply would not have been possible without the group of dedicated folks that gave up many of their nights and weekends to help ensure that the quality was the highest possible. Any credit should be given to all of the great people involved; any mistakes are mine alone.

First, I need to thank my O'Reilly editors, Brett McLaughlin and Robert Eckstein, two of the most dedicated and sincere editors that I have worked with. I hope we have a chance to work together on future projects. Your advice and leadership made the task much easier than I could have imagined. I also would like to thank Kyle Hart from O'Reilly's marketing department. Your help was dearly appreciated.

Next, I would like to acknowledge the team of fine developers that I first learned Struts with. The bond that our little NV team had was something special that comes around only once in a while. I really enjoyed working with all of you.

The following people played a special role by giving me advice on the book's content and direction: Steve Ardis, Jill Entinger, See Yam Lim, and Ted Husted (although Ted may not realize that he contributed in this way).

When I first decided to post the draft chapters of the book, I made a comment that if any reviewers went beyond the call of duty, I would personally thank them in the acknowledgments of the book. Little did I realize how many would take me up on it! There are so many that I can't thank each and every one individually. Over 100 people contributed feedback for one or more chapters of this book. The Struts community is by far one of the best. Almost every person on the Struts mailing list has contributed in one way or another. To each of you, thank you!

Thanks to the following people: John Guthrie, David Karr, Brent Kyle, Stefano Scheda, and Rick Reumann for asking all the right questions, Mark Galbreath for reminding me of my 10th-grade English teacher, and James Mitchell and James Holmes for getting me involved with the Atlanta Struts group.

I need to say a special thanks to Tim Drury for his help on Chapter 16. His Ant skills are known worldwide. Special thanks also to Brian Keeton, who wrote Chapter 13 because I'm too slow—he's the smartest EJB developer I know. Both of you are great friends and simply the finest humans that I've ever met. Just knowing you has made me a better person. I hope we can work together again.

The group at TheServerSide.com deserves special thanks from me and the reviewers for allowing the draft chapters of this book to be available for download. This is a great example of what the future holds for book publishing.

I would be remiss if I didn't thank the entire Struts community. I have met and corresponded with many smart developers who also strike me as just really fun people to hang around with. The feedback and suggestions I received during this process were awesome. I hope that all of you got some benefit out of this, and I appreciate everyone's patience while some of this was figured out as I went.

Finally, all Struts developers should give thanks to Craig McClanahan for having the wits about him to create the framework and make it freely available to the community. He could have tried to make a profit from it by starting Struts, Inc., but he realized that he would be rewarded ten-fold anyway, and I'm sure he has been. Craig, it's a nice framework, you should be proud. And to all of the committers on the Struts project, what would it really be without you? Thanks for all of your help.

# CHAPTER 1

# Introduction

The Struts open source framework was created to make it easier for developers to build web applications based on the Java Servlet and JavaServer Pages (JSP) technologies. Like a building, a web application must have a solid foundation from which the rest of the structure can grow. The Struts framework provides developers with a unified infrastructure upon which Internet applications can be based. Using Struts as the foundation allows developers to concentrate on building the business application rather than on the infrastructure.

The Struts framework was created by Craig R. McClanahan and donated to the Apache Software Foundation (ASF) in 2000. The project now has several committers from around the world, and many developers are contributing to the overall good of the framework. The Struts framework is one of many well-known and successful Apache Jakarta projects. Others include Ant, *log4j*, and Tomcat. The overall mission of the Jakarta project is to provide commercial-quality server solutions, based on the Java platform, in an open and cooperative fashion.

## A Brief History of the Web

No book on web technology would be complete without a brief look at how the World Wide Web (WWW) has become as popular as it is today. The Web has come a long way since the days when the first hypertext documents were sent over the Internet. In 1989, when the physicists at the CERN laboratory proposed the idea of sharing research information between researchers using hypertext documents, they had no idea how big the Web would grow or how essential it would become to daily life for much of the industrialized world. The Web is now an accepted part of our vernacular.

It took a while for the benefits of using the Web to become clear to others outside of CERN, but as we all know, it eventually erupted into what we use today. From its beginnings, the Web was designed for dealing with static documents, but it was a natural progression to want the ability to generate document content dynamically.

The *Common Gateway Interface* (CGI) was created to do that very thing. CGI is a standard that allows web servers to interact with external applications in such a way that hypertext pages no longer have to be static. A CGI program can retrieve results from a database and insert those results as a table in a hypertext document. Likewise, data entered into a hypertext page can be inserted into the database. This technology opened up infinite possibilities and, in fact, started the Internet craze of the mid-1990s and today.

Although CGI applications are very good at what they do, there are some serious limitations to this approach. For one thing, CGI applications are very resource-intensive. A new operating system (OS) heavyweight process is created to handle every request that comes from a browser. Once the CGI script is finished executing, the process has to be reclaimed by the OS. This constant starting and stopping of heavyweight processes is terribly inefficient. You can imagine how bad the response time might be if hundreds of concurrent users were making requests to the same web application. Another major limitation of CGI is that it's difficult to link to other stages of request processing, because it is running in a separate process from the web server. This makes it difficult to handle things such as authorization, workflow, and logging.

A few alternatives to standard CGI applications have been put forward. One alternative is *FastCGI*, a language-independent extension to CGI that doesn't have the same process model as standard CGI. It's able to create a single heavyweight process for each FastCGI program, allowing multiple requests to run within the same process space. However, when clients interact concurrently with the same FastCGI program, the program needs to create a pool of processes to handle each request. This is not much better than standard CGI. Another problem with FastCGI applications is that they're only as portable as the languages in which they are written. Other alternatives to CGI include mod_perl for Apache, NSAPI for Netscape, and ISAPI for Microsoft's IIS web server. While these solutions often offer better performance and scalability than standard CGI programs, they still have portability issues.

In 1997, while the Java language was experiencing tremendous growth and use by application developers, the Java Servlet technology was created. This new web technology opened up an entirely new avenue for web developers to explore.

# What Are Java Servlets?

Java servlets have become the mainstay for extending and enhancing web applications using the Java platform. They provide a component-based, platform-independent method for building web applications. Servlets don't suffer from the same performance limitations that standard CGI applications incur. Servlets are more efficient than the standard CGI threading model because they create a single heavyweight process and allow each user request to use a much more lightweight thread, which is maintained by the Java Virtual Machine (JVM), to fulfill the request. Multiple user requests can be threaded through the same instance of a servlet. A servlet is mapped to one or more *uniform resource locators* (URLs), and when the server receives a request to one of the servlet URLs, the service method in the servlet is invoked and it responds. Because each user request is associated with a separate thread, multiple threads or users can invoke the service method at the same time. This multithreaded nature of servlets is one of the main reasons that they are more scalable than standard CGI applications. Also, because servlets are written in Java, they are not proprietary to a platform or OS.

Another significant advantage of being written in the Java language is that servlets are able to exploit the entire suite of Java application programming interfaces (APIs), including Java DataBase Connectivity™ (JDBC) and Enterprise JavaBeans (EJB). This was one of the factors in servlets becoming part of the mainstream so quickly; there already was a rich Java library in place for them to leverage.

Servlets are not executed directly by a web server. They require a servlet container, sometimes referred to as a servlet engine, to host the servlet. This servlet container is loosely coupled to a particular instance of a web server, and together they cooperate to service requests. Figure 1-1 illustrates how a web server and servlet container cooperate to service a request from a web browser.

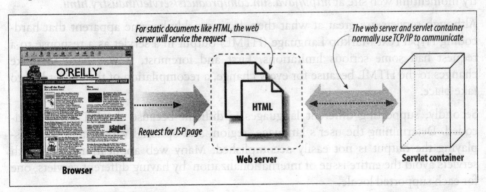

*Figure 1-1. Processing a client request*

Developers are free to choose from one of many servlet containers available to host their servlets; they are not locked into a particular vendor or platform. Servlets can be ported to any of these containers without recompiling the source code. This leads to a "best of breed" solution for web applications—you get the best product or component for a specialized need, while at the same time avoiding the high risk normally associated with a single solution.

There are several popular servlet containers on the market. Some are standalone servlet containers that must be connected to an external web server to work, while others provide both the web server and servlet container in the same product. There are even a few that are integrated into application servers and provide much more functionality than just a servlet container. Table 1-1 lists some of the more popular servlet containers. Some of the products in this list are commercial products while others listed have a small or insignificant cost to use.

*Table 1-1. Popular servlet containers*

| Servlet container | URL |
|---|---|
| Borland Enterprise Server | http://www.inprise.com |
| Sun One Application Server | http://www.sun.com |
| Jetty | http://jetty.mortbay.org/jetty/index.html |
| JRun | http://www.macromedia.com/software/jrun |
| Orion Application Server | http://www.orionserver.com |
| Resin | http://www.caucho.com |
| Apache Tomcat | http://jakarta.apache.org/tomcat |
| Weblogic Application Server | http://www.bea.com |
| WebSphere | http://www-4.ibm.com/software/webservers/appserv |
| EAServer | http://www.sybase.com |

For a more complete listing of available servlet containers, visit Sun's servlet industry momentum web site at *http://java.sun.com/products/servlet/industry.html*.

Although servlets are great at what they do, it quickly became apparent that hardcoding HyperText Markup Language (HTML) output in a servlet as a response to a request had some serious limitations. First and foremost, it was hard to make changes to the HTML because for every change, a recompilation of the servlet had to take place.

Secondly, supporting different languages is difficult because the HTML is hardcoded. Determining the user's language, region, and optional variant and then displaying the output is not easily accomplished. Many web applications built with servlets avoid the entire issue of internationalization* by having different servlets, one for each supported locale.

Finally, because HTML was embedded within the servlet, there was a problem with responsibility. Web designers build HTML pages; they are not usually experienced with Java programming, let alone skilled at object-oriented design and programming. When you mix HTML and Java code within the servlet, it becomes hard to separate the page design and programming duties. Even when a developer has the necessary skills to perform both functions, modifications to the page layout require recompilation, which adds to development and testing time.

---

* Interrnationalization is commonly referred to as "I18N" because the word begins with the letter I, ends with the letter N, and contains 18 characters in between.

Servlet programming is such a broad topic that it can't be covered in great detail here. If you feel that you need more information on Java Servlet technology, a great source of material is Jason Hunter's *Java Servlet Programming* (O'Reilly). You can also find more information at the Sun Servlet web site *(http://java.sun.com/products/servlet/index.html)*.

JavaServer Pages was the next step in the linear progression of developing web technologies based on the Java platform. The introduction of JSP pages, as they are commonly referred to, helped to alleviate the servlet limitations mentioned earlier and opened up many new doors for web developers.

# JavaServer Pages

The first thing to understand about JavaServer Pages is that it's a natural extension to the Java Servlet technology. In fact, after some preprocessing by a translator, JSP pages end up being nothing more than Java servlets. This is a point that many beginning developers have a hard time understanding. JSP pages are text documents that have a *.jsp* extension and contain a combination of static HTML and XML–like tags and scriptlets. The tags and scriptlets encapsulate the logic that generates the content for the pages. The *.jsp* files are preprocessed and turned into *.java* files. At this point, a Java compiler compiles the source and creates a *.class* file that can be executed by a servlet container.

The translator that turns the *.jsp* file into a *.java* file takes care of the tedious work of creating a Java servlet from the JSP page. Figure 1-2 illustrates how a JSP page is translated and compiled into a servlet.

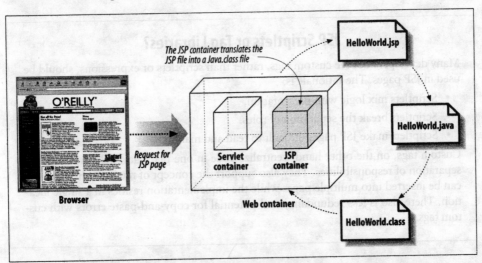

*Figure 1-2. A JSP page is translated and compiled into a Java servlet*

JSP technology has become an extremely popular solution for building web applications using the Java platform. JSP offers several advantages over its competitors:

- JSP is a specification, not a product. Developers are able to choose a "best of breed" approach.

- JSP pages are compiled, not interpreted, which can lead to better performance.

- JSP pages support both scripting and access to the full Java language and can be extended through the use of custom tags.

- JSP pages share the Write Once, Run Anywhere™ characteristics of Java technology.

As mentioned in the previous section, one of the limitations of using hardcoded HTML inside of servlets is the problem of separating page design and application logic programming responsibilities. This separation is easier with JSP pages, because the HTML designers are free to create web pages with whatever tools they choose (many of today's popular tools are capable of working with JSP and custom tags). When they are comfortable with the page layout, the JSP developers can insert JSP scriptlets and custom tags and save the files with a *.jsp* extension. That's pretty much all there is to it. When the time comes to change either the page layout or page logic, the developer modifies the JSP page as needed and allows it to be recompiled automatically.

Together, JSP pages and servlets are an attractive alternative to other types of dynamic web programming. Because both are based on the Java language, they offer platform-independence, extensibility into the enterprise, and, most importantly, ease of development.

---

## JSP Scriptlets or Tag Libraries?

Many developers believe custom tags, rather than scriptlets or expressions, should be used in JSP pages. The rationale is:

- Scriptlets mix logic with presentation.
- Scriptlets break the separation of roles.
- Scriptlets make JSP pages difficult to read and maintain.

Custom tags, on the other hand, centralize code in one place and help maintain the separation of responsibilities. They also support the concept of reuse, as the same tag can be inserted into multiple pages while the implementation resides in a single location. There also is less redundancy and potential for copy-and-paste errors with custom tags.

---

## JSP Model 1 and Model 2 Architectures

The early JSP specifications presented two approaches for building web applications using JSP technology. These two approaches were the JSP *Model 1* and *Model 2* architectures. Although these terms are no longer used in the JSP specification, they still are widely used throughout the web tier development community.

The two JSP architectures differ in several key areas. The major difference is in how and by which component the processing of a request is handled. With the Model 1 architecture, the JSP page handles all of the processing of the request and is responsible for displaying the output to the client. This is illustrated in Figure 1-3.

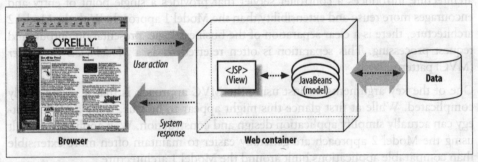

*Figure 1-3. JSP Model 1 architecture*

Notice that there is no servlet involved in the process. The client request is sent directly to a JSP page, which may communicate with JavaBeans or other services, but ultimately the JSP page selects the next page for the client. The next view is determined based on either the JSP selected or parameters within the client's request.

In contrast, in the Model 2 architecture, the client request is first intercepted by a servlet, commonly referred to as a *controller servlet*. This servlet handles the initial processing of the request and determines which JSP page to display next. This approach is illustrated in Figure 1-4.

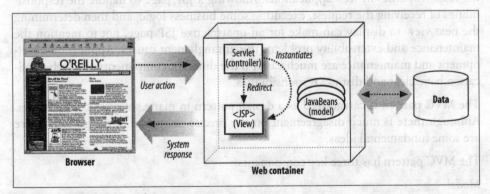

*Figure 1-4. JSP Model 2 architecture*

As shown in the figure, a client never sends a request directly to a JSP page in the Model 2 architecture. This allows the servlet to perform front-end processing, including authentication and authorization, centralized logging, and help with internationalization. Once request processing has completed, the servlet directs the request to the appropriate JSP page. How the next page is determined varies widely across different applications. For example, in simpler applications, the next JSP page to display may be hardcoded in the servlet based on the request, parameters, and current application state. In more sophisticated web applications, a workflow/rules engine might possibly be used.

As you can see, the main difference between the two approaches is that the Model 2 architecture introduces a controller servlet that provides a single point of entry and encourages more reuse and extensibility than the Model 1 approach. With the Model 2 architecture, there is a clear separation of the business logic, presentation output, and request processing. This separation is often referred to as a *Model-View-Controller* (MVC) pattern.

One of the key arguments against using the MVC approach is that it seems overly complicated. While at first glance this might appear to be true, using a MVC strategy can actually simplify application design and construction. Web applications built using the Model 2 approach are generally easier to maintain often more extensible than comparable applications built around the Model 1 architecture.

# Why Is Model-View-Controller So Important?

The MVC architectural pattern is not directly related to web applications or Java for that matter. In fact, it's quite common in Smalltalk applications, which generally have nothing to do with the Web.

As we saw in the previous section, the Model 2 approach is concerned with separating responsibilities in web applications. Allowing a JSP page to handle the responsibilities of receiving the request, executing some business logic, and then determining the next view to display can make for an unattractive JSP page, not to mention the maintenance and extensibility problems this entanglement causes. Application development and maintenance are much easier if the different components of a web application have clear and distinct responsibilities.

The MVC pattern is categorized as a design pattern in many software design books. Although there is much disagreement on the precise definition of the pattern, there are some fundamental ideas.

The MVC pattern has three key components:

*Model*
    Responsible for the business domain state knowledge

*View*
  Responsible for a presentation view of the business domain
*Controller*
  Responsible for controlling the flow and state of the user input

With the MVC pattern, a form of event notification usually takes place to notify the view when some portion of the model changes. However, because a browser in a typical web application has a stateless connection, the notification from the model to the view cannot occur easily.\* Of course, an application could perform some type of push mechanism to push notification or data all the way to a client, but this is overkill for most web applications. A user can close the browser at any time, and generally no notification is sent to the server. A great deal of overhead is necessary to manage remote clients from the server side. This type of behavior is not necessary for typical web applications.

With standard web applications, a client typically sends another request to the server to learn about any changes to the model. This is known as a "pull" approach. For example, if a user is viewing pricing information for an item and at the same time the administrator changes the price for that item, the user will not know it changed until he refreshes the page.

## The MVC Model

Depending on the type of architecture your application uses, the model portion of the MVC pattern can take many different forms. In a two-tier application, where the web tier interacts directly with a data store such as a database, the model classes may be a set of regular Java objects. These objects may be populated manually from a ResultSet returned by a database query, or they may be instantiated and populated automatically by an *object-to-relational mapping* (ORM) framework such as TopLink or CocoBase.

In a more complex enterprise application (where the web tier communicates with an EJB server, for example), the model portion of the MVC pattern will be Enterprise JavaBeans. Although the EJB 2.0 specification made performance improvements through the use of local interfaces, there still can be a significant performance impact if the web tier attempts to use entity beans directly as the model portion of the application, due to the overhead of making remote calls. In many cases, JavaBeans are returned from session beans and used within the web tier. These JavaBeans, commonly referred to as data transfer objects, are used within the views to build the dynamic content.

---

\* Web applications are considered stateless because the browser doesn't maintain a constant open connection to the web server. However, a web application still may maintain session data for a user or even store data within the browser on behalf of the user.

## The MVC View

The views within the web tier MVC pattern typically consist of HTML and JSP pages. HTML pages are used to serve static content, while JSP pages can be used to serve both static and dynamic content. Most dynamic content is generated in the web tier. However, some applications may require client-side JavaScript. This does not interfere with or infringe upon the MVC concept.

HTML and JSP are not the only choice for the view. You easily can support WML, for example, instead of HTML. Because the view is decoupled from the model, you can support multiple views, each for a different client type, using the same model components.

## The MVC Controller

The controller portion of the web tier MVC design generally is a Java servlet. The controller in a web tier application performs the following duties:

1. Intercepts HTTP requests from a client
2. Translates each request into a specific business operation to perform
3. Either invokes the business operation itself or delegates it to a handler
4. Helps to select the next view to display to the client
5. Returns the view to the client

The *Front Controller* pattern, which is part of the Java 2 Platform, Enterprise Edition (J2EE) Design Patterns (found at *http://java.sun.com/blueprints/patterns/index.html*), describes how a web tier controller should be implemented. Because all client requests and responses go through the controller, there is a centralized point of control for the web application. This helps when adding new functionality. Code that would normally need to be put in every JSP page can be put in the controller servlet, which processes all the requests. The controller also helps to decouple the presentation components (views) from the business operations, further aiding development.

## What Is a Framework?

I have been using the term *framework* in this chapter without having defined what exactly it is, or how it adds value in software development. In its simplest form, a framework is a set of classes and interfaces that cooperate to solve a specific type of software problem. A framework has the following characteristics:

- A framework comprises multiple classes or components, each of which may provide an abstraction of some particular concept.
- The framework defines how these abstractions work together to solve a problem.
- Framework components are reusable.
- A framework organizes patterns at a higher level.

A good framework should provide generic behavior that many different types of applications can make use of.

There are many interpretations of what constitutes a framework. Some might consider the classes and interfaces provided by the Java language a framework, but these are really a library. There's a subtle, but very important, difference between a software library and a framework. A software library contains functions or routines that your application can invoke. A framework, on the other hand, provides generic, cooperative components that your application extends to provide a particular set of functions. The places where the framework can be extended are known as *extension points*. A framework commonly is referred to as an "upside-down" library because of the alternate manner in which it operates. Figure 1-5 illustrates the subtle differences between frameworks and software libraries.

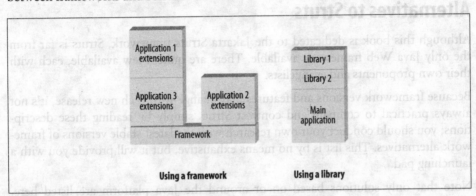

*Figure 1-5. A framework and a library are not the same thing*

## Creation of the Struts Framework

The Struts framework was created by Craig R. McClanahan and donated to the ASF in 2000. Craig is deeply involved in the expert groups for the Servlet and JSP specifications and wrote a large portion of the Tomcat implementation. He also speaks at various conferences, including JavaOne and ApacheCon.

Several committers[*] have joined the Struts project, and even more developers have volunteered their time and effort to improve it and increase its value. As a result, the framework has gone through several beta releases and a few general availability (GA) releases, and although many new features have been added, the framework hasn't strayed far from its core ideas.

---

[*] A *committer* is a developer who provides expert direction and advice to steer the Struts framework on the correct course. A committer has the ability to modify the source code repository and can cast votes that affect the future of the framework.

## Contribution to the Struts Project

The Struts group always welcomes new participants. To become a contributor, it's recommended that you first join the Struts User mailing list. If you like what you see there, take a look at the Struts Developers mailing list. This is the best way to get started and become familiar with the direction of the project. You should read the mailing list guidelines, at *http://jakarta.apache.org/site/mail.html*, before joining. You can then join one or more of the Jakarta Project's mailing lists, including those for Struts, from the URL *http://jakarta.apache.org/site/mail2.html*.

The main project web site for Struts is located at *http://jakarta.apache.org/struts/*. For more information on downloading and installing Struts, see Appendix B.

# Alternatives to Struts

Although this book is dedicated to the Jakarta Struts framework, Struts is far from the only Java Web framework available. There are quite a few available, each with their own proponents and evangelists.

Because framework versions and features may change with each new release, it's not always practical to compare and contrast Struts simply by reading these descriptions; you should conduct your own research with the latest stable versions of framework alternatives. This list is by no means exhaustive, but it will provide you with a launching pad.

Note that only solutions based on or around the Java platform are listed here. Microsoft also offers a competing technology based on Active Server Pages (ASP). Although the goal of ASP is similar to that of JSP, ASP and ASP+ are not discussed here—they're better left for a book on JSP and servlets. Furthermore, the Struts framework goes well beyond what is offered by JSP alone, and comparing ASP or other technologies similar to Struts wouldn't make sense.

Microsoft also has also introduced an "Application Block" called User Interface Process (UIP). UIP shares some of the same goals as MVC frameworks like Struts, but is meant for use with for the .NET programming model. Although interesting, it won't be presented here either.

## Building Your Own Framework

At first, it might seem strange to include building your own framework as an alternative to using Struts. Why would you want to build frameworks from scratch when they already exist in readily-available products? The answer is the same reason that other open source or commercial products are developed. The available selection of products just might not be close enough to your desired framework, and it might be preferable to build it in-house.

The best advice I can give regarding building your own framework is to ask yourself several questions:

1. Have I taken the time to inspect what's available and build a prototype using an available framework?
2. What does my application need that doesn't exist in one of the available frameworks?
3. Can I extend an existing framework to suit my needs or find what I need at another source and add it?
4. Do I know enough about building this type of framework to be able to meet my requirements?
5. Am I willing to provide support for bug fixes and feature enhancements for my framework for at least one year?

Depending on the honest answers to these questions, you might find that building your own framework isn't the best decision. A good guideline to which many in the software-development industry subscribe is that if it pertains to your core business, you should build it in-house. However, if the software component is not directly related to your core business, it might be wise to get it elsewhere. Play to your team's strengths and minimize its weaknesses.

## Barracuda

The Barracuda presentation framework is a type of Model 2 architecture similar to Struts, but it goes a step further and provides a model event-notification mechanism. Unlike a strictly JSP approach, the Barracuda framework has created a template engine component, which is supposed to allow for more flexibility and extensibility. The framework leverages code-content separation provided by the XMLC approach of creating user interfaces. XMLC is a Java-based compiler that uses either an HTML or XML document and creates Java classes that can recreate the document when executed. The generated Java classes can be used to insert dynamic content into the document at runtime by manipulating Document Object Model (DOM) interfaces. The separation of markup and application logic allows web designers to focus on markup and programmers to focus on coding. It also includes a Form mapping and Validation package for taking HTML form data and automatically validating it.

The available documentation for Barracuda is abundant, which makes it easy to get started. You can find more information on the Barracuda presentation framework at *http://barracudamvc.org/Barracuda/index.html*.

## Cocoon

Stefano Mazzocchi founded the Cocoon project in January 1999 as an open source project under the ASF. The goal of Cocoon is to help separate the content style, logic, and management functions for XML-based web sites. Cocoon leverages XML, Extensible Stylesheet Language Transformations (XSLT), and Simple API for XML (SAX) technologies to help create, deploy, and maintain XML server applications. With the release of 2.0, Cocoon has been raised to a higher level by providing a pipe-line-style of assembling components. This allows for easier assembly of its various components and allows Cocoon to fit inside your existing web architecture.

Most types of data sources, including RDBMS, LDAP, and File Systems, are supported. More information on Cocoon can be found at *http://cocoon.apache.org*.

## Expresso

The Expresso framework from Jcorporate is an application development framework that provides a component-based framework for developing applications. It provides a set of core components, compatible with both EJB and non-EJB applications alike. Although completely independent of Struts and other frameworks, the Expresso components can also be integrated into Struts in order to add security capabilities, object-to-relational mapping, background job handling and scheduling, and many other features. More information on the Expresso framework can be found at *http:// www.jcorporate.com*.

## Freemarker, Velocity, and WebMacro

These three products are grouped together because they all represent similar types of template engines.

Freemarker is an open source HTML template engine for Java servlets. With Freemarker, you store the HTML in templates, which eventually get compiled into template objects. These template objects then generate HTML dynamically, using data provided by servlets. Freemarker uses its own template language and claims speeds approaching those of static HTML pages. The software is free and licensed under a BSD-style License. You can find more information about Freemarker at *http:/ /freemarker.sourceforge.net*.

Velocity is another Jakarta project like Struts. It is a Java-based template engine that is similar in many ways to Freemarker, but it is capable of more than just creating dynamic content for web sites. Velocity can generate SQL, PostScript, and XML from templates, for example, and can be used either as a standalone utility for generating source code and reports or as an integrated component of other systems. Velocity also provides template services for the Turbine web application framework. Many other frameworks either support the Velocity scripting syntax or actually depend on it. For more information on Velocity, go to *http://jakarta.apache.org/velocity*.

WebMacro is an open source Java servlet framework used by several large web sites. The WebMacro framework uses a lightweight scripting language that allows separation of how a page looks from the page logic. WebMacro can be run in standalone mode or with a servlet container. More information about WebMacro can be found at *http://www.webmacro.org*.

## Maverick

The Maverick MVC framework offers the ability to render views using JSP, the Velocity scripting language, or XSLT. Maverick is an MVC-type architecture, but it actually provides a view template mechanism. One neat feature of Maverick is that it can use reflection on JavaBeans in the presentation layer to create a DOM interface, so no XML generation or parsing is required. This allows for a little less clutter and probably better performance when using XSLT to generate the views. You can find more information on the Maverick framework at *http://mav.sourceforge.net*.

## SiteMesh

SiteMesh is a web page layout and integration system that makes it easier to create web sites that need a consistent look and feel. SiteMesh intercepts requests to any web page, whether it's static or dynamically generated, parses the content, and generates a final page. This process is based on the well-known Decorator pattern.*

SiteMesh is built with Servlet, JSP, and XML technologies, which makes it appropriate for J2EE applications. However, it also claims to be easy to integrate with other web technologies, such as CGI. More information on SiteMesh can be found at *http://www.opensymphony.com/sitemesh*.

## Jakarta Turbine

Turbine is a servlet-based framework and an open source Jakarta project.

Turbine appears to be focused on providing a collection of reusable components. A large set of components is included with the framework, including components for using relational databases, security, and scheduling—just to name a few. More information on Turbine can be found at *http://jakarta.apache.org/turbine*.

## WebWork

WebWork has now moved under the umbrella project known as OpenSymphony. OpenSymphony is a SourceForge project dedicated to providing open source J2EE applications and components. You can find information on OpenSymphony at *http://www.opensymphony.com*.

---

* The Decorator pattern is a structural design pattern mentioned in the book *Design Patterns* (Addison Wesley), by Gamma, Helm, Johnson, and Vlissides, affectionately known as the "gang of four."

WebWork is a web application framework that uses the Pull Hierarchical Model View Controller (HMVC) design. With a standard MVC design, changes made to the model are pushed to the view. In the case of WebWork, the views pull the data when they need it. Interestingly, WebWork doesn't seem to be tied to a servlet; therefore, it can support other types of clients such as Swing. More information on the Web-Work framework can be found at *http://www.opensymphony.com/webwork*.

## Spring Framework

Spring is a relatively new J2EE application framework developed by Rod Johnson and included in his J2EE design book. Spring is not just a web framework—it's strength lies in the ability be integrated with other disparate components. More information on Spring can be found at *http://www.springframework.org*.

## JavaServer Faces

In 2001, a new Java Specification Request (JSR) was issued for a new Java technology called JavaServer Faces (JSF). The goal of this JSR is to lessen the burden on Servlet and JSP developers by providing a standard set of JSP Tags and classes to aid in the management of complicated HTML forms, event handling, and presentation state. The proposal also attempts to account for various platforms and client types by allowing pluggable rendering kits.

The JSR defines the architecture and a set of APIs for the creation and maintenance of Java server web applications—it's simply a set of standard APIs, not an actual implementation. Vendors can create their own implementations, so developers have more than one implementation to choose from.

The JSR indicates that the creators of JSF are aware that other projects (such as Struts) already have addressed many of the problems that this specification attempts to solve. The JSR is aimed at creating a standard that will help unify this fragmented area. Keep your eye on this specification, as it may have a huge impact on Struts and the entire web application area as a whole. The good news for Jakarta Struts users is that one of the primary authors of Struts, Craig McClanahan, is co–specification lead for JavaServer Faces. His influence will surely help ensure a smooth transition for the Struts framework.

At the time of this writing, the Java Specification Request (JSR) has moved past the 2nd public review and a final specification is expected in the near future. More information on the specification can be found in Chapter 18 and online at *http://www.jcp. org/jsr/detail/127.jsp*.

# CHAPTER 2

# Inside the Web Tier

This chapter discusses the relationship between the architectural tiers and their roles in an application. Special attention is given to the web tier, which allows an application to communicate and interoperate with clients over the Web. In particular, this chapter focuses on the physical and logical aspects of designing and using a web tier for your applications.

The Struts framework is based on the Java Servlet technology and, to a lesser extent, JavaServer Pages, and therefore is dependent on a web container. For Struts developers, understanding how the web container processes client requests is fundamental to a deeper understanding of the framework itself. This chapter illustrates the various components that are part of the web container and discusses each component's responsibilities.

## An Architecture Overview

This section presents a high-level architectural view of a Struts application. Although this section shows an architecture for an enterprise application, not all applications written using Struts will be of this size and makeup. However, this type of application does allow us to present many facets of how Struts applications may be configured.

Many applications—especially J2EE applications—can be described in terms of their *tiers*. The application's functionality is separated across these tiers, or functional layers, to provide separation of responsibility, reusability, improved scalability, and many other benefits. The separation of tiers may be a physical separation where each is located on a separate hardware resource, or it may be purely logical. In the latter case, one or more tiers are collocated (i.e., arranged or grouped together) on the same hardware resource, and the separation exists in terms of software components. Figure 2-1 illustrates the tiers that may be used by a typical Struts application.

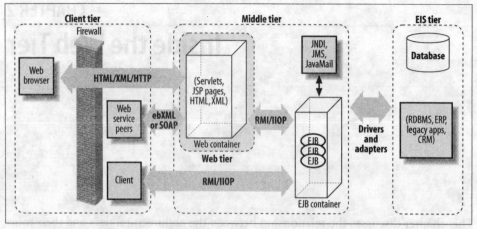

*Figure 2-1. Functional application tiers*

Not every Struts application will contain all of the tiers illustrated in Figure 2-1. For many smaller applications, the middle tier may consist primarily of a web container that interacts directly with a database in the enterprise information system (EIS) tier.

---

## What Is a Container?

There are many different types of containers—EJB containers, web containers, servlet containers, and so on. In general, containers provide a hosting environment for software components to run in. Containers provide general services that the components within the environment can use, so that the component developers don't have to worry about providing these services. A web container allows servlets, JSP components, and other Java classes to be deployed and executed within the container. Services such as the Java Naming and Directory Interface (JNDI), connection pooling, and transaction services can be configured at the container level—similar to the way in which EJB containers manage security, transactions, and bean pooling—and the component developers don't have to worry about managing these resources.

When using the services provided by a container, component developers may have to give up some control of the environment to the container. Third-party vendors, who must follow certain guidelines that are explicitly laid out in public specifications, build these containers. Although each vendor is allowed to implement certain portions of the container in a proprietary manner, they must follow the specifications to ensure that applications are portable.

---

## The Client Tier

The client tier provides a way for users to interact with the application. This interaction may be through a web browser, or it may be programmatic, through a web services interface. Regardless of the type of client, the interaction includes submitting a request and receiving some type of response from the middle tier.

In the case of the Struts framework, the most common type of client is a web browser. However, it is also possible to have clients such as wireless devices and Java applets.

## The Web Tier

Figure 2-1 shows the middle tier as an aggregate of the web tier plus some type of application server component (in this case, an EJB container). These two tiers often are combined, and many application servers include web tier functionality.

The web tier allows the client tier to communicate and interact with application logic that resides in other tiers. In more traditional web applications, it's not uncommon for some or all of the application logic to reside in this tier. In larger, enterprise-scale applications, the web tier acts as a translator and maps HTTP requests into service invocations on the middle tier.

The web tier also is responsible for managing screen flow based on application and user state. The web tier communicates with either a database or, in the case of an enterprise application, an application server. The web tier is the glue that binds client applications to the core backend business systems.

The components that reside in the web tier allow developers to extend the basic functionality of a web service. In the case of Struts, it does this through framework components that run in a servlet container.

## The Middle Tier

The middle tier is often referred to as the "application tier" or "server." This is due in part to the fact that there is often an application server within this tier. Not all Struts applications have an application tier. This is especially true for small web applications—many small projects forgo using a large application server and communicate directly with a database or some other data store. When an application server is present, the web tier communicates with it using some variation of Remote Method Invocation (RMI). If an EJB server is present in the application tier, the communication protocol is RMI over IIOP (Internet Inter-ORB Protocol).

When included, the application tier might provide a more scalable, fault-tolerant, and highly available architecture. One of the main purposes of using an application tier is to separate the responsibilities of presentation from those of the model and the business rules for the application. Today, many web applications use EJB servers for their application tiers. They may not use all available aspects of the J2EE architecture, such as EJBs, but there are other benefits that can be leveraged from a J2EE server such as JavaMail, JDBC and JMS to name a few.

## RMI over IIOP

Remote Method Invocation (RMI) allows methods to be invoked on remote objects. Java's implementation of RMI, known as the Java Remote Method Protocol (JRMP), has been around for quite some time and is specifically designed for Java-to-Java remote communications.

One of the issues with JRMP is that a JVM must be running on both the client and the server. With the number of so-called legacy applications that are written in languages such as C++, Java needed a way to communicate with these systems. This is where RMI over IIOP helps out.

The Internet Inter-ORB Protocol (IIOP) was designed to allow distributed components to communicate with one another using TCP/IP. IIOP is language- and platform-independent.

By using RMI on top of IIOP, Java can communicate with applications written in many other languages and on various platforms. RMI/IIOP, as it often is written, is required to be supported by all EJB servers and exists in the EJB and J2EE specifications.

## The Enterprise Information System Tier

The EIS tier contains data and services that are used throughout the enterprise. It provides access to enterprise resources such as databases, mainframes, customer relationship management (CRM) applications, and resource-planning systems.

The middle tier communicates with components in the EIS tier using resource-specific protocols. For example, to communicate with a relational database, the middle tier normally will use a JDBC driver. For enterprise resource planning (ERP) systems, a proprietary adapter b is used, although some ERP systems and other enterprise resources are starting to support a more web service–like access approach.

## Where Does Struts Fit In?

As illustrated in Figure 2-2, the Struts framework resides in the web tier. Struts applications are hosted by a web container and can make use of services provided by the container, such as handling requests via the HTTP and HTTPS protocols. This frees developers to focus on building applications that solve business problems.

## The HTTP Request/Response Phase

To better illustrate how the web server and servlet container work together to service clients, this section discusses the protocol for an HTTP request and response, from the time a client request is received until the server returns a response. Struts makes heavy use of the request and response objects, and a complete understanding of the round-trip process will help clarify some topics discussed later in the book.

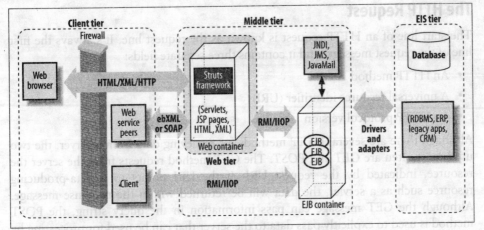

Figure 2-2. The Struts framework is used within the web tier

 Although the browser is not the only type of client that can be used with Struts, it certainly is the most common. More and more developers are starting to use Struts for wireless applications and even some interaction with web services, but the web browser remains the predominant client.

HTTP is based on a request/response model, so there are two types of HTTP messages: the request and the response. The browser opens a connection to a server and makes a request. The server processes the client's request and returns a response. Figure 2-3 illustrates this process.

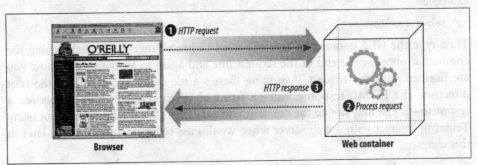

Figure 2-3. The HTTP request/response model

Both types of messages consist of a start line, zero or more header fields, and an empty line that indicates the end of the message headers. Both message types also may contain an optional message body.

The format and makeup of the request and response messages are very similar, but there are a few differences. We'll discuss each type of message separately.

# The HTTP Request

The start line of an HTTP request is known as the request line. It's always the first line of the request message, and it contains three separate fields:

- An HTTP method
- A universal resource identifier (URI)
- An HTTP protocol version

Although there are several HTTP methods for retrieving data from a server, the two used most often are *GET* and *POST*. The GET method requests from the server the resource, indicated by the request URI. If the URI points to a data-producing resource such as a servlet, the data will be returned within the response message. Although the GET message can pass information in the query string, the POST method is used to explicitly pass data to the server that can be used for processing by the request URI.

The URI identifies the resource that should process the request. For the purposes of this discussion, it can be either an absolute or a relative path. A request with an invalid URI will return an error code (typically 404).

The HTTP request protocol version identifies to the server which version of the HTTP specification the request conforms to. The following example illustrates the request line for a sample GET request:

```
GET /index.html HTTP/1.0
```

You can execute this example by opening up a Telnet session to a server running a web server. You must specify the hostname and port number of the web server. For example:

```
telnet localhost 80
```

Then type the GET command. You will need to press Enter twice after issuing the command: once for the end of the request line and again to let the server know you are finished with the request. Assuming there's a file called *index.html* in the root directory, the HTML response will be returned. (Actually, you will always see a response—it just may not be the one that you expected.) We'll talk more about using Telnet to interact with a web server when we discuss redirects and forwards later in this chapter.

As mentioned earlier, the HTTP request may contain zero or more header fields. Request header fields allow the client to pass to the server additional information about the request and the client itself. The format of a header field, for both the request and the response, is the name of the header field, followed by a colon (:) and the value. If multiple values are specified for a single header field, they must be separated with commas. Table 2-1 lists some of the more commonly used request headers.

*Table 2-1. Common HTTP request header fields*

| Name | Purpose |
|------|---------|
| Accept | Indicates the media types that are acceptable for the response. If no Accept header field is present, the server can safely assume that the client accepts all media types. An example of an Accept header value is "image/gif, image/jpeg". |
| Accept-Charset | Indicates what character sets are acceptable for the response. If the Accept-Charset header is not present in the request, the server can assume that any character set is acceptable. The ISO-8859-1 character set can be assumed to be acceptable by all user agents. |
| Accept- Encoding | Similar to the Accept header field, but further restricts the content-encoding values that are acceptable by the client. An example of an Accept-Encoding header value is "compress, gzip". |
| Accept-Language | Indicates which languages the client would prefer the response to be in. An example of an Accept-Language header value is "en-us, de-li, es-us". |
| Content- Encoding | Indicates what encoding mechanism has been applied to the body of the message and, therefore, what decoding mechanism must be used to get the information. An example of a Content-Encoding header value is "gzip". |
| Content-Type | Indicates the media type of the body sent to the recipient. An example of a Content-Type header value is "text/html; charset=ISO-8859-1". |
| Host | Indicates the hostname and port number of the resource being requested, as obtained from the original URL. An example of a Host header value is "www.somehost.com". |
| Referer | Allows the client to specify the address (URI) of the resource from which the request URI was obtained. This header is used mainly for maintenance and tracking purposes. |
| User-Agent | Contains information about the client that originated the request. This header is used mainly for statistical purposes and tracing of protocol violations. An example of a User-Agent header value is "Mozilla/4.0 (compatible; MSIE 6.0; Windows NT 5.0)". |

The message body for a request is used to carry to the server data associated with the request. The data included within the body is different from the values used by the header fields in terms of both format and content. The header fields can be thought of as metadata about the message body.

## The HTTP Response

Once the server has received and processed the request, it must return an HTTP response message to the client. The response message consists of a status line and zero or more header fields, followed by an empty line. It also may have an optional message body.

The first line of the HTTP response message is known as the status line. It consists of the HTTP protocol version that the response conforms to, followed by a numeric status code and its textual explanation. Each field is separated from the next by a space. An example response status line is shown here:

```
HTTP/1.1 200 OK
```

The status code is a three-digit numeric value that corresponds to the result code of the server's attempt to satisfy the request. The status code is for programmatic applications, while the text that accompanies it is intended for human readers. The first digit of the status code defines the category of the result code. Table 2-2 lists the allowed first digits and the corresponding categories.

*Table 2-2. Status code categories*

| Numeric value | Meaning |
| --- | --- |
| 100–199 | Informational—The request was received and is being processed. |
| 200–299 | Success—The action was successfully received, understood, and accepted. |
| 300–399 | Redirection—Further action must be taken to complete the request. |
| 400–499 | Client Error—The request contains bad syntax or cannot be fulfilled. |
| 500–599 | Server Error—The server failed to fulfill an apparently valid request. |

Quite a few status codes have been defined. They also are extensible, which allows applications to extend the behavior of the server. If a client application doesn't recognize a status code returned by the server, it can determine the general meaning of the response by using the first digit of the returned status code. Table 2-3 lists some of the most common response status codes.

*Table 2-3. Common HTTP response status codes*

| Code | Meaning |
| --- | --- |
| 200 | OK—The request succeeded. |
| 302 | Moved Temporarily —The request resides temporarily at a different URI. If the new URI is a location, the Location header field in the response will give the new URL. This code typically is used when the client is being redirected. |
| 400 | Bad Request—The server couldn't understand the request due to malformed syntax. |
| 401 | Unauthorized—The request requires authentication and/or authorization. |
| 403 | Forbidden—The server understood the request but for some reason is refusing to fulfill it. The server may or may not reveal why it is refusing the request. |
| 404 | Not Found—The server has not found anything matching the request URI. |
| 500 | Internal Server Error—The server encountered an unexpected condition that prevented it from fulfilling the request. |

The header fields in the response are similar in format to those found in the request message. They allow the server to pass to the client additional information that cannot be placed in the status line. These fields give information about the server and about further access to the URI contained within the request. After the last response header, which is followed by an empty line, the server can insert the response message body. In many cases, the response message body is HTML output. Figure 2-4 illustrates an example response to the following request:

```
GET /hello.html HTTP/1.0
```

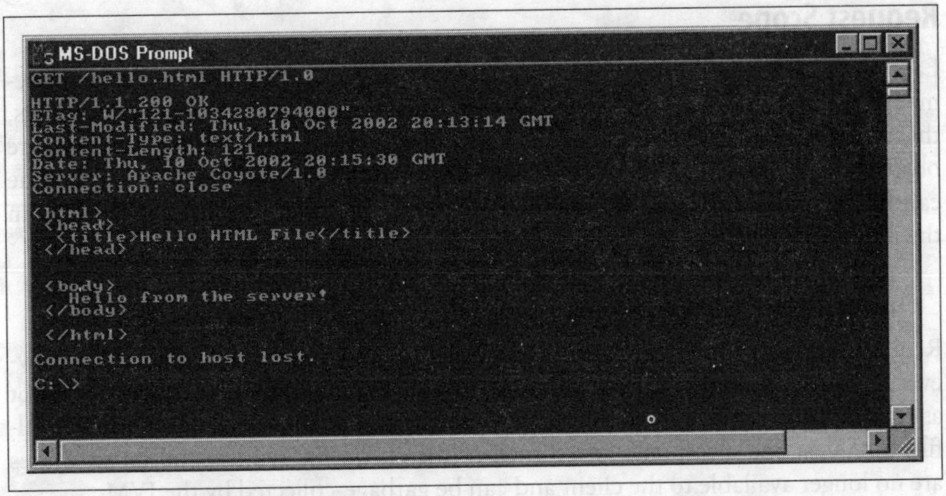

```
MS-DOS Prompt                                    _ □ X
GET /hello.html HTTP/1.0

HTTP/1.1 200 OK
ETag: W/"121-1034280794000"
Last-Modified: Thu, 10 Oct 2002 20:13:14 GMT
Content-Type: text/html
Content-Length: 121
Date: Thu, 10 Oct 2002 20:15:30 GMT
Server: Apache Coyote/1.0
Connection: close

<html>
 <head>
  <title>Hello HTML File</title>
 </head>

 <body>
  Hello from the server!
 </body>

</html>
Connection to host lost.

C:\>
```

*Figure 2-4. An example HTTP response message*

## HTTP Versus HTTPS

You've probably noticed that the request and response message text shown in the previous examples all have been standard readable text. This is fine when you don't need to protect the data; however, you would never want to send confidential data in the clear. When you need to ensure the integrity and privacy of information that is sent over a network, especially an open one like the Internet, one of the options is to use the HTTPS protocol, rather than standard HTTP.

HTTPS is normal HTTP wrapped by a *Secure Sockets Layer* (SSL). SSL is a communication system that ensures privacy when communicating with other SSL-enabled applications. It's really just a protocol that runs on top of the TCP/IP layer. It encrypts the data through the use of symmetric encryption and digital certificates. An SSL connection can be established between a client and server only when both systems are running in SSL mode and are able to authenticate each other.

The fact that SSL encrypts the transmitted data has no impact on the underlying request and response messages. The encryption and subsequent decryption on the other side occur after the message body is constructed and is decoupled from the HTTP portion of the message.

## Struts and Scope

The Struts framework uses various shared resource areas to store objects. The shared resource areas all have a lifetime and visibility rule that defines the *scope* of the resource. This section discusses these resources, their scopes, and how the framework uses them.

# Request Scope

Each time a client issues an HTTP request, the server creates an object that implements the javax.servlet.http.HttpServletRequest interface. Among other things, this object contains a collection of key/value attribute pairs that can be used to store objects for the lifetime of the request. The key of each pair is a String, and the value can be any type of Object. The methods to store objects in and retrieve them from the request scope are:

```
public void setAttribute( String name, Object obj );
public Object getAttribute( String name );
```

Request-scope attributes can be removed using the removeAttribute( ) method; however, because the scope of the attribute is only for the lifetime of the request, it is not as important to remove them as it is for other scoped attributes. Once the server fulfills a request and a response is returned to the client, the request and its attributes are no longer available to the client and can be garbage-collected by the JVM.

The Struts framework provides the ability to store JavaBeans in a request, so that they can be used by presentation components such as JSP pages. This makes it much easier to access JavaBeans data, without having to do a manual cleanup of the objects later. There's seldom a need to remove objects from request scope; the web container takes care of it for you. Objects stored at the request level are visible only to resources that have access to that request. Once the response has been returned to the client, the visibility is gone. Objects that are stored in one request are not visible to any other client request.

# Session Scope

The next-higher level of visibility is session scope. The web container creates an object that implements the javax.servlet.http.HttpSession interface to identify a user across multiple page requests. When the session is created depends on the application and the container implementation. The user's session will persist for a period of time that is based on how often the user makes requests. This allowed inactivity time is configurable through the application deployment descriptor. It also can be destroyed prematurely by calling the invalidate( ) method on the session object.

The session also allows for a collection of objects to be stored based on a key/value pair schema, as with the request object. The only difference between this one and the one provided by the request is the duration of the objects. Because sessions exist across multiple requests, objects stored in the session scope live longer than those at the request level. The Struts framework uses session attributes extensively. An example of an object that may be stored as a session attribute is the Locale object for the user. This allows the entire framework access to the user's locale to perform localized behavior. Objects stored in one user's session are not visible to users with a different session.

The web container provides no synchronization for objects stored in the session. If multiple threads attempt to access an object stored in the session and modify the value, it's up to the developer to provide synchronization. Although the need to synchronize access to the session is quite low, the developer is responsible for protecting the resources. For example, if your application uses frames, or if you have a process that takes a long time to complete, multiple threads might be accessing the session at the same time.

## Application Scope

An even higher level of visibility and duration comes with objects stored at the application-scope level. Application-scoped objects are visible to all clients and threads of the current web application. They live until they are programmatically removed or until the application is terminated. The servlet container creates an object that implements the javax.servlet.ServletContext interface for each and every web application that is installed within the container. This is done when the container is first started.

Beyond the scope for the request and session objects, the ServletContext allows application objects to be stored and retrieved by the entire application and to persist for the lifetime of the application. The Struts framework uses application scope to store JavaBeans that need to be visible to all users. Normally, objects are stored in this scope during application startup and remain there until the application exits.

## Page Scope

The last scope we will discuss, page scope, has to do exclusively with JSP pages. Objects with page scope are stored in the javax.servlet.jsp.PageContext for each page and are accessible only within the JSP page in which they were created. Once the response is sent to the client or the page forwards to another resource, the objects are no longer available.

Every JSP page has an implicit object reference named pageContext that can be used to store and retrieve page-level objects. It includes the same getAttribute() and setAttribute() methods that the other scopes offer, and they function in the same manner.

# Using URL Parameters

URL parameters are strings that are sent to the server with the client request. The parameters are inserted into the HttpServletRequest object from the URI query string and data that is sent in a POST method. The parameters are formatted as key/value pairs and are accessed by applications as request parameters. URL parameters play an important role in all web applications, and the Struts framework is no exception.

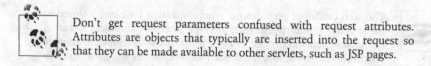

Don't get request parameters confused with request attributes. Attributes are objects that typically are inserted into the request so that they can be made available to other servlets, such as JSP pages.

# Forward Versus Redirect

It's often necessary for more than one component to share control of a request. For example, one servlet may be responsible for authenticating and authorizing a client, while it's the job of a different servlet to retrieve some data for the user. The sharing of a request can be accomplished in several different ways.

There are important differences between how a web container processes a forward request versus how it processes a redirect. The Struts front controller servlet, discussed in Chapter 1, will always perform one or the other for a typical request, so it's important that you understand these differences and the impact that each mechanism will have on your application.

## Using a Redirect

When the sendRedirect() method is invoked, it causes the web container to return to the browser a response indicating that a new URL should be requested. Because the browser issues a completely new request, any objects that are stored as request attributes before the redirect occurs will be lost. This is one of the biggest differences between a forward and redirect. Figure 2-5 illustrates why this occurs.

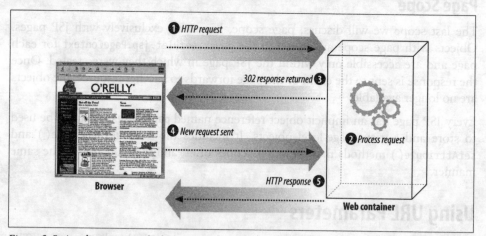

*Figure 2-5. A redirect causes the browser to issue a new request*

Because of the extra round trip that occurs, a redirect is slower than a forward. Example 2-1 provides an example servlet that performs a redirect for a JSP page called *result.jsp* when a request for the servlet is issued.

*Example 2-1. A Java servlet that performs a redirect when it receives a request*

```java
package com.oreilly.struts.chapter2examples;

import java.io.IOException;
import javax.servlet.ServletException;
import javax.servlet.http.HttpServlet;
import javax.servlet.http.HttpServletRequest;
import javax.servlet.http.HttpServletResponse;
import javax.servlet.RequestDispatcher;

public class RedirectServlet extends HttpServlet {

  public void doPost(HttpServletRequest request, HttpServletResponse response)
    throws ServletException,IOException {
    redirect(request, response);
  }

  public void doGet(HttpServletRequest request, HttpServletResponse response)
    throws ServletException,IOException {
    redirect(request, response);
  }

  /**
   * Set a few URL parameters and objects for the request to see what happens
   * to them during a redirect.
   */
  protected void redirect(HttpServletRequest req, HttpServletResponse resp)
    throws ServletException,IOException {

    log("A request arrived for " + req.getServletPath());

    req.setAttribute("firstName", "John");
    req.setAttribute("lastName", "Doe");

    String contextPath = req.getContextPath();
    String redirectStr = contextPath + "/result.jsp?username=foo&password=bar";
    log("redirecting to " + redirectStr);

    // Always call the encodeRedirectURL method when perfoming a redirect
    resp.sendRedirect(resp.encodeRedirectURL(redirectStr));
  }
}
```

When the servlet in Example 2-1 receives either a GET or POST request, it calls the redirect( ) method and passes to it the HttpServletRequest and HttpServletResponse objects. The method sets two String objects into the request, to demonstrate that they will not be available after the redirect, and it creates a String that will become the URL for which the client is told to make a new request. After the encodeRedirectURL( ) method is called and passed the redirect string, the sendRedirect( ) method is invoked on the response object.

All URLs passed to the sendRedirect() method should be run through the encodeRedirectURL() method, so that the session ID can be included if the browser doesn't support cookies and session tracking needs to occur. The Struts framework performs this step automatically in the RequestProcessor during normal action processing.

The JSP page to which the servlet will redirect is shown in Example 2-2.

*Example 2-2. The result.jsp page*

```html
<html>
 <head>
  <title>Struts Redirect/Forward Example</title>
 </head>

<body>
 <img src="images\tomcat-power.gif">
 <br>
<%
 String firstName = (String)request.getAttribute( "firstName" );
 if ( firstName == null ){
   firstName = "Not found in request";
 }


 String lastName = (String)request.getAttribute( "lastName" );
 if ( lastName == null ){
   lastName = "Not found in request";
 }
%>

 <b>First Name:</b> <%=firstName%><br>
 <b>Last Name:</b> <%=lastName%><br>

</body>
</html>
```

When you enter the URL for this servlet (*http://localhost:8080/servlet/com.oreilly. struts.chapter2examples.RedirectServlet*) in a browser, the browser output will look like Figure 2-6.

Notice that the first name and last name arguments that were set in the servlet were not found in the request. This is because a second request actually was issued for this page. Fortunately, we can peek behind the scenes and observe what's taking place.

The URL parameters username and password were included in this example just to illustrate that they are still present after a redirect occurs. You should never add confidential information such as passwords to the query string.

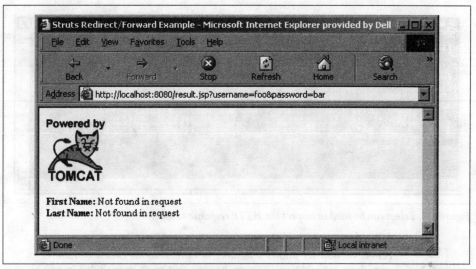

*Figure 2-6. The output page when the RedirectServlet is called*

Let's look at the HTTP response that comes back to the client when the Redirect-Servlet is requested. We can view the response using a standard Telnet session. An HTTP connection uses a simple network socket to communicate with the server, so we can partially simulate the interaction between a browser and a server using the Telnet application. You can establish a connection to a web server using Telnet by connecting to the port on which the server is listening (usually port 80 or, in the case of Tomcat, 8080):

```
telnet localhost 8080
```

You can do this from the command line, whether you're using a DOS shell or Unix. The Telnet session will alert you if it's unable to connect to a server with the specified hostname and port number.

If a connection is established, the Telnet session will sit and wait for you to enter the HTTP request information. The only information you are required to enter is the first line of the request, which tells the server what resource the client wants. Each line in the request is a text line, separated by a newline character. The request header ends with a blank line, so you actually have to press Enter twice to let Telnet know you are done with the request. Figure 2-7 shows the HTTP response message Tomcat returns when a request is made for the RedirectServlet resource.

In Figure 2-7, the first line of the request issues a GET and a path for a resource. The path is the portion of the HT.TP request that comes after the hostname and includes the preceding / character. The HTTP/1.0 string at the end of the GET request is the HTTP version protocol.

*Figure 2-7. Telnet can be used to inspect the HTTP response headers*

HTTP Version 1.1 added a number of optimizations over 1.0. However, there are additional request headers that must be included in an HTTP 1.1 request, which would make this example more complicated than necessary. Therefore, 1.0 was used to issue the request.

Everything after the first line is a response from the server. The entire HTML output at the bottom comes from Tomcat; it indicates that the original request has performed a redirect and that the client should request a new URL.

If you look at the Location response header, which is the third line in Figure 2-7, you can see that the server has informed the client what the URL for the new request should be. Any URL parameters attached to the original request will be present in the new request. When the browser issues the new request, these parameters will be sent along with it. This technique of using Telnet provides a simple way of interacting with a web server and viewing what responses it sends back to the client.

Hopefully, you now have a better understanding of how a redirect works. It should also be clear why any objects placed into the original request are not available to the redirected resource. This will become very important later, when we discuss the Struts framework.

Notice that in Example 2-1, the redirect string didn't explicitly contain the hostname and port that the client needed to use for the new request. It's the job of the servlet container to translate the relative URL to a fully qualified URL for transmission back to the client.

## Using a Forward

A forward differs from a redirect in several ways. When you invoke a forward for a request, the request is sent to another resource on the server, without the client being informed that a different resource is going to process the request. This process occurs completely within the web container, and the client is never the wiser. Unlike with a redirect, objects can be stored in the request and passed along for the next resource to use. Figure 2-8 illustrates the steps that take place when a request is forwarded.

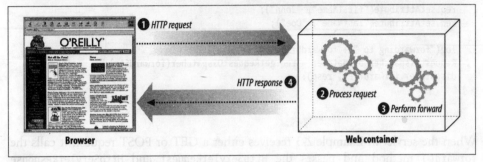

Figure 2-8. When a forward occurs, the client is not notified

Because a forward takes place completely on the server and there is no communication with the client, the performance is better than with a redirect. However, there are some differences in how a forward deals with relative URLs. Example 2-3 should make this clearer.

Example 2-3. A Java servlet that performs a forward when it receives a request

```
package com.oreilly.struts.chapter2examples;

import java.io.IOException;
import javax.servlet.ServletException;
import javax.servlet.http.HttpServlet;
import javax.servlet.http.HttpServletRequest;
import javax.servlet.http.HttpServletResponse;
import javax.servlet.RequestDispatcher;
public class ForwardServlet extends HttpServlet {

  public void doPost(HttpServletRequest request, HttpServletResponse response)
    throws ServletException,IOException {
    forward(request, response);
  }

  public void doGet(HttpServletRequest request, HttpServletResponse response)
    throws ServletException,IOException {
    forward(request, response);
  }

  /**
   * Set a few URL parameters and objects for the request to see what happens
   * to them during a redirect.
   */
  protected void forward(HttpServletRequest req, HttpServletResponse resp)
    throws ServletException,IOException {
```

*Example 2-3. A Java servlet that performs a forward when it receives a request (continued)*

```
    log("A request arrived for " + req.getServletPath());

    String forwardStr = "/result.jsp?username=foo&password=bar";

    req.setAttribute("firstName", "John");
    req.setAttribute("lastName", "Doe");

    log("forwarding to " + forwardStr);
    RequestDispatcher dispatcher = req.getRequestDispatcher(forwardStr);
    dispatcher.forward(req, resp);
  }
}
```

When the servlet in Example 2-3 receives either a GET or POST request, it calls the forward( ) method and passes the HttpServletRequest and HttpServletResponse objects to it. As with the redirect example, two String objects are set into the request. However, in contrast with the redirect example, the objects will be available after the forward. Next, the servlet creates a path to which the request will be passed. A RequestDispatcher is created, and the forward( ) method is invoked on it. We'll use the same JSP page from Example 2-2. In the browser, we enter a URL such as *http://localhost:8080/servlet/com.oreilly.struts.chapter2examples.ForwardServlet*.

The browser output should look similar to Figure 2-9.

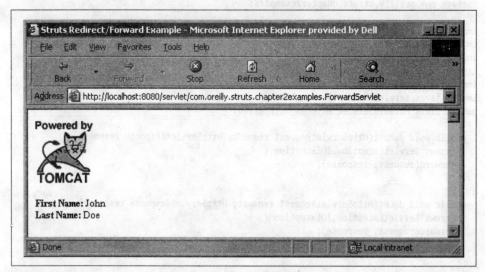

*Figure 2-9. The output page when the ForwardServlet is called*

There are two things to note about Figure 2-9. The first is that the first and last name fields have values. This is because the objects were placed into the request before the forward occurred, and *result.jsp* was able to retrieve the values and use them in the page.

The second is the URL in the address bar. Notice that the URL back in Figure 2-6 showed the new URL, whereas it didn't change in Figure 2-9. This shows further that the client is not aware that a forward occurred—the browser was not notified that a different servlet handled the request.

 The forward( ) method of the RequestDispatcher class can be called only when no output has been committed to the client. Writing something to the response object and then calling forward( ) may result in an IllegalStateException being thrown by the container.

## Which Is Best for Struts?

It's difficult to decree whether Struts applications should use redirects or forwards, as we haven't discussed the framework yet. However, there are some key points about using each approach. Both mechanisms have their pros and cons within Struts and web applications in general. For many situations, a forward is recommended over a redirect, because objects that are stored in the request scope are easily available to the presentation components. In fact, using a forward is the default for the Struts framework. Another advantage of forwards is that they're much more efficient, as the client is not required to issue a new request.

There are some situations, however, where a redirect is necessary or preferred over a forward. When forwards are used, the URLs are not always consistent with the state of the client application. If the browser's Refresh button is pressed, an incorrect request may occur. This problem will be explored further in Chapter 5.

If you are using relative paths for images and other resources in your JSP pages, forwards can be problematic. Because the browser has no indication that a forward has occurred, the relative paths will be relative to the initial servlet, not to the JSP to which it was forwarded. As you'll see in Chapter 8, the Struts framework provides a JSP custom tag that can help to alleviate the hassle associated with this behavior.

# CHAPTER 3

# Overview of the Struts Framework

It's finally time to introduce the Struts framework. Familiarity with the material from the previous two chapters will allow you to absorb the information here much faster. This chapter provides an overview of the Struts framework. It does not attempt to cover all of its features or go into significant depth; instead, it emphasizes how all the pieces fit into the MVC and Model 2 architecture presented in Chapter 1.

The rest of the book will be spent pulling back the layers and uncovering the details of the framework, expanding on the basic concepts and terminology introduced here. It is important that you have a firm grasp of the fundamentals presented in this chapter—even if you are familiar with the basic concepts of the Struts framework, you should read through this chapter before going on.

## A Banking Account Example

This section introduces an online banking application that will be used to familiarize you with Struts. The example presented here is not complete, but it provides an overview of the major components that are present in all Struts applications and shows how those components fit together. A more comprehensive and thorough shopping-cart example will be used throughout the rest of the book.

Most people are familiar with the concept of online banking, so we won't spend too much time explaining the business requirements. In short, the online banking application will allow an end user to log in to the financial institution's web site, view account information, and transfer funds from one account to another (assuming the user has more than one account). The user must present a valid set of credentials to enter the site—in this case, an access number and a personal identification number (PIN).

If the user leaves one or both fields blank, the application will display a formatted message informing the user that both fields are required. If the user enters values for both fields but the authentication fails, the login screen will be redisplayed, along with a formatted error message informing the user that the login has failed. Figure 3-1 shows the online banking login screen after an invalid login attempt has been detected.

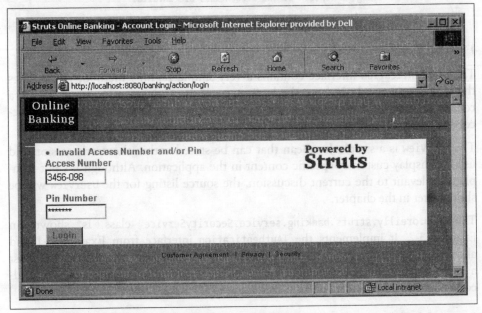

*Figure 3-1. Login screen for the online banking application*

If the proper credentials are entered for an account, the user is taken to the account information screen. This screen shows all of the accounts that the user has with the financial institution, as well as the current balance for each account.

For this example, we are not going to provide a robust, full-fledged security service and security realm. Handling security in a web application can be complicated, and there's no reason to muddy the waters with it at the moment. For the purposes of this chapter, we'll use a simple Java interface that contains a single login() method to authenticate users. The IAuthentication interface is shown in Example 3-1.

*Example 3-1. The IAuthentication interface used by the banking application*

```
package com.oreilly.struts.banking.service;

import com.oreilly.struts.banking.view.UserView;
/**
 * Provides methods that the banking security service should implement.
 */
public interface IAuthentication {
  /**
   * The login method is called when a user wants to log in to
   * the online banking application.
   * @param accessNumber- The account access number.
```

```
 * @param pin- The account private id number.
 * @returns a DTO object representing the user's personal data.
 * @throws InvalidLoginException if the credentials are invalid.
 */
public UserView login( String accessNumber, String pin )
  throws InvalidLoginException;
}
```

The IAuthentication interface contains a very simple login( ) method, which takes the accessNumber and pin from the login page. If the authentication is successful, a com.oreilly.struts.banking.view.UserView object is returned. If the login is unsuccessful, an InvalidLoginException is thrown.

The UserView is a simple JavaBean that can be stored within the user's session and used to display customer-specific content in the application. Although it's not completely relevant to the current discussion, the source listing for the UserView will be shown later in the chapter.

The com.oreilly.struts.banking.service.SecurityService class is shown in Example 3-2. It implements the IAuthentication interface from Example 3-1 and allows the application to authenticate users. We are not going to authenticate against a security realm for this example, so the SecurityService class will contain hard-coded logic to authenticate users.

*Example 3-2. The security service used by the example banking application*

```
package com.oreilly.struts.banking.service;

import com.oreilly.struts.banking.view.UserView;
/**
 * Used by the example banking application to simulate a security service.
 */
public class SecurityService implements IAuthentication {

  public UserView login( String accessNumber, String pin )
    throws InvalidLoginException {

    // A real security service would check the login against a security realm.
    // This example is hardcoded to let in only 123/456.
    if( "123".equals(accessNumber) && "456".equals(pin) ){
      /* Dummy a UserView for this example.
       * This data/object would typically come from the business layer
       * after proper authentication/authorization had been done.
       */
      UserView userView = new UserView( "John", "Doe" );
      userView.setId( "39017" );
      return userView;
    }
    else {
      // If the login method is invalid, throw an InvalidLoginException.
```

*Example 3-2. The security service used by the example banking application (continued)*

```
        // Create a msg that can be inserted into a log file.
        String msg = "Invalid Login Attempt by " + accessNumber + ":" + pin;
        throw new InvalidLoginException( msg );
    }
  }
}
```

For this example application, we will authenticate the user only if the accessNumber entered is "123" and the pin entered is "456".

 If the SecurityService were being used in a real application, it would have to check the credentials against some type of security realm, such as a relational database or an LDAP server.

Once the user has logged in successfully, she may perform two actions:

- View an account detail
- Log out

Figure 3-2 shows the account information screen to which the user is taken after a successful login. The user can view detailed information about an account by clicking on that account. Figure 3-3 shows the account detail screen for the checking account listed in Figure 3-2.

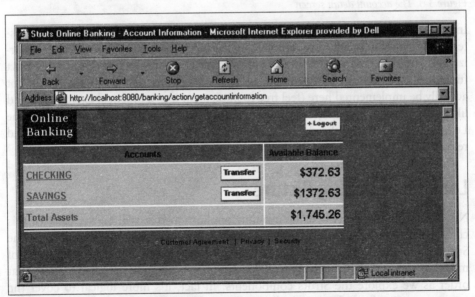

*Figure 3-2. The account information screen*

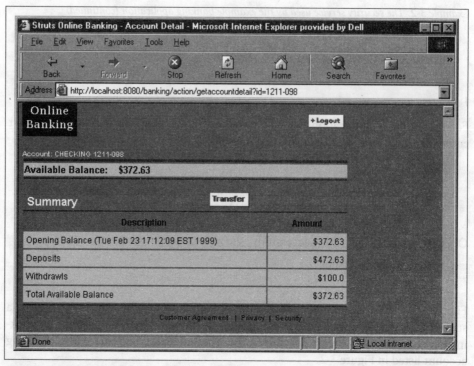

*Figure 3-3. The account detail screen*

In a typical online banking application, the user would also have the ability to transfer funds from one account to another. As the purpose of this chapter is to familiarize you with the components of the Struts framework, not to teach you the correct functionality of a web banking application, the funds-transfer functionality will not actually be implemented here (feel free to implement it as a practical exercise if you'd like!). Finally, the user may log out of the application altogether by clicking on the Logout button. When she does so, she will be logged out of the application and returned to the login screen.

## Looking at the Big Picture

Now that we have described the example application that will be the basis of this chapter's discussion, it's time to start looking at how we can implement it using the Struts framework. Although Chapter 1 discussed the MVC pattern in the order of model, view, and then controller, it doesn't necessarily make sense to follow that order as we explore the Struts components. In fact, it's more logical to cover the components in the order in which the Struts framework uses them to process a request. Thus, we'll discuss the components that make up the controller portion of the framework first.

# The Struts Component Packages

The Struts framework is made up of approximately 300 Java classes, divided into 8 core packages ("approximately" is an appropriate term because the framework is continuously growing and being shaped). In this chapter, we'll focus on only the top-level packages. Figure 3-4 shows the top-level packages and their dependencies within the framework.

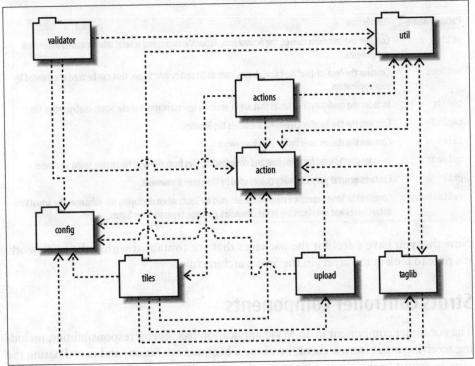

*Figure 3-4. The eight top-level packages in the Struts framework*

 The validator package shown in Figure 3-4 does not represent the entire set of classes and interfaces necessary for the Validator framework. These are only the Struts-specific extensions necessary to use the Validator framework with Struts. There is also a ninth top-level package named config, which consists of a single Java class. We'll ignore this package for now; it's not relevant to the discussion in this chapter.

The framework components are not arranged by what role they play in the MVC pattern—actually, they are arranged a little haphazardly. You might have noticed this by some of the circular dependencies shown in Figure 3-4. This has more to do with how fast the framework has evolved than with poor decisions made by the designers.

For example, the action package contains some classes for the controller, some that are used by the view domain, and even a few that probably would have been better off in the util package. While this may be confusing at first, you'll eventually become accustomed to where everything is. Table 3-1 enumerates the top-level packages and provides brief descriptions of their purposes. A few of these top-level packages also contain subpackages, which will be covered in later chapters.

*Table 3-1. Top-level packages in the Struts framework*

| Package name | Description |
|---|---|
| action | Contains the controller classes, the ActionForm, ActionMessages, and several other required framework components. |
| actions | Contains the "out-of-box" Action classes, such as DispatchAction, that can be used or extended by your application. |
| config | Includes the configuration classes that are in-memory representations of the Struts configuration file. |
| taglib | Contains the tag handler classes for the Struts tag libraries. |
| tiles | Contains the classes used by the Tiles framework. |
| upload | Includes classes used for uploading and downloading files from the local filesystem, using a browser. |
| util | Contains general-purpose utility classes used by the entire framework. |
| validator | Contains the Struts-specific extension classes used by Struts when deploying the validator. The actual Validator classes and interfaces are in the commons package, separate from Struts. |

Now that you have a feel for the packages that are contained within the framework, it's time to look at the layers in the Struts architecture.

# Struts Controller Components

The controller component in an MVC application has several responsibilities, including receiving input from a client, invoking a business operation, and coordinating the view to return to the client. Of course, the controller may perform many other functions, but these are a few of the primary ones.

For an application built using the JSP Model 2 approach, the controller is implemented by a Java servlet. This servlet is the centralized point of control for the web application. The controller servlet maps user actions into business operations and then helps to select the view to return to the client based on the request and other state information. As a reminder, Figure 3-5 shows the figure used in Chapter 1 to illustrate how this works.

In the Struts framework, however, the controller responsibilities are implemented by several different components, one of which is an instance of the org.apache.struts. action.ActionServlet class.

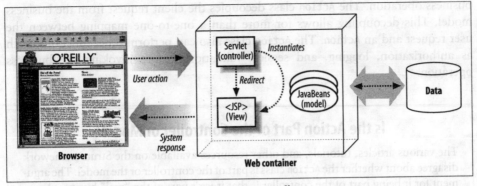

*Figure 3-5. The Struts framework uses a servlet as a controller*

# The Struts ActionServlet

The `ActionServlet` extends the `javax.servlet.http.HttpServlet` class and is responsible for packaging and routing HTTP traffic to the appropriate handler in the framework. The `ActionServlet` class is not abstract and therefore can be used as a concrete controller by your applications. Prior to Version 1.1 of the Struts framework, the `ActionServlet` was solely responsible for receiving the request and processing it by calling the appropriate handler. In Version 1.1, a new class, called `org.apache.struts.action.RequestProcessor`, was introduced to process the request for the controller. The main reason for decoupling the request processing from the `ActionServlet` is to provide you with the flexibility to subclass the `RequestProcessor` with your own version and modify how the request is processed.

For the banking application example, we will keep it simple and use the default `ActionServlet` and `RequestProcessor` classes provided by the framework. For brevity in this chapter, we will refer to these two components simply as "the controller." Chapter 5 describes in detail how these classes can be extended to modify the default controller behavior and explains the roles and responsibilities of each component.

Like any other Java servlet, the Struts `ActionServlet` must be configured in the deployment descriptor for the web application. We won't go into detail about the deployment descriptor here, though—it's covered in Chapter 4.

Once the controller receives a client request, it delegates the handling of the request to a helper class. This helper knows how to execute the business operation associated with the requested action. In the Struts framework, this helper class is a descendant of the `org.apache.struts.action.Action` class.

# Struts Action Classes

An `org.apache.struts.action.Action` class in the Struts framework is an extension of the controller component. It acts as a bridge between a client-side user action and a business operation. The Action class decouples the client request from the business model. This decoupling allows for more than a one-to-one mapping between the user request and an Action. The Action class also can perform other functions, such as authorization, logging, and session validation, before invoking the business operation.

---

## Is the Action Part of the Controller or Model?

The various articles, tutorials, and other resources available on the Struts framework disagree about whether the Action class is part of the controller or the model. The argument for it being part of the controller is that it isn't part of the "real" business logic. If Struts were replaced with an alternative framework, chances are the Action class would be replaced with something else. Therefore, it really isn't part of the model domain, but rather is tightly coupled to the Struts controller. It doesn't make sense to put business logic into the Action, because other types of clients can't easily reuse it.

Another reason to consider the Struts Action class part of the controller is that it has access to the ActionServlet, and therefore all of the controller resources, which the model domain shouldn't know about. Hypothetically, the Action class's behavior could have been left in the servlet, and the servlet would call the appropriate method on itself. If this were the case, there would be no doubt about whether this was controller or model functionality.

With all of that said, the Action class may invoke operations on the business model, and many developers end up trying to insert too much of their business logic into the Action classes. Eventually, the line becomes blurry. Perhaps this is why some developers consider it part of the model. However, this book will take the approach that the Action class is part of the controller.

---

The Struts Action class contains several methods, but the most important is the execute( ) method. Here is the method signature:

```
public ActionForward execute(ActionMapping mapping,
                ActionForm form,
                HttpServletRequest request,
                HttpServletResponse response)
    throws Exception;
```

The execute( ) method is called by the controller when a request is received from a client. The controller creates an instance of the Action class if one doesn't already exist. The Struts framework will create only a single instance of each Action class in your application. Because there is only one instance for all users, you must ensure that all of your Action classes operate properly in a multithreaded environment, just as you would do when developing a servlet. Figure 3-6 illustrates how the execute( ) method is invoked by the controller components.

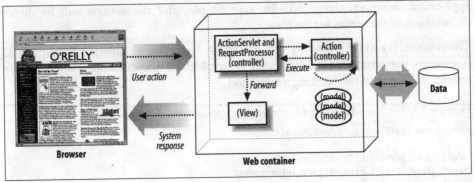

*Figure 3-6. The execute( ) method is called by the controller*

Although the execute( ) method is not abstract, the default implementation returns null, so you will need to create your own Action class implementation and override this method.

There is some debate over how best to implement Action classes using Struts. Whether you create a different Action class for each operation or put several business operations in the same Action class is subjective, and each approach has pros and cons.

> In Chapter 5, we'll discuss an action provided by the Struts framework called org.apache.struts.actions.DispatchAction. This action gives you the ability to create a single Action class and implement several similar operations, such as *Create, Read, Update, and Delete* (CRUD), within it. This has the effect of creating a smaller number of Action classes, but it might make maintenance a little more cumbersome.

For the banking application, we will create a unique Action class for each action that the user can perform:

- Login
- Logout
- GetAccountInformation
- GetAccountDetail

Each of the banking Action classes will extend the Struts Action class and will override the execute( ) method to carry out a specific operation. In Chapter 5, you'll learn that it's best to create an abstract base Action class, which all of your other Action classes extend. The application-specific base Action extends the Struts Action class and provides you with added flexibility and extensibility by allowing common Action behavior to be handled by a single parent class. For example, if you want to verify for each request that the user's session has not timed out, you can put this behavior in the abstract base Action before calling the subclass. For the banking application, however, things will be kept simple, and the actions will be direct descendants of the Struts Action class.

The com.oreilly.struts.banking.action.LoginAction class is shown in Example 3-3. It extends the Struts Action class and is invoked by the controller when a user attempts to log in to the banking application.

*Example 3-3. The LoginAction used by the banking application*

```java
package com.oreilly.struts.banking.action;

import javax.servlet.http.HttpServletRequest;
import javax.servlet.http.HttpServletResponse;
import javax.servlet.http.HttpSession;
import org.apache.struts.action.Action;
import org.apache.struts.action.ActionMapping;
import org.apache.struts.action.ActionForm;
import org.apache.struts.action.ActionForward;
// Non Struts Imports
import com.oreilly.struts.banking.IConstants;
import com.oreilly.struts.banking.service.IAuthentication;
import com.oreilly.struts.banking.service.SecurityService;
import com.oreilly.struts.banking.service.InvalidLoginException;
import com.oreilly.struts.banking.view.UserView;
import com.oreilly.struts.banking.form.LoginForm;
/**
 * This Action is called by the ActionServlet when a login attempt
 * is made by the user. The ActionForm should be an instance of
 * a LoginForm and contain the credentials needed by the SecurityService.
 */
public class LoginAction extends Action {
  public ActionForward execute( ActionMapping mapping,
                                ActionForm form,
                                HttpServletRequest request,
                                HttpServletResponse response )
    throws Exception {

      // The ActionForward to return when completed
      ActionForward forward = null;
      UserView userView = null;

      // Get the credentials from the LoginForm
      String accessNbr = ((LoginForm)form).getAccessNumber();
      String pinNbr = ((LoginForm)form).getPinNumber();

      /*
       * In a real application, you would typically get a reference
       * to a security service through something like JNDI or a factory.
       */
      IAuthentication service = new SecurityService();

      // Attempt to log in
      userView = service.login(accessNbr, pinNbr);
```

*Example 3-3. The LoginAction used by the banking application (continued)*

```
    // Since an exception wasn't thrown, login was successful

    // Invalidate existing session if it exists
    HttpSession session = request.getSession(false);
    if(session != null) {
      session.invalidate();
    }

    // Create a new session for this user
    session = request.getSession(true);

    // Store the UserView into the session and return
    session.setAttribute( IConstants.USER_VIEW_KEY, userView );
    forward = mapping.findForward(IConstants.SUCCESS_KEY );
    return forward;
  }
}
```

The LoginAction in Example 3-3 gets the credentials from the ActionForm that was passed in as an argument in the execute( ) method.

> The ActionForm class will be discussed later in this chapter in "Struts View Components."

A SecurityService is then created, and the security credentials are passed to the login( ) method. If the login succeeds, a new HttpSession is created for the user, and the UserView returned from the login( ) method is put into the session. If authentication fails, an InvalidLoginException is thrown. Note that there is no try/catch block for the InvalidLoginException in the execute( ) method. This is because one of the new features of Struts 1.1 is its declarative exception-handling capabilities, which remove much of the burden of exception handling from the developer. With the declarative exception handling in Struts, you specify what exceptions can be thrown from the actions and what you want the framework to do with them. You specify this information in the Struts configuration file:

```
<global-exceptions>
 <exception
     key="global.error.invalidlogin"
     path="/login.jsp"
      scope="request"
      type="com.oreilly.struts.banking.service.InvalidLoginException"/>
</global-exceptions>
```

This fragment from the banking configuration file tells the framework that if an InvalidLoginException is thrown by any action, it should forward the request to the *login.jsp* resource and build an error message using the key global.error. invalidlogin from the resource bundle. You also have the ability to override the default exception-handling behavior with whatever functionality you need it to perform. Exception handling is covered at length in Chapter 10.

## Mapping the Actions

At this point, you might be asking yourself, "How does the controller know which Action instance to invoke when it receives a request?" It determines this by inspecting the request information and using a set of action mappings.

Action mappings are part of the Struts configuration information that is configured in a special XML file. This configuration information is loaded into memory at startup and made available to the framework at runtime. Each action element is represented in memory by an instance of the org.apache.struts.action. ActionMapping class. The ActionMapping object contains a path attribute that is matched against a portion of the URI of the incoming request. We'll talk more about action mappings and the Struts configuration file in Chapter 4.

The following XML fragment illustrates the login action mapping from the configuration file used by the banking application:

```
<action
  path="/login"
  type="com.oreilly.struts.banking.action.LoginAction"
  scope="request"
  name="loginForm"
  validate="true"
  input="/login.jsp">
  <forward name="Success" path="/action/getaccountinformation" redirect="true"/>
  <forward name="Failure" path="/login.jsp" redirect="true"/>
</action>
```

The login action mapping shown here maps the path "/login" to the Action class com.oreilly.struts.banking.LoginAction. Whenever the controller receives a request where the path in the URI contains the string "/login", the execute( ) method of the LoginAction instance will be invoked. The Struts framework also uses the mappings to identify the resource to forward the user to once the action has completed. We'll talk more about configuring action mappings in Chapter 4.

## Determining the Next View

So far, we've discussed how the controller receives the request and determines the correct Action instance to invoke. What hasn't been discussed is how or what determines the view to return to the client.

If you looked closely at the execute( ) method signature in the Action class from the previous section, you might have noticed that the return type for the method is an org.apache.struts.action.ActionForward class. The ActionForward class represents a destination to which the controller may send control once an Action has completed.

Instead of specifying an actual JSP page in the code, you can declaratively associate an action forward mapping with the JSP and then use that `ActionForward` throughout your application.

The action forwards are specified in the configuration file, similar to action mappings. They can be specified at an `Action` level, as this forward is for the `logout` action mapping:

```
<action
  path="/logout"
  type="com.oreilly.struts.banking.action.LogoutAction"
  scope="request">
  <forward name="Success" path="/login.jsp" redirect="true"/>
</action>
```

The `logout` action declares a `forward` element named "Success", which forwards to the "/login.jsp" resource. The `redirect` attribute is specified and set to "true". Now, instead of performing a forward using a `RequestDispatcher`, the request will be redirected.

The action forward mappings also can be specified in a global section, independent of any specific action mapping. In the previous case, only the `logout` action mapping could reference the action forward named "Success", However, all action mappings can reference forwards declared in the `global-forwards` section. Here is an example `global-forwards` section from the banking configuration file:

```
<global-forwards>
  <forward name="SystemFailure" path="/systemerror.jsp" />
  <forward name="SessionTimeOut" path="/sessiontimeout.jsp" />
</global-forwards>
```

The forwards defined in this section are more general and don't apply to specific action mappings. Notice that every forward must have a `name` and `path`, but the `redirect` attribute is optional. If you don't specify a `redirect` attribute, its default value of "false" is used, and thus the framework will perform a forward. The `path` attribute in an action forward also can specify another Struts `Action`. You'll see an example of how to do this in Chapter 5.

Now that you understand from a high level how the Struts controller components operate, it's time to look at the next piece of the MVC puzzle—the model.

# Struts Model Components

There are several different ways to look at what constitutes a model for Struts. The lines between business and presentation objects can get quite blurry when dealing with web applications—one application's business objects are another's data transfer objects (DTOs).

It's important to keep the business objects separate from the presentation so that the application is not tightly coupled to one type of presentation. It's likely that the look and feel of a web site will change over time. Studies show that the freshness of a web site's appearance helps to attract new customers and keep existing customers coming back. This may not be as true in the business-to-business (B2B) world, but it's definitely true for business-to-consumer (B2C) applications, which make up the majority of the web applications used today.

## Using Data Transfer Objects

DTOs (sometimes referred to as value objects) often are used to provide a coarse-grained view of remote, fine-grained data. If your application were using entity beans, for example, instead of making several remote calls to get individual state about the object, you could make a single call that would return a local DTO containing all the data you need. Sometimes there is a summary and a detailed version for the remote object to mitigate how much data is returned.

Although the DTO represents the remote business object, it doesn't necessarily contain the same business logic. In fact, it generally doesn't contain any business logic at all—it represents a "snapshot" of the remote object at a particular instance in time, namely, when the client requested the data. DTOs also can be used to update the business object. However, this gets a little more complicated because of issues such as optimistic locking and synchronization.

For performance reasons, using DTOs in a distributed application is almost a necessity. It helps to reduce the network bandwidth and improve response time. It's also a good idea to use the same technique for smaller applications. Using a DTO in a Struts application helps to decouple the business objects from the presentation, making maintenance and future enhancements easier.

The type of model components that you use might also depend on whether you're building a traditional two-tier application or a multi-tiered distributed application. Typically, with a two-tiered application, the business objects are collocated with the web application. *Collocation* means that objects are deployed within the same JVM. This makes it easier to use these business objects to retrieve data for the views. However, just because it's easier doesn't necessarily make this a smart thing to do. The business objects may be made up of deep object graphs and may contain references to many other nonpresentation resources. If you're not careful, the business objects quickly can become coupled to a specific presentation, which can have unintended side effects each time the look and feel of the web site changes.

One benefit of separating your business objects from the presentation is that you can build coarse-grained objects that your JSP pages and custom tags will have an easier time dealing with. All of your business logic should remain separate from the presentation, and the presentation views should simply retrieve data from the DTO and display it.

The LoginAction class shown in Example 3-3 didn't contain the actual authentication logic. Because the Action class is part of the controller functionality, it delegates the handling of the business logic to another service. In the case of the LoginAction, it relies on a SecurityService component. The SecurityService component may be a session EJB, or just a wrapper around some JDBC code that performs the authentication. In either case, the LoginAction doesn't know or care how the service is implemented. This is helpful, because even if the implementation changes drastically, no code will have to change as long as the IAuthentication interface remains unchanged and is implemented by the service.

This approach also helps with reuse. Say you have another type of client, such as a Swing GUI, that needs to be authenticated. Because the logic is encapsulated in a separate component and not in the Action class, you are free to reuse this security service.

You should strive to keep business logic out of the Action classes to protect against change. In the case of the LoginAction, the login() method returns an object of class com.oreilly.struts.banking.view.UserView. This is an example of a DTO. Example 3-4 shows the UserView used in the example application.

*Example 3-4. The UserView value object used by the presentation tier*

```
package com.oreilly.struts.banking.view;

import java.util.Set;
import java.util.HashSet;
/**
 * A value object that wraps all of the user's security information
 */
public class UserView implements java.io.Serializable {
  private String id;
  private String lastName;
  private String firstName;

  // A unique collection of permission String objects
  private Set permissions = null;

  public UserView(String first, String last) {
    this(first, last, new HashSet());
  }

  public UserView(String first, String last, Set userPermissions) {
    super();
    firstName = first;
    lastName = last;
    permissions = userPermissions;
  }
```

```
  public boolean containsPermission(String permissionName) {
    return permissions.contains(permissionName);
  }

  public String getLastName() {
    return lastName;
  }

  public void setLastName(String name) {
    lastName = name;
  }

  public String getFirstName() {
    return firstName;
  }

  public void setFirstName(String name) {
    firstName = name;
  }

  public String getId() {
    return id;
  }

  public void setId(String id) {
    this.id = id;
  }
}
```

The UserView provides a coarse-grained view of a remote object. There might be five security tables, all joined by foreign keys that contain the data, but when the web tier gets a UserView, it already has been consolidated and made easier to access. In fact, one implementation of this application could get the data from a relational database and another from an LDAP instance. The nice thing about encapsulating the authentication behind the security service is that the presentation tier does not have to change if the security realm is switched. The Action is free to put the UserView object in the request or session and then forward it to a JSP, where the data can be extracted and presented to the user.

The Struts framework doesn't have a great deal of support in the way of model components. This is better left for EJB, CORBA, or some other type of component framework. You can access a database directly from the framework, but you still should attempt to separate that layer from all other parts of the framework. You can do this by making use of the appropriate design patterns to encapsulate the behavior.

# Struts View Components

The last of the MVC components to discuss are the view components. Arguably, they are the easiest to understand. The view components typically employed in a Struts application are:

- HTML
- Data transfer objects
- Struts ActionForms
- JavaServer Pages
- Custom tags
- Java resource bundles

## Using the Struts ActionForm

Struts ActionForm objects are used in the framework to pass client input data back and forth between the user and the business layer. The framework automatically collects the input from the request and passes this data to an Action using a form bean, which then can be passed along to the business layer. To keep the presentation layer decoupled from the business layer, you should not pass the ActionForm itself to the business layer; rather, create the appropriate DTO using the data from the ActionForm. The following steps illustrate how the framework processes an ActionForm for every request:

1. Check the mapping for the action and see if an ActionForm has been configured.
2. If an ActionForm is configured for the action, use the name attribute from the action element to look up the form bean configuration information.
3. Check to see if an instance of the ActionForm already has been created.
4. If an ActionForm instance is present in the appropriate scope and it's the same type as needed for the new request, reuse it.
5. Otherwise, create a new instance of the required ActionForm and store it in the appropriate scope (set by the scope attribute for the action element).
6. Call the reset( ) method on the ActionForm instance.
7. Iterate through the request parameters, and populate every parameter name that has a corresponding setter method in the ActionForm with the value for that request parameter.
8. Finally, if the validate attribute is set to "true", invoke the validate( ) method on the ActionForm instance and return any errors.

For every HTML page where form data is posted, you should use an ActionForm. The same ActionForm can be used for multiple pages if necessary, as long as the HTML fields and ActionForm properties match up.

Example 3-5 shows the com.oreilly.struts.banking.form.LoginForm that is used with the banking application.

*Example 3-5. The LoginForm used by the banking application*

```java
package com.oreilly.struts.banking.form;

import javax.servlet.http.HttpServletRequest;
import org.apache.struts.action.Action;
import org.apache.struts.action.ActionError;
import org.apache.struts.action.ActionErrors;
import org.apache.struts.action.ActionForm;
import org.apache.struts.action.ActionMapping;
import org.apache.struts.util.MessageResources;
/**
 * This ActionForm is used by the online banking appliation to validate
 * that the user has entered an accessNumber and a pinNumber. If one or
 * both of the fields are empty when validate( ) is called by the
 * ActionServlet, error messages are created.
 */
public class LoginForm extends ActionForm {
  // The user's private ID number
  private String pinNumber;
  // The user's access number
  private String accessNumber;

  public LoginForm() {
    super();
    resetFields();
  }
  /**
   * Called by the framework to validate the user has entered values in the
   * accessNumber and pinNumber fields.
   */
  public ActionErrors validate(ActionMapping mapping, HttpServletRequest req ){
    ActionErrors errors = new ActionErrors();

    // Get access to the message resources for this application.
    // There's no easy way to access the resources from an ActionForm.
    MessageResources resources =
      (MessageResources)req.getAttribute( Action.MESSAGES_KEY );

    // Check and see if the access number is missing.
    if(accessNumber == null || accessNumber.length() == 0) {
      String accessNumberLabel = resources.getMessage( "label.accessnumber" );
      ActionError newError =
        new ActionError("global.error.login.requiredfield", accessNumberLabel );
      errors.add(ActionErrors.GLOBAL_ERROR, newError);
    }

    // Check and see if the pin number is missing.
    if(pinNumber == null || pinNumber.length() == 0) {
      String pinNumberLabel = resources.getMessage( "label.pinnumber" );
      ActionError newError =
```

*Example 3-5. The LoginForm used by the banking application (continued)*

```
      new ActionError("global.error.login.requiredfield", pinNumberLabel );
      errors.add(ActionErrors.GLOBAL_ERROR, newError);
    }
    // Return the ActionErrors, if any.
    return errors;
  }

  /**
   * Called by the framework to reset the fields back to their default values.
   */
  public void reset(ActionMapping mapping, HttpServletRequest request) {
    // Clear out the accessNumber and pinNumber fields.
    resetFields();
  }
  /**
   * Reset the fields back to their defaults.
   */
  protected void resetFields() {
    this.accessNumber = "";
    this.pinNumber = "";
  }

  public void setAccessNumber(String nbr) {
    this.accessNumber = nbr;
  }

  public String getAccessNumber() {
    return this.accessNumber;
  }

  public String getPinNumber() {
    return this.pinNumber;
  }
  public void setPinNumber(String nbr) {
    this.pinNumber = nbr;
  }
}
```

The `ActionForm` class provided by the Struts framework implements several methods, but by far the two most important are the reset( ) and validate( ) methods:

```
    public void reset( ActionMapping mapping, HttpServletRequest request );
    public ActionErrors validate( ActionMapping mapping, HttpServletRequest request );
```

The default implementation for both methods in the Struts `ActionForm` class doesn't perform any default logic. You'll need to override these two methods in your `ActionForm` classes, as was done in the `LoginForm` class shown in Example 3-5.

The controller calls the reset( ) method right before it populates the `ActionForm` instance with values from the request. It gives the `ActionForm` a chance to reset its properties back to the default state. This is very important, as the form bean instance may be shared across different requests or accessed by different threads. However, if you are using an `ActionForm` instance across multiple pages, you might not want to implement the `reset()` method so that the values don't get reset until you're completely done with the instance. Another approach is to implement your own `resetFields()` method and call this method from the `Action` class after a successful update to the business tier.

The `validate()` method is called by the controller after the values from the request have been inserted into the `ActionForm`. The `ActionForm` should perform any input validation that can be done and return any detected errors to the controller. Business logic validation should be performed in the business objects, not in the `ActionForm`. The validation that occurs in the `ActionForm` is presentation validation only. Where to perform certain types of validation logic will be covered in detail in Chapters 6 and 7.

The `validate()` method in the `LoginForm` in Example 3-5 checks to see if the access number and/or pin number is missing and creates error messages if they are. If no errors are generated, the controller passes the `ActionForm` and several other objects to the `execute()` method. The `Action` instance can then pull the information out of the `ActionForm`.

 You might have noticed that the `execute()` method in the `Action` class contains an argument that is always of the type `ActionForm`. You will need to cast this argument to the appropriate subclass to retrieve the needed properties. To see an example of this, look back at Example 3-3.

Once you have coded your `ActionForm` classes, you need to inform your Struts application that they exist and tell it which action mappings should use which `ActionForms`. This is done in the configuration file. The first step is to configure all of the `ActionForms` for your application in the `form-beans` section of the configuration file. The following fragment from the banking configuration file informs Struts of the three `ActionForm` beans used by the banking application:

```
<form-beans>
  <form-bean
    name="loginForm"
    type="com.oreilly.struts.banking.form.LoginForm"/>
  <form-bean
    name="accountInformationForm"
    type="org.apache.struts.action.DynaActionForm">
    <form-property name="accounts" type="java.util.ArrayList"/>
  </form-bean>
  <form-bean
    name="accountDetailForm"
    type="org.apache.struts.action.DynaActionForm">
    <form-property
      name="view"
      type="com.oreilly.struts.banking.view.AccountDetailView"/>
  </form-bean>
</form-beans>
```

The name attribute for each form bean must be unique, and the type attribute must define a fully qualified Java class that extends the Struts ActionForm class. The next step is to use one of the form-bean names from the form-beans section in one or more action elements. The following fragment shows the mapping for the LoginAction, which you've already seen earlier in this chapter:

```
<action
    path="/login"
    type="com.oreilly.struts.banking.action.LoginAction"
    scope="request"
    name="loginForm"
    validate="true"
    input="/login.jsp">
    <forward name="Success" path="/action/getaccountinformation" redirect="true"/>
    <forward name="Failure" path="/login.jsp" redirect="true"/>
</action>
```

Notice that the name attribute of the login mapping matches one of the names in the form-beans section from earlier.

 Instances of the ActionForm class commonly are referred to as "form beans." I use this term throughout the book to refer to an object of type ActionForm.

One of the new features in Struts 1.1 is shown in the previous form-beans fragment. With previous versions of the framework, you always had to extend the ActionForm class with your own subclass, even if the ActionForm performed very generic behavior. With Struts 1.1, a new type of action form, called org. apache.struts.action. DynaActionForm, has been added. This class can be configured for an action mapping and will automatically handle the data passed from the HTML form to the Action. The DynaActionForm is able to deal with the data generically because it uses a Map to store the values internally. Chapter 7 will cover the DynaActionForm in more detail.

You may be wondering what the difference is between an ActionForm and the DTOs mentioned earlier. This is a good question, and one that is a little confusing for developers new to Struts.

The view components can use both ActionForms and DTOs to populate dynamic content. When no ActionForm is configured for a mapping, you can use DTOs to build the views. And when a form bean is defined for the mapping, there are several ways to handle extracting the data from the bean. One approach is to always wrap a form bean around one or more DTOs returned from the business tier and to force the Struts view components to access the DTO data through the form bean. Likewise, when a client submits an HTML page, Struts will invoke the form bean setter methods, which can shove the data back into the DTO after the validation method has completed successfully. This provides a single, cohesive interface to which the views can retrieve and submit the HTML data to. We'll discuss the various pros and cons of this and other approaches in Chapter 7.

## Using JSP for Presentation

JSP pages make up the majority of what has to be built for the Struts view components. Combined with custom tag libraries and HTML, JSP makes it easy to provide a set of views for an application.

Although JSP is the technology most commonly used by organizations and developers to display dynamic content, it's not the only option. Many developers feel that JSP has the following problems:

- Developers are free to embed application logic into the JSP pages, which can lead to applications that are difficult to maintain (with JSP 2.0, you can configure JSP pages to not allow scriptlets).

- Developers must learn the JSP syntax and how to program custom tags (although this will not be true when JSP 2.0 is final and the new expression language is available).

- The container must recompile the JSP page when a change is made to the page.

Some developers do not see these issues as a major problem, and many sites have been built using the JSP technology. However, for those that want alternatives, there are other forms of presentation technologies that can be combined with the Struts framework. One popular alternative is the XML/XSLT combination. This model combines the controller servlet from the Struts framework with XSLT and beans serialized from DTOs to render the views.

## Using Custom Tag Libraries

The Struts framework provides six core tag libraries that your applications can use. Each one has a different purpose and can be used individually or alongside others. You also may extend the Struts tags or create your own custom tags if you need additional functionality. The custom tag libraries that are included with the framework are the HTML, Bean, Logic, Template, Nested, and Tiles tag libraries.

To use these libraries in your application, you first need to register them with the web application in the *web.xml* file. You need to register only the tag libraries that you plan to use in your application. For example, if you are planning on using the HTML and Logic tag libraries, you must add the following fragment to the deployment descriptor for the web application:

```
<web-app>
  <taglib>
    <taglib-uri>/WEB-INF/struts-html.tld</taglib-uri>
    <taglib-location>/WEB-INF/struts-html.tld</taglib-location>
  </taglib>
  <taglib>
    <taglib-uri>/WEB-INF/struts-logic.tld</taglib-uri>
    <taglib-location>/WEB-INF/struts-logic.tld</taglib-location>
  </taglib>
</web-app>
```

More information on installing and configuring Struts for your application is provided in Appendix B.

The next step is to create your JSP pages and include the necessary `taglib` elements, depending on which tag libraries the page will need:

```
<%@ taglib uri="/WEB-INF/struts-html.tld" prefix="html" %>
<%@ taglib uri="/WEB-INF/struts-logic.tld" prefix="logic" %>
```

Once this is done and the JAR files are in the web application's CLASSPATH, you can use the custom tags in your JSP pages. Example 3-6 illustrates the usage of several of the Struts custom tags inside the *login.jsp* page for the banking application.

*Example 3-6. The login.jsp page used by the banking application*

```
<%@ taglib uri="/WEB-INF/struts-bean.tld" prefix="bean" %>
<%@ taglib uri="/WEB-INF/struts-html.tld" prefix="html" %>

<html:html>
<head>
  <html:base/>
  <title><bean:message key="title.login"/></title>
  <link rel="stylesheet" href="stylesheets/login_style_ie.css" type="text/css">
</head>

<body topmargin="0" leftmargin="5" marginheight="0" marginwidth="0" bgcolor="#6699FF">

<html:form action="login" focus="accessNumber">

<table border="0" cellpadding="0" cellspacing="0" width="100%" bgcolor="#6699FF">
  <tr><td>
    <html:img srcKey="image.logo" width="79" height="46"
      altKey="image.logo.alt" border="0"/>
  </td></tr>
</table>

<table border="0" cellpadding="0" cellspacing="0" width="100%">
 <tr><td bgcolor="#000000">
    <table border="0" cellpadding="0" cellspacing="0" width="1" height="2"></table>
  </td></tr>
</table>

<table border="0" cellpadding="0" cellspacing="0" width="1" height="1">
  <tr><td></td></tr>
</table>

<table>
  <tr><td></td></tr>
</table>

<table border="0" cellpadding="0" cellspacing="0" width="590">
 <tr><td width="15" height="31"></td><td width="12"></td></tr>
 <tr>
  <td width="15"></td>
```

```
  <td width="575" bgcolor="#FFFFFF" colspan="2">
      <table cellpadding="0" cellspacing="0" border="0" width="575" height="3">
 <tr><td></td></tr>
</table>
    </td>
</tr>
</table>

<table border="0" cellpadding="0" cellspacing="0" width="590" bgcolor="#ffffff">
  <tr>
    <td width="15" bgcolor="#6699FF"></td>
    <td width="15"></td><td width="379"></td>
    <td width="15"></td>
    <td width="15"></td>
    <td width="15"></td>
  </tr>
  <tr>
    <td bgcolor="#6699FF" width="15"></td>
    <td></td>
    <td valign="top">
       <table border="0" cellpadding="0" cellspacing="0">
    <tr class="fieldlabel">
      <td><bean:message key="label.accessnumber"/></td>
    </tr class="fieldlabel">
    <tr>
      <td><html:text property="accessNumber" size="9" maxlength="9"/></td>
      <td class="error"><html:errors/></td>
    </tr>
    <tr class="fieldlabel"><td height="10"></td></tr>
    <tr class="fieldlabel"><td><bean:message key="label.pinnumber"/></td></tr>
    <tr class="fieldlabel">
      <td><html:password property="pinNumber" size="4" maxlength="4"/></td>
    </tr>
    <tr><td height="10"></td></tr>
    <tr><td><html:submit styleClass="fieldlabel" value="Login"/></td></tr>
    <tr><td></td></tr>
</table>
</td>
  <td width="151" valign="top">
    <html:img srcKey="image.strutspower" altKey="image.strutspower.alt"/>
  </td>
</tr>
</table>
<%@include file="include/footer.jsp"%>
<br>

</html:form>
</body>
</html:html>
```

One of the first things that should strike you about the login page in Example 3-6 is that there's no Java code in it. Instead, you see mostly HTML formatting tags and several uses of Struts tag libraries. This is exactly the purpose of using custom tag libraries. No Java programming is necessary, so HTML designers can work freely with the page layout without being burdened by the programming aspects of the page. The other nice feature is that many JSP pages can use the same tags. For more information on tag libraries, see Chapter 8.

## Using Message Resource Bundles

One of the hardest customizations that developers face is to quickly and effortlessly customize a web application for multiple languages. Java has several built-in features that help support internationalization; Struts builds on those features to provide even more support.

The Java library includes a set of classes to support reading message resources from either a Java class or a properties file. The core class in this set is the java.util. ResourceBundle. The Struts framework provides a similar set of classes, based around the org.apache.struts.util.MessageResources class, that provides similar functionality but allows for more of the flexibility that the framework requires.

With a Struts application, you must provide a resource bundle for each language you want to support. The name of the class or properties file must adhere to the guidelines listed in the JavaDocs for the java.util.ResourceBundle class. Example 3-7 shows the properties file used by the example banking application.

*Example 3-7. The resource bundle for the banking application*

```
# Labels
label.accessnumber=Access Number
label.pinnumber=Pin Number
label.accounts=Accounts
label.balance=Balance
label.totalassets=Total Assets
label.account=Account
label.balance=Available Balance
label.description=Description
label.amount=Amount
label.deposits=Deposits
label.withdrawls=Withdrawls
label.openingbalance=Opening Balance


# Links
link.customeragreement=Customer Agreement
link.privacy=Privacy
link.security=Security
link.viewaccountdetail=View Account Detail
```

*Example 3-7. The resource bundle for the banking application (continued)*

```
# Page Titles
title.login=Struts Online Banking - Account Login
title.accountinfo=Struts Online Banking - Account Information
title.accountdetail=Struts Online Banking - Account Detail

# Button Labels
label.button.login=Login

# Error messages
global.error.invalidlogin=<li>Invalid Access Number and/or Pin</li>

global.error.login.requiredfield=<li>The {0} is required for login</li>

# Images
image.logo=images/logo.gif
image.logo.alt=Struts Online Banking

image.logout=images/logout.gif
image.logout.alt=Logout

image.strutspower=images/struts-power.gif
image.strutspower.alt=Powered By Struts

image.transfer=images/transfer.gif
image.transfer.alt="Transfer Funds"

image.clear=images/clear.gif
```

If you look back at the *login.jsp* page in Example 3-6, you can see how the messages from the bundle are used. For example, the following fragment from the login page illustrates the key *title.login* from Example 3-6 being used and inserted between the HTML title tags in the page.

```
<title><bean:message key="title.login"/></title>
```

The Struts org.apache.struts.taglib.bean.MessageTag is one of several custom tags included in the framework that can take advantage of the resource bundle. JSP pages can retrieve values from the resource bundle using the MessageTag based on a key, as shown in the login page in Example 3-6. The key in the message tag must correspond to a value on the left side of the equals sign in the bundle. Case is important, and the value must match exactly.

 A message resource bundle can be used for more than just localization—it also can save you time during application maintenance. For example, if you use the same text messages or labels throughout various parts of your web site or application, when one or more of these values need to change, you need make the change only in a single location. Even if you don't have internationalization requirements, you still should use resource bundles.

With Struts 1.1, you can define multiple `MessageResources` for an application. This allows you to isolate certain types of resources into separate bundles. For example, you might want to store the image resources for an application in one bundle and the rest of the resources in another. How you organize your application's resources is up to you, but you now have the flexibility to separate them based on some criteria. For example, some applications choose to separate along component lines: all resources relating to the catalog go into one bundle, order and shopping-cart resources go into another, and so on.

## Multiple Application Support

Prior to Version 1.1, each Struts application was limited to a single configuration file. The single instance of the file, normally called *struts-config.xml*, was specified in the web application deployment descriptor. It was the sole provider of the configuration information for the Struts application. The fact that there was only one place to put configuration information made it very difficult for larger projects, because it often became a bottleneck and caused contentions to use and modify this file.

With the advent of multi-application support in Version 1.1, this problem has been alleviated. You now can define multiple configuration files, allowing developers to work better in parallel. Applications modules, as they currently are known, are discussed further in Chapters 4, 5, 6, and 7.

## Summary

The Struts framework provides an implementation for the MVC structure, tailored for a web application. The Struts `ActionServlet`, `RequestProcessor`, and `Action` classes provide the controller components; the `Action` communicates with your application's model components; and the combination of the `ActionForm`, DTOs, JSP pages, and tag libraries make up the view.

This chapter focused on Struts at a high level and left out many of the details that make the framework even better. Struts, like other valuable software frameworks, allows you to focus on developing the business logic, instead of spending expensive development time on low-level infrastructure functionality such as request dispatching and field-level validation. Hopefully, this peripheral discussion has enticed you to read on and explore the framework details in the rest of the book.

# CHAPTER 4

# Configuring Struts Applications

The Struts framework uses two separate but somewhat related types of configuration files, which must be configured properly before an application will work correctly. Due to the popularity, flexibility, and self-describing nature of XML, both types of configuration files are based on XML.

The web application deployment descriptor named *web.xml* is described fully in the Java Servlet specification.* This configuration file is necessary for all web applications, not just those built with the Struts framework. However, there is Struts-specific deployment information within it that must be configured when building Struts applications.

 Although the Struts framework supports the 2.2 Servlet specification, many servlet containers already have support for Version 2.3. This book includes coverage of the 2.2 and 2.3 specifications.

The second configuration file that we will examine is the Struts configuration file. It is commonly named *struts-config.xml*, but you can name it just about anything you want. The Struts configuration file makes it possible for you to declaratively configure many of your application's settings. You can think of the Struts configuration file as the rules for the web application.

## The Storefront Application

Throughout the rest of this book, we will construct a shopping-cart type application to use for all of the examples. By the end of the book, we should have a fairly complete application that uses most of the Struts 1.1 features. Figure 4-1 shows the main page of the Storefront example application.

---

* See the Java Servlet Specification Version 2.3, Chapter SRV.13.

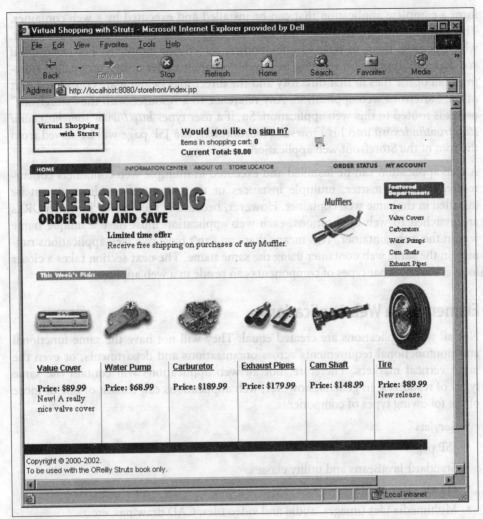

*Figure 4-1. The main page of the Storefront application*

The Storefront application will demonstrate an e-commerce automotive parts supplier, but you can substitute any items you want as long as you have your own images and data to put into the application. In the end, the Storefront application will be a complete web archive (WAR) file that can be deployed into any compliant web container and used as an example for many different purposes.

# What Is a Web Application?

Applications built using the Struts framework are, at their core, web applications. A *web application* is a collection of individual components that, once bound together,

---

form a complete application that can be installed and executed by a web container. The components are tied together because they reside in the same web context, which permits them to refer to one another, directly or indirectly. For example, if you have an application running in a web container under a directory called *storefront*, all of the files in that directory and the directories below it are considered part of the Storefront web application. Any reference to a resource with the "storefront" prefix is routed to this web application. So, if a user types *http://www.somehost.com/storefront/index.jsp* into his browser's location bar, the JSP page will be served from the root of the Storefront web application.

A web application can be installed and executed in multiple web containers concurrently. For that matter, multiple instances of the same web application can be installed in the same web container. However, because of the manner in which URLs are matched to web applications, each web application must have a unique name within the web container. This means that you can't have two web applications running in the same web container using the same name. The next section takes a closer look at exactly what types of components can reside in a web application.

## Elements of a Web Application

Not all web applications are created equal. They will not have the same functional and nonfunctional requirements across organizations and departments, or even the same vertical markets. Therefore, not all web applications will contain the same types of resources. In general, however, web applications can consist of one or more of the following types of components:

- Servlets
- JSP pages
- Standard JavaBeans and utility classes
- HTML documents
- Multimedia files (images, audio and video files, CAD drawings, etc.)
- Client-side applets, stylesheets, and JavaScript files
- Text documents
- Meta-information, which ties together all of the above components

## The Web Application Directory Structure

A web application typically consists of a structured hierarchy of directories. Although the Servlet specification does not require servlet containers to support a hierarchical structure, it recommends that they do so, and most, if not all, comply with this recommendation. The root directory of the hierarchy serves as the document root for the web application. As discussed earlier, requests made using a web application's root context path are served out of the directory for that web application.

Within the web application directory hierarchy, a special directory named *WEB-INF* must be created. This directory is the repository for meta-information relating to the web application. It is a private directory; no resource within it is accessible to a client. However, the resources in the *WEB-INF* directory are visible to servlets and Java classes that reside within the web application.

Because the Servlet specification requires that the *WEB-INF* directory should not be visible to a web client, this is an ideal location for files and other resources that you do not want to expose outside the application. Web application resources such as XML configuration files and other private application resources should be placed within this directory. As you'll see later in this chapter, the Struts configuration file is also normally located here.

The *WEB-INF* directory is where the deployment descriptor for the web application should be placed. The deployment descriptor is covered in detail in the next section.

There are two special directories underneath *WEB-INF* that get special treatment by the web container. The *WEB-INF/classes* directory is used for servlets and utility classes that can be used by the web application. If the Java classes are scoped within a Java package, the *classes* directory must contain the proper subdirectories that match the package name. For example, suppose you had a Java servlet named com.oreilly.struts.framework.StorefrontController for a web application named Storefront. The StorefrontController.class file would have to be placed in the framework directory as shown in Figure 4-2.

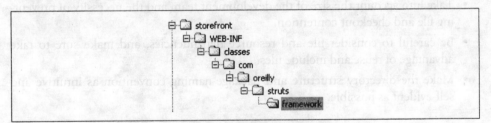

*Figure 4-2. Java classes must be in the proper directories*

The other special subdirectory is *WEB-INF/lib*. This subdirectory is where Java Archive (JAR) files can be deployed and will be picked up by the class loader for the web application.

Based on the 2.3 Servlet specification, the web application class loader must load classes first from the *WEB-INF/classes* directory, then from library JARs located in the *WEB-INF/ lib* directory.

Other than these special requirements, the directory structure for a web application is left up to the developer. It should be based on the functional and nonfunctional needs of the application. With smaller web applications, files and resources may be combined into a few common directories. For larger web applications, however, each component may need to have a separate directory underneath the web application root directory. This will allow for easier development and maintenance. Figure 4-3 shows the directory structure for the Storefront web application.

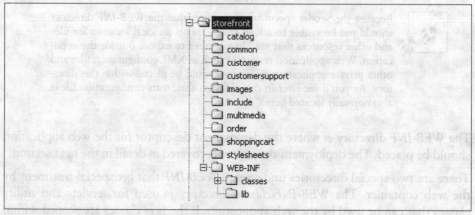

*Figure 4-3. The directory structure for the Storefront web application*

Consider these tips when choosing the directories for your Struts application:

- Keep optional components separate from required ones so that partial deployment will be easier to support.

- Take into account the size of the development team and the necessity of preventing file and checkout contention.

- Be careful to consider file and resource dependencies, and make sure to take advantage of reuse and include files.

- Make the directory structure and package-naming convention as intuitive and self-evident as possible.

 For many containers, directory and filenames are case-sensitive. Make sure that you are consistent with whatever case convention you choose for your application.

## Web Application Archive Files

Web applications are often packaged as web archive (WAR) files, which must have an extension of *.war*. For example, if we packaged the Storefront application as a WAR file, it would be named *storefront.war*. When a web application is packaged as a WAR file, it must maintain its relative directory structure, as illustrated in Figure 4-3.

Although there are some subtle differences, a WAR file is really just a ZIP file with a different extension. In fact, you can also use a ZIP utility application such as WinZip to create and unpack WAR files.

Web containers are capable of loading a WAR file and exploding the resources back into the structure required by the container. The WAR file format is most useful when you need to distribute an application. It also can be part of a much larger distributable file called an enterprise archive (EAR) file. Chapter 16 discusses the best practices of packaging your application using these different formats.

# The Web Application Deployment Descriptor

The web application deployment descriptor conveys configuration information between application developers, deployers, and assemblers. Web containers also use the descriptor to configure and load web applications when the container is started.

All servlet containers that are compliant with the 2.3 Servlet specification are required to support the following types of deployment information:

- Initialization parameters
- Session configuration
- Servlet declarations
- Servlet mappings
- Application lifecycle listener classes
- Filter definitions and mappings
- MIME type mappings
- Welcome file list
- Error pages

Security configuration information is not required unless the servlet container is part of a J2EE implementation. The following elements are not required unless the servlet container is using JSP pages or is part of a J2EE application server:

- Tag library mappings
- JNDI References

 Much of the functionality described in this list was added in the 2.3 version of the Servlet specification. If you are using a 2.2-compliant container, it will not be available to you. Struts 1.1 supports the 2.2 and 2.3 Servlet specifications.

# Web Application Deployment Descriptor DTD

The format for both the web application deployment descriptor and the Struts configuration file is based on a *Document Type Definition* (DTD), which defines the legal building blocks that may be used in the XML files. From the DTD point of view, all XML documents, including the web application deployment descriptor and the Struts configuration file, are made up of the following elements:

- Elements
- Tags
- Attributes
- Entities
- PCDATA
- CDATA

Using these components, DTDs help to specify valid and well-formed XML documents.* The DTD for the 2.3 web application deployment descriptor can be downloaded from *http://java.sun.com/dtd/index.html*.

The following DTD declaration shows the top-level elements that make up the deployment descriptor for a web application:

```
<!ELEMENT web-app (icon?, display-name?, description?,
    distributable?, context-param*, filter*, filter-mapping*,
    listener*, servlet*, servlet-mapping*, session-config?, mime-
    mapping*, welcome-file-list?, error-page*, taglib*, resource-
    env-ref*, resource-ref*, security-constraint*, login-config?,
    security-role*, env-entry*, ejb-ref*, ejb-local-ref*)
>
```

The web-app element is the root of the deployment descriptor for a web application. The other elements inside the parentheses are child elements, which must be placed inside the root web-app element within the XML file. The symbols next to the child elements indicate the allowed multiplicity of the child elements within the XML file. Table 4-1 provides a brief explanation of the symbols.

The order of the child elements is implied by their order inside of the parent element. For instance, in the web-app syntax, the servlet element must come before the servlet-mapping element, the servlet-mapping element must come before the taglib element, and so on.

---

* A well-formed XML document is one that is properly formatted with all beginning tags closed with end tags, all attributes quoted properly, all entities declared, and so on. When an XML document is well-formed, it is easier for a computer program to parse it and deliver it over a network. A valid XML document is one that declares a DTD and adheres to the rules set forth in that DTD. For more information, see *Java & XML* by Brett McLaughlin (O'Reilly).

*Table 4-1. Multiplicity symbols of child elements within a DTD*

| Symbol | Meaning |
|---|---|
| No symbol | Indicates that the child element must occur once and only once within the parent element. |
| + | Declares that the child element can occur one or more times within the parent element. |
| * | Declares that the child element can occur zero or more times within the parent element. This symbol is used quite often. |
| ? | Declares that the child element can occur zero or one time within the parent element. In other words, the child element is optional. This symbol is used quite often. |

# Configuring the web.xml File for Struts

Although the *web.xml* file is used for configuring any generic web application, there are a few Struts-specific configuration options that you must configure within this file when using the Struts framework. The next section describes the necessary steps that you'll need to perform to ensure that your Struts application is properly configured.

## Mapping the Struts ActionServlet

The first and perhaps most important step that you need to perform is to configure the ActionServlet that will receive all incoming requests for the application.

 You need to configure only a single ActionServlet, regardless of the number of application modules that are being used. Some developers choose to set up multiple controller servlets to handle different functional areas of the application. Because servlets are multithreaded, you don't gain any real performance or scalability value by using multiple ActionServlet mappings.

There are two steps in configuring the Struts controller servlet in the *web.xml* file. The first step is to use the servlet element to configure the servlet instance that can later be mapped in the servlet-mapping element. The child elements that can be used in the servlet element are shown here:

```
<!ELEMENT servlet (icon?, servlet-name, display-name?, description?,
    (servlet-class|jsp-file), init-param*, load-on-startup?, run-
    as?, security-role-ref*)
>
```

The child elements that we are most interested in are servlet-name, servlet-class, and init-param. The servlet-name element specifies the name used by the deployment descriptor to reference the servlet throughout the remainder of the file. When you're configuring the servlet-class element for a Struts application, this element must specify a fully qualified class that extends the org.apache.struts.action. ActionServlet class.

Because the Struts ActionServlet class is not abstract, you are free to use that class and avoid having to create a subclass of the ActionServlet for your application. With earlier versions of the Struts framework, it was more important to extend the ActionServlet class with one of your own because most of the processing occurred there, and subclassing allowed you to override that functionality with your own. With Version 1.1, however, most of the processing functionality has been moved to another class, which you can configure declaratively (as you'll see later in this chapter). There is little reason to create your own ActionServlet class, although you are still free to do so.

The following *web.xml* fragment illustrates how to use the servlet element to configure the servlet class:

```
<web-app>
 <servlet>
  <servlet-name>storefront</servlet-name>
  <servlet-class>org.apache.struts.action.ActionServlet</servlet-class>
 </servlet>
</web-app>
```

The next step that needs to be performed to configure the Struts controller servlet in the deployment descriptor is to configure the servlet mapping. This is done using the servlet-mapping element. The following partial deployment descriptor illustrates how to combine the servlet-mapping element with the servlet element shown previously:

```
<web-app>
 <servlet>
  <servlet-name>storefront</servlet-name>
  <servlet-class>org.apache.struts.action.ActionServlet</servlet-class>
 </servlet>
 <servlet-mapping>
  <servlet-name>storefront</servlet-name>
  <url-pattern>*.do</url-pattern>
 </servlet-mapping>
</web-app>
```

Notice that the value in the servlet-name element within the servlet element must match the value in the servlet-name element within the servlet-mapping element. This tells the web container that the ActionServlet should service all requests having an extension of *.do*.

### Mapping requests to servlets

This is a good time to digress for a moment and discuss how the URLs that a user types into a browser are mapped to the correct web application and servlet. When a web application is installed in a container, the container is responsible for assigning a ServletContext to it. There is a single instance of a ServletContext object for each web application deployed in a container.

If the container is distributable and uses more than one JVM, the web application may have a separate `ServletContext` instance for each JVM.

The `ServletContext` provides an external view of the web container environment for a servlet. A servlet can use the `ServletContext` object to gain access to external resources, log events, and store attributes and objects that other servlet instances in the same context can access. It's essentially an application-scope shared resource.

Because a servlet is associated with a specific web application, all requests that begin with a specific request path (known as the *context path*) are routed to the web application associated with that servlet. Servlets associated with the default application have an empty string (" ") as the context path.

When a web container receives a client request, it must determine the correct web application to forward it to. The web container determines this by matching the URL with the longest context path that matches an installed web application.

For example, suppose that there are two web applications installed in a container. One web application is given the name Storefront and is located off the root directory of the container at */storefront*. The second web application is called Storefront_demo and is located off the root directory at */storefront_demo*.

If a client request arrives at the server with a URL of *http://www.somehost.com/storefront_demo/login.do*, the server will match it to the web application that has the closest match, which in this case would be the Storefront_demo application. Once the container determines the correct context or web application, it must determine which servlet in the web application should process the request. The web container uses the request URL, minus the context path, to determine the path that will be used to map the request to the correct servlet.

The web container uses the following guidelines to find the first successful match:

1. The container attempts to locate an exact match of the request path to the path of a servlet.

2. The container recursively tries to match the longest path prefix. The servlet that contains the longest match, if any, is selected.

3. If the URL path contains an extension—for example, *.do*—the servlet container tries to match a servlet that handles requests for that extension. The extension is defined as the part of the segment after the last dot (.).

4. If none of the previous rules produces a match, the container attempts to use a default servlet, if one is configured. Otherwise, the request returns an error response.

The web container uses case-sensitive string comparisons when checking for a match.

The concept of extension mappings was mentioned in Step 3 of the matching guidelines. There is another type of mapping that can be used, known as *path mapping*. A servlet-mapping that uses path mapping allows a URL that doesn't contain an extension to match to the servlet. Using the earlier Storefront servlet mapping, the following partial *web.xml* file illustrates how path mapping is configured:

```
<web-app>
 <servlet>
  <servlet-name>storefront</servlet-name>
  <servlet-class>org.apache.struts.action.ActionServlet</servlet-class>
 </servlet>
 <servlet-mapping>
  <servlet-name>storefront</servlet-name>
  <url-pattern>/action/*</url-pattern>
 </servlet-mapping>
</web-app>
```

Using path mapping, all requests mapped to this web application that contain the string "/action" in the request URL will be serviced by the Storefront servlet, regardless of what is in place of the * character.

## Specifying Multiple Application Modules

As was briefly discussed in Chapter 3, the Struts 1.1 release added the ability to define multiple Struts configuration files, one for each supported application module. In previous versions of the framework, you specified a relative path to the single Struts configuration file using the config initialization parameter. With Version 1.1 and introduction of the concept of application modules, you can now create multiple Struts configuration files and specify them in the *web.xml* file using multiple config initialization parameters and the application module prefix. The next section discusses the initialization parameters that can be configured for a servlet.

## Declaring the Initialization Parameters

Initialization parameters are used to make configuration options available to a servlet. This allows the developer to declaratively affect the runtime environment of the servlet. Initialization parameters are configured within the servlet element using init-param elements, as shown in the following *web.xml* fragment:

```
<web-app>
 <servlet>
 <servlet-name>storefront</servlet-name>
 <servlet-class>org.apache.struts.action.ActionServlet</servlet-class>
 <init-param>
```

```
      <param-name>config</param-name>
      <param-value>/WEB-INF/struts-config.xml</param-value>
    </init-param>
    <init-param>
      <param-name>host</param-name>
      <param-value>localhost</param-value>
    </init-param>
    <init-param>
      <param-name>port</param-name>
      <param-value>7001</param-value>
    </init-param>
  </servlet>

  <servlet-mapping>
    <servlet-name>storefront</servlet-name>
    <url-pattern>*.do</url-pattern>
  </servlet-mapping>
</web-app>
```

You can specify any parameter you need within the init-param element, as long as it's a name/value pair. For example, the previous web deployment descriptor included initialization parameters for a host and port. If you were using EJB, this might be a way to include the server connection information. Zero or more init-param elements are allowed.

There are specific initialization parameters that can be specified for the Struts servlet. In earlier versions of Struts, many of the configuration options that are now in the Struts configuration file were configured by adding init-param elements. Although applications that were built and tested with Version 1.0 will continue to work using Version 1.1, you may want to move some of the initialization parameters that currently are specified in the web deployment descriptor to the proper location in the Struts configuration file. Although the framework includes functionality that allows the previous initialization parameters to work in the *web.xml* file, we will cover the 1.1 parameters here. Table 4-2 identifies the initialization parameters that can be specified for Struts 1.1.

*Table 4-2. Initialization parameters for web.xml using Struts 1.1*

| Name | Purpose/default value |
| --- | --- |
| config | A context-relative path to the default Struts configuration file. The default value is /WEB-INF/struts-config.xml, which serves as the default application. Starting with Struts 1.1, you can specify a comma-separated list of configuration files for this paramter. |
| config/sub1 | Specify additional application modules by using the value config/ and the prefix of the module. In this example, the init-param name would be config/module1, and the value might be WEB-INF/struts-sub1-config.xml. This tells the controller to load the application module mod1 from the additional Struts configuration file. You can declare as many application modules as you need. |
| convertNull | Force simulation of the Struts 1.0 behavior when populating forms. If set to true, the numeric Java wrapper class types such as java.lang.Integer will default to null rather than 0. The default is false. |
| validating | A validating XML parser is used to process the configuration file. This is strongly recommended. The default value is true. |

There are several initialization parameters that have been deprecated in Version 1.1. Most of them are now supported through the Struts configuration file, which is discussed later in the chapter.

## Using Multiple Struts Configuration Files

We've briefly mentioned using multiple application modules with Struts 1.1, but now you can use multiple configuration files as well. This is possible because the previously monolithic Struts configuration file has now been separated into individual XML files, making it possible to declare each them with the config initialization parameter. This is helpful because no single Struts configuration file now contends for resources during development. Using multiple files also makes is easier to support optional functionality. If, for example, you don't need to deploy certain Struts actions or other configuration elements, you can group them into a single file and remove all of them at once by removing that file from the list in *web.xml*. The following init-param fragment shows how to include more than one Struts configuration file:

```
<init-param>
  <param-name>config</param-name>
  <param-value>/WEB-INF/struts-config.xml,/WEB-INF/other-struts-config.xml
  </param-value>
</init-param>
```

You can declare as many configuration files as needed.

## Configuring the Tag Libraries

The Struts framework provides several JSP tag libraries that you must configure in the web application deployment descriptor if you choose to use them. You inform the container of these tag libraries by declaring one or more taglib elements within the web deployment descriptor. The following partial *web.xml* file illustrates how the tag libraries are configured within the web-app element:

```
<web-app>
 <servlet>
  <servlet-name>storefront</servlet-name>
  <servlet-class>org.apache.struts.action.ActionServlet</servlet-class>
  <init-param>
   <param-name>config</param-name>
   <param-value>/WEB-INF/struts-config.xml</param-value>
  </init-param>
  <init-param>
   <param-name>host</param-name>
   <param-value>localhost</param-value>
  </init-param>
  <init-param>
   <param-name>port</param-name>
   <param-value>7001</param-value>
  </init-param>
 </servlet>
```

```
<servlet-mapping>
  <servlet-name>storefront</servlet-name>
  <url-pattern>*.do</url-pattern>
</servlet-mapping>

<taglib>
  <taglib-uri>/WEB-INF/struts-html.tld</taglib-uri>
  <taglib-location>/WEB-INF/struts-html.tld</taglib-location>
</taglib>

<taglib>
  <taglib-uri>/WEB-INF/struts-bean.tld</taglib-uri>
  <taglib-location>/WEB-INF/struts-bean.tld</taglib-location>
</taglib>

<taglib>
  <taglib-uri>/WEB-INF/struts-logic.tld</taglib-uri>
  <taglib-location>/WEB-INF/struts-logic.tld</taglib-location>
</taglib>
</web-app>
```

The taglib element has two subelements: taglib-uri and taglib-location. The taglib-uri element specifies a URI identifying a tag library that is used by the web application. The value may be either a relative or an absolute URI. It must be a valid URI, but here it's used as a unique identifier for the tag library. The taglib-location element specifies the location (as a resource) of the tag library descriptor file.

The Struts tag libraries are not the only ones that can be declared in the web application deployment descriptor. If you create any of your own custom tag libraries, you should create taglib elements for them here as well.

## Setting Up the Welcome File List

The welcome-file-list element allows you to configure default resources that should be used when a valid but partial URI is entered for a web application. You can specify multiple welcome files, and they will be used in the order in which they are listed.

Suppose we configured the welcome-file-list element for the Storefront application as in Example 4-1.

*Example 4-1. The welcome-file-list element for the Storefront application*

```
<welcome-file-list>
 <welcome-file>index.jsp</welcome-file>
</welcome-file-list>
```

This indicates that a request to the server for *http://www.somehost.com/storefront*, which is the root of the Storefront application, should resolve to *http://www.somehost.com/storefront/index.jsp*. This is beneficial because most containers would, by default, look for *index.html* or *index.htm* instead. You can specify multiple welcome-file elements within the welcome-file-list. This might be helpful if, for example, you deployed your application on various types of containers and the first welcome-file resource was not found on the server. The container would continue to try to match the welcome files up to the request URI until it found one on the server and served that resource to the client. The order of the welcome file entries in the deployment descriptor is used for the matching process.

There should be no trailing or leading "/" characters in the welcome-file element. If no welcome files are declared for the web application or the URI entered by a client, the web container may handle the request appropriately—for example, it may return a 404 (File Not Found) error response or a directory listing. It's a good idea to configure a welcome file for at least the root web application.

### Using a Struts action in the welcome file list

Because the web containers don't use the servlet mappings for resources in the welcome-file-list, you can't directly set up a welcome-file element to use a Struts action.

However, there is an alternate way that allows you to achieve the same results. First, create a global forward in the Struts configuration file for the action that you would like to invoke:

```
<global-forwards>
  <forward name="welcome" path="viewsignin.do"/>
</global-forwards>
```

Then create a JSP page called *welcome.jsp* (the name actually can be anything you want) and use the Struts forward tag to forward to the global forward when the page is loaded. The *welcome.jsp* page only has to contain:

```
<%@ taglib uri="/WEB-INF/struts-logic.tld" prefix="logic" %>
<html>
  <body>
    <logic:forward name="welcome"/>
  </body>
</html>
```

You then need to add a welcome-file element for the *welcome.jsp* page:

```
<welcome-file-list>
  <welcome-file>welcome.jsp</welcome-file>
</welcome-file-list>
```

Containers using the *welcome.jsp* resource will automatically forward to the forward named welcome, which was defined in the global-forwards section. The welcome forward in turn invokes the viewsignin.do action and achieves the desired result.

## Configuring Error Handling in web.xml

Although the Struts framework provides a suitable error-handling mechanism, there are times that problems slip through the exception-handling crack and users are shown a servlet or JSP exception. To absolutely prevent this from happening, you should use the error-page element available to the web application deployment descriptor. Example 4-2 shows a partial *web.xml* file that uses the error-page element to prevent users from seeing a 404 or a 500 (Internal Server) error.

*Example 4-2. Using the error-page element*

```
<web-app>
  <!-- Other elements go here -->

  <error-page>
    <error-code>404</error-code>
    <location>/common/404.jsp</location>
  </error-page>

  <error-page>
    <error-code>500</error-code>
    <location>/common/500.jsp</location>
  </error-page>
</web-app>
```

When an error status code is set in the response, the container consults the list of error-page declarations for the web application. If a match is found, the container returns the resource indicated by the location element. The value of the location element must begin with a "/" character, and it must refer to a resource within the web application.

If you need to refer to a resource outside of the web application, you can use the HTML Refresh meta tag. To do this, refer to a static HTML document in the location element that contains only the following line:

```
<meta http-equiv="Refresh" content="0;URL=http://www.somehost.com/404.jsp">
```

When the error occurs, the Refresh meta tag will reload immediately, but it will use the alternate URL provided. This strategy also is a good way to allow users to refer to resources with a static extension, such as *.htm*, but then reload to a dynamic page, such as a JSP page.

> For example, you can use this approach to show a "Still Processing" page. You might want to set the reload time to a value greater than zero. The URL can be a Struts action—if the processing isn't finished, it will just call the same page again. If processing has completed, it can forward to a completed page.

A servlet also can generate exceptions for which you can declare error pages. Instead of specifying the error-code element, you can specify a fully qualified Java class using the exception-type element. Servlets can throw the following exceptions during processing:

- RuntimeException or Error
- ServletException or subclasses
- IOException or subclasses

The Java exception class declared in the exception-type element must be one of these.

Example 4-3 illustrates how you would substitute the exception-type element for the error-code.

*Example 4-3. Using the exception-type instead of the error-code element*

```
<web-app>
 <error-page>
  <exception-type>javax.servlet.ServletException</exception-type>
  <location>/common/system_error.jsp</location>
 </error-page>
</web-app>
```

For the majority of this chapter, you have been shown partial deployment descriptors. This was done mainly to save space, but also so that we could ease our way into the various supported elements. Now it's time to include a complete example of a web deployment descriptor. Example 4-4 shows the web deployment descriptor for the Storefront application.

*Example 4-4. A complete web.xml file configured for Struts 1.1*

```
<?xml version="1.0" encoding="UTF-8"?>

<!DOCTYPE web-app
    PUBLIC "-//Sun Microsystems, Inc.//DTD Web Application 2.3//EN"
    "http://java.sun.com/dtd/web-app_2_3.dtd">

<web-app>
 <servlet>
  <servlet-name>storefront</servlet-name>
  <servlet-class>org.apache.struts.action.ActionServlet</servlet-class>
  <init-param>
   <param-name>config</param-name>
   <param-value>/WEB-INF/struts-config.xml</param-value>
  </init-param>

  <load-on-startup>1</load-on-startup>
 </servlet>

 <servlet-mapping>
  <servlet-name>storefront</servlet-name>
  <url-pattern>/action/*</url-pattern>
 </servlet-mapping>

 <welcome-file-list>
  <welcome-file>index.jsp</welcome-file>
 </welcome-file-list>
```

```
<error-page>
  <error-code>404</error-code>
  <location>/common/404.jsp</location>
</error-page>
<error-page>
  <error-code>500</error-code>
  <location>/common/500.jsp</location>
</error-page>

<taglib>
  <taglib-uri>/WEB-INF/struts-html.tld</taglib-uri>
  <taglib-location>/WEB-INF/struts-html.tld</taglib-location>
</taglib>
<taglib>
  <taglib-uri>/WEB-INF/struts-bean.tld</taglib-uri>
  <taglib-location>/WEB-INF/struts-bean.tld</taglib-location>
</taglib>
<taglib>
  <taglib-uri>/WEB-INF/struts-logic.tld</taglib-uri>
  <taglib-location>/WEB-INF/struts-logic.tld</taglib-location>
</taglib>
</web-app>
```

# The Struts Configuration File

The Struts framework depends on one or more configuration files to be able to load and create the necessary application-specific components at startup. The configuration files allow the behavior of the framework components to be specified declaratively, rather than having the information and behavior hardcoded. This gives developers the flexibility to provide their own extensions, which the framework can discover dynamically.

The configuration file is based on the XML format and can be validated against the Struts DTD *struts-config_1_1.dtd*. Although there are some similarities between the 1.0 and 1.1 versions of the framework with respect to the configuration file, there are at least as many differences. Fortunately, the designers of the framework have made backward compatibility a goal of the Struts 1.1 release; therefore, your 1.0 applications should continue to work properly with the new version.

## Configuring Multiple Application Modules

Application modules were mentioned briefly in Chapter 3, but we haven't yet fully introduced this new feature. With application modules, you can define multiple Struts configuration files, one for each supported module. Each application module can provide its own configuration information, including message resources, and be completely independent from other modules.

Application modules allow a single Struts application to be split into separate projects, making parallel development easier to accomplish. Although the functionality for application modules exists in the framework, you are not required to implement more than one (the default application module). We'll discuss application modules further in Chapters 5, 6, and 7. For now, we'll concentrate on configuring the default application; we'll see how easy it is to add additional modules later.

## The org.apache.struts.config Package

The org.apache.struts.config package was added to Struts 1.1. The framework uses JavaBeans at runtime to hold the configuration information it reads from the Struts configuration files. Figure 4-4 shows the essential classes from the config package.

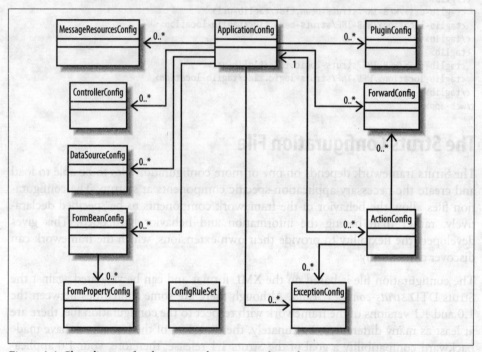

Figure 4-4. Class diagram for the org.apache.struts.config package

Each class in the config package holds information from a specific section of the configuration file. After the configuration file has been validated and parsed, the Struts framework uses instances of these beans to represent in-memory versions of the information that has been declared in the configuration file. These classes act as runtime containers of the configuration information and are used by the framework components as needed.

The org.apache.struts.config.ConfigRuleSet class shown in Figure 4-4 has a slightly different, but related, job—it contains the set of rules that are required to parse a

Struts configuration file. Its job is to construct instances of the configuration Java-Beans mentioned in the previous paragraph when the application is started.

## The ApplicationConfig Class

The `org.apache.struts.config.ApplicationConfig` class deserves a special introduction, as it plays a very important role in the framework. As Figure 4-4 indicates, it is central to the entire `config` package and holds onto the configuration information that describes an entire Struts application. If multiple application modules are being used, there is one `ApplicationConfig` object for each module. The `ApplicationConfig` class will surface throughout the remainder of our discussion of the framework.

## The Struts Configuration DTD

As the web application's DTD is used to validate the *web.xml* file, the Struts DTD is used to validate the Struts configuration file.

A complete *struts-config.xml* file is shown later, in Example 4-5. It may help to refer to that example following the discussion of these elements.

The following Struts DTD declaration indicates that the `struts-config` element is the root element for the XML file and that it has eight child elements:

```
<!ELEMENT struts-config (data-sources?, form-beans?, global-exceptions?, global-
    forwards?, action-mappings?, controller?, message-resources*, plug-in*)
>
```

### The data-sources element

The `data-sources` element allows you to set up a rudimentary data source that you can use from within the Struts framework. A data source acts as a factory[*] for database connections and provides a single point of control. Many data source implementations use a connection-pooling mechanism to improve performance and scalability.

Many vendors provide their own implementations of data source objects. The Java language provides the `javax.sql.DataSource` interface, which all implementations must implement. Most application servers and some web containers provide built-in data source components. All of the major database vendors also provide data source implementations.

---

[*] See the discussion of the Abstract Factory pattern in the Gang of Four's *Design Patterns: Elements of Reusable Object-Oriented Software* (Addison Wesley).

The data-sources element can contain zero or more data-source elements:

```
<!ELEMENT data-sources (data-source*)>
```

The data-source element allows for multiple set-property elements to be specified:

```
<!ELEMENT data-source (set-property*)>
```

The set-property element allows you to configure properties that are specific to your data source implementation.

Throughout the discussion of the Struts configuration elements in the rest of this chapter, you will notice a child element called set-property in many of the major elements of the configuration file. The set-property element specifies the name and value of an additional JavaBeans configuration property whose setter method will be called on the object that represents the surrounding element. This element is especially useful for passing additional property information to an extended implementation class. The set-property element is optional, and you will use it only if you need to pass additional properties to a configuration class.

 The set-property element defines three attributes, including the id attribute, which is seldom used. The property attribute is the name of the JavaBeans property whose setter method will be called. The value attribute is a string representing the value that will be passed to the setter method after proper conversion. This section provides an example of using the set-property element. The same format is replicated wherever the set-property element is declared.

The attributes for the data-source element are listed in Table 4-3.

*Table 4-3. Attributes of the data-source element*

| Name | Description |
| --- | --- |
| id | Not currently used. |
| className | The implementation class of the configuration bean that will hold the data source information. If specified, it must be a descendant of org.apache.struts.config.DataSourceConfig, which is the default class when no value is specified. This attribute is optional. |
| key | The servlet context attribute under which this data source will be stored. This attribute is optional; the default value is Globals.DATA_SOURCE_KEY. |
| type | The fully qualified Java class name of the data source implementation class. The class represented by this value must implement javax.sql.DataSource and be configurable from JavaBeans properties. |

 The GenericDataSource class included with the Struts framework has been deprecated in favor of the Database Connection Pool (DBCP) project from Jakarta or an implementation from your container.

The following code illustrates how to configure a data source within the Struts configuration file:

```
<data-sources>
 <data-source>
   <set-property property="autoCommit" value="true"/>
   <set-property property="description" value="MySql Data Source"/>
   <set-property property="driverClass" value="com.caucho.jdbc.mysql.Driver"/>
   <set-property property="maxCount" value="10"/>
   <set-property property="minCount" value="2"/>
   <set-property property="user" value="admin"/>
   <set-property property="password" value="admin"/>
   <set-property property="url"
               value="jdbc:mysql-caucho://localhost:3306/storefront"/>
 </data-source>
</data-sources>
```

This code illustrates a data-source element configured to connect to a MySQL database using a JDBC driver from Caucho Technology, the developers of the Resin™ servlet/EJB container.

You can specify multiple data sources within the configuration file, assign each one a unique key, and access a particular data source in the framework by its key. This gives you the ability to access multiple databases if necessary. There are several other popular data source implementations you can use. Table 4-4 lists a few of the more popular alternative implementations.

*Table 4-4. Alternative data source implementations*

| Name | Vendor | URL |
| --- | --- | --- |
| Poolman | Open source | http://sourceforge.net/projects/poolman/ |
| Expresso | Jcorporate | http://www.jcorporate.com |
| JDBC Pool | Open source | http://www.bitmechanic.com/projects/jdbcpool/ |
| DBCP | Jakarta | http://jakarta.apache.org/commons/dbcp/ |

 The creator of the Poolman open source library is no longer supporting it. Although it works well and still is available on SourceForge.net, it has not been updated for quite some time. Of course, since it's open source, you can make necessary fixes and changes yourself.

### The form-beans element

The form-beans element allows you to configure multiple ActionForm classes that are used by the views. Within the form-beans section, you can configure zero or more form-bean child elements. Each form-bean element also has several child elements.

```
<!ELEMENT form-bean (icon?, display-name?, description?, set-property*, form-
    property*)
>
```

Each form-bean element also has four attributes that you can specify. Table 4-5 lists the attributes.

*Table 4-5. Attributes of the form-bean element*

| Name | Description |
| --- | --- |
| className | If you don't want to use the standard configuration bean org.apache.struts.config. FormBeanConfig, you can specify your own class here. It must extend the FormBeanConfig class. This attribute is optional; the framework will use an instance of the FormBeanConfig class if it's not specified. |
| dynamic | If the class identified by the type attribute is an instance of org.apache.struts.action. DynaActionForm or a subclass, this value should be set to true. Otherwise, this value is false. This has been deprecated and the framework will now determine this automatically. |
| name | A unique identifier for this bean, which is used to reference it throughout the framework. This value is required and must be unique within a application module. |
| type | The fully qualified name of a Java class that extends the Struts ActionForm class. If this value is specified as org.apache.struts.action.DynaActionForm, Struts will dynamically generate an instance of the DynaActionForm. This attribute is required. |

 Be careful when configuring the value for the type attribute. It must be the fully qualified name of the ActionForm implementation class. If you misspell the name, it can be very hard to debug this problem.

As mentioned in Chapter 3, a form bean is a JavaBeans class that extends the org. apache.struts.action.ActionForm class. The following code shows how the form-beans element can be configured in the Struts configuration file:

```
<struts-config>
 <form-beans>
  <form-bean
    name="loginForm"
    type="org.apache.struts.action.DynaActionForm">
     <form-property name="username" type="java.lang.String"/>
     <form-property name="password" type="java.lang.String"/>
  </form-bean>

  <form-bean
    name="shoppingCartForm"
    type="com.oreilly.struts.order.ShoppingCartForm"/>
 </form-beans>
</struts-config>
```

One of the form-bean elements in this code uses a feature new in Struts 1.1, called *dynamic action forms*. Dynamic action forms were discussed briefly in Chapter 3 and will be discussed in detail in Chapter 7.

You can pass one or more dynamic properties to an instance of the org.apache. struts.action.DynaActionForm class using the form-property element. It is supported only when the type attribute of the surrounding form-bean element is org.apache. struts.action.DynaActionForm, or a descendant class.

Each `form-property` element also has four attributes that you can specify. Table 4-6 lists the attributes allowed in the `form-property` element.

*Table 4-6. Attributes of the form-property element*

| Name | Description |
|------|-------------|
| className | If you don't want to use the standard configuration bean `org.apache.struts.config.FormPropertyConfig`, you can specify your own class here. This attribute is not required. |
| initial | A string representation of the initial value for this property. If not specified, primitives will be initialized to zero, and objects to their zero-argument instantiation of that object class. This attribute is not required. |
| name | The JavaBeans property name of the property being described by this element. This attribute is required. |
| type | The fully qualified Java class name of the implementation class of this bean property, optionally followed by "[ ]" to indicate that this property is indexed. This attribute is required. |

The following `form-bean` fragment illustrates the use of the `form-property` element:

```
<form-bean
  name="checkoutForm"
    type="org.apache.struts.action.DynaActionForm">
    <form-property name="firstName" type="java.lang.String"/>
    <form-property name="lastName" type="java.lang.String"/>
    <form-property name="age" type="java.lang.Integer" initial="18"/>
  </form-bean>
```

### The global-exceptions element

The global-exceptions section allows you to configure exception handlers declaratively. The `global-exceptions` element can contain zero or more exception elements:

```
<!ELEMENT global-exceptions (exception*)>
```

Later in this chapter, when action mappings are discussed, you will see that the exception element also can be specified in the action element. If an exception element is configured for the same type of exception both in the global- exceptions element and in the action element, the action level will take precedence. If no exception element mapping is found at the action level, the framework will look for exception mappings defined for the exception's parent class. Eventually, if a handler is not found, a ServletException or IOException will be thrown, depending on the type of the original exception. Chapter 10 deals with both declarative and programmatic exception handling in detail. This section illustrates how to configure declarative exception handling for your applications.

The exception element describes a mapping between a Java exception that may occur during processing of a request and an instance of org.apache.struts. action. ExceptionHandler that is responsible for dealing with the thrown exception. The declaration of the exception element illustrates that it also has several child elements:

```
<!ELEMENT exception (icon? display-name? description? set-property*)>
```

Probably more important than the child elements are the attributes that can be specified in the exception element. The attributes are listed in Table 4-7.

*Table 4-7. Attributes of the exception element*

| Name | Description |
| --- | --- |
| className | The implementation class of the configuration bean that will hold the exception information. If specified, it must be a descendant of org.apache.struts.config.ExceptionConfig, which is the default class when no value is specified. |
| handler | The fully qualified Java class name of the exception handler that will process the exception. If no value is specified, the default class org.apache.struts.action.ExceptionHandler will be used. If a class is specified for this attribute, it must be a descendant of the ExceptionHandler class. |
| key | A message key that is specified in the resource bundle for this module. This value is used by the ActionError instance. |
| path | The application-relative path of the resource to forward to if this exception occurs. |
| scope | The identifier of the scope level where the ActionError instance should be stored. The attribute value must be either request or session. This attribute is optional and will default to request if not specified. |
| type | The fully qualified Java class name of the exception that is to be handled. This attribute is required because it identifies the exception, which can't be assumed by the framework. |
| bundle | The ServletContext attribute that identifies a resource bundle from which the key attribute of this element should come. |

The following is an example of a global-exceptions element:

```
<global-exceptions>
  <exception
    key="global.error.invalidlogin"
    path="/security/signin.jsp"
    scope="request"
    type="com.oreilly.struts.framework.exceptions.InvalidLoginException"/>
</global-exceptions>
```

## The global-forwards element

Every action that is executed finishes by forwarding or redirecting to a view. This view is a JSP page or static HTML page, but might be another type of resource. Instead of referring to the view directly, the Struts framework uses the concept of a forward to associate a logical name with the resource. So, instead of referring to *login.jsp* directly, a Struts application may refer to this resource as the login forward, for example.

The global-forwards section allows you to configure forwards that can be used by all actions within an application. The global-forwards section consists of zero or more forward elements:

```
<!ELEMENT global-forwards (forward*)>
```

The forward element maps a logical name to an application-relative URI. The application can then perform a forward or redirect, using the logical name rather than the literal URI. This helps to decouple the controller and model logic from the view. The forward element can be defined in both the global-forwards and action elements. If a forward with the same name is defined in both places, the action level will take precedence.

The declaration of the forward element illustrates that it also has child elements:

```
<!ELEMENT forward(icon?, display-name?, description, set-property*)>
```

As with the exception element, the attributes probably are more interesting than the child elements. The attributes for the forward element are shown in Table 4-8.

*Table 4-8. Attributes of the forward element*

| Name | Description |
| --- | --- |
| className | The extension class of the configuration bean that will hold the forward information. The default class is org.apache.struts.action.ForwardConfig when no value is specified. This attribute is not required. |
| contextRelative | Set to true to indicate that the resource specified in the path attribute should be interpreted as relative to the entire web application if the path starts with a "/" character. This is so the resource specified by the path attribute can reside in another module. This attribute is not required; the default value is false. |
| Name | A unique value that is used to reference this forward in the application. This attribute is required. |
| Path | A module relative (if the contextRelative attribute is false) or context-relative (if the contextRelative attribute is true) URI to which control should be forwarded or redirected. This attribute is required and must begin with a "/" character. |
| redirect | A Boolean value that determines whether the RequestProcessor should perform a forward or a redirect when using this forward mapping. This attribute is not required; the default value is false, which means that a forward will be performed. |

Here's an example of a global-forwards element from the Storefront application:

```
<global-forwards>
  <forward name="Login" path="/security/signin.jsp" redirect="true"/>
  <forward name="SystemFailure" path="/common/systemerror.jsp"/>
  <forward name="SessionTimeOut" path="/common/sessiontimeout.jsp" redirect="true"/>
  <forward name="Welcome" path="/viewsignin"/>
</global-forwards>
```

The org.apache.struts.action.ActionForward class is used to hold the information configured in the controller element (discussed later). The ActionForward class now extends org.apache.struts.config.ForwardConfig for backward compatibility.

## The action-mappings element

The action-mappings element contains a set of zero or more action elements for a Struts application:

```
<!ELEMENT action-mappings (action*)>
```

The action element describes a mapping from a specific request path to a corresponding Action class. The controller selects a particular mapping by matching the URI path in the request with the path attribute in one of the action elements. The action element contains the following child elements:

```
<!ELEMENT action (icon?, display-name?, description, set-property*, exception*,
    forward*)>
```

Two child elements should stand out in the list of children for the action element, because you've already seen them earlier in this chapter: exception and forward.

We talked about the exception element when we discussed the global-exceptions element. We mentioned then that exception elements could be defined at the global or at the action level. The exception elements defined within the action element take precedence over any of the same type defined at the global level. The syntax and attributes are the same, regardless of where they are defined.

We introduced the forward element when we discussed the global-forwards element. As with exception elements, a forward element can be defined both at the global level and at the action level. The action level takes precedence if the same forward is defined in both locations. The action element contains quite a few attributes, shown in Table 4-9.

Table 4-9. Attributes of the action element

| Name | Description |
| --- | --- |
| attribute | The name of the request- or session-scope attribute under which the form bean for this action can be accessed. A value is allowed here only if there is a form bean specified in the name attribute. This attribute is optional and has no default value. If both this attribute and the name attribute contain a value, this attribute will take precedence. |
| className | The implementation class of the configuration bean that will hold the action information. The org.apache.struts.action.ActionMapping class is the default class when no value is specified. This attribute is optional. |
| forward | The application-relative path to a servlet or JSP resource that will be forwarded to, instead of instantiating and calling the Action class. The attributes forward, include, and type are mutually exclusive, and exactly one must be specified. This attribute is optional. org.apache.struts.actions.ForwardAction can be used to achieve the same behavior. This action is discussed in Chapter 5. |
| include | The application-relative path to a servlet or JSP resource that will be included with the response, instead of instantiating and calling the Action class. The attributes forward, include, and type are mutually exclusive, and exactly one must be specified. This attribute is optional. org.apache.struts.actions.IncludeAction can be used to achieve the same behavior. This action is discussed in Chapter 5. |
| input | Module-relative path of the action or other resource to which control should be returned if a validation error is encountered. Valid only when "name" is specified. Required if "name" is specified and the input bean returns validation errors. Optional if "name" is specified and the input bean does not return validation errors |
| name | The name of the form bean associated with this action. This value must be the name attribute from one of the form-bean elements defined earlier. This attribute is optional and has no default value. |

*Table 4-9. Attributes of the action element (continued)*

| Name | Description |
|------|-------------|
| path | The application-relative path to the submitted request, starting with a "/" character and without the filename extension if extension mapping is used. In other words, this is the name of the action—for example, /addToShoppingCart. This value is required. This attribute probably should have been called "name" because it really is the name of the action. |
| parameter | A general-purpose configuration parameter that can be used to pass extra information to the action instance selected by this action mapping. The core framework does not use this value. If you provide a value here, you can obtain it in your Action by calling the getParameter() method on the ActionMapping passed to the execute() method. |
| prefix | Used to match request parameter names to form bean property names. For example, if all of the properties in a form bean begin with "pre_", you can set the prefix attribute so the request parameters will match to the ActionForm properties. You can provide a value here only if the name attribute is specified. |
| roles | A comma-delimited list of security role names allowed to invoke this Action. When a request is processed, the RequestProcessor verifies that the user has at least one of the roles identified within this attribute. This attribute is optional. |
| scope | Used to identify the scope in which the form bean is placed—either request or session. This attribute can be specified only if the name attribute is present. The default value is session. |
| suffix | Used to match request parameter names to form bean property names. For example, if all of the properties in a form bean end with "_foo", you can set the suffix attribute so the request parameters will match to the ActionForm properties. You can provide a value here only if the name attribute is specified. |
| type | A fully qualified Java class name that extends the org.apache.struts.action.Action class. This attribute is used to process the request if the forward and include attributes are not specified. The attributes forward, include, and type are mutually exclusive, and exactly one must be specified. |
| unknown | A Boolean value indicating whether this action should be configured as the default for this application. If this attribute is set to true, this action will handle any request that is not handled by another action. Only one action mapping per application can have this value set to true. This attribute is optional and defaults to false. This is a good place to set up a default action that will catch any invalid action URL entered by the user. The name of this attribute would have been better as "default". |
| validate | A Boolean value indicating whether the validate() method of the form bean, specified by the name attribute, should be called prior to calling the execute() method of this action. This attribute is optional and defaults to true. |

The following is an example of the "signin" action element from the Storefront application:

```
<action
  path="/signin"
  type="com.oreilly.struts.storefront.security.LoginAction"
  scope="request"
  name="loginForm"
  validate="true"
  input="/security/signin.jsp">
  <forward name="Success" path="/index.jsp" redirect="true"/>
  <forward name="Failure" path="/security/signin.jsp" redirect="true"/>
</action>
```

The org.apache.struts.action.ActionMapping class is used to represent the information configured in the action element. The ActionMapping class extends org.apache.struts.config.ActionConfig for backward compatibility.

## The controller element

The controller element is new to Struts 1.1. Prior to Version 1.1, the ActionServlet contained the controller functionality, and you had to extend that class to override the functionality. In Version 1.1, however, Struts has moved most of the controller functionality to the RequestProcessor class. The ActionServlet still receives the requests, but it delegates the request handling to an instance of the RequestProcessor. This allows you to declaratively assign the processor class and modify its functionality.

If you're familiar with Version 1.0, you'll notice that many of the parameters that were configured in the *web.xml* file for the controller servlet now are configured using the controller element. Because the controller and its attributes are defined in the *struts-config.xml* file, you can define a separate controller element for each module. The controller element has a single child element:

```
<!ELEMENT controller (set-property*)>
```

The controller element can contain zero or more set-property elements and many different attributes. The attributes are shown in Table 4-10.

*Table 4-10. Attributes of the controller element*

| Name | Description |
|---|---|
| bufferSize | The size of the input buffer used when processing file uploads. This attribute is optional; the default value is 4096. |
| className | The implementation class of the configuration bean that will hold the controller information. If specified, it must be a descendant of org.apache.struts.config.ControllerConfig, which is the default class when no value is specified. This attribute is not required. |
| contentType | The default content type and optional character encoding that gets set for each response. This attribute is not required; the default value is text/html. Even when a value is specified here, an action or a JSP page may override it. |
| forwardPattern | A replacement pattern defining how the path attribute of a forward element is mapped to a context-relative URL when it starts with a slash (and when the contextRelative property is false). This value may consist of any combination of the following:<br>• $M—Replaced by the module prefix of this module<br>• $P—Replaced by the path attribute of the selected forward element<br>• $$—Causes a literal dollar sign to be rendered<br>• $x (where x is any character not defined above)—Silently swallowed, reserved for future use<br>If not specified, the default forwardPattern is $M$P, which is consistent with previous hardcoded behavior of forwards. |

*Table 4-10. Attributes of the controller element (continued)*

| Name | Description |
| --- | --- |
| inputForward | Set to true if you want the input parameters of action elements to be the names of local or global forward elements used to calculate the ultimate URLs. Set to false (the default) to treat the input parameters of action elements as module-relative paths to the resources used for the input form. |
| locale | A Boolean value indicating whether the user's preferred locale is stored in the user's session if not already present. This attribute is not required; the default value is true. |
| maxFileSize | The maximum size (in bytes) of a file to be accepted as a file upload. This value can be expressed as a number followed by "K", "M", or "G" (interpreted to mean kilobytes, megabytes, or gigabytes, respectively). This attribute is not required; the default value is 250M. |
| memFileSize | The maximum size (in bytes) of a file whose contents will be retained in memory after uploading. Files larger than this threshold will be written to some alternative storage medium, typically a hard disk. Can be expressed as a number followed by a "K", "M", or "G", which are interpreted to mean kilobytes, megabytes, or gigabytes, respectively. The default value is 256K. |
| multipartClass | The fully qualified Java class name of the multipart request-handler class to be used. This is used when uploading files from a user's local filesystem to the server. This attribute is not required; the default value is the CommonsMultipartRequestHandler class in the org.apache.struts.upload package. |
| nocache | A Boolean value indicating whether the framework should set nocache HTTP headers in every response. This attribute is not required; the default value is false. Note that the letter "c" in nocache is lowercase. To be consistent with the other attributes shown here, it should have been noCache, but it's not. |
| pagePattern | A replacement pattern defining how the page attributes of custom tags using it are mapped to context-relative URLs of the corresponding resources. This value may consist of any combination of the following:<br><br>• $M—Replaced by the module prefix of this module<br>• $P—Replaced by the value of the page attribute<br>• $$—Causes a literal dollar sign to be rendered<br>• $x (where x is any character not defined above)—Silently swallowed, reserved for future use<br><br>If not specified, the default pagePattern is $M$P, which is consistent with previous hardcoded behavior of URL evaluation for page attributes. |
| processorClass | The fully qualified Java class name of the request-processor class to be used to process requests. The value specified here should be a descendant of org.apache.struts.action.RequestProcessor, which is the default value. This attribute is not required. |
| tempDir | Specifies the temporary working directory that is used when processing file uploads. This attribute is not required; the servlet container will assign a default value for each web application. |

The org.apache.struts.config.ControllerConfig class is used to represent the information configured in the controller element in memory. The following fragment shows an example of how to configure the controller element:

```
<controller
    contentType="text/html;charset=UTF-8"    locale="true"
    nocache="true"
    processorClass="com.oreilly.struts.framework.CustomRequestProcessor"/>
```

## The message-resources element

The `message-resources` element specifies characteristics of the message resource bundles that contain the localized messages for an application. Each Struts configuration file can define one or more message resource bundles; therefore, each module can define its own bundles. The `message-resources` element contains only a `set-property` element:

```
<!ELEMENT message-resources (set-property*)>
```

Table 4-11 lists the attributes supported by the `message-resources` element.

*Table 4-11. Attributes of the message-resources element*

| Name | Description |
|------|-------------|
| className | The implementation class of the configuration bean that will hold the `message-resources` information. If specified, it must be a descendant of `org.apache.struts.config.MessageResourcesConfig`, which is the default class when no value is specified. This attribute is optional. |
| factory | The fully qualified Java class name of the `MessageResourcesFactory` class that should be used. This attribute is optional. The `PropertyMessageResources` class of the package `org.apache.struts.util` is the default. |
| key | The servlet context attribute with which this message resource bundle will be stored. This attribute is optional. The default value is specified by the string constant `Globals.MESSAGES_KEY`. Only one resource bundle can be the default bundle. |
| null | A Boolean value indicating how the `MessageResources` subclass should handle the case when an unknown message key is used. If this value is set to `true`, an empty string will be returned. If set to `false`, a message that looks something like *"???global.label.missing???"* will be returned. The actual message will contain the bad key. This attribute is optional. The default value is `true`. |
| parameter | The base name of the resource bundle. For example, if the name of your resource bundle is `Application Resources.properties`, you should set the parameter value to `ApplicationResources`. This attribute is required. If your resource bundle is within a package, you must provide the fully qualified name in this attribute. |

The following example shows how to configure multiple `message-resources` elements for a single application. Notice that the second element had to specify the key attribute, because only one can be stored with the default key:

```
<message-resources
  null="false"
  parameter="StorefrontMessageResources"/>
<message-resources
  key="IMAGE_RESOURCE_KEY"
  null="false"
  parameter="StorefrontImageResources"/>
```

## The plug-in element

The concept of a plug-in was added in Struts 1.1. This powerful feature allows your Struts applications to discover resources dynamically at startup. For example, if you need to create a connection to a remote system at startup and you didn't want to hardcode this functionality into the application, you can use a plug-in, and the Struts application will discover it dynamically. To use a plug-in, create a Java class that implements the org.apache.struts.action.PlugIn interface and add a plug-in element to the configuration file. The PlugIn mechanism itself will be discussed further in Chapter 9.

The plug-in element specifies a fully qualified class name of a general-purpose application plug-in module that receives notification of application startup and shutdown events. An instance of the specified class is created for each element; the init() method is called when the application is started, and the destroy() method is called when the application is stopped. The class specified here must implement the org.apache.struts.action.PlugIn interface and implement the init() and destroy() methods.

The plug-in element may contain zero or more set-property elements, so that extra configuration information may be passed to your PlugIn class:

```
<!ELEMENT plug-in (set-property*)>
```

The allowed attribute for the plug-in element is shown in Table 4-12.

*Table 4-12. Attribute of the plug-in element*

| Name | Description |
| --- | --- |
| className | The fully qualified Java class name of the PlugIn class. It must implement the PlugIn interface. |

The following fragment shows two plug-in elements being used:

```
<plug-in
  className="com.oreilly.struts.storefront.service.StorefrontServiceFactory"/>

<plug-in
  className="org.apache.struts.validator.ValidatorPlugIn">
  <set-property
    property="pathnames"
    value="/WEB-INF/validator-rules.xml,/WEB-INF/validation.xml"/>
</plug-in>
```

The ValidatorPlugIn shown in the second plug-in element displays how the Struts framework initializes the Validator. The Validator framework is discussed in Chapter 11.

## A Complete struts-config.xml File

Up to this point, you haven't seen a complete example of a Struts configuration file. Example 4-5 provides a complete listing.

*Example 4-5. A complete Struts configuration file*

```xml
<?xml version="1.0" encoding="UTF-8" ?>
<!DOCTYPE struts-config PUBLIC
      "-//Apache Software Foundation//DTD Struts Configuration 1.1//EN"
      "http://jakarta.apache.org/struts/dtds/struts-config_1_1.dtd">

<struts-config>

  <data-sources>
   <data-source>
    <set-property property="autoCommit" value="true"/>
    <set-property property="description" value="Resin Data Source"/>
    <set-property property="driverClass" value="com.caucho.jdbc.mysql.Driver"/>
    <set-property property="maxCount" value="10"/>
    <set-property property="minCount" value="2"/>
    <set-property property="user" value="admin"/>
    <set-property property="password" value="admin"/>
    <set-property
      property="url"
      value="jdbc:mysqlcaucho://localhost:3306/storefront"/>
   </data-source>
  </data-sources>

  <form-beans>
   <form-bean
     name="loginForm"
     type="com.oreilly.struts.storefront.security.LoginForm"/>
   <form-bean
       name="itemDetailForm"
       type="org.apache.struts.action.DynaActionForm">
       <form-property name="view" type="com.oreilly.struts.catalog.view.ItemView"/>
   </form-bean>
  </form-beans>

  <global-exceptions>
   <exception
    key="global.error.invalidlogin"
    path="/security/signin.jsp"
    scope="request"
    type="com.oreilly.struts.framework.exceptions.InvalidLoginException"/>
  </global-exceptions>

  <global-forwards>
   <forward name="Login" path="/security/signin.jsp" redirect="true"/>
   <forward name="SystemFailure" path="/common/systemerror.jsp"/>
   <forward
    name="SessionTimeOut"
    path="/common/sessiontimeout.jsp"
    redirect="true"/>
  </global-forwards>

  <action-mappings>
   <action
```

*Example 4-5. A complete Struts configuration file (continued)*

```
    path="/viewsignin"
    parameter="/security/signin.jsp"
    type="org.apache.struts.actions.ForwardAction"
    scope="request"
    name="loginForm"
    validate="false"
    input="/index.jsp">
</action>
<action
  path="/signin"
  type="com.oreilly.struts.storefront.security.LoginAction"
  scope="request"
  name="loginForm"
  validate="true"
  input="/security/signin.jsp">
  <forward name="Success" path="/index.jsp" redirect="true"/>
  <forward name="Failure" path="/security/signin.jsp" redirect="true"/>
</action>
<action
  path="/signoff"
  type="com.oreilly.struts.storefront.security.LogoutAction"
  scope="request"
  validate="false"
  input="/security/signin.jsp">
  <forward name="Success" path="/index.jsp" redirect="true"/>
</action>
<action
  path="/home"
  parameter="/index.jsp"
  type="org.apache.struts.actions.ForwardAction"
  scope="request"
  validate="false">
</action>
<action
  path="/viewcart"
  parameter="/order/shoppingcart.jsp"
  type="org.apache.struts.actions.ForwardAction"
  scope="request"
  validate="false">
</action>
<action path="/cart"
  type="com.oreilly.struts.storefront.order.ShoppingCartActions"
  scope="request"
  input="/order/shoppingcart.jsp"
  validate="false"
  parameter="method">
  <forward name="Success" path="/action/viewcart" redirect="true"/>
</action>
  <action
    path="/viewitemdetail"
    name="itemDetailForm"
    input="/index.jsp"
```

*Example 4-5. A complete Struts configuration file (continued)*

```
        type="com.oreilly.struts.storefront.catalog.GetItemDetailAction"
        scope="request"
        validate="false">
        <forward name="Success" path="/catalog/itemdetail.jsp"/>
    </action>
    <action
        path="/begincheckout"
        input="/order/shoppingcart.jsp"
        type="com.oreilly.struts.storefront.order.CheckoutAction"
        scope="request"
        validate="false">
        <forward name="Success" path="/order/checkout.jsp"/>
    </action>
    <action
        path="/getorderhistory"
        input="/order/orderhistory.jsp"
        type="com.oreilly.struts.storefront.order.GetOrderHistoryAction"
        scope="request"
        validate="false">
        <forward name="Success" path="/order/orderhistory.jsp"/>
    </action>
</action-mappings>

<controller
    contentType="text/html;charset=UTF-8"
    locale="true"
    nocache="true"
    processorClass="com.oreilly.struts.framework.CustomRequestProcessor"/>

<message-resources
    parameter="StorefrontMessageResources"
    null="false"/>
<message-resources
    key="IMAGE_RESOURCE_KEY"
    parameter="StorefrontImageResources"
    null="false"/>
<plug-in
    className="com.oreilly.struts.storefront.service.StorefrontServiceFactory"/>
<plug-in
    className="org.apache.struts.validator.ValidatorPlugIn">
    <set-property
        property="pathnames"
        value="/WEB-INF/validator-rules.xml,/WEB-INF/validation.xml"/>
</plug-in>
</struts-config>
```

## Using Multiple Application Modules

Now that you've seen how to configure the default application for Struts, the last step is to discuss how you include multiple application modules. With Struts 1.1, you have the ability to set up multiple Struts configuration files. Although the application modules are part of the same web application, they act independently of one another. You also can switch back and forth between application modules if you like.

Using multiple application modules allows for better organization of the components within a web application. For example, you can assemble and configure one application module for everything that deals with catalogs and items, while another module can be organized with the configuration information for a shopping cart and ordering. Separating an application into components in this way facilitates parallel development.

The first step is to create the additional Struts configuration files. Suppose we created a second configuration file named *struts-order-config.xml*. We must modify the *web.xml* file for the application and add an additional init-param element for the new module. This was shown earlier in the chapter, but it's repeated here for convenience. Example 4-6 shows the servlet instance mapping from before with an additional init-param for the second Struts configuration file.

*Example 4-6. A partial web.xml file that illustrates how to configure multiple modules*

```
<servlet>
  <servlet-name>storefront</servlet-name>
  <servlet-class>org.apache.struts.action.ActionServlet</servlet-class>

  <init-param>
   <param-name>config</param-name>
   <param-value>/WEB-INF/struts-config.xml</param-value>
  </init-param>

  <init-param>
   <param-name>config/order</param-name>
   <param-value>/WEB-INF/struts-order-config.xml</param-value>
  </init-param>

  <load-on-startup>1</load-on-startup>
</servlet>
```

Notice that the param-name value for the nondefault application module in Example 4-6 begins with config/. All nondefault application modules' param- name elements must begin with config/; the default application's param-name element contains the config value alone. The part that comes after config/ is known as the *application module prefix* and is used throughout the framework for intercepting requests and returning the correct resources.

With the current version of the Struts framework, only extension mapping is supported when using multiple application modules. Path mapping is not yet supported.

Pay special attention to the configuration attributes available in the various Struts XML elements. Some of them, as mentioned in this chapter, have a profound effect on how an application operates in a multiapplication module environment.

## Specifying a DOCTYPE Element

To ensure that your Struts configuration file is valid, it can and should be validated against the Struts DTD. To do this, you must include the DOCTYPE element at the beginning of your Struts configuration XML file:

```
<?xml version="1.0" encoding="ISO-8859-1" ?>

<!DOCTYPE struts-config PUBLIC
          "-//Apache Software Foundation//DTD Struts Configuration 1.1//EN"
          "http://jakarta.apache.org/struts/dtds/struts-config_1_1.dtd">
```

In earlier versions of the framework, there were some issues with applications not being able to start up if they couldn't get to the Jakarta site and access the DTD from there. This is no longer the case, as Struts now provides local copies of the DTDs.

Some users prefer to specify a SYSTEM DOCTYPE tag, rather than a PUBLIC one. This allows you to specify an absolute path instead of a relative one. Although this may solve a short-term problem, it creates more long-term ones. You can't always guarantee the directory structure from one target environment to another. Also, different containers act differently when using a SYSTEM DOCTYPE tag. You probably are better off not using it. However, if you decide that you need to do so, it should look something like the following:

```
<?xml version="1.0" encoding="ISO-8859-1" ?>
<!DOCTYPE struts-config SYSTEM "file:///c:/dtds/struts-config_1_1.dtd">

<struts-config>
   <!-The rest of the struts configuration file goes next -->
```

As you can see, the location of the DTD is an absolute path. If the path of the target environment is not the same, you'll have to modify the XML file. This is why this approach is not recommended.

# The Digester Component

When a Struts application is initialized, one of the first things that it must do is to read and parse the configuration file, which, as you've seen in this chapter, is in XML. The Digester component is a separate Jakarta project made up of several classes that read XML files and create and initialize Java objects based on those files.

The Digester component uses a set of rules, written as a Java class, to invoke callback methods. These methods instantiate and populate the objects with data read from the Struts configuration file.

The Struts framework uses the Digester to parse the configuration files and to create the necessary configuration objects within the `org.apache.struts.config` package. The rules that the Digester uses for Struts are contained within the `org.apache.struts.config.ConfigRuleSet` class. There is little need to modify the `ConfigRuleSet` class unless you need to extend the configuration file. If this is necessary for your application, you should view the documentation for the Digester component before you get started. This can be found at *http://jakarta.apache.org/commons/digester.html*.

## The Struts Console Tool

When you're developing a small application, the Struts configuration is manageable. It's still XML, but typically it's not much of a problem. Some developers use XML editors, while others use ordinary text editors. Both of these are fine when the application is relatively small, but when you are working on a large Struts project, the size and complexity of the file can be staggering.

The Struts Console application was created by James Holmes to solve this and other problems associated with managing large configuration files. It is a Swing-based application that provides an easy-to-use interface for editing the various elements of the Struts configuration file.

You can download the Struts Console for free from *http://www.jamesholmes.com/struts/console*, even though it's not open source software. No license currently is necessary, but you should check the web site to make sure this hasn't changed.

 The formatting of your Struts configuration file might be modified when you save the file using the Console. The Console uses an XML parser to read in the configuration file, and the parser can't maintain complete knowledge of how the file was originally formatted. The Console does provide several output options that you can use to format the XML file based on different formats.

Figure 4-5 shows the action screen from the Struts Console.

The Struts Console application also plugs into multiple popular Java integrated development environments (IDEs). Currently, the supported IDEs include:

- JBuilder (4.0 or higher)
- Eclipse (1.0 or higher)
- NetBeans (3.2 or higher)
- Oracle JDeveloper (9i or higher)
- Sun One Studio (3.0 or higher)

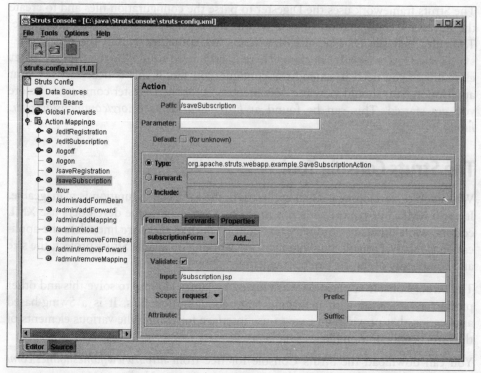

*Figure 4-5. The action configuration screen from the Struts Console*

Figure 4-6 shows what the Console application looks like in JBuilder.

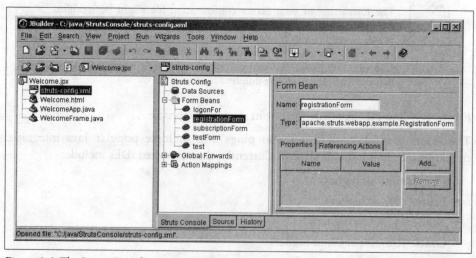

*Figure 4-6. The Struts Console running in the JBuilder IDE*

# Reloading the Configuration Files

The web deployment descriptor is loaded and parsed when the web container is first started. By default, changes to the descriptor are not detected and reloaded while the container is running. In fact, not many containers even provide this functionality—it's typically not a wanted feature, due to the possible security issues involved. The Struts configuration files also are loaded and parsed when the container is launched, and changes to these configuration files also are not automatically detected; the same security issues are present.

Some applications might require the ability to reload the Struts configuration files without restarting the web container. If your application is one of them, there are ways you can do this. One approach is to create a Struts action that will reinitialize the ActionServlet (you may want to restrict which users can call this action). Once the ActionServlet is reinitialized, everything will be new and the application can again service requests, just like before.

A second strategy is to create a thread that monitors the lastModifiedTime of the configuration file. It can sleep for a few seconds and, upon awakening, compare the lastModifiedTime of the file against the one stored in a variable. If they are different, the file has changed and it's time to reload the application. This approach is nice because you don't have to worry about an unwelcome user reloading your application. However, the time that it gets reloaded is entirely up to the thread.

# CHAPTER 5

# Struts Controller Components

As discussed in Chapter 1, the controller components are responsible for detecting user input, possibly updating the domain model, and selecting the next view for the client. The controller helps to separate the presentation of the model from the model itself. This separation gives you much more freedom to develop a variety of presentations based on a single domain model.

Using a controller provides a centralized point of control where all client requests are initially processed. Centralizing control in this way realizes two requirements of MVC design. First, the controller acts as the mediator/translator between client input and the model, providing common functionality such as security, logging, and other important services on behalf of each client request. Second, because all requests are filtered through the controller, the view is decoupled both from the business logic and from other view components. The view returned to the client is entirely up to the controller. This makes your applications much more flexible.

The Struts framework uses a servlet to process incoming requests. However, it relies on many other components that are part of the controller domain to help carry out its responsibilities. The Struts controller components were mentioned briefly in previous chapters, but it's time to take an in-depth look at what components have responsibility for the controller functionality in the framework.

## The Controller Mechanism

The J2EE Front Controller design pattern uses a single controller to funnel all client requests through a central point. Among the many advantages this pattern brings to application functionality is that services such as security, internationalization, and logging are concentrated in the controller. This permits the consistent application of these functions across all requests. When the behavior of these services needs modification, changes potentially affecting the entire application need to be made only to a relatively small and isolated area of the program.

As discussed in Chapter 1, the Struts controller has several responsibilities. Chief among these are:

- Intercepting client requests.
- Mapping each request to a specific business operation.
- Collecting results from the business operation and making them available to the client.
- Determining the view to display to the client based on the current state and result of the business operation.

In the Struts framework, several components are responsible for the controller duties. Figure 5-1 is a simple class diagram of the components in the Struts framework that share some portion of the controller responsibility.

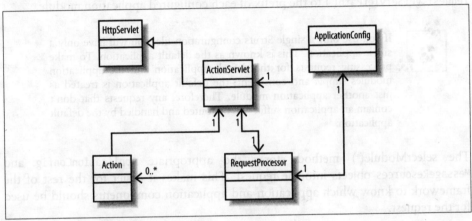

*Figure 5-1. Struts controller components*

There also are secondary helper components that assist those in Figure 5-1 in fulfilling their responsibilities, but for now, let's focus on the ones in Figure 5-1.

## The ActionServlet Class

The `org.apache.struts.action.ActionServlet` class acts as an interceptor for a Struts application. All requests from the client tier must pass through the `ActionServlet` before proceeding anywhere else in the application.

When an instance of the `ActionServlet` receives an `HttpRequest`, through either the `doGet()` or `doPost()` method, the `process()` method is called to handle the request. The `process()` method of `ActionServlet` is shown in Example 5-1.

*Example 5-1. The ActionServlet process() method*

```
protected void process(HttpServletRequest request, HttpServletResponse response)
      throws IOException, ServletException {

    RequestUtils.selectModule(request, getServletContext());
    getRequestProcessor(getModuleConfig(request)).process(request, response);
}
```

The process() method might not look complicated, but the methods invoked within it are. First, the static selectModule() method in the org.apache.struts.util. RequestUtils class is called and passed the current request and the ServletContext for the web application. The job of the selectModule() method is to select an application module to handle the current request by matching the path returned from the request.getServletPath() to the prefix of each configured application module.

 If you use only a single Struts configuration file, you will have only a single application. This is known as the default application. To make processing requests for the default application and the application modules simple and consistent, the default application is treated as just another application module. Therefore, any requests that don't contain an application suffix will be routed and handled by the default application.

The selectModule() method stores the appropriate ApplicationConfig and MessageResources objects into the request. This makes it easier for the rest of the framework to know which application and application components should be used for the request.

### Extending the ActionServlet class

Prior to Struts 1.1, the ActionServlet class contained much of the code to process each user request. Starting with 1.1, however, most of that functionality has been moved to the org.apache.struts.action.RequestProcessor class, which is discussed in a moment. This new controller component was added to help relieve the ActionServlet class of most of the controller burden.

Although the framework still allows you to extend the ActionServlet class, the benefit is not as great as with earlier versions because most of the functionality lies in the new RequestProcessor class. If you still want to use your own version, just create a class that extends ActionServlet and configure the framework to use this class instead of the ActionServlet itself. Example 5-2 shows a Java servlet that extends the Struts ActionServlet and overrides the init() method.

*Example 5-2. The Struts ActionServlet can be extended to perform custom initialization*

```
package com.oreilly.struts.storefront.framework;

import javax.servlet.ServletException;
import javax.servlet.UnavailableException;
import org.apache.struts.action.ActionServlet;
import com.oreilly.struts.storefront.service.IStorefrontService;
import com.oreilly.struts.storefront.service.StorefrontServiceImpl;
import com.oreilly.struts.storefront.framework.util.IConstants;
import com.oreilly.struts.storefront.framework.exceptions.DatastoreException;
/**
 * Extend the Struts ActionServlet to perform your own special
 * initialization.
 */
public class ExtendedActionServlet extends ActionServlet {

  public void init() throws ServletException {

    // Make sure to always call the super's init() first
    super.init();

    // Initialize the persistence service
    try{
      // Create an instance of the service interface
      IStorefrontService serviceImpl = new StorefrontServiceImpl();

      // Store the service into the application scope
      getServletContext().setAttribute( IConstants.SERVICE_INTERFACE_KEY,
                                        serviceImpl );
    }catch( DatastoreException ex ){
      // If there's a problem initializing the service, disable the web app
      ex.printStackTrace();
      throw new UnavailableException( ex.getMessage() );
    }
  }
}
```

Overriding the init( ) method is just an example; you can override any method you need to. If you do override init( ), make sure that you call the super.init( ) method so that the default initialization occurs.

 Don't worry about what the code in Example 5-2 is doing for now. The goal is to understand how to extend the ActionServlet.

To configure the framework to use your ActionServlet subclass instead of the default in the Struts framework, you will need to modify the *web.xml* file as follows:

```
<servlet>
  <servlet-name>storefront</servlet-name>
  <servlet-class>
```

```
        com.oreilly.struts.storefront.framework.ExtendedActionServlet
      </servlet-class>
    </servlet>
```

## Struts initialization process

Depending on the initialization parameters configured in the *web.xml* file, the servlet container will load the Struts `ActionServlet` either when the container is first started or when the first request arrives for the servlet. In either case (as with any other Java servlet) the `init()` method is guaranteed to be called and must finish before any request is processed by the servlet. The Struts framework performs all of the compulsory initialization when `init()` is called. Let's take a look at what goes on during that initialization process. Understanding these details will make debugging and extending your applications much easier.

The following steps occur when the `init()` method of the Struts `ActionServlet` is invoked by the container:

1. Initialize the framework's internal message bundle. These messages are used to output informational, warning, and error messages to the log files. The `org.apache.struts.action.ActionResources` bundle is used to obtain the internal messages.

2. Load from the *web.xml* file the initialization parameters that control various behaviors of the `ActionServlet` class. These parameters include `config`, `debug`, `detail`, and `convertNull`. For information on how these and other servlet parameters affect the behavior of an application, refer to "Declaring the Initialization Parameters" in Chapter 4.

3. Load and initialize the servlet name and servlet mapping information from the *web.xml* file. These values will be used throughout the framework (mostly by tag libraries) to output correct URL destinations when submitting HTML forms. During this initialization, the DTDs used by the framework also are registered. The DTDs are used to validate the configuration file in the next step.

4. Load and initialize the Struts configuration data for the default application, which is specified by the `config` initialization parameter. The default Struts configuration file is parsed and an `ApplicationConfig` object is created and stored in the `ServletContext`. The `ApplicationConfig` object for the default application is stored in the `ServletContext` with a key value of `org.apache.struts.action.APPLICATION`.

5. Each message resource that is specified in the Struts configuration file for the default application is loaded, initialized, and stored in the `ServletContext` at the appropriate location, based on the key attribute specified in each `message-resources` element. If no key is specified, the message resource is stored at the key value `org.apache.struts.action.MESSAGE`. Only one message resource can be stored as the default because the keys have to be unique.

6. Each data source declared in the Struts configuration file is loaded and initialized. If no data-sources elements are specified, this step is skipped.

7. Load and initialize each plug-in specified in the Struts configuration file. The init() method will be called on each and every plug-in specified.

8. Once the default application has been properly initialized, the servlet init() method will determine if any application modules are specified and, if so, will repeat Steps 4 through 7 for each one.

Figure 5-2 uses a sequence diagram to illustrate the eight major steps that occur during the initialization of the ActionServlet.

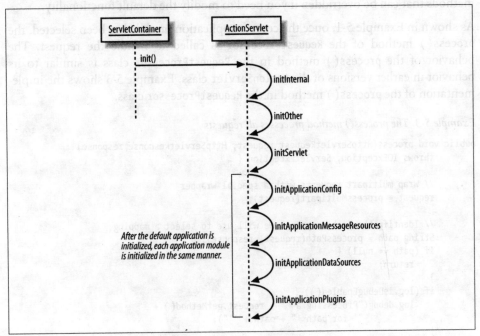

*Figure 5-2. Sequence diagram for the ActionServlet init() method*

You may be tempted to set up multiple Struts controller servlets for a single application in an attempt to achieve better performance. This most likely will not get better performance or scalability and is discouraged by the Struts architects. Servlets are multithreaded and allow many clients to execute simultaneously. A single servlet is capable of servicing many clients at once. In fact, the Struts 1.1 framework assumes that there is only one servlet mapping. You should not attempt to set up multiple servlet mappings.

# The RequestProcessor Class

The second step in Example 5-1 is to call the process( ) method of the org.apache. struts.action.RequestProcessor class. It's called by the ActionServlet instance and passed the current request and response objects.

The RequestProcessor class was added to the framework to allow developers to customize the request-handling behavior for an application. Although this type of customization was possible in previous versions by extending the ActionServlet class, it was necessary to introduce this new class to allow each application module to have its own customized request handler. The RequestProcessor class contains many methods that can be overridden if you need to modify the default functionality.

As shown in Example 5-1, once the correct application module has been selected, the process( ) method of the RequestProcessor is called to handle the request. The behavior of the process( ) method in the RequestProcessor class is similar to its behavior in earlier versions of the ActionServlet class. Example 5-3 shows the implementation of the process( ) method in the RequestProcessor class.

*Example 5-3. The process() method processes all requests*

```
public void process(HttpServletRequest request, HttpServletResponse response)
     throws IOException, ServletException {

    // Wrap multipart requests with a special wrapper
    request = processMultipart(request);

    // Identify the path component we will use to select a mapping
    String path = processPath(request, response);
    if (path == null) {
        return;
    }
    if (log.isDebugEnabled()) {
        log.debug("Processing a '" + request.getMethod() +
                "' for path '" + path + "'");
    }

    // Select a Locale for the current user if requested
    processLocale(request, response);

    // Set the content type and no-caching headers if requested
    processContent(request, response);
    processNoCache(request, response);

    // General purpose preprocessing hook
    if (!processPreprocess(request, response)) {
        return;
    }

    // Identify the mapping for this request
    ActionMapping mapping = processMapping(request, response, path);
```

*Example 5-3. The process() method processes all requests  (continued)*

```
if (mapping == null) {
    return;
}

// Check for any role required to perform this action
if (!processRoles(request, response, mapping)) {
    return;
}

// Process any ActionForm bean related to this request
ActionForm form = processActionForm(request, response, mapping);
processPopulate(request, response, form, mapping);
if (!processValidate(request, response, form, mapping)) {
    return;
}

// Process a forward or include specified by this mapping
if (!processForward(request, response, mapping)) {
    return;
}
if (!processInclude(request, response, mapping)) {
    return;
}

// Create or acquire the Action instance to process this request
Action action = processActionCreate(request, response, mapping);
if (action == null) {
    return;
}

// Call the Action instance itself
ActionForward forward =
    processActionPerform(request, response, ,
                          action, form, mapping);

// Process the returned ActionForward instance
processForwardConfig(request, response, forward);

}
```

As Example 5-3 shows, there's quite a lot going on in the process( ) method of the
RequestProcessor. Let's go through the method step by step:

1. The processMultipart( ) method is called. If the HttpServletRequest method is a
   POST and the contentType of the request starts with multipart/form-data, the
   standard request object is wrapped with a special version from the Struts framework that deals exclusively with multipart requests. If the request method is a
   GET or the contentType is not multipart, the original request is returned. Unless
   your application supports uploading files, you don't need to worry about multipart functionality in Struts.

2. The processPath( ) method is called to determine the path component from the URI for the request. Among other things, this information is used to select the appropriate Struts Action to invoke.

3. The processLocale( ) method is called to determine the locale of the user making the request and to store a Locale object into the user's HttpSession object. The locale isn't always obtained into the user's session—it depends on the locale attribute in the controller configuration element. See Chapter 4 for more details on the attributes of the controller element.

4. Determine the content type and optional encoding of the request by calling the processContent( ) method. The content type may be configured in the configuration settings and also overridden by the JSPs. The default content type is text/html.

5. The processNoCache( ) method is called to determine whether the noCache attribute is set to true. If it is, add the proper header parameters in the response object to prevent the pages from being cached in the browser. The header parameters include Pragma, Cache-Control, and Expires.

6. The processPreprocess( ) method is called next. It's a general-purpose preprocessing hook that, by default, just returns true. However, subclasses can override this method and perform conditional logic to decide whether to continue processing the request. Because this method gets called before an Action is invoked, this is a good place to validate whether the user contains a valid session. If this method returns true, processing of the request will continue. If it returns false, processing will stop. It's up to you to programmatically redirect or forward the request—the controller will assume that you are handling the request and will not send a response to the client.

7. Determine the ActionMapping for the request using the path information by calling the processMapping( ) method. If a mapping can't be found using the path information, an error response will be returned to the client.

8. Check to see if any security roles are configured for the Action by calling the processRoles( ) method. If there are roles configured, the isUserInRole( ) method is called on the request. If the user doesn't contain the necessary role, processing will end here and an appropriate error message will be returned to the client.

9. Call the processActionForm( ) method to determine whether an ActionForm is configured for the ActionMapping. If an ActionForm has been configured for the mapping, an attempt will be made to find an existing instance in the appropriate scope. Once an ActionForm is either found or created, it is stored within the proper scope using a key that is configured in the name attribute for the Action element.

10. The processPopulate( ) method is called next, and if an ActionForm is configured for the mapping, its properties are populated from the request parameter values. Before the properties are populated from the request, however, the reset( ) method is called on the ActionForm.

11. The processValidate() method is called, and if an ActionForm has been configured and the validate attribute is set to true for the action element, the validate() method is called. If the validate() method detects errors, it will store an ActionErrors object into the request scope, and the request automatically will be forwarded to the resource specified by the input attribute for the action mapping. If no errors were detected from the validate() method or there was no ActionForm for the action mapping, processing of the request continues. You can configure the controller element to interpret the input attributes as defined forwards. See Chapter 4 for more information on this feature.

12. Determine if a forward or an include attribute is configured for the action mapping. If so, call the forward() or include() method on the RequestDispatcher, depending on which one is configured. The processing of the request ends at this point if either one of these is configured. Otherwise, continue processing the request.

13. Call the processActionCreate() method to create or acquire an Action instance to process the request. An Action cache will be checked to see if the Action instance already has been created. If so, that instance will be used to process the request. Otherwise, a new instance will be created and stored into the cache.

14. Call the processActionPerform() method, which in turn calls the execute() method on the Action instance. The execute() call is wrapped with a try/catch block so that exceptions can be handled by the RequestProcessor.

15. Call the processActionForward() method and pass it the ActionForward object returned from the execute() method. The processActionForward() method determines whether a redirect or a forward should occur by checking with the ActionForward object, which in turn depends on the redirect attribute in the forward element.

## Extending the RequestProcessor class

It's easy to create your own custom RequestProcessor class. Let's look at an example of how and why you might do this. Suppose your application needs to allow the user to change her locale at any time during the session. The default behavior of the processLocale() method in RequestProcessor is to set the user's Locale only if it hasn't already been stored in the session, which typically happens during the first request.

 The default behavior of the Struts framework is not to store the Locale in the user's session. This can easily be overridden using the locale attribute of the controller element.

Example 5-4 shows a customized RequestProcessor class that checks the request for a locale each time and updates the user's session if it has changed from the previous one. This allows the user to change her locale preference at any point during the application.

*Example 5-4. Customized RequestProcessor that overrides the default Locale processing*

```
package com.oreilly.struts.framework;

import javax.servlet.http.*;
import java.util.Locale;
import org.apache.struts.action.Action;
import org.apache.struts.action.RequestProcessor;

/**
 * A customized RequestProcessor that checks the user's preferred locale
 * from the request each time. If a Locale is not in the session or
 * the one in the session doesn't match the request, the Locale in the
 * request is set in the session.
 */
public class CustomRequestProcessor extends RequestProcessor {

  protected void processLocale(HttpServletRequest request,
                               HttpServletResponse response) {

    // Are we configured to select the Locale automatically?
    if (!appConfig.getControllerConfig().getLocale()){
      // The locale is configured not to be stored, so just return
      return;
    }

    // Get the Locale (if any) that is stored in the user's session
    HttpSession session = request.getSession();
    Locale sessionLocale = (Locale)session.getAttribute(Action.LOCALE_KEY);

    // Get the user's preferred locale from the request
    Locale requestLocale = request.getLocale();

    // If the Locale was never added to the session or it has changed, set it
    if (sessionLocale == null || (sessionLocale != requestLocale) ){
      if (log.isDebugEnabled()) {
        log.debug(" Setting user locale '" + requestLocale + "'");
      }
      // Set the new Locale into the user's session
      session.setAttribute( Action.LOCALE_KEY, requestLocale );
    }
  }
}
```

To configure the `CustomizedRequestProcessor` for your application, you will need to add a `controller` element to the Struts configuration file and include the `processorClass` attribute as shown here:

```
<controller
  contentType="text/html;charset=UTF-8"
  debug="3"
  locale="true"
  nocache="true"
  processorClass="com.oreilly.struts.framework.CustomRequestProcessor"/>
```

You need to specify the fully qualified class name of the `CustomizedRequest-Processor`, as shown in this fragment. Although not every application has a reason to create a custom request processor, having one available in your application can act as a placeholder for future customizations. Therefore, it's a good idea to create one for your application and specify it in the configuration file. It doesn't have to override anything when you create it; you can add to it as the need arises. For more information on the controller element, see "The Struts Configuration DTD" in Chapter 4.

## The Action Class

The `org.apache.struts.action.Action` class is the heart of the framework. It's the bridge between a client request and a business operation. Each `Action` class typically is designed to perform a single business operation on behalf of a client. A single business operation doesn't mean the `Action` can perform only one task. Rather, the task that it performs should be cohesive and centered around a single functional unit. In other words, the tasks performed by the `Action` should be related to one business operation. For instance, you shouldn't create an `Action` that performs shopping-cart functionality as well as handling login and logout responsibilities. These areas of the application are not closely related and shouldn't be combined.

 Later in this chapter, we'll introduce the `DispatchAction` provided by the framework, which supports multiple operations in a single class. These multiple operations still should be cohesive and handle a common functional unit of the application.

Once the correct `Action` instance is determined, the `processActionPerform()` method is invoked. The `processActionPerform()` method of the `RequestProcessor` class is shown in Example 5-5.

*Example 5-5. The processActionPerform() method*

```
protected ActionForward processActionPerform(HttpServletRequest request,
                                             HttpServletResponse response,
                                             Action action,
                                             ActionForm form,
                                             ActionMapping mapping)

  throws IOException, ServletException {
```

*Example 5-5. The processActionPerform( ) method (continued)*

```
    try {
      return (action.execute(mapping, form, request, response));
    }catch (Exception e){
      return (processException(request, response, e, form, mapping));
    }
}
```

The processActionPerform( ) method is responsible for calling the execute( ) method on the Action instance. In earlier versions of the Struts framework, the Action class contained only a perform( ) method. The perform( ) method has been deprecated in favor of the execute( ) method in Struts 1.1. This new method is necessary because the perform( ) method declares that it throws only IOExceptions and ServletExceptions. Due to the added declarative exception-handling functionality, the framework needs to catch all instances of java.lang.Exception from the Action class.

Instead of changing the method signature for the perform( ) method and breaking backward compatibility, the execute( ) method was added. The execute( ) method invokes the perform( ) method, but eventually the perform( ) method will go away. You should use the execute( ) method in place of the perform( ) method in all of your Action classes.

 If you look at the source code for the Action class, you'll see that there are two different versions of the execute( ) and perform( ) methods. One version takes a non-HTTP request and response, while the second version contains the HTTP versions. Generally, you'll need only to use the HTTP version, unless you are using a non-HTTP servlet. For now, the non-HTTP versions just attempt to cast the request and response objects to their HTTP counterparts and invoke the HTTP versions of their respective methods.

You will need to extend the Action class and provide an implementation of the execute( ) method. Example 5-6 shows the LoginAction from the Storefront application.

*Example 5-6. The LoginAction class from the Storefront application*

```
package com.oreilly.struts.storefront.security;

import java.util.Locale;
import javax.servlet.http.*;
import org.apache.struts.action.*;
import com.oreilly.struts.storefront.customer.view.UserView;
import com.oreilly.struts.storefront.framework.exceptions.BaseException;
import com.oreilly.struts.storefront.framework.UserContainer;
import com.oreilly.struts.storefront.framework.StorefrontBaseAction;
import com.oreilly.struts.storefront.framework.util.IConstants;
import com.oreilly.struts.storefront.service.IStorefrontService;
```

*Example 5-6. The LoginAction class from the Storefront application  (continued)*

```java
/**
 * Implements the logic to authenticate a user for the Storefront application.
 */
public class LoginAction extends StorefrontBaseAction {
  /**
   * Called by the controller when the user attempts to log in to the
   * Storefront application.
   */
  public ActionForward execute( ActionMapping mapping,
                                ActionForm form,
                                HttpServletRequest request,
                                HttpServletResponse response )
  throws Exception{

    // The email and password should have already been validated by the ActionForm
    String email = ((LoginForm)form).getEmail();
    String password = ((LoginForm)form).getPassword();

    // Log in through the security service
    IStorefrontService serviceImpl = getStorefrontService();
    UserView userView = serviceImpl.authenticate(email, password);

    // Create a single container object to store user data
    UserContainer existingContainer = null;
    HttpSession session = request.getSession(false);
    if ( session != null ){
      existingContainer = getUserContainer(request);
      session.invalidate();
    }else{
      existingContainer = new UserContainer();
    }

    // Create a new session for the user
    session = request.getSession(true);

    // Store the UserView in the container and store the container in the session
    existingContainer.setUserView(userView);
    session.setAttribute(IConstants.USER_CONTAINER_KEY, existingContainer);

    // Return a Success forward
    return mapping.findForward(IConstants.SUCCESS_KEY);
  }
}
```

When the execute( ) method in LoginAction is called, the email and password values are retrieved and passed to the authenticate( ) method. If no exception is thrown by the authenticate( ) business operation, a new HttpSession is created and a JavaBean that contains user information is stored into the user's session.

A common bug that inexperienced Struts developers sometimes introduce into their applications is to not implement the execute( ) method correctly. If you misspell it or don't implement the signature exactly, the method will never be called. Unfortunately, you will not get a compiler error or even a runtime error telling you this, because the Struts Action class, which all action classes must extend, has a default execute( ) method that returns null.

The UserView class contains simple properties such as firstName and lastName that can be used by the presentation. These types of presentation JavaBeans are commonly referred to as value objects (VOs), but are more formally called data transfer objects (DTOs) because they are used to transfer data from one layer to another. In the UserView class shown in Example 5-7, the data is transferred from the security service to the presentation layer.

*Example 5-7. The UserView DTO*

```
package com.oreilly.struts.storefront.customer.view;

import com.oreilly.struts.storefront.framework.view.BaseView;
/**
 * Mutable data representing a user of the system.
 */
public class UserView extends BaseView {
  private String lastName;
  private String firstName;
  private String emailAddress;
  private String creditStatus;

  public UserView( ){
    super( );
  }

  public String getFirstName() {
    return firstName;
  }

  public void setFirstName(String firstName) {
    this.firstName = firstName;
  }

  public void setLastName(String lastName) {
    this.lastName = lastName;
  }

  public String getLastName() {
    return lastName;
  }

  public String getEmailAddress() {
    return emailAddress;
```

*Example 5-7. The UserView DTO (continued)*

```
}

  public void setEmailAddress(String emailAddress) {
    this.emailAddress = emailAddress;
  }

  public void setCreditStatus(String creditStatus) {
    this.creditStatus = creditStatus;
  }
  public String getCreditStatus() {
    return creditStatus;
  }
}
```

Data transfer objects are discussed in Chapter 6.

 Example 5-6 also uses a class called UserContainer. This class has not yet been fully introduced, so don't worry about having missed something. The UserContainer class is a wrapper around any data that might normally be put directly into the user's session. Using this object and storing everything within it makes retrieval and cleanup much easier. It's a good idea to use a container like this for your applications as well.

### The Action class cache

Because Action instances are expected to be thread-safe, only a single instance of each Action class is created for an application. All client requests share the same instance and are able to invoke the execute( ) method at the same time.

The RequestProcessor contains a HashMap, the keys of which are the names of all the Action classes that are specified in the configuration file; the value for each key is the single instance of that Action. During the processActionCreate( ) method of the RequestProcessor class, the framework checks the HashMap to see whether an instance already has been created. If it has, this instance is returned. Otherwise, a new instance of the Action class is created, stored into the HashMap, and returned. The section of the code that creates a new Action instance is synchronized to ensure that only one thread will create an instance. Once a thread creates an instance and inserts it into the HashMap, all future threads will use the instance from the cache.

## The ActionForward class

As you saw in the discussion of the Action class, the execute( ) method returns an ActionForward object. The ActionForward class represents a logical abstraction of a web resource. This resource typically is a JSP page or a Java servlet.

The `ActionForward` is a wrapper around the resource, so there's less coupling of the application to the physical resource. The physical resource is specified only in the configuration file (as the name, path, and redirect attributes of the forward element), not in the code itself. The `RequestDispatcher` may perform either a forward or redirect for an `ActionForward`, depending on the value of the redirect attribute.

To return an `ActionForward` from an `Action`, you can either create one dynamically in the `Action` class or, more commonly, use the action mapping to locate one that has been preconfigured in the configuration file. The following code fragment illustrates how you can use the action mapping to locate an `ActionForward` based on its logical name:

```
return mapping.findForward( "Success" );
```

Here, an argument of "Success" is passed to the `findForward()` method of an `ActionMapping` instance. The argument in the `findFoward()` method must match either one of the names specified in the `global-forwards` section or one specific to the action from which it's being called. The following fragment shows forward elements defined for the *signin* action mapping:

```
<action
    input="/security/signin.jsp"
    name="loginForm"
    path="/signin"
    scope="request"
    type="com.oreilly.struts.storefront.security.LoginAction"
    validate="true">
    <forward name="Success" path="/index.jsp" redirect="true"/>
    <forward name="Failure" path="/security/signin.jsp" redirect="true"/>
</action>
```

The `findForward()` method in the `ActionMapping` class first calls the `findForwardConfig()` method to see if a forward element with the corresponding name is specified at the action level. If not, the `global-forwards` section is checked. When an `ActionForward` that matches is found, it's returned to the `RequestProcessor` from the `execute()` method. Here's the `findForward()` method from the `ActionMapping` class:

```
public ActionForward findForward(String name) {

    ForwardConfig config = findForwardConfig(name);
    if (config == null) {
        config = getModuleConfig().findForwardConfig(name);
    }
    return ((ActionForward) config);

}
```

If the `findForward()` method does not find a forward that matches the name argument, it will not complain. A null will be returned, and you will receive a blank page because no output will be written to the response.

# Creating Multithreaded Action Classes

A single Action instance is created for each Action class in the framework. Every client request will share the same instance, just as every client request shares the same ActionServlet instance. Thus, as with servlets, you must ensure that your Action classes operate properly in a multithreaded environment.

To be thread-safe, it's important that your Action classes do not use instance variables to hold client-specific state. You may use instance variables to hold state information; it just shouldn't be specific to one client or request. For example, you can create an instance variable of type org.apache.commons.logging.Log to hold onto a logger, as the Struts RequestProcessor class does. The log instance can be used by all requests because the logger is thread-safe and does not hold state for a specific client or request.

For client-specific state, however, you should declare the variables inside the execute() method. These local variables are allocated in a different memory space than instance variables. Each thread that enters the execute() method has its own stack for local variables, so there's no chance of overriding the state of other threads.

# Business Logic and the Action Class

Some developers get confused about what logic belongs in an Action class. The Action class is not the proper place to put your application's business logic. If you look back to Figure 3-6, you can see that the Action class is still part of the controller; it's just been separated out from the ActionServlet and RequestProcessor for the sake of convenience.

Business logic belongs in the model domain. Components that implement this logic may be EJBs, CORBA objects, or even services written on top of a data source and a connection pool. The point is that the business domain should be unaware of the type of presentation tier that's accessing it. This allows your model components to be more easily reused by other applications. Example 5-8 illustrates the GetItemDetailAction from the Storefront application, which calls the model to retrieve the detail information for an item in the catalog.

*Example 5-8. The Action class should delegate the business logic to a model component*

```
package com.oreilly.struts.storefront.catalog;

import javax.servlet.http.*;
import org.apache.struts.action.*;
import com.oreilly.struts.storefront.framework.exceptions.BaseException;
import com.oreilly.struts.storefront.framework.UserContainer;
import com.oreilly.struts.storefront.framework.StorefrontBaseAction;
import com.oreilly.struts.storefront.catalog.view.ItemDetailView;
import com.oreilly.struts.storefront.framework.util.IConstants;
import com.oreilly.struts.storefront.service.IStorefrontService;
```

```
/**
 * An action that gets an ItemView based on an id parameter in the request and
 * then inserts the item into an ActionForm and forwards to whatever
 * path is defined as Success for this action mapping.
 */
public class GetItemDetailAction extends StorefrontBaseAction {
  public ActionForward execute( ActionMapping mapping,
                                ActionForm form,
                                HttpServletRequest request,
                                HttpServletResponse response )

    throws Exception {
    // Get the primary key of the item from the request
    String itemId = request.getParameter( IConstants.ID_KEY );

    // Call the storefront service and ask it for an ItemView for the item
    IStorefrontService serviceImpl = getStorefrontService();
    ItemDetailView itemDetailView = serviceImpl.getItemDetailView( itemId );

    // Set the returned ItemView into the Dynamic Action Form
    // The parameter name 'view' is what is defined in the struts-config
    ((DynaActionForm)form).set("view", itemDetailView);

    // Return the ActionForward that is defined for the success condition
    return mapping.findForward( IConstants.SUCCESS_KEY );
  }
}
```

The GetItemDetailAction class in Example 5-8 delegates to the Storefront service the real work of getting the item information. This a good approach because the Action doesn't know the internals of the Storefront service or the getItemDetailView( ) method. It can be a local object that performs JDBC calls, a session bean performing a remote call to an application server, or some other implementation. If the model implementation changes (which it will when we discuss EJB in Chapter 13), the Action will be protected from that change. Because the Storefront service is unaware of the type of client using it, clients other than Struts can use it. Decoupling the Action classes from the business objects is explored further in the next chapter.

## Using the Prebuilt Struts Actions

The Struts framework includes five out-of-the-box Action classes that you can integrate into your applications easily, saving yourself development time. Some of these are more useful than others, but all of them deserve some attention. The classes are contained within the org.apache.struts.actions package.

### The org.apache.struts.actions.ForwardAction class

There are many situations where you just need to forward from one JSP page to another, without really needing to go through an Action class. However, calling a JSP directly should be avoided, for several reasons. The controller is responsible for selecting the correct application module to handle the request and storing the ApplicationConfig and MessageResources for that application module in the request. If this step is bypassed, functionality such as selecting the correct messages from the resource bundle may not work properly.

Another reason that calling a JSP directly is not a good idea is that it violates the component responsibilities of MVC. The controller is supposed to process all requests and select a view for the client. If your application were allowed to call the page directly, the controller would not be able to fulfill its obligations to the MVC contract.

To solve these problems and to prevent you from having to create an Action class that performs only a simple forward, you can use the provided ForwardAction. This Action simply performs a forward to a URI that is configured in the parameter attribute. In the Struts configuration file, you specify an action element using the ForwardAction as the type attribute:

```
<action
    input="/index.jsp"
    name="loginForm"
    path="/viewsignin"
    parameter="/security/signin.jsp"
    scope="request"
    type="org.apache.struts.actions.ForwardAction"
    validate="false"/>
</action>
```

When the */viewsignin* action is selected, the perform( ) method of the ForwardAction class gets called. When you use the ForwardAction in an action element, the parameter attribute (instead of an actual forward element) is used to specify where to forward to. Other than this difference, you call the ForwardAction in the same way as any other Action.

The ForwardAction class comes in handy when you need to integrate your Struts application with other servlets or JSP pages while still taking advantage of the controller functionality. The ForwardAction class is one of the most valuable of the prebuilt Action classes included with the framework.

### The org.apache.struts.actions.IncludeAction class

The IncludeAction class is similar in some respects to the ForwardAction class. It originally was created to make it easier to integrate existing servlet-based components into Struts-based web applications. If your application is using the include( ) method of a RequestDispatcher, you can implement the same behavior using the IncludeAction.

You specify the IncludeAction in an action element in the same manner that you do for ForwardAction, except that you use IncludeAction in the type attribute:

```
<action
    input="/subscription.jsp"
    name="subscriptionForm"
    path="/saveSubscription"
    parameter="/path/to/processing/servlet"
    scope="request"
    type="org.apache.struts.actions.IncludeAction"/>
```

You must include the parameter attribute and specify a path to the servlet you want to include.

## The org.apache.struts.actions.DispatchAction class

The purpose of the DispatchAction class is to allow multiple operations that normally would be scattered throughout multiple Action classes to reside in a single class. The idea is that there is related functionality for a service, and instead of being spread over multiple Action classes, it should be kept together in the same class. For example, an application that contains a typical shopping-cart service usually needs the ability to add items to the cart, view the items in the cart, and update the items and quantities in the cart. One design is to create three separate Action classes (e.g., AddItemAction, ViewShoppingCartAction, and UpdateShoppingCartAction).

Although this solution is a valid approach, all three Action classes probably would perform similar functionality before carrying out their assigned business operations. By combining them, you would be making it easier to maintain the application—if you exchanged the current shopping-cart implementation for an alternate version, all of the code would be located in a single class.

To use the DispatchAction class, create a class that extends it and add a method for every function you need to perform on the service. Your class should not contain the typical execute( ) method, as other Action classes do. The execute( ) method is implemented by the abstract DispatchAction class.

You must include one method in your DispatchAction for every Action you want to invoke for this DispatchAction. Example 5-9 will help illustrate this. One thing should be noted about this example, however. Instead of extending the Struts DispatchAction, it actually extends a Storefront version called StorefrontDispatchAction. This was done to allow for utility-type behavior to exist as a superclass without modifying the Struts version. It's a fairly common practice.

*Example 5-9. The shopping-cart functionality is put into a single DispatchAction*

```
package com.oreilly.struts.storefront.order;

import java.io.IOException;
import java.text.Format;
import java.text.NumberFormat;
```

```java
import java.util.*;
import javax.servlet.ServletException;
import javax.servlet.http.*;
import org.apache.struts.action.*;
import org.apache.struts.actions.DispatchAction;
import com.oreilly.struts.storefront.service.IStorefrontService;
import com.oreilly.struts.storefront.catalog.view.ItemDetailView;
import com.oreilly.struts.storefront.framework.UserContainer;
import com.oreilly.struts.storefront.framework.util.IConstants;
import com.oreilly.struts.storefront.framework.ShoppingCartItem;
import com.oreilly.struts.storefront.framework.ShoppingCart;
import com.oreilly.struts.storefront.framework.StorefrontDispatchAction;
/**
 * Implements all of the functionality for the shopping cart.
 */
public class ShoppingCartActions extends StorefrontDispatchAction {
  /**
   * This method just forwards to the success state, which should represent
   * the shoppingcart.jsp page.
   */
  public ActionForward view(ActionMapping mapping,
                            ActionForm form,
                            HttpServletRequest request,
                            HttpServletResponse response)
    throws Exception {

    // Call to ensure that the user container has been created
    UserContainer userContainer = getUserContainer(request);
    return mapping.findForward(IConstants.SUCCESS_KEY);
  }


/**
 * This method updates the items and quantities for the shopping cart from the
 * request.
 */
public ActionForward update(ActionMapping mapping,
                            ActionForm form,
                            HttpServletRequest request,
                            HttpServletResponse response)
    throws Exception {

    updateItems(request);
    updateQuantities(request);
    return mapping.findForward(IConstants.SUCCESS_KEY);
  }

/**
 * This method adds an item to the shopping cart based on the id and qty
 * parameters from the request.
 */
public ActionForward addItem(ActionMapping mapping,
                             ActionForm form,
```

```
                              HttpServletRequest request,
                              HttpServletResponse response)
    throws Exception {

    UserContainer userContainer = getUserContainer(request);

    // Get the id for the product to be added
    String itemId = request.getParameter( IConstants.ID_KEY );
    String qtyParameter = request.getParameter( IConstants.QTY_KEY );

    int quantity;
    if(qtyParameter != null) {
      Locale userLocale = userContainer.getLocale( );
      Format nbrFormat = NumberFormat.getNumberInstance(userLocale);
      try {
        Object obj = nbrFormat.parseObject(qtyParameter);
        quantity = ((Number)obj).intValue( );
      }
      catch(Exception ex) {
        // Set the default quantity
        quantity = 1;
      }
    }

    // Call the Storefront service and ask it for an ItemView for the item
    IStorefrontService serviceImpl = getStorefrontService( );
    ItemDetailView itemDetailView = serviceImpl.getItemDetailView( itemId );

    // Add the item to the cart and return
    userContainer.getCart( ).addItem(
      new ShoppingCartItem(itemDetailView, quantity));

    return mapping.findForward(IConstants.SUCCESS_KEY);
}

/**
 * Update the items in the shopping cart. Currently, only deletes occur
 * during this operation.
 */
private void updateItems(HttpServletRequest request) {
    // Multiple checkboxes with the name "deleteCartItem" are on the
    // form. The ones that were checked are passed in the request.
    String[] deleteIds = request.getParameterValues("deleteCartItem");

    // Build a list of item ids to delete
    if(deleteIds != null && deleteIds.length > 0) {
      int size = deleteIds.length;
      List itemIds = new ArrayList( );
      for(int i = 0;i < size;i++) {
        itemIds.add(deleteIds[i]);
      }
      // Get the ShoppingCart from the UserContainer and delete the items
```

*Example 5-9. The shopping-cart functionality is put into a single DispatchAction (continued)*

```
    UserContainer userContainer = getUserContainer(request);
    userContainer.getCart().removeItems(itemIds);
  }
}

/**
 * Update the quantities for the items in the shopping cart.
 */
private void updateQuantities(HttpServletRequest request) {
  Enumeration enum = request.getParameterNames();
  // Iterate through the parameters and look for ones that begin with
  // "qty_". The qty fields in the page were all named "qty_" + itemId.
  // Strip off the id of each item and the corresponding qty value.
  while(enum.hasMoreElements()) {
    String paramName = (String)enum.nextElement();
    if(paramName.startsWith("qty_")) {
      String id = paramName.substring(4, paramName.length());
      String qtyStr = request.getParameter(paramName);
      if(id != null && qtyStr != null) {
        ShoppingCart cart = getUserContainer(request).getCart();
        cart.updateQuantity(id, Integer.parseInt(qtyStr));
      }
    }
  }
}
```

The `com.oreilly.struts.storefront.order.ShoppingCartActions` class contains the methods `addItem()`, `update()`, and `view()`. Each of these methods would normally be put into a separate `Action` class. With the `DispatchAction` class, they can be kept together in the same one.

 There are two other methods in the `ShoppingCartActions` class that we didn't mention: `updateItems()` and `updateQuantities()`. These methods are private utility methods used by the other action methods within the class. They are not called outside of this `Action` class. You can tell this by noting they do not have the required method signature.

To use your specialized `DispatchAction` class, you need to configure each action element that uses it a little differently than the other mappings. Example 5-10 illustrates how the `ShoppingCartActions` class from Example 5-9 is declared in the configuration file.

*Example 5-10. Specifying the parameter attribute when using a DispatchAction subclass*

```
<action path="/cart"
  input="/order/shoppingcart.jsp"
  parameter="method"
```

```
          scope="request"
          type="com.oreilly.struts.storefront.order.ShoppingCartActions"
          validate="false">
      <forward name="Success" path="/order/shoppingcart.jsp" redirect="true"/>
    </action>
```

The */cart* action mapping shown in Example 5-10 specifies the parameter attribute and sets the value to be the literal string "method". The value specified here becomes very important to the DispatchAction instance when invoked by a client. The DispatchAction uses this attribute value to determine which method in your specialized DispatchAction to invoke. Instead of just calling the */cart* action mapping, an additional request parameter is passed; the key is the value specified for the parameter attribute from the mapping. The value of this request parameter must be the name of the method to invoke. To invoke the addItem() method on the Storefront application, you might call it like this:

```
    http://localhost:8080/storefront/action/cart?method=addItem&id=2
```

The request parameter named method has a value of addItem. This is used by the DispatchAction to determine which method to invoke. You must have a method in your DispatchAction subclass that matches the parameter value. The method name must match exactly, and the method must include the parameters normally found in the execute() method. The following fragment highlights the method signature for the addItem() method from Example 5-9:

```
    public ActionForward addItem( ActionMapping mapping,
                                  ActionForm form,
                                  HttpServletRequest request,
                                  HttpServletResponse response )
        throws Exception;
```

DispatchAction uses reflection to locate a method that matches the same name as the request parameter value and contains the same number and type of arguments. Once found, the method will be invoked and the ActionForward object will be returned, just as with any other Action class.

> Although the DispatchAction does use Java reflection to invoke the correct method, the performance of the reflection APIs in Java 1.3 and newer are so much better that it's not a problem for this small amount of work. Because reflection is being used, however, the method must be declared public, or the perform() method in the abstract DispatchAction will not be able to invoke it. You can still declare other private or protected methods, but the ones to be called by DispatchAction must be declared public.

## The org.apache.struts.actions.LookupDispatchAction class

LookupDispatchAction, as you might guess, is a subclass of the DispatchAction class. From a high level, it performs a similar task as the DispatchAction.

Like DispatchAction, the LookupDispatchAction class allows you to specify a class with multiple methods, where one of the methods is invoked based on the value of a special request parameter specified in the configuration file. That's about where the similarity ends. While DispatchAction uses the value of the request parameter to determine which method to invoke, LookupDispatchAction uses the value of the request parameter to perform a reverse lookup from the resource bundle using the parameter value and match it to a method in the class.

An example will help you understand this better. First, create a class that extends LookupDispatchAction and implements the getKeyMethodMap( ) method. This method returns a java.util.Map containing a set of key/value pairs.

The keys of this Map should match those from the resource bundle. The value that is associated with each key in the Map should be the name of the method in your LookupDispatchAction subclass. This value will be invoked when a request parameter equal to the message from the resource bundle for the key is included.

The following fragment shows an example of the getKeyMethodMap( ) method for ProcessCheckoutAction in the Storefront application:

```
protected Map getKeyMethodMap( ) {
  Map map = new HashMap( );
  map.put("button.checkout", "checkout" );
  map.put("button.saveorder", "saveorder" );
  return map;
}
```

For the purposes of this discussion, let's suppose we have the following resources in the message resource bundle:

```
button.checkout=Checkout
button.saveorder=Save Order
```

and that we have specified the following action element in the Struts configuration file:

```
<action path="/processcheckout"
  input="/checkout.jsp"
  name="checkoutForm"
  parameter="action"
  scope="request"
  type="com.oreilly.struts.storefront.order.ProcessCheckoutAction">
  <forward name="Success" path="/order/ordercomplete.jsp"/>
</action>
```

Then create a JSP that performs a POST using the processcheckout action. A URL parameter of action="Checkout" will be sent in the request header. Example 5-11 shows the JSP that calls the processcheckout action.

*Example 5-11. The checkout.jsp file that calls the ProcessCheckoutAction when posted*

```
<%@ taglib uri="/WEB-INF/struts-html.tld" prefix="html" %>
<%@ taglib uri="/WEB-INF/struts-logic.tld" prefix="logic" %>
<%@ taglib uri="/WEB-INF/struts-bean.tld" prefix="bean" %>

<html:html>
<head>
<title>Virtual Shopping with Struts</title>
<html:base/>
<script language=javascript src="include/scripts.js"></script>
<link rel="stylesheet" href="../stylesheets/format_win_nav_main.css" type="text/css">
</head>

<body topmargin="0" leftmargin="0" bgcolor="#FFFFFF">

<!-- Header Page Information -->
<%@ include file="../include/head.inc"%>

<!-- Nav Bar -->
<%@ include file="../include/menubar.inc"%>

<br>

Display order summary and take credit card information here

<html:form action="/processcheckout">
    <html:submit property="action">
     <bean:message key="button.checkout"/>
    </html:submit>
</html:form>
<%@ include file="../include/copyright.inc"%>
</body>

</html:html>
```

The key to understanding how all of this works is that the submit button in Example 5-11 will have a name of "action" and its value will be the value returned from the <bean:message> tag. This is more evident when you see the HTML source generated from this JSP page. The following fragment shows the source generated inside the <html:form> tag:

```
<form
  name="checkoutForm"
  method="POST"
  action="/storefront/action/processcheckout">
     <input type="submit" name="action" value="Checkout" alt="Checkout">
</form>
```

You can see in this HTML source that when the checkoutForm is posted, the action="Checkout" URL parameter will be included. ProcessCheckoutAction will take the value "Checkout" and find a message resource key that has this value. In the instance, the key will be button.checkout, which, according to the getKeyMethodMap() method shown earlier, maps to the method checkout().

---

Whew! That's a long way to go just to determine which method to invoke. The intent of this class is to make it easier when you have an HTML form with multiple submit buttons with the same name. One submit button may be a Checkout action and another might be a Save Order action. Both buttons would have the same name (for example, "action"), but the value of each button would be different. This may not be an Action class that you will use often, but in certain situations, it can save you scarce development time.

### The org.apache.struts.actions.SwitchAction class

The SwitchAction class is new to the framework. It was added to support switching from one application module to another and then forwarding control to a resource within the application.

There are two required request parameters. The prefix request parameter specifies the application prefix, beginning with a "/", of the application module to which control should be switched. If you need to switch to the default application, use a zero-length string (" "). The appropriate ApplicationConfig object will be stored in the request, just as it is when a new request arrives at the ActionServlet.

The second required request parameter is the page parameter. This parameter should specify the application-relative URI, beginning with a "/", to which control should be forwarded once the correct application module is selected. This Action is very straightforward. You'll need it only if you use more than one Struts application module.

## The Utilities Classes

When building web applications, many of the tasks to retrieve and process requests are quite repetitive. Like any good framework, Struts places most of this tedious functionality into utility classes, so it can be shared and used by many different components and applications. This separation of utilitarian functionality from regular application-specific functionality allows for greater reuse and less redundancy throughout the framework and within your applications.

The utility classes used by Struts are located in several packages. Many of the utility components were so generic and beneficial to so many applications that they have been moved out of the Struts framework and into the larger Jakarta Commons project. These packages include BeanUtils, Collections, and the Digester component mentioned in Chapter 3.

One of the Java packages that remain in the Struts package hierarchy is org.apache. struts.util. Everything from the MessageResources class to StrutsValidatorUtil (part of the new Validator component added to the core framework in 1.1) is part of this package. This package contains many classes with different purposes and responsibilities. Although the Struts framework classes have strong dependencies on the utility classes, utility classes generally should have dependencies only on other utility classes and framework components that are lower in the food chain. This is mostly true in the Struts framework, with a few minor exceptions.

The utility classes within the util package assist the rest of the framework in solving mundane problems that all web applications encounter. We will not cover all of the classes in the package, but instead will highlight some of the more useful components.

## The RequestUtils Class

The org.apache.struts.util.RequestUtils class provides general-purpose utility methods that are common when processing a servlet request within Struts. You've already seen several examples that use the RequestUtils class. One of the most important, and the first to be invoked for a request, is the selectApplication() method that is called by the ActionServlet when a new request arrives. Every method in the RequestUtils class is designed to be thread-safe and doesn't declare any instance variables. In fact, every method in the class also is static.

You seldom need to modify any of the methods within the RequestUtils class. However, you should become familiar with the methods implemented by the RequestUtils class, so you don't replicate that same behavior in your application. Another reason to be familiar with the methods is that it will help you understand what the entire framework is doing on your behalf.

## The ResponseUtils Class

The purpose of the org.apache.struts.util.ResponseUtils class is similar to that of the RequestUtils class except that it aids in building a response rather than handling a request.

There are only a few methods within the class, but the JSP tag libraries included with Struts use them extensively for filtering and writing data destined for the response object.

## The Commons BeanUtils Package

The org.apache.commons.beanutils package contains several classes that are used throughout the Struts framework. From the standpoint of the Struts framework, the two most important are the BeanUtils and PropertyUtils classes.

The BeanUtils class is used with JavaBeans. Struts components primarily use just three of the methods in the BeanUtils class:

populate()

Fills a JavaBean with data, using a map of key/value pairs. The method signature for the populate() method is shown here:

```
public static void populate( Object bean, Map properties )
  throws IllegalAccessException, InvocationTargetException;
```

getProperty( )

Returns a String representation of the property stored in the variable with the name that matches the value of the name parameter. Here is the method signature for the getProperty( ) method:

```
public static String getProperty( Object bean, String name )
    throws IllegalAccessException, InvocationTargetException,
    NoSuchMethodException;
```

Regardless of the type of property that the name argument references, it will be converted and returned as a String.

getArrayProperty( )

Returns the value of the specified array property of the specified bean as a String array. Here is the method signature for the getArrayProperty( ) method:

```
public static String[] getArrayProperty(Object bean, String name)
    throws IllegalAccessException, InvocationTargetException,
    NoSuchMethodException;
```

Although the Java language provides reflection and introspection as part of its core APIs, the BeanUtils class provides convenience wrappers around these APIs.

The other class the Struts framework uses is PropertyUtils. Only the getProperty( ) method of this class currently is used. The getProperty( ) method in the PropertyUtils class returns the value of the specified property, without attempting to convert the type. Here is its method signature:

```
public static Object getProperty(Object bean, String name)
    throws IllegalAccessException, InvocationTargetException, NoSuchMethodException;
```

Much of the code in the PropertyUtils class originally was implemented in the BeanUtils class. It was moved to its own class because BeanUtils was becoming so large.

## The Commons Collection Package

Although Java 1.3 added the much-requested and needed Collection classes, a few holes were left unfilled by the new additions. The classes within the Commons Collection package address these remaining deficiencies.

Among the features of the Collection package are:

- Implementations of Lists and Maps that are designed for fast access
- Methods to utilize set-theory properties of collections, such as unions, intersections, and the closure properties
- Adaptor classes that allow conversions between Java 1.1 containers and Java 1.2–style containers

Currently, the Struts framework uses only the FastHashMap class from the Collection package. The FastHashMap class is designed to operate in a multithreaded environment, where most of the calls are read-only. The FastHashMap extends java.util. HashMap and provides two different modes, *slow* and *fast*. In slow mode, all access is synchronized. This is appropriate for when initialization is taking place. Once initialization is complete and mostly read-only calls occur, the Map can be switched to fast mode by calling setFast(true). In fast mode, read access is not synchronized, and write calls use cloning for performance.

## Security in the Action Classes

Action classes, if designed and scoped properly, can perform some very important functionality for an application. To prevent unauthorized users from finding a way to execute an action, Action classes should have a way to authorize certain users to perform the intended action. The processRoles() method is designed to check whether any roles are defined in the configuration file for the Action and, if so, to call the isUserInRole() method on the request. The problem with this approach is that not all applications can define their roles ahead of time. In some applications, roles can be added and removed dynamically and can be enumerated beforehand. In this case, there must be an alternative approach to dealing with users, roles, and permissions— container-managed security might not be enough, and an application might have to handle more of the details programmatically.

# CHAPTER 6

# Struts Model Components

This chapter introduces the components that make up the model portion of a Struts application. The model represents the business data for an application and should closely resemble the real-world entities and business processes for the organization. In this chapter, we'll explore the roles and responsibilities of the model components within the Struts framework and focus on building an architecturally correct implementation for the Storefront application. Special attention will be given to using a persistence framework that can easily and effortlessly be integrated into a Struts application.

## The "M" in MVC

The model components of an application arguably are the most valuable software artifacts to an organization. The model includes the business entities and the rules that govern access to and modification of the data. It's vital that this be kept in a single location in order to maintain valid data integrity, reduce redundancy, and increase reusability.

The model should remain independent of the type of client that's being used to access the business objects and their associated rules. In fact, the components within the model should not be aware of what type of client or framework is using it. There's an axiom that goes, "Dependencies go down, data goes up." The idea is that when using a layered architecture, the upper layer may have dependencies on lower layers, but the lower layers should not depend on the layers above them. Figure 6-1 illustrates how this principle is applied to a typical Struts architecture.

If you find yourself importing packages or classes from the Struts framework into your model, you are violating this principle. Coupling a lower layer to an upper one will make maintenance, reuse, and future enhancements more difficult.

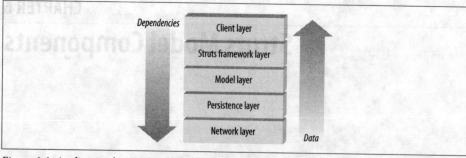

*Figure 6-1. Application layers should depend only on lower layers*

Before we get into the details of designing and building a model for a Struts application, let's look at the different types of models and how each one is relevant to a project.

## Types of Models

The term "model" has many different meanings. In very general terms, a model is a representation of some aspect of reality, such as a shop where products are bought and sold, an auction house where bids are placed, or a way to predict how a weather storm will move. All of these examples are based on real concepts. The main purpose of creating a model is to help understand, describe, or simulate how things work in the real world.

In software development, the term "model" is used to indicate both the logical representation of real-world entities and the physical creation of classes and interfaces that programs can use. The first step, however, always should be to perform a thorough analysis of the problem domain. Once use-cases are complete, the next step should be to develop a conceptual model.

### The conceptual model

During analysis of the problem domain, a conceptual model should be developed based on the real-life entities within the problem space. The entities in a conceptual model have less to do with the software components of the system and more to do with the physical entities that are fundamental to the business. The conceptual model usually illustrates the concepts, the relationships between them, and the attributes that belong to each concept. The behavior usually is not represented in this type of model.

The conceptual model is developed from a set of use-cases for the system. The purpose of building the model is to help identify the entities that most likely will become classes in the design stage and to better understand the problem domain. Figure 6-2 illustrates a conceptual model for the Storefront application. Notice that only relationships and the attributes for the entities are shown; no methods are specified.

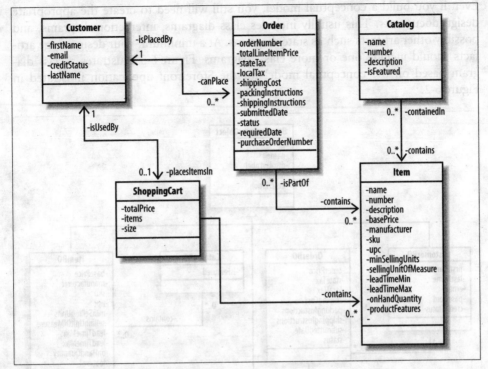

*Figure 6-2. The Storefront conceptual model*

 If you are familiar with Entity-Relationship (E-R) diagrams, you shouldn't be too confused by the conceptual model. They are very similar.

The value of a conceptual model is that it clearly shows the entities that are used by the problem domain. Everyone involved in the business, technical or not, should be able to look at the conceptual model and make sense of it. They also should be able to quickly point out problems with the model. For example, maybe an item can't belong to more than one catalog at a time. By examining the conceptual model, someone would be able to point this out, and the analysts could make the change early. The later in the design and development cycle that a change is required, the more costly that change becomes.

## The design model

The conceptual model is just one artifact of the analysis stage; there can be many others. In smaller development groups or on smaller projects, the conceptual model may be skipped in favor of moving to the design stage sooner. The risk of doing this, however, is that you might leave the analysis stage without a clear and concise understanding of the requirements.

Even if you build a conceptual model, you still will need to create the appropriate design documents. This usually includes class diagrams, interaction diagrams, and possibly other artifacts such as state diagrams. At a minimum, your design-stage artifacts should include one or more class diagrams. Figure 6-3 illustrates a class diagram based on the conceptual model for the Storefront application illustrated in Figure 6-2.

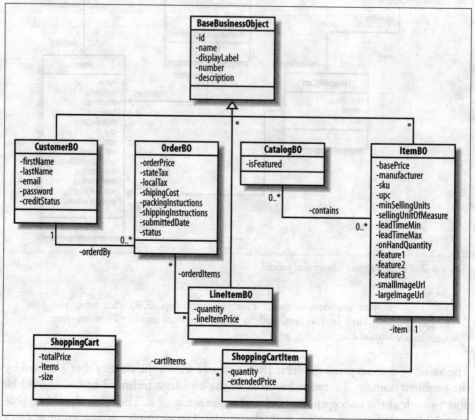

Figure 6-3. The class diagram for the Storefront business objects

The class diagram in Figure 6-3 shows the business objects used within the Storefront application. For brevity, only the attributes and relationships are shown here.

The way you arrive at the proper design for your application is definitely beyond the scope of this book. There are a multitude of excellent analysis and design books available. One of the more popular references is *Applying UML and Patterns* by Craig Larman (Prentice Hall).

The exact type and structure of business objects and processing rules obviously are dependent on the domain of your application, and no two applications are exactly the same. Even within a single application, it's understood that requirements change. However, conducting a thorough analysis of the problem domain and constructing a resilient design goes a long way toward protecting your application from unexpected change.

# What Is a Business Object?

This question may sound a little too simplistic for a book on Struts. However, the term "business object" has many connotations, and some developers use it when they really mean something else. A business object (BO) is simply a software abstraction of a real-world entity. It represents a person, place, thing, or concept from the business domain. So, concepts such as items, orders, and customers are all business objects from the Storefront business domain.

Business objects consist of state and behavior. The OrderBO, for example, is aware of information relating to a single customer purchase order, including price, tax, and order status. An OrderBO also should know who the customer is and be able to provide this information. Having both state and behavior is an important criterion for a class to be considered a business object. Let's examine a few other business object characteristics.

## Requirements for Business Objects

For a class to be considered a business object, several conditions should be met:

- Consists of state and behavior
- Represents a person, place, thing, or concept from the business domain
- Is reusable

Business objects also can be grouped into different classifications. Generally, there are three types:

- Entity business object
- Process business object
- Event business object

Probably the most familiar, an *entity BO* represents a person, place, thing, or concept. These usually are extracted straight from the business domain by considering the nouns in the business. Again, these are concepts such as customers, orders, items, and so on. In an EJB application, these are modeled as entity beans (hence the name). In a more traditional web application, these may be regular JavaBeans that contain the state and behavior of the business application.

*Process BOs* represent business processes or workflow tasks within an application. They usually are dependent on entity BO objects and are the verbs of the business. In an EJB application, these normally are modeled as session beans or, in some cases, message-driven beans. In a non-EJB application, these may be regular JavaBeans that contain specialized behavior to operate as a manager or controller for the application. Even though these types of business objects are used for processing workflow, they still can hold state for an application. With EJB, for example, there are stateless and stateful session beans.

The final category of business object is the *event BO*. An event BO represents some event in the application (exception, alert, timed event) that causes or is generated by some action in the system. In a Java Swing application, for example, when you press a button, an event is raised notifying the underlying framework so that an event handler can handle the button press.

## The Importance of Business Objects

Using business objects in an application has several benefits. Probably the most important is that business objects provide common terminology and ideas that can be shared across an organization by technical and nontechnical people alike. Because they represent real-world concepts and ideas, they are very intuitive and should make sense to the entire organization. If multiple applications from the same business domain exist, it's likely that the same business objects exist across the application boundaries. This reuse of information and behavior allows for faster application development and reduces redundancy.

Business objects also have the ability to evolve with the organization through modifications to the original object or through proper specialization. This is very important because as an organization changes, the information and behavior must adapt and change with it.

Finally, business objects have well-defined interfaces—not interfaces in the Java sense, but a clear and cohesive set of functionalities. The internal implementation should be hidden from the client to protect the callers from changes to the implementation details. For example, suppose you have a business object that uses a java.util.ArrayList. Instead of exposing the type ArrayList, you should expose java.util.List. If the implementation changes internally from ArrayList to LinkedList, the caller will not be impacted because the client is programming against the List interface, not the implementation class.

By now, you should be fully aware of the importance that business objects have in an organization. They are present in all but the most trivial applications. You also know that they contain state and behavior that, in most cases, acts on that data. So the next questions should be, where does that state originate and where does it go when the application is stopped? This leads us into the topic of object persistence.

# Persistence

In general, *persistence* means that the data that is input into an application, either by a human user or by other means, will exist beyond the lifetime of the application. Even though the application may exit or the computer may shut down, the information will survive. This obviously is very important to an organization. Every small, medium, and large organization has the need to persist data.

## Persisting Business Objects

When objects are created in memory for an application, they can't stay there forever. Eventually, they must either be cleaned up or persisted to a data store. Memory is volatile, and an application might crash or need to be stopped for maintenance. Without data persistence, there's no record to indicate what was ordered, for example, or whom to charge.

Business objects represent information that must be kept. To be of value, orders, items, and customer information must be persisted for an application like the Storefront. Losing a customer's order is not going to make the customer a customer for long. Once the data has been persisted, it can be retrieved and used to reconstruct the business objects at a later time.

## Storing Objects into a Relational Model

Although there are many different types of data stores, relational databases are used quite frequently to store the data for an organization, especially with applications like the Storefront. Relational databases are a necessity, and their use is widespread. There are, however, several obstacles that must be overcome to use them successfully. One of the biggest challenges is solving the so-called "impedance mismatch."

### The impedance mismatch

Objects hold state and behavior and can be traversed through their relationships with other objects. The relational paradigm, on the other hand, is based on storing data and joining sets of data by matching overlapping fields. Essentially, a relational database is a very "flat" view of the data. This difference leads to a challenging mismatch between the two worlds: objects must be flattened before they can be stored into a relational database, but the relationships that objects have to one another also must be persisted in order for the object hierarchy to be reassembled correctly.

 Object databases don't require the data to be flattened out. However, they are not yet as widespread as relational databases.

There's not enough room in this chapter for a detailed tutorial on mapping objects to a relational model. Suffice it to say that there are many challenges. Fortunately, many resources and references are available to help in overcoming these challenges. A definitive source of information on how to correctly map objects to a relational database can be found in Scott Ambler's white paper, "Mapping Objects to Relational Databases" (see *http://www.ambysoft.com/mappingObjects.pdf*).

As you'll see shortly, there are many object-to-relational mapping (ORM) frameworks that make this job much easier for the Java developer. Such frameworks don't completely eliminate your need for a good understanding of the problems, but they can hide many of the ugly chores that no developer wants to perform.

# What Does Struts Offer for the Model?

To be honest, the Struts framework doesn't offer much in the way of building model components, but this probably is as it should be. Many frameworks and component models are already available for dealing with the business domain of an application, including Enterprise JavaBeans and Java Data Objects (JDO), or you can use regular JavaBeans and an ORM. The good news is that the Struts framework does not limit you to one particular model implementation. This chapter will present one approach. In Chapter 13, we'll take a completely different approach and see how the framework is affected by this change.

## Building the Storefront Model

After all this discussion of what constitutes a model for a Struts application, it's finally time to apply the previously discussed concepts using the Storefront application as the business domain. Obviously, the Storefront is a fictitious example and doesn't represent a complete model for what a "real" e-commerce application would need to support. However, it does provide enough of an object model for you to understand the semantics of this chapter.

## Accessing a Relational Database

The state of the Storefront application will be persisted using a relational database. This is, in fact, how it would be done if Storefront were a real application. Of course, an ERP system often is used in conjunction with the relational database, but many e-commerce applications use a relational database closer to the frontend for performance and ease of development. When both are deployed in an enterprise, there's usually a middleware service to keep the data between the two synchronized, either in real time or using batch mode.

As you probably are aware, there are many relational databases to choose from. You can choose one of several major database vendors or, if your requirements don't call for such a large and expensive implementation, you can choose one of the cheaper or free products on the market. Because we will not be building out every aspect of the application and our intended user load is small, our requirements for a database are not very stringent. That said, the database-specific examples in this chapter should be fine for most database platforms. If you understand the SQL Data Definition Language (DDL), you can tweak the DDL for the database that's available to you.

We have quite a bit of work to do before we can start using the Storefront model. The following tasks need to be completed before we are even ready to involve the Struts framework:

- Create the business objects for the Storefront application
- Create the database for the Storefront application
- Map the business objects to the database
- Test that the business objects can be persisted in the database

As you can see, none of these tasks mentions the Struts framework. You should approach this part of the development phase without a particular client in mind. The Struts Storefront web application is just one potential type of client to the business objects. If designed and coded properly, many different types may be used. The business objects are used to query and persist information regarding the Storefront business. They should not be coupled to a presentation client.

To help insulate the Struts framework from changes that may occur in the business objects, we also will look at using the *Business Delegate* design pattern within the Storefront application. The business delegate acts as a client-side business abstraction. It hides the implementation of the actual business service, which helps to reduce the coupling between the client and the business objects.

## Creating the Storefront Business Objects

Business objects contain data and behavior. They are a virtual representation of one or more records within a database. In the Storefront application, for example, an OrderBO object represents a physical purchase order placed by a customer. It also contains the business logic that helps to ensure that the data is valid and remains valid.

The first step is to create the business objects with which we'll need to interact. For this implementation, they will just be regular JavaBean objects. Many component models are specific to a single implementation. Entity beans, for example, will work only within an EJB container. For this example, the Storefront business objects will not be specific to a particular implementation. If later we want to use these same business objects with an EJB container, we can wrap them with entity beans or just delegate the call from a session bean method to one of these objects. In Chapter 13, we'll show how this can be done without impacting the Storefront application.

# Where Does Business Validation Belong?

Deciding where to put your validation logic in a Struts application can be frustrating. On the one hand, it seems to belong within the framework itself, as this is the first place that the user data can be obtained and validated. The problem with placing business-logic validation within the `Action` or `ActionForm` class is that the validation then becomes coupled to the Struts framework, which prevents the validation logic from being reused by any other clients.

There is a different type of validation, called *presentation validation,* that can and should occur within the framework. Presentation validation, or "input validation," as it's sometime called, can be grouped into three distinct categories:

- Lexical
- Syntactic
- Semantic

*Lexical validation* checks to make sure data is well formed. For example, is the quantity value an integer? *Syntactic validation* goes one step further and makes sure that values made from a composite are valid and well formed. For example, date fields in a browser typically are accepted as month/day/year values. Syntactic validation ensures that the value entered is in the proper format. However, it doesn't ensure that the values make a valid date. Ensuring that the date entered is valid and meaningful is the job of *semantic validation*, which ensures that the values entered have meaning for the application. For example, putting a quantity value of -3 in the order quantity field for an item is lexically and syntactically valid but not semantically valid.

Presentation validation belongs within the Struts framework, but business validation does not. The business objects have the final responsibility of ensuring that any data inserted into the database is valid, and therefore it should have the rules necessary to perform this duty.

Because all the business objects share several common properties, we are going to create an abstract superclass for the business objects. Every business object will be a subclass of the `BaseBusinessObject` class shown in Example 6-1.

*Example 6-1. BaseBusinessObject is the superclass for all business objects*

```
package com.oreilly.struts.storefront.businessobjects;

/**
 * An abstract superclass that many business objects will extend.
 */
abstract public class BaseBusinessObject implements java.io.Serializable {
  private Integer id;
  private String displayLabel;
  private String description;

  public Integer getId() {
```

*Example 6-1. BaseBusinessObject is the superclass for all business objects (continued)*

```
    return id;
  }

  public void setId(Integer id) {
    this.id = id;
  }

  public void setDescription(String description) {
    this.description = description;
  }

  public String getDescription() {
    return description;
  }

  public void setDisplayLabel(String displayLabel) {
    this.displayLabel = displayLabel;
  }

  public String getDisplayLabel() {
    return displayLabel;
  }
}
```

The BaseBusinessObject prevents each business object from needing to declare these common properties. We also can put common business logic here if the opportunity presents itself.

Example 6-2 shows the OrderBO business object that represents a customer purchase order in the Storefront application. There's nothing that special about the OrderBO class; it's an ordinary JavaBean object. Other than the recalculatePrice( ) method, the class just provides setter and getter methods for the order properties.

*Example 6-2. The OrderBO object represents an order placed by a customer*

```
package com.oreilly.struts.storefront.businessobjects;

import java.sql.Timestamp;
import java.util.Iterator;
import java.util.List;
import java.util.LinkedList;

/**
 * The OrderBO, which represents a purchase order that a customer
 * has placed or is about to place.
 */
public class OrderBO extends BaseBusinessObject{

  // A list of line items for the order
  private List lineItems = new LinkedList();
  // The customer who placed the order
  private CustomerBO customer;
```

```java
// The current price of the order
private double totalPrice;
// The id of the customer
private Integer customerId;
// Whether the order is in process, shipped, canceled, etc.
private String orderStatus;
// The date and time that the order was received
private Timestamp submittedDate;

public OrderBO( Integer id, Integer custId, String orderStatus,
                Timestamp submittedDate, double totalPrice ){
  this.setId(id);
  this.setCustomerId(custId);
  this.setOrderStatus(orderStatus);
  this.setSubmittedDate(submittedDate);
  this.setTotalPrice(totalPrice);
}

public void setCustomer( CustomerBO owner ){
  customer = owner;
}

public CustomerBO getCustomer(){
  return customer;
}

public double getTotalPrice(){
  return this.totalPrice;
}

private void setTotalPrice( double price ){
  this.totalPrice = price;
}

public void setLineItems( List lineItems ){
  this.lineItems = lineItems;
}

public List getLineItems(){
  return lineItems;
}

public void addLineItem( LineItemBO lineItem ){
  lineItems.add( lineItem );
}

public void removeLineItem( LineItemBO lineItem ){
  lineItems.remove( lineItem );
}

public void setCustomerId(Integer customerId) {
  this.customerId = customerId;
}
```

*Example 6-2. The OrderBO object represents an order placed by a customer (continued)*

```java
public Integer getCustomerId() {
  return customerId;
}

public void setOrderStatus(String orderStatus) {
  this.orderStatus = orderStatus;
}

public String getOrderStatus() {
  return orderStatus;
}

public void setSubmittedDate(Timestamp submittedDate) {
  this.submittedDate = submittedDate;
}

public Timestamp getSubmittedDate() {
  return submittedDate;
}

private void recalculatePrice(){
  double totalPrice = 0.0;

  if ( getLineItems() != null ){
    Iterator iter = getLineItems().iterator();
    while( iter.hasNext() ){
      // Get the price for the next line item and make sure it's not null
      Double lineItemPrice = ((LineItemBO)iter.next()).getUnitPrice();
      // Check for an invalid lineItem. If found, return null right here.
      if (lineItemPrice != null){
        totalPrice += lineItemPrice.doubleValue();
      }
    }
    // Set the price for the order from the calcualted value
    setTotalPrice( totalPrice );
  }
}
}
```

We won't show all of the business objects here; they all have similar implementations to the OrderBO class.

When designing your business objects, don't worry about how they will be mapped to the database. There will be plenty of time for that. Don't be afraid to use object-oriented techniques such as inheritance and polymorphism, just as you would with any other object model. The BaseBusinessObject in Example 6-1 will not actually be mapped to a table in the database, but its properties will get mapped with the respective subclasses. Although most persistence mapping frameworks support multiple approaches to mapping inheritance in the database, adding the properties to each table allows fewer SQL joins to occur, which may have a positive impact on performance.

## The Storefront Data Model

Once all the business objects have been created for the Storefront application, we need to create a database model and schema. The details of creating a database schema for the Storefront application are beyond the scope of this book. It's seemingly easy to throw a bunch of tables into a database and add columns to them. However, it's quite another thing to understand the trade-offs between database normalization and issues that surface due to the object-relational mismatch discussed earlier.

If the application is small enough, almost anyone can create a database schema, especially with the tools available from database vendors and third-party sources. If your schema is more than just a few tables, or if the complexity of foreign keys, triggers, and indexes is high, it's best to leave creating a schema to the experts. The Storefront schema is quite small, mainly because we've chosen to implement only a portion of what normally would be required. Figure 6-4 shows the data model that will be implemented for the Storefront application.

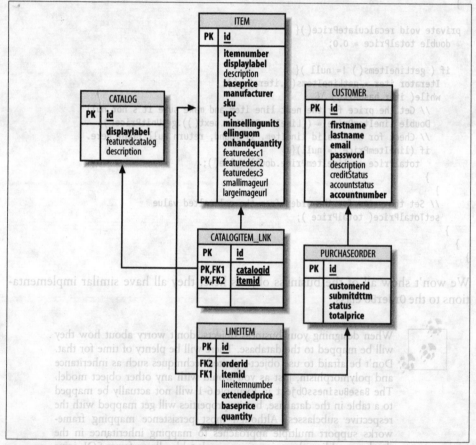

*Figure 6-4. The Storefront data model*

The table definitions in Figure 6-4 are fairly self-explanatory. There are several items of interest that should be pointed out, however. The first is that every table, except for the many-to-many link table CATALOGITEM_LNK, has been assigned an *object identifier* (OID). OIDs simplify the navigation between objects, and should have no business meaning at all. Values that are based on business semantics will sooner or later change, and basing your keys on values that change is very problematic. In the database world, using the OID strategy is known as using *surrogate keys*.

To generate the schema for the data model shown in Figure 6-4, we need to create the DDL. The SQL DDL is used to create the physical entities in the database. The Storefront SQL DDL that will create the set of tables in Figure 6-4 is shown in Example 6-3.

*Example 6-3. The Storefront SQL DDL*

```
DROP DATABASE storefront;

CREATE DATABASE storefront;

use storefront;

CREATE TABLE CATALOG(
    id int NOT NULL,
    displaylabel varchar(50) NOT NULL,
    featuredcatalog char(1) NULL,
    description varchar(255) NULL
);

ALTER TABLE CATALOG ADD
    CONSTRAINT PK_CATALOG PRIMARY KEY(id);

CREATE TABLE CUSTOMER (
    id int NOT NULL,
    firstname varchar(50) NOT NULL,
    lastname varchar(50) NOT NULL,
    email varchar(50) NOT NULL,
    password varchar(15) NOT NULL,
    description varchar(255) NULL,
    creditStatus char(1) NULL,
    accountstatus char(1) NULL,
    accountnumber varchar(15) NOT NULL
);

ALTER TABLE CUSTOMER ADD
    CONSTRAINT PK_CUSTOMER PRIMARY KEY(id);

CREATE TABLE ITEM (
    id int NOT NULL,
    itemnumber varchar (255) NOT NULL,
    displaylabel varchar(50) NOT NULL,
    description varchar (255) NULL,
    baseprice decimal(9,2) NOT NULL,
    manufacturer varchar (255) NOT NULL,
```

*Example 6-3. The Storefront SQL DDL (continued)*

```
    sku varchar (255) NOT NULL,
    upc varchar (255) NOT NULL,
    minsellingunits int NOT NULL,
    sellinguom varchar (255) NOT NULL,
    onhandquantity int NOT NULL,
    featuredesc1 varchar (255) NULL,
    featuredesc2 varchar (255) NULL,
    featuredesc3 varchar (255) NULL,
    smallimageurl varchar (255) NULL,
    largeimageurl varchar (255) NULL
)

ALTER TABLE ITEM ADD
    CONSTRAINT PK_ITEM PRIMARY KEY(id);


CREATE TABLE CATALOGITEM_LNK(
    catalogid int NOT NULL,
    itemid int NOT NULL
)

ALTER TABLE CATALOGITEM_LNK ADD
    CONSTRAINT PK_CATALOGITEM_LNK PRIMARY KEY(catalogid, itemid);

ALTER TABLE CATALOGITEM_LNK ADD
    CONSTRAINT FK_CATALOGITEM_LNK_CATALOG FOREIGN KEY
    (catalogid) REFERENCES CATALOG(id);

ALTER TABLE CATALOGITEM_LNK ADD
    CONSTRAINT FK_CATALOGITEM_LNK_ITEM FOREIGN KEY
    (itemid) REFERENCES ITEM(id);

CREATE TABLE PURCHASEORDER (
    id int NOT NULL,
    customerid int NOT NULL,
    submitdttm timestamp NOT NULL,
    status varchar (15) NOT NULL,
    totalprice decimal(9,2) NOT NULL,
)

ALTER TABLE PURCHASEORDER ADD
    CONSTRAINT PK_PURCHASEORDER PRIMARY KEY(id);


ALTER TABLE PURCHASEORDER ADD
    CONSTRAINT FK_PURCHASEORDER_CUSTOMER FOREIGN KEY
    (customerid) REFERENCES CUSTOMER(id);

CREATE TABLE LINEITEM (
    id int NOT NULL,
    orderid int NOT NULL,
    itemid int NOT NULL,
    lineitemnumber int NULL,
    extendedprice decimal(9, 2) NOT NULL,
```

*Example 6-3. The Storefront SQL DDL (continued)*

```
  baseprice decimal(9, 2) NOT NULL,
  quantity int NOT NULL
)

ALTER TABLE LINEITEM ADD
  CONSTRAINT PK_LINEITEM PRIMARY KEY(id);

ALTER TABLE LINEITEM ADD
  CONSTRAINT FK_LINEITEM_ORDER FOREIGN KEY
  (orderid) REFERENCES PURCHASEORDER(id);

ALTER TABLE LINEITEM ADD
  CONSTRAINT FK_LINEITEM_ITEM FOREIGN KEY
  (itemid) REFERENCES ITEM(id);
```

 The DDL shown in Example 6-3 has been tested on Microsoft SQL Server 2000. If you plan to use it with other database platforms, it might be necessary to modify the ALTER statements. For example, due to the limitations of foreign keys with MySQL, you may have to eliminate the FOREIGN KEY statements entirely. The only parts that are absolutely necessary to run the example are the CREATE TABLE sections and the primary keys, which all databases should support. It might also be necessary to execute the first couple of statements one at a time until the database is created and then execute the CREATE TABLE statements.

Once you have executed the DDL from Example 6-3, you will need to insert some data for the tables. The data must be in the database for the Storefront application to work properly. You can either use the administrative tools to enter data for the application or execute INSERT statements in the same manner as you did when creating the tables. As an example, to insert catalog data, you can execute the following statements:

```
  INSERT INTO CATALOG(id, displaylabel) VALUES(1,'Import');
  INSERT INTO CATALOG(id, displaylabel) VALUES(2,'Domestic');
  INSERT INTO CATALOG(id, displaylabel) VALUES(3,'Lager');
  INSERT INTO CATALOG(id, displaylabel) VALUES(4,'Light');
  INSERT INTO CATALOG(id, displaylabel) VALUES(5,'Import');
  INSERT INTO CATALOG(id, displaylabel) VALUES(6,'Malt Liquor');
```

## Mapping the Business Objects to the Database

When it comes time to connect or map the business objects to the database, there are a variety of approaches from which you can choose. Your choice depends on several factors that may change from application to application and situation to situation. A few of the approaches are:

- Use straight JDBC calls
- Use a "home-grown" ORM approach (a.k.a. the "roll-your-own" approach)

- Use a proprietary ORM framework
- Use a nonintrusive, nonproprietary ORM framework
- Use an object database

Keeping in mind that some tasks are better done in-house and others are better left to the experts, building a Java persistence mechanism is one that typically you should avoid doing. Remember that the point of building an application is to solve a business problem. You generally are better off acquiring a persistence solution from a third party.

There are many issues that must be dealt with that are more complicated than just issuing a SQL select statement through JDBC, including transactions, support for the various associations, virtual proxies or indirection, locking strategies, primary-key increments, caching, and connection pooling, just to name a few. Building a persistence framework is an entire project in and of itself. You shouldn't be spending valuable time and resources on something that isn't the core business. The next section lists several solutions that are available.

## Object-to-Relational Mapping Frameworks

There are a large number of ORM products available for you to choose from. Some of them are commercially available and have a cost that is near to or exceeds that of most application servers. Others are free and open source. Table 6-1 presents several commercial and noncommercial solutions that you can choose from.

*Table 6-1. Object-to-relational mapping frameworks*

| Product | URL |
| --- | --- |
| TopLink | http://otn.oracle.com/products/ias/toplink/index.html |
| CocoBase | http://www.cocobase.com |
| Torque | http://db.apache.org/torque/index.html |
| Hibernate | http://www.hibernate.org |
| ObJectRelationalBridge | http://db.apache.org/ojb |
| FrontierSuite | http://www.objectfrontier.com |
| Castor | http://castor.exolab.org |
| FreeFORM | http://chimu.com/projects/form |
| Expresso | http://www.jcorporate.com |
| JRelationalFramework | http://jrf.sourceforge.net |
| VBSF | http://www.objectmatter.com |
| JGrinder | http://sourceforge.net/projects/jgrinder |

Although Table 6-1 is not an exhaustive list of available products, it does present many solutions to choose from. Regardless of whether you select a commercial or noncommercial product, you should make sure that the mapping framework implementation does not "creep" into your application. Recall from Figure 6-1 that dependencies always should go down the layers, and there should not be a top layer depending on the persistence framework. It's even advantageous to keep the business objects ignorant about how they are being persisted. Some persistence frameworks force you to import their classes and interfaces, but this is problematic if you ever need to change your persistence mechanism. Later in this chapter, you'll see how you can use the Business Delegate pattern and the Data Access Object (DAO) pattern to limit the intrusion of the persistence framework.

 You can find a complete list of ORM product vendors at *http://www.service-architecture.com/products/object-relational_mapping.html*.

Another thing to be careful of is that a few of the persistence frameworks need to alter the Java bytecode of the business objects after they are compiled. Depending on how you feel about this, it could introduce some issues. Just make sure you fully understand how a persistence framework needs to interact with your application before investing time and resources into using it.

## The Storefront Persistence Framework

We could have chosen almost any solution from Table 6-1 and successfully mapped the Storefront business objects to the database. Our requirements are not that stringent, and the model isn't that complicated. We evaluated several options, but our selection process was very informal and quick, an approach you should not follow for any serious project. The criteria that the frameworks were judged against were:

- The cost of the solution
- The amount of intrusion the persistence mechanism needed
- How good the available documentation was

Cost was a big factor. We needed a solution that you could use to follow along with the examples in this book without incurring any monetary cost. All of the solutions evaluated for this example performed pretty well and were relatively easy to use, but we finally selected the open source Hibernate product to use for the Storefront example. We could have just as easy used ObJectRelationalBridge (OJB), which is another very popular open source ORM framework.

 Just because this solution was chosen for this example, don't assume that it will be the best solution for your application. Take the necessary time and evaluate the products based on your specific criteria.

The documentation for Hibernate is pretty good, considering that documentation for open source projects tends to be one of the last tasks completed. Essentially, the mapping of the business objects to the database tables takes place within XML files. The files are parsed by the mapping framework at runtime and used to execute SQL to the database. The portion of the mapping file that maps the customer business object is shown in Example 6-4.

 At the time that this source was written, the newest version of Hibernate was 2.1.2. For the latest Hibernate changes, go to *http://www.hibernate.org*.

*Example 6-4. The mapping XML for the CustomerBO class*

```xml
<?xml version="1.0"?>
<!DOCTYPE hibernate-mapping PUBLIC
    "-//Hibernate/Hibernate Mapping DTD 2.0//EN"
    "http://hibernate.sourceforge.net/hibernate-mapping-2.0.dtd">
<hibernate-mapping package="com.oreilly.struts.storefront.businessobjects">

    <class name="CustomerBO" table="CUSTOMER">
      <id name="id">
        <generator class="native"/>
      </id>
      <property name="firstName"/>
      <property name="lastName"/>
      <property name="password"/>
      <property name="email"/>
      <property name="accountStatus"/>
      <property name="creditStatus"/>

        <set name="submittedOrders" lazy="true">
        <key column="customerid"/>
        <one-to-many class="OrderBO"/>
      </set>
    </class>
</hibernate-mapping>
```

The rest of the mappings are mapped in a similar manner. Once all of the mappings are specified, you must configure the database connection information to allow the JDBC driver to connect to the correct database. With Hibernate, you configure the connection information in the *hibernate.cfg.xml* file. This is shown in Example 6-5.

*Example 6-5. The respository.xml file contains the database connection information*

```xml
<?xml version='1.0' encoding='utf-8'?>
<!DOCTYPE hibernate-configuration PUBLIC
        "-//Hibernate/Hibernate Configuration DTD 2.0//EN"

    "http://hibernate.sourceforge.net/hibernate-configuration-2.0.dtd">

<hibernate-configuration>
```

```
<!-- a SessionFactory instance listed as /jndi/name -->
<session-factory name="java:comp/env/hibernate/SessionFactory">

    <!-- properties -->
    <property name="connection.datasource">datasource/storefront</property>
    <property name="dialect">net.sf.hibernate.dialect.SQLServerDialect</property>
    <property name="show_sql">false</property>
    <property name="use_outer_join">true</property>
    <property name="transaction.factory_class">
    net.sf.hibernate.transaction.JTATransactionFactory
    </property>
    <property name="jta.UserTransaction">java:comp/UserTransaction</property>

    <!-- mapping files -->
    <mapping resource="customer.hbm.xml"/>

</session-factory>
</hibernate-configuration>
```

You need to configure the settings in this file for your specific environment and all add all of the mappings for your application—Example 6.5 adds only the mapping for the Customer business object. That's really all there is to configuring the persistence framework for your application. To initialize the framework within your application, you simply call a few initialization methods, as shown later in this section.

 Hibernate offers a rich and user-friendly API that you can use to create, query, update and delete your objects. You can read the documentation and tutorials to get a complete understanding of the API. The Storefront application will not need to scale for multiple servers. This means that the persistence framework is running within the same JVM as the Storefront application itself. This makes our design much simplier.

There's not enough room in this chapter for a better explanation of the Hibernate framework. For more detailed information, review the documentation for the product at *http://www.hibernate.org*. Don't forget that you will need to have an appropriate database and a JDBC driver in your web application's classpath.

## The Business Delegate and DAO Patterns in Action

The final piece of the puzzle is to create a service interface that the Storefront Action classes can use instead of interacting with the persistence framework directly. Again, the idea is to decouple the persistence from as much of the application as possible. Before we show the details of how we are going to accomplish this for the Storefront example, we need to briefly discuss the Data Access Object (DAO) pattern.

The purpose of the DAO pattern is to decouple the business logic of an application from the data access logic. When a persistence framework is being used, the pattern should help to decouple the business objects from that framework. A secondary goal is to allow the persistence implementation to easily be replaced with another, without negatively affecting the business objects.

There are actually two independent design patterns contained within the DAO—the Bridge and the Adaptor—both of which are structural design patterns explained in the Gang of Four's *Design Patterns: Elements of Reusable Object-Oriented Software* (Addison Wesley).

For the Storefront application, we are going to combine the DAO and Business Delegate patterns to insulate the Action and business object classes from the persistence implementation. The abstract approach is shown in Figure 6-5.

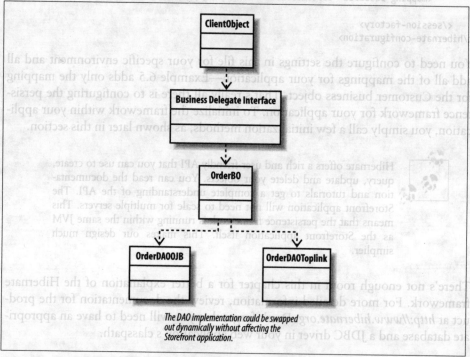

The DAO implementation could be swapped out dynamically without affecting the Storefront application.

*Figure 6-5. The Business Delegate and DAO patterns combined*

The client object in Figure 6-5 represents the Struts Action classes. They will acquire a reference to a service interface, which is referred to in the diagram as the Business Delegate Interface. The Storefront business interface is shown in Example 6-6.

*Example 6-6. The Storefront business interface*

```
package com.oreilly.struts.storefront.service;

import java.util.List;
import com.oreilly.struts.storefront.catalog.view.ItemDetailView;
import com.oreilly.struts.storefront.catalog.view.ItemSummaryView;
import com.oreilly.struts.storefront.framework.exceptions.DatastoreException;
import com.oreilly.struts.storefront.framework.security.IAuthentication;
/**
 * The business interface for the Storefront application. It defines all
 * of the methods that a client may call on the Storefront application.
 * This interface extends the IAuthentication interface to provide a
 * single cohesive interface for the Storefront application.
 */
public interface IStorefrontService extends IAuthentication {

  public List getFeaturedItems() throws DatastoreException;

  public ItemDetailView getItemDetailView( String itemId )
    throws DatastoreException;
}
```

The IStorefrontService interface in Example 6-6 defines all of the methods a client may call on the Storefront application. In our case, the client will be the set of Action classes in the Storefront application. The IStorefrontService is designed so that there is no web dependency. It's feasible that other types of clients could use this same service.

The IStorefrontService extends the IAuthentication class to encapsulate the security methods. The IAuthentication class, shown in Example 6-7, contains only two methods for this simple example.

*Example 6-7. The IAuthentication interface*

```
package com.oreilly.struts.storefront.framework.security;

import com.oreilly.struts.storefront.customer.view.UserView;
import com.oreilly.struts.storefront.framework.exceptions.InvalidLoginException;
import com.oreilly.struts.storefront.framework.exceptions.ExpiredPasswordException;
import com.oreilly.struts.storefront.framework.exceptions.AccountLockedException;
import com.oreilly.struts.storefront.framework.exceptions.DatastoreException;
/**
 * Defines the security methods for the system.
 */
public interface IAuthentication {

  /**
   * Log the user out of the system.
   */
  public void logout(String email);

  /**
```

*Example 6-7. The IAuthentication interface (continued)*

```
    * Authenticate the user's credentials and either return a UserView for the
    * user or throw one of the security exceptions.
    */
    public UserView authenticate(String email, String password)
      throws InvalidLoginException, ExpiredPasswordException,
             AccountLockedException, DatastoreException;
}
```

One implementation for the IStorefrontService interface is shown in Example 6-8. The implementation could be swapped out with other implementations, as long as the new implementations also implement the IStorefrontService interface. No clients would be affected because they are programmed against the interface, not the implementation.

 You'll see an example of switching the implementation of the IStorefrontService interface in Chapter 13, when we substitute an EJB tier into the Storefront application.

*Example 6-8. The Storefront service implementation class*

```
public class StorefrontServiceImpl implements IStorefrontService{

  // The SessionFactory
  SessionFactory sessionFactory = null;

  /**
   * Create the service, which includes initializing the persistence
   * framework.
   */
  public StorefrontServiceImpl() throws DatastoreException {
    super();
    init();
  }

  /**
   * Return a list of items that are featured.
   */
  public List getFeaturedItems() throws DatastoreException {
    List items = null;
    Session session = null;

    try{
      session = sessionFactory.openSession();
      Query q = session.createQuery("from ItemBO item");
      List results = q.list();

      int size = results.size();
      items = new ArrayList();

      for( int i = 0; i < size; i++ ){
```

*Example 6-8. The Storefront service implementation class (continued)*

```
        ItemBO itemBO = (ItemBO)results.get(i);
        ItemSummaryView newView = new ItemSummaryView();
        newView.setId( itemBO.getId().toString() );
        newView.setName( itemBO.getDisplayLabel() );
        newView.setUnitPrice( itemBO.getBasePrice() );
        newView.setSmallImageURL( itemBO.getSmallImageURL() );
        newView.setProductFeature( itemBO.getFeature1() );
        items.add( newView );
      }
      session.close();

    }catch( Exception ex ){
      ex.printStackTrace();
      throw DatastoreException.datastoreError(ex);
    }
    return items;
}

/**
 * Return an detailed view of an item based on the itemId argument.
 */
public ItemDetailView getItemDetailView( String itemId )
throws DatastoreException{
  ItemBO itemBO = null;
  Session session = null;

  try{
    session = sessionFactory.openSession();
    itemBO = (ItemBO) session.get(ItemBO.class, itemId);
    session.close();

  }catch( Exception ex ){
    ex.printStackTrace();
    throw DatastoreException.datastoreError(ex);
  }

  //
  if (itemBO == null ){
    throw DatastoreException.objectNotFound();
  }

  // Build a ValueObject for the Item
  ItemDetailView view = new ItemDetailView();
  view.setId( itemBO.getId().toString() );
  view.setDescription( itemBO.getDescription() );
  view.setLargeImageURL( itemBO.getLargeImageURL() );
  view.setName( itemBO.getDisplayLabel() );
  view.setProductFeature( itemBO.getFeature1() );
  view.setUnitPrice( itemBO.getBasePrice() );
  view.setTimeCreated( new Timestamp(System.currentTimeMillis() ));
  view.setModelNumber( itemBO.getModelNumber() );
```

*Example 6-8. The Storefront service implementation class (continued)*

```
      return view;
}

/**
 * Authenticate the user's credentials and either return a UserView for the
 * user or throw one of the security exceptions.
 */
public UserView authenticate(String email, String password) throws
  InvalidLoginException,ExpiredPasswordException,AccountLockedException,
  DatastoreException {

    List results = null;
    try{
      Session session = sessionFactory.openSession();
      results =
        session.find(
        "from CustomerBO as cust where cust.email = ? and cust.password = ?",
        new Object[] { email, password },
        new Type[] { Hibernate.STRING, Hibernate.STRING } );

    }catch( Exception ex ){
      ex.printStackTrace();
      throw DatastoreException.datastoreError(ex);
    }

    // If no results were found, must be an invalid login attempt
    if ( results.isEmpty() ){
      throw new InvalidLoginException();
    }

    // Should only be a single customer that matches the parameters
    CustomerBO customer  = (CustomerBO)results.get(0);

    // Make sure the account is not locked
    String accountStatusCode = customer.getAccountStatus();
    if ( accountStatusCode != null && accountStatusCode.equals( "L" ) ){
      throw new AccountLockedException();
    }

    // Populate the Value Object from the Customer business object
    UserView userView = new UserView();
    userView.setId( customer.getId().toString() );
    userView.setFirstName( customer.getFirstName() );
    userView.setLastName( customer.getLastName() );
    userView.setEmailAddress( customer.getEmail() );
    userView.setCreditStatus( customer.getCreditStatus() );

    return userView;
  }

/**
```

*Example 6-8. The Storefront service implementation class (continued)*

```
 * Log the user out of the system.
 */
public void logout(String email){
  // Do nothing with right now, but might want to log it for auditing reasons
}

public void destroy(){
  // Do nothing for this example
}

private void init() throws DatastoreException {

  try{
    sessionFactory = new Configuration().configure().buildSessionFactory();
  }catch( Exception ex ){
    throw DatastoreException.datastoreError(ex);
  }
 }
}
```

The service implementation provides all of the required methods of the IStorefrontService interface. Because the IStorefrontService interface extends the IAuthentication interface, the StorefrontServiceImpl class also must implement the security methods. Again, notice that the implementation knows nothing about the Struts framework or web containers in general. This allows it to be reused across many different types of applications. This was our goal when we set out at the beginning of this chapter.

We mentioned earlier that we have to call a few methods of the Hibernate framework so that the mapping XML can be parsed and the connections to the database can be made ready. This initialization is shown in the init() method in Example 6-8. When the constructor of this implementation is called, the XML file is loaded and parsed. Upon successful completion of the constructor, the persistence framework is ready to be called.

The constructor needs to be called by the client. In the case of the Storefront application, we'll use a factory class, which will also be a Struts PlugIn. The factory is shown in Example 6-9.

*Example 6-9. The StorefrontServiceFactory class*

```
package com.oreilly.struts.storefront.service;

import javax.servlet.ServletContext;
import javax.servlet.ServletException;
import org.apache.struts.action.PlugIn;
import org.apache.struts.action.ActionServlet;
import org.apache.struts.config.ModuleConfig;
import com.oreilly.struts.storefront.framework.util.IConstants;
```

*Example 6-9. The StorefrontServiceFactory class (continued)*

```
/**
 * A factory for creating Storefront Service Implementations. The specific
 * service to instantiate is determined from the initialization parameter
 * of the ServiceContext. Otherwise, a default implementation is used.
 * @see com.oreilly.struts.storefront.service.StorefrontDebugServiceImpl
 */
public class StorefrontServiceFactory implements IStorefrontServiceFactory, PlugIn{
  // Hold onto the servlet for the destroy method
  private ActionServlet servlet = null;
  // The default is to use the debug implementation
  String serviceClassname =
    "com.oreilly.struts.storefront.service.StorefrontDebugServiceImpl";

  public IStorefrontService createService() throws
    ClassNotFoundException, IllegalAccessException, InstantiationException {
    String className = servlet.getInitParameter( IConstants.SERVICE_CLASS_KEY );

    if (className != null ){
      serviceClassname = className;
    }

    IStorefrontService instance =
      (IStorefrontService)Class.forName(serviceClassname).newInstance();

    return instance;
  }
  public void init(ActionServlet servlet, ModuleConfig config)
    throws ServletException{
    // Store the servlet for later
    this.servlet = servlet;

    /* Store the factory for the application. Any Storefront service factory
     * must either store itself in the ServletContext at this key, or extend
     * this class and don't override this method. The Storefront application
     * assumes that a factory class that implements the IStorefrtonServiceFactory
     * is stored at the proper key in the ServletContext.
     */
    servlet.getServletContext().setAttribute( IConstants.SERVICE_FACTORY_KEY, this );
  }

  public void destroy(){
    // Do nothing for now
  }
}
```

The StorefrontServiceFactory class in Example 6-9 reads an initialization parameter from the *struts-config.xml* file, which tells it the name of the IStorefrontService implementation class to instantiate. If it doesn't have an property for this value, a default implementation class (in this case, the debug implementation) is created.

Because the factory class implements the PlugIn interface, it will be instantiated at startup, and the init() method will be called. The init() method stores an instance of the factory into the application scope, where it can be retrieved later. To create an instance of the Storefront service, a client just needs to retrieve the factory from the ServletContext and call the createService() method. The createService() method calls the no-argument constructor on whichever implementation class has been configured.

The final step that needs to be shown is how we invoke the Storefront service interface from an Action class. The relevant methods are highlighted in Example 6-10.

*Example 6-10. The LoginAction from the Storefront application*

```
package com.oreilly.struts.storefront.security;

import java.util.Locale;
import javax.servlet.http.*;
import javax.servlet.ServletContext;
import org.apache.struts.action.*;
import org.apache.struts.util.MessageResources;
import com.oreilly.struts.storefront.customer.view.UserView;
import com.oreilly.struts.storefront.framework.exceptions.*;
import com.oreilly.struts.storefront.framework.UserContainer;
import com.oreilly.struts.storefront.framework.StorefrontBaseAction;
import com.oreilly.struts.storefront.framework.util.IConstants;
import com.oreilly.struts.storefront.service.IStorefrontService;
import org.apache.commons.logging.Log;
import org.apache.commons.logging.LogFactory;
/**
 * Implements the logic to authenticate a user for the storefront application.
 */
public class LoginAction extends StorefrontBaseAction {
  protected static Log log = LogFactory.getLog( StorefrontBaseAction.class );
  /**
   * Called by the controller when the a user attempts to login to the
   * storefront application.
   */
  public ActionForward execute( ActionMapping mapping,
                                ActionForm form,
                                HttpServletRequest request,
                                HttpServletResponse response )
  throws Exception{

    // Get the user's login name and password. They should have already
    // validated by the ActionForm.
    String email = ((LoginForm)form).getEmail();
    String password = ((LoginForm)form).getPassword();

    // Get the StorefrontServiceFactory
    IStorefrontServiceFactory factory = (IStorefrontServiceFactory)
    servlet.getServletContext().getAttribute( IConstants.SERVICE_FACTORY_KEY );

    // Create the Service
```

```
try{
    service = factory.createService();
}catch( Exception ex ){
    log.error( "Problem creating the Storefront Service", ex );
}
return service;

    // Attempt to authenticate the user
    UserView userView = service.authenticate(email, password);

    // Store the user object into the HttpSession
    UserContainer existingContainer = getUserContainer(request);
    existingContainer.setUserView(userView);
    return mapping.findForward(IConstants.SUCCESS_KEY);
    }
}
```

The first step in the LogoutAction is to acquire an instance of the service on which it will authenticate the user. As you have seen in the previous examples, an instance of the Storefront service can be obtained through the factory, as Example 6-10 shows.

Once you have written the code to acquire the factory and the service in several Action classes, you my be tempted to move this code up to an abstract base Action class from which all others can extend. Once implemented, concrete Action classes would need only to call a getStorefrontService( ) method. This method is located in the superclass called StorefrontBaseAction.

The implementation for the getStorefrontService( ) method retrieves the factory and calls the createService( ) method. The StorefrontBaseAction class, which includes the getStorefrontService( ) method, is shown in Example 6-11.

*Example 6-11. The Storefront Base Action class*

```
package com.oreilly.struts.storefront.framework;

import java.util.Collection;
import java.util.LinkedList;
import java.util.List;
import java.util.Locale;
import java.util.Iterator;
import javax.servlet.http.*;
import org.apache.struts.action.*;
import org.apache.commons.logging.Log;
import org.apache.commons.logging.LogFactory;
import com.oreilly.struts.storefront.framework.util.IConstants;
import com.oreilly.struts.storefront.framework.exceptions.*;
import com.oreilly.struts.storefront.service.IStorefrontService;
import com.oreilly.struts.storefront.service.IStorefrontServiceFactory;
/**
 * An abstract Action class that all Storefront action classes should
 * extend.
```

*Example 6-11. The Storefront Base Action class (continued)*
```
*/
abstract public class StorefrontBaseAction extends Action {
  Log log = LogFactory.getLog( this.getClass() );

  protected IStorefrontService getStorefrontService(){
    IStorefrontServiceFactory factory = (IStorefrontServiceFactory)getApplicationObject(
IConstants.SERVICE_FACTORY_KEY );
    IStorefrontService service = null;

    try{
      service = factory.createService();
    }catch( Exception ex ){
      log.error( "Problem creating the Storefront Service", ex );
    }
    return service;
  }

  /**
   * Retrieve a session object based on the request and the attribute name.
   */
  protected Object getSessionObject(HttpServletRequest req,
                                    String attrName) {

    Object sessionObj = null;
    HttpSession session = req.getSession(false);
    if ( session != null ){
        sessionObj = session.getAttribute(attrName);
    }
    return sessionObj;
  }

  /**
   * Return the instance of the ApplicationContainer object.
   */
  protected ApplicationContainer getApplicationContainer() {
    return (ApplicationContainer)getApplicationObject(IConstants.APPLICATION_CONTAINER_
KEY);
  }

  /**
   * Retrieve the UserContainer for the user tier to the request.
   */
  protected UserContainer getUserContainer(HttpServletRequest request) {

    UserContainer userContainer = (UserContainer)getSessionObject(request, IConstants.
USER_CONTAINER_KEY);

    // Create a UserContainer for the user if it doesn't exist already
    if(userContainer == null) {
      userContainer = new UserContainer();
      userContainer.setLocale(request.getLocale());
      HttpSession session = request.getSession(true);
      session.setAttribute(IConstants.USER_CONTAINER_KEY, userContainer);
    }
```

*Example 6-11. The Storefront Base Action class (continued)*

```
    return userContainer;
  }

  /**
   * Retrieve an object from the application scope by its name. This is
   * a convience method.
   */
  protected Object getApplicationObject(String attrName) {
    return servlet.getServletContext().getAttribute(attrName);
  }

  public boolean isLoggedIn( HttpServletRequest request ){
    UserContainer container = getUserContainer(request);
    if ( container.getUserView() != null ){
      return true;
    }else{
      return false;
    }
  }
}
```

The getApplicationObject() method is just a convenience method for the Storefront Action classes; it calls the getAttribute() method on the ServletContext object.

Once the service is obtained in Example 6-10, the authenticate() method is called and a value object called UserView is returned back to the Action:

```
    UserView userView = serviceImpl.authenticate(email, password);
```

This object is placed inside a session object, and the Action returns. If no user with a matching set of credentials is found, the authenticate() method will throw an InvalidLoginException.

Notice that the Action class is using the IStorefrontService interface, not the implementation object. As we said, this is important to prevent alternate implementations from having a ripple effect on the Action classes.

## Conclusion

We covered a lot of ground in this chapter, and it may be little overwhelming if you are new to the concepts of models and persistence. Some of the future chapters will assume that these topics are familiar to you and will not spend any time discussing them, so make sure you understand this material before moving on.

Obviously much of this chapter dealt with issues not directly related to Struts. As mentioned earlier, the Struts framework doesn't offer much for the model. Most of the work is spent integrating an existing model architecture into Struts, as we did throughout this chapter. And although this material may seem irrelevant to the topic of the book, it's just as important as anything else you'll have to do with Struts.

# CHAPTER 7

# Struts View Components

This chapter introduces the components that make up the view portion of the Struts framework. The framework uses the view components to render dynamic content for the client. Based primarily on JavaServer Pages, the components provide support for internationalization, user-input acceptance, validation, and error handling, making it easier for the developer to focus on business requirements. This chapter concludes the three-part discussion of how the Struts framework implements the MVC pattern.

## What Is a View?

In a general sense, a view represents a display of the domain model in a user interface. There can be many different views of the same model. As discussed in Chapter 5, the domain model contains the business entities, which hold the state for the application. Metaphorically speaking, a view is a window that clients can use to look at the state of the model, and the perspective may be different depending on which window a client looks through. For example, in the Storefront application, the front page shows a set of featured items in the catalog. It doesn't show all of the information about each item, only a small portion. This "summary" view is used in the Storefront application wherever real estate is scarce, such as on the main page (shown in Figure 7-1).

When a user selects one of the items for sale, all of the item details are displayed. The user is still looking at the same business model, but the view is different. This alternate view of the model is shown in Figure 7-2.

A more detailed view of the business model is necessary for this page—there may be different JSP pages, images, multimedia files, and other view-related components. These two different perspectives are in fact two different views of the same model.

Because business objects don't have a natural way of representing themselves externally, it's up to the view components to present the domain model information to the clients. This presentation may be in the form of XML and XSLT, SOAP messages

*Figure 7-1. The Storefront main page is one perspective of the model*

returned to a web service client, or, in the case of the Storefront application, HTML rendered in a browser. A different type of client, such as a wireless device, could look at a completely different set of views but still use the same model. The model is used to represent the state of the application, while the views are used to present the model, or a portion of it, to the client.

Although the Storefront demo is a B2C application, it's possible to have a B2B application use the same model to make part-ordering functionality available to partners. As long as the proper separation is maintained between the model and the presentation layer, you can build any number of views for any number of clients on top of the same domain model.

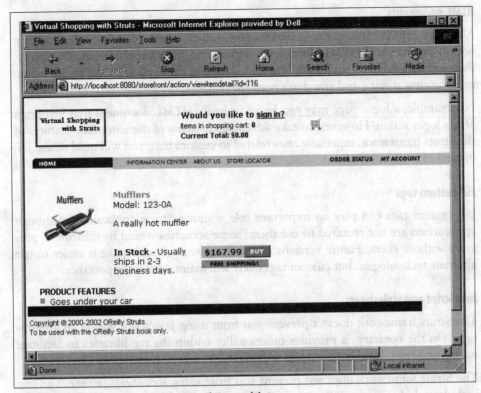

Figure 7-2. An alternate view of the Storefront model

# Using Views Within the Struts Framework

Generally speaking, the views in the Struts framework are built using JSP pages. Other approaches and frameworks are available for performing the same functions, but JSP is the most widely used presentation technology in the Struts community. Additional components that can be used by or in conjunction with JSP pages to render the views include:

- HTML documents
- JSP custom tag libraries
- JavaScript and stylesheets
- Multimedia files
- Message resource bundles
- `ActionForm` classes

## HTML documents

Although HTML documents generate only static content, there's nothing wrong with using standard HTML documents within your Struts applications. Obviously, they will be unable to render any dynamic data, but they still are valid to use whenever the view is static and you don't need the dynamic capabilities of JSP.

For example, a login page may just be an ordinary HTML document that invokes a Struts login action. However, to take advantage of many of the automatic features of the Struts framework, especially ones related to custom tags, you will need to use JSP instead of straight HTML.

## JSP custom tags

JSP custom tags can play an important role within a Struts application. Although applications are not required to use them, some scenarios would be difficult to program without them. Future versions of the framework should make it easier to use alternate technologies, but custom tags likely will maintain their importance.

## JavaScript and stylesheets

The Struts framework doesn't prevent you from using JavaScript within an application. On the contrary, it provides functionality within the tag libraries to facilitate using JavaScript. JavaScript support within custom tags is discussed in Chapter 8.

The Struts framework does not prevent you from using stylesheets, either. You can include stylesheets in a JSP page, and they will be rendered in the browser just as standard HTML pages would be.

Stylesheets are used to help web designers gain more control over the appearance of a web site. Features such as character size, color, font, and other look-and-feel characteristics can be changed in a central location and have an immediate effect throughout the entire site.

## Multimedia files

Multimedia files are used in just about every web application. These include but are not limited to:

- Images (*.gif*, *.jpg*, etc.)
- Audio (*.wav*, *.mp3*, etc.)
- Video (*.avi*, *.mpg*, etc.)

Images probably are the most widely used, although for B2B applications, audio and video files also are prevalent (e.g., for displaying CAD drawings and specifications). The Struts framework supports using multimedia files within an application. This support is achieved mainly through the use of custom tags, but you can also use standard HTML to render these types of resources.

There are a few sore spots when it comes to rendering images using custom tags. Differences between absolute and relative paths can cause some images not to display properly. The best advice is to decide whether you are going to need relative or absolute paths and then be as consistent as possible.

### Message resource bundles

Message resource bundles, commonly referred to simply as resource bundles, are a very important component for Struts applications. They provide a means to support localization and also help to reduce maintenance time and redundancy throughout an application.

For example, suppose your web application uses certain text labels or messages in multiple locations. Instead of hardcoding the string in every page, you can specify it in the bundle and retrieve it using one of the custom tags. Then, if the text label or message needs to change, you need to modify it only in one location. This helps to reduce maintenance time.

Some developers consider the resource bundles as belonging to the model, rather than the view. This is because application data (in the form of messages) is stored within the bundles. However, because the bundles also contain labels and strings for such things as text fields, checkbox labels, page titles, and so on, a valid argument can be made either way.

## Using JavaBeans Within the View Components

It might seem weird to talk about JavaBeans within a chapter on views. However, because JavaBeans make up a large portion of how the model data is used within the framework, it makes sense to discuss them briefly.

### Quick refresher

JavaBeans itself is a portable, platform-independent component model written in the Java programming language. The JavaBeans component architecture allows developers to create reusable components that can be used on any platform that supports a JVM. The JavaBeans model supports properties, events, methods, and persistence.

The Struts framework (and Java web applications in general) uses only a small portion of the capabilities defined in the JavaBeans specification. JavaBeans in Struts applications are used like ordinary Java objects, but they must follow certain guidelines:

- Must provide a zero-argument constructor.
- Should provide both a get<PropertyName> and set<PropertyName> method for all properties defined within the bean.

- For Boolean properties, if the method is<PropertyName> is present, it will be used to return the property value.

- For indexed properties where a property like <PropertyElement>[] is defined, the following methods should be present: get<PropertyName>(int a) and set<PropertyName>(int a, PropertyElement b).

These guidelines are necessary for the beans to be introspected at runtime by the framework.

One of the common traps that Struts developers fall into when dealing with JavaBeans is to use a return type that's different from the parameter type. If you create a method in a JavaBean that passes a String as an argument:

```
public void setDescription( String newDescription );
```

you must have a corresponding get method that returns the same type:

```
public String getDescription();
```

If the return type differs from the parameter type, the Struts framework may not recognize it as a bean, and you likely will get an error message stating that "No getter method could be found" or "No setter method could be found" for the property name.

### How Struts applications use JavaBeans

In a strict MVC architecture, as shown in Figure 7-3, the view gets updates directly from the model when it receives a notification that something has changed within the model. With web applications, this notification is not possible, or at least is difficult to achieve. Normally, it's up to the client to issue a request to the controller to refresh a view from the model state. In other words, the client "pulls" the view from the model, instead of the model "pushing" changes out to the view.

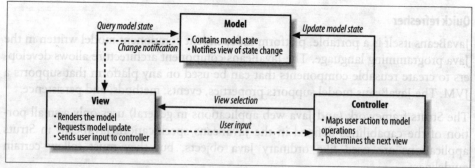

Figure 7-3. The view queries the model for state information

### The Data Transfer Object pattern

Chapter 6 discussed one approach to building the model components for a Struts application. The one thing that was intentionally left out was exactly how the view accesses the data from the model. To understand this, it will help to understand the *Data Transfer Object* (DTO) pattern (sometimes referred to as the *Value Object* or *Replicate Object* pattern).

The DTO pattern is used quite frequently in J2EE applications, where distributed components making remote calls can suffer serious performance setbacks from using too many remote invocations. It is used in other technologies as well, under different names and guises.

A DTO is a coarse-grained view of what is typically fine-grained information. It aggregates various attributes from one or more business entities and puts this information into a JavaBean instance. This instance can then be passed throughout the local application, or even be serialized and sent over the network, and clients can retrieve the model information from a local object without suffering any negative performance impact.

The DTO normally doesn't provide any business logic or validation; it just provides access to the properties of the bean. Some documentation on this pattern suggests that the bean should be immutable, to help reinforce that the object is local and that changes will not be reflected in the system. However, this can cause problems because the JavaBeans specification requires that all private properties have get<PropertyName> and set<PropertyName> methods. It is up to you to determine how best to handle the mutability of DTOs based on your requirements.

DTOs effectively are part of the model—they are just local, possibly immutable copies of the business objects. Within Struts applications, they are used by the view to deliver the model data that is rendered along with the static information in the page.

# What Are ActionForms?

Almost every web application has to accept input from users. Some examples of user input are usernames and passwords, credit card information, and billing and shipping address information. HTML provides the necessary components to render the input fields in a browser, including text boxes, radio buttons, checkboxes, and buttons. When you're building these types of pages, you must nest the input components inside HTML form elements. Example 7-1 illustrates a very basic sign-in page, similar to the one used in the Storefront application.

*Example 7-1. A simple sign-in page*

```
<html>
<head>
<title>Example 7-1. OReilly Struts Book</title>
```

*Example 7-1. A simple sign-in page (continued)*

```html
<link rel="stylesheet" href="stylesheets/main.css" type="text/css">
</head>

<body>

<form method="post" action="/action/signin">

<!-- The table layout for the email and password fields -->
<table BORDER="0" cellspacing="0" cellpadding="0">
<tr>
  <td>Email: </td>
  <td>  </td>
  <td>
    <input type="text" name="email" size="20" maxlength="20"/>
  </td>
</tr>

<tr>
  <td>Password:</td>
  <td>  </td>
  <td class="alignformslist">
    <input type="text" name="password" size="20" maxlength="25"/>
  </td>
</tr>

<!-- The table layout for the signin button -->
<table width="250" border="0">
<tr>
  <td>
    <input type="submit" name="Submit" value="Signin" class="Buttons">
  </td>
</tr>
</table>
</form>
</body>
</html>
```

When the user presses the Signin button on the HTML form from Example 7-1, the values within the fields are submitted along with the HTTP request. The server application can retrieve the values that were entered, perform input validation on the data, and then pass the data to another component in the application where the actual authentication process occurs. If the input data fails the input validation rules, the application should return to the previous location, redisplay some or all of the values entered, and display an error message indicating that the login attempt failed.

Manually performing all of this functionality, retrieving the values, executing the validation, and displaying error messages on failure can be a daunting task. This type of behavior is performed in many places throughout a web application, and it would be nice to have it taken care of by the framework and to be able to reuse it across applications.

Fortunately, the Struts framework does provide this functionality and will handle these tasks on behalf of your application. The Struts framework relies on the org. apache.struts.action.ActionForm class as the key component for handling these tasks.

The ActionForm class is used to capture input data from an HTML form and transfer it to the Action class. Because users often enter invalid data, web applications need a way to store the input data temporarily so that it can be redisplayed when an error occurs. In this sense, the ActionForm class acts as a buffer to hold the state of the data the user entered while it is being validated. The ActionForm also acts as a "firewall" for your application in that it helps to keep suspect or invalid input out of your business tier until it has been scrutinized by the validation rules. Lastly, when data is returned from the business tier, a particular ActionForm can be populated and used by a JSP page to render the input fields for an HTML form. This allows more consistency for your HTML forms, as they always pull data from the ActionForm, not from different JavaBeans.

When the user-input data does pass input validation, the ActionForm is passed into the execute( ) method of the Action class. From there, the data can be retrieved from the ActionForm and passed on to the business tier.

 Because the ActionForm imports packages from the Servlet API, you shouldn't pass the ActionForm to the business tier—doing so would couple the business methods to the Servlet API and make it more difficult to reuse the business tier components. Instead, the data within the ActionForm should be transferred to an object from the domain model. A common approach is to create a DTO and populate it with the data from the ActionForm.

You don't have to declare an ActionForm for every HTML form in your application. The same ActionForm can be associated with one or more action mappings. This means that they can be shared across multiple HTML forms. For example, if you had a wizard interface where a set of data was entered and posted across multiple pages, you could use a single ActionForm to capture all of this data, a few fields at a time.

## ActionForms and Scope

ActionForms can have two different levels of scope: request and session. If request scope is used, the ActionForm is available only until the end of the request/ response cycle. Once the response has been returned to the client, the ActionForm and the data within it are no longer accessible.

If you need to keep the form data around for longer than a single request, you can configure an ActionForm to have session scope. This might be necessary if your application captures data across multiple pages, like a wizard dialog does. An ActionForm that has been configured with session scope will remain in the session until it's removed or replaced with another object, or until the session times out. The framework doesn't have a built-in facility for automatically cleaning up session-scoped ActionForm objects. As with any other object placed into the HttpSession, it's up to the application to routinely perform cleanup on the resources stored there. This is slightly different from what happens with objects placed into request scope, because once the request is finished, they no longer can be referenced and so can be reclaimed by the garbage collector.

Unless you need to hold the form data across multiple requests, you should use request scope for your ActionForm objects.

 If you don't specify the scope attribute for an action mapping, the ActionForm will default to session scope. To be safe, you should always explicitly specify the scope of the ActionForm. To see how to specify the scope for an action element, see "The Struts Configuration DTD" in Chapter 4.

When the controller receives a request, it attempts to recycle an ActionForm instance from either the request or the session, depending on the scope that the ActionForm has in the action element. If no instance is found, a new instance is created.

## The Lifecycle of an ActionForm

The section "Using the Struts ActionForm" in Chapter 3 described the steps the framework takes when an ActionForm is being used by an application. From these steps, it's easy to get a picture of the lifecycle of an ActionForm. Figure 7-4 illustrates the main steps taken by the framework that have some effect on the ActionForm.

Figure 7-4 shows only the steps that are relevant to an ActionForm, not all those that a request goes through during request processing. Notice that when an ActionForm detects one or more validation errors, it performs a forward back to the resource identified in the input attribute. The data that was sent in the request is left in the ActionForm so that it can be used to repopulate the HTML fields.

## Creating an ActionForm

The ActionForm class provided by the Struts framework is abstract, and you need to create subclasses of it to capture your application-specific form data. Within your subclass, you should define a property for each field that you want to capture from the HTML form. For example, suppose you want to capture the email and password fields from a form, similar to the one in Example 7-1. Example 7-2 illustrates the LoginForm for the Storefront application that can be used to store and validate the email and password fields.

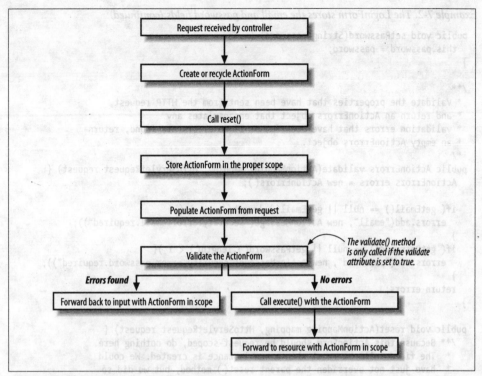

The validate() method is only called if the validate attribute is set to true.

Errors found

No errors

*Figure 7-4. The lifecycle of an ActionForm*

*Example 7-2. The LoginForm stores the email and password fields*

```
package com.oreilly.struts.storefront.security;

import javax.servlet.http.HttpServletRequest;
import org.apache.struts.action.*;

public class LoginForm extends ActionForm {
  private String email = null;
  private String password = null;

  public void setEmail(String email) {
    this.email = email;
  }

  public String getEmail() {
    return (this.email);
  }

  public String getPassword() {
    return (this.password);
  }
```

*Example 7-2. The LoginForm stores the email and password fields (continued)*

```java
public void setPassword(String password) {
  this.password = password;
}

/**
 * Validate the properties that have been sent from the HTTP request,
 * and return an ActionErrors object that encapsulates any
 * validation errors that have been found. If no errors are found, return
 * an empty ActionErrors object.
 */
public ActionErrors validate(ActionMapping mapping, HttpServletRequest request) {
  ActionErrors errors = new ActionErrors();

  if( getEmail() == null || getEmail().length() < 1 ) {
    errors.add("email", new ActionMessage("security.error.email.required"));
  }
  if( getPassword() == null || getPassword().length() < 1 ){
    errors.add("password", new ActionMessage("security.error.password.required"));
  }
  return errors;
}

public void reset(ActionMapping mapping, HttpServletRequest request) {
  /** Because this ActionForm should be request-scoped, do nothing here.
   *  The fields will be reset when a new instance is created. We could
   *  have just not overriden the parent reset() method, but we did so
   *  to provide an example of the reset() method signature.
   */
}
}
```

When the form is submitted, an instance of the LoginForm will be created and populated from the request parameters. The framework does this by matching each request parameter name against the corresponding property name in the ActionForm class.

 The ActionForm is populated from request parameters, not request attributes. If you are forwarding from one action to another, you can't add a request attribute and expect that the ActionForm will be populated from it. Request parameters and request attributes are two separate resources.

### The validate( ) method

The RequestProcessor may call the validate( ) method for every request. Whether it's called depends on two things. First, an ActionForm must be configured for an action mapping. This means that the name attribute for an action element must correspond to the name attribute of one of the form-bean elements in the configuration file.

The second condition that must be met for the RequestProcessor to invoke the validate() method is that the validate attribute in the action mapping must have a value of true. The following fragment shows an action element that uses the LoginForm from Example 7-2 and meets both requirements:

```
<action
    path="/signin"
    type="com.oreilly.struts.storefront.security.LoginAction"
    scope="request"
    name="loginForm"
    validate="true"
    input="/security/signin.jsp">
    <forward name="Success" path="/index.jsp" redirect="true"/>
    <forward name="Failure" path="/security/signin.jsp" redirect="true"/>
</action>
```

When the *signin* action is invoked, the framework will populate an instance of a LoginForm using the values it finds in the request. Because the validate attribute has a value of true, the validate() method in the LoginForm will be called. Even if the validate attribute is set to false, the ActionForm still will be populated from the request.

 The validate() method in the base ActionForm class simply returns null. If you want to perform validation on the data submitted with the request, you'll need to override the validate() method in your ActionForm subclasses, as in Example 7-2.

The validate() method may return an ActionErrors object, depending on whether any validation errors were detected; it also can return null if there are no errors. The framework will check for both null and an empty ActionErrors object. This saves you from having to create an instance of ActionErrors when there are no errors. The ActionError class and its parent class, ActionMessage, are discussed later in this chapter.

### The reset() method

The reset() method has been a bane for much of the Struts user community at one time or another. Exactly when the reset() method is called and what should be done within it almost always are misinterpreted. This doesn't mean that one implementation is more correct than another, but many new Struts developers pick up misconceptions about reset() that they have a hard time shaking.

As Figure 7-4 showed, the reset() method is called for each new request, regardless of the scope of the ActionForm, before the ActionForm is populated from the request. The method was originally added to the ActionForm class to facilitate resetting Boolean properties back to their defaults. To understand why they need to be reset, it's helpful to know how the browser and the HTML form-submit operation process checkboxes.

When an HTML form contains checkboxes, only the values for the checkboxes that are checked are sent in the request. Those that are not checked are not included as a request parameter. The reset( ) method was added to allow applications to reset the Boolean properties in the ActionForm to false–because false wasn't included in the request, it was possible for the Boolean values to be stuck in the true state.

The reset( ) method in the base ActionForm contains no default behavior, as no properties are defined in this abstract class. Applications that extend the ActionForm class are allowed to override this method and reset the ActionForm properties to whatever state they want. This may include setting Boolean properties to true or false, setting String values to null or some initialized value, or even instantiating instances of other objects that the ActionForm holds on to. For an ActionForm that has been configured with request scope, the framework will create a new instance for each new request; hence, there's not much need to reset the values back to any default state. ActionForms that are configured with session scope are different, however, and this is where the reset( ) method comes in handy.

## Declaring ActionForms in the Struts Configuration File

Once you have created a class that extends ActionForm, you need to configure the class in the Struts configuration file. The first step is to add a new form-bean element to the form-beans section of the file:

```
<form-beans>
  <form-bean
    name="loginForm"
    type="com.oreilly.struts.storefront.security.LoginForm"/>
</form-beans>
```

The value for the type attribute must be a fully qualified Java class name that is a descendant of ActionForm.

Once you have defined your form-bean, you can use it in one or more action elements. It's common to share one ActionForm across several actions. For example, suppose there was an admin application that managed the items in the Storefront application. There would need to be an HTML form for adding new items to the system. This might be the *createItem* action. There also would need to be a *getItemDetail* action to show the details of an existing item. These HTML forms would look similar, but they might be submitted to different actions. Still, because they contained the same properties, both forms could use the same ActionForm.

To use an ActionForm in an action element, you need to specify a few attributes for each action mapping that uses the ActionForm. These attributes are name, scope, and validate:

```
<action
  path="/signin"
  input="/security/signin.jsp"
  name="loginForm"
  scope="request"
  type="com.oreilly.struts.storefront.security.LoginAction"
  validate="true">
  <forward name="Success" path="/index.jsp" redirect="true"/>
  <forward name="Failure" path="/security/signin.jsp" redirect="true"/>
</action>
```

For more information on the attributes of the action element, see "The Struts Configuration DTD" in Chapter 4.

## Using an ActionForm in an Action

Once you have configured the ActionForm for a particular Action, you can insert values into it and retrieve values from it within the execute( ) method, as Example 7-3 illustrates.

*Example 7-3. The ActionForm is available within the execute() method*

```
public ActionForward execute( ActionMapping mapping,
                              ActionForm form,
                              HttpServletRequest request,
                              HttpServletResponse response )
  throws Exception{

    // Get the user's login name and password. They should already have
    // been validated by the ActionForm.
    String email = ((LoginForm)form).getEmail();
    String password = ((LoginForm)form).getPassword();

    // Log in through the security service.
    IStorefrontService serviceImpl = getStorefrontService();
    UserView userView = serviceImpl.authenticate(email, password);

    UserContainer existingContainer = null;
    HttpSession session = request.getSession(false);
    if ( session != null ){
      existingContainer = getUserContainer(request);
      session.invalidate();
    }else{
      existingContainer = new UserContainer();
    }

    // Create a new session for the user.
    session = request.getSession(true);
    existingContainer.setUserView(userView);
    session.setAttribute(IConstants.USER_CONTAINER_KEY, existingContainer);

    return mapping.findForward(IConstants.SUCCESS_KEY);
}
```

It's not mandatory that you use an ActionForm to capture the data from an HTML form. Even if you don't declare an ActionForm for a form, the data is still available from the request. However, your application will have to manually handle the process of validation and error handling from the Action class.

## Declaring ActionForm Properties as Strings

All request parameters that are sent by the browser are strings. This is true regardless of the type that the value will eventually map to in Java. For example, dates, times, Booleans, and other values all are strings when they are pulled out of the request, and they will be converted into strings when they are written back out to the HTML page. Therefore, all of the ActionForm properties where the input may be invalid should be of type String, so that the data can be displayed back to the user in its original form when an error occurs. For example, say a user types in "12Z" for a property expecting an Integer. There's no way to store "12Z" into an int or Integer property, but you can store it into a String until it can be validated. This value can be used to render the input field with the value, so the user can see his mistake. Even the most inexperienced users have come to expect and look for this functionality.

---

### ActionForms Are Not the Model

Many developers get confused when they learn about the ActionForm class. Although it can hold state for an application, the state that it holds should be limited and constrained to the user input that is received from the client, and the ActionForm should hold it only until it can be validated and transferred to the business tier.

You've already seen why it's important to separate the model from the presentation tier in an application. Business objects can be persisted and should contain the business logic for an application. They also should be reusable. This set of criteria does not match up well when compared against ActionForms. For one thing, the ActionForm class is tied to the Struts framework and explicitly to a web container, as it imports javax. servlet packages. It would be very difficult to port ActionForm classes to a different type of framework, such as a Swing application.

ActionForms are designed exclusively to capture the HTML data from a client, allow "presentation validation" to occur, and provide a transport vehicle for the data back to the more persistent business tier. They also transport data from the business tier forward to the views. Apart from these uses, you should keep the ActionForms separate from your business components.

---

## Using ActionForms Across Multiple Pages

Many applications require wizard-like functionality where data is captured across multiple pages. ActionForms can be used for this but the scope must be set to session to ensure that the data collected from a previous page will be present throughout the set of wizard pages.

When programming this type of functionality into your application, you must be careful to validate only the fields that are ready to be validated. For instance, if you go from page 1 to page 2, only the properties populated from page 1 should be validated. You also must be careful with the reset( ) method. You don't want to reset fields that already have been entered, but, you might want to reset the properties for the upcoming page. This can be a little tricky, but keeping these thoughts in mind will save time.

# Using ActionErrors

Earlier in this chapter in Example 7-2, we saw that the validate( ) method returns an ActionErrors object. The ActionErrors class encapsulates one or more errors that have been discovered by the application. Each problem discovered is represented by an instance of org.apache.struts.action.ActionError.

It should be pointed out that in Example 7-2, instances of the ActionMessage class and not ActionError were added to the ActionErrors collection. ActionMessage is actually the parent of ActionError. We will talk more about the usage of the ActionMessage class in the next section. For now, when you see ActionError mentioned, just know that you can substitute ActionMessage in most cases.

An ActionErrors object has request scope. Once an instance is created and populated by the validate( ) method, it is stored into the request. Later, the JSP page can retrieve the object from the request and use the ActionError objects contained within it to display error messages to the user.

The Struts framework includes several JSP custom tags that make retrieving and displaying the messages very easy. Two of them, ErrorsTag and MessagesTag, are discussed in Chapter 8.

An instance of ActionErrors can be instantiated in the validate( ) method and populated by adding instances of the ActionMessage class to it. The LoginForm from Example 7-2 demonstrated this and is illustrated again here for convenience:

```
public ActionErrors validate(ActionMapping mapping, HttpServletRequest request){
    ActionErrors errors = new ActionErrors();
```

```
if( getEmail() == null || getEmail().length() < 1 ){
  errors.add("email", new ActionMessage("security.error.email.required"));
}

if( getPassword() == null || getPassword().length() < 1 ){
  errors.add("password", new ActionMessage("security.error.password.required"));
}
return errors;
}
```

The validate( ) method in this fragment checks to make sure that the email and password fields have been set with values other than an empty string. If not, ActionMessage objects are added to the ActionErrors instance.

The ActionMessage class contains several useful constructors; a few are listed here:

```
public ActionError(String key);
public ActionError(String key, Object value0);
public ActionError(String key, Object value0, Object value1);
public ActionError(String key, Object[] values);
```

The key argument is a String value that corresponds to a key from one of the application's resource bundles. The custom tags MessagesTag and ErrorsTag use this value to look up the message to display to the user. The remaining arguments are used as parametric replacement values for the message. For example, if you had a bundle message defined like this:

```
global.error.login.requiredfield=The {0} field is required for login
```

you could create an instance of an ActionMessage like this:

```
ActionMessage message = new ActionMessage("global.error.login.requiredfield",
"Email");
```

The message displayed to the user after substituting in the "Email" string would be:

```
The Email field is required for login
```

If building I18N applications is a requirement for you, you must be careful when using hardcoded String values, as in the previous example. The string "Email" can't easily be localized, because it's hardcoded into the source code.

In this case, you should get the localized value from the bundle as well before passing it as an argument in the ActionMessage constructor.

When adding instances of the ActionMessage class to the ActionErrors object, the first argument in the add( ) method is a property that can be used to retrieve a specific ActionMessage instance. For example, if you have a login input field and a password field and you want to display a particular message next to each corresponding field, you could do:

```
errors.add("login",
           new ActionMessage("security.error.login.required"));
```

```
errors.add("password",
        new ActionMessage ("security.error.password.required"));
```

By associating a specific name with each error, you can retrieve the respective error in the JSP page using the MessagesTag tag, which we'll discuss in the next chapter.

If instead you want to show all of the errors at the top of the page, you can use the constant ActionMessages.GLOBAL_MESSAGE, like this:

```
errors.add(ActionMessages.GLOBAL_MESSAGE,
        new ActionMessage("security.error.password.required"));
```

## The ActionMessage Class

In Struts 1.1, a new message class was added that also can be used to display messages to a user. The org.apache.struts.action.ActionMessage class operates in the same manner that the ActionError class does—in fact, it was added as the superclass to the ActionError class.

The main reason that the ActionMessage class was added to the framework was that the name ActionError implies that it shouldn't be used for general-purpose informational or warning messages, although it is used that way by many developers. A more general-purpose message class made sense.

The ActionMessage is used exactly like the ActionError class, except that it can represent a less severe message that needs to be displayed to the user. Instances of this class are created the same way and added to an ActionMessages object instead of an ActionErrors object. Because ActionError is just a specialized message, it extends the ActionMessage class. Figure 7-5 illustrates the relationship between these classes.

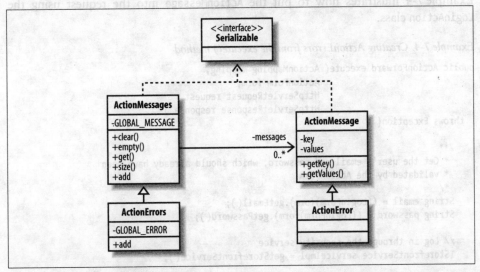

*Figure 7-5. ActionErrors are specialized ActionMessages*

Starting with Struts 1.2, you should expect the `ActionError` class to be deprecated. You should make all attempts to start using the `ActionMessage` class instead. The `ActionErrors` class will a little harder for the Struts developers to remove as it is tied into the framework quite tightly. Nonetheless, the writing is on the wall and you may eventually be using `ActionMessages` exclusively.

## Creating ActionErrors in the Action Class

The `ActionForm` is not the only place that you can create `ActionMessages` or `ActionErrors`. You also can create them in other parts of the framework. If, for example, a business operation called from an `Action` raised an exception and you wanted to insert an error message informing the user, you could create an `ActionMessage` from the `Action` class itself. The Struts `Action` class includes functionality to support this.

When the business operation throws the exception, the `Action` class catches it and takes the appropriate steps—usually returning to the previous page and displaying an error message to the user. Returning to the previous state can be accomplished by returning the appropriate `ActionForward`, but the `ActionMessage` needs to be put in the request before the forward occurs.

In Chapter 10, you'll learn how to take advantage of the declarative exception handling in Struts 1.1 and thus avoid having to deal with the exceptions in the `Action` class completely.

Example 7-4 illustrates how to put the `ActionMessage` into the request using the `LoginAction` class.

*Example 7-4. Creating ActionErrors from the execute() method*

```
public ActionForward execute( ActionMapping mapping,
                              ActionForm form,
                              HttpServletRequest request,
                              HttpServletResponse response )
  throws Exception{

  /**
   * Get the user's email and password, which should already have been
   * validated by the ActionForm.
   */
  String email = ((LoginForm)form).getEmail();
  String password = ((LoginForm)form).getPassword();

  // Log in through the security service
  IStorefrontService serviceImpl = getStorefrontService();

  UserView userView = null;
```

*Example 7-4. Creating ActionErrors from the execute() method (continued)*

```
try{
    userView = serviceImpl.authenticate(email, password);
}catch( InvalidLoginException ex ){
    ActionMessages messages = new ActionMessages();
    ActionMessage newMessage = new ActionMessage ( "security.login.failed" );
    messages.add(ActionMessages.GLOBAL_MESSAGE, newMessage);
    saveMessages( request, messages );
    // Return back to the previous state
    return mapping.findForward( mapping.getInput() );
}


// Authenticate was successful
UserContainer existingContainer = null;
HttpSession session = request.getSession(false);
if ( session != null ){
    existingContainer = getUserContainer(request);
    session.invalidate();
}else{
    existingContainer = new UserContainer();
}


// Create a new session for the user
session = request.getSession(true);
existingContainer.setUserView(userView);
session.setAttribute(IConstants.USER_CONTAINER_KEY, existingContainer);

    return mapping.findForward(IConstants.SUCCESS_KEY);
}
```

In Example 7-4, when an InvalidLoginException is thrown by the authenticate() method, the exception is caught and an ActionMessage is created. The saveMessages() method exists in the Struts base Action class and stores the ActionMessages object into the request.

Once the ActionError or ActionMessage is stored in the request and control is forwarded to a JSP page, one of the framework's JSP custom tags can be used to print out the messages to the user. These tags are discussed in the next chapter.

# Performing Presentation Validation

This chapter has touched on performing your application's input validation in the validate() method of the ActionForm. You can create whatever presentation validation rules you need in this method. For example, the LoginForm from Example 7-2 validated that the email and password fields were entered and were not empty strings. Although this is a trivial example, you can validate anything you like. A common validation rule is to ensure that a string value that should be a number is in fact a string representation of a valid number. The validate() routine for this rule might look like the one in Example 7-5.

*Example 7-5. Performing a number validation rule*

```
public ActionErrors validate(ActionMapping mapping, HttpServletRequest request) {
  ActionErrors errors = new ActionErrors();

  String orderQtyStr = getQuantity();

  if( orderQtyStr == null || orderQtyStr.length() < 1 ){
    errors.add( ActionMessages.GLOBAL_MESSAGE,
               new ActionMessage( "order.quantity.required" ));
  }

  // Validate that the qty entered was in fact a number
  try{
    // Integer.parse was not used because it's not really I18N-safe
    java.text.Format format = java.text.NumberFormat.getNumberInstance();
    Number orderQty = (Number)format.parseObject( orderQtyStr );
  }catch( Exception ex ){
    // The quantity entered by the user was not a valid qty
    errors.add( ActionMessages.GLOBAL_MESSAGE,
               new ActionMessage( "order.quantity.invalid" ));
  }
  return errors;
}
```

As you can imagine, web applications often need to check for required values or validate that data entered fits a certain format or is of a certain type. Because all data that is retrieved from a request is of type String, you must ensure that the data is not going to corrupt your business components.

Although you can perform the validation programmatically, the Struts framework provides an alternative that can be external to the ActionForm and the validate() method. In fact, most of the standard validation rules already are defined, so you don't have to write any code for them. All you need to do is to declaratively configure the rules that you need in an extra XML file. The Struts Validator will be covered in Chapter 11.

# Using the DynaActionForm Class

Using the ActionForm class has many advantages over performing the functionality yourself in the Action class or some set of helper utility classes. Because the behavior the ActionForm class provides is needed in nearly every web application and often many times in the same application, using the framework to perform the work can really reduce the development time and your frustration level. However, there are a few very important downsides to using ActionForms.

The biggest problem with using ActionForms is the sheer number of classes that it can add to a project. Even if you share ActionForm definitions across many pages, the additional classes make it more difficult to manage and maintain a project. This is why some developers create a single `ActionForm` and implement the properties for all of the HTML forms within it. The problem with this approach, of course, is that combining the fields into one class makes it a point of contention on a project that has more than just a few developers.

Another major liability is the requirement to define the properties in the `ActionForm` that need to be captured from the HTML form. If a property is added or removed from the HTML form, the `ActionForm` class may need to be modified and recompiled.

For these reasons, a new type of `ActionForm`, which is dynamic in nature and allows you to avoid having to create concrete `ActionForm` classes for your application, was added to the framework. The dynamic `ActionForm` is implemented by the base class `org.apache.struts.action.DynaActionForm`, which extends the `ActionForm` class. There are only three real differences between the `ActionForms` for any application:

- The properties that the `ActionForm` defines
- The validate( ) method
- The reset( ) method

The properties for a `DynaActionForm` are configured in the Struts configuration file and will be illustrated in the next section. The reset( ) method is called at exactly the same time during request processing as it is for a standard `ActionForm`. The one difference is that you have a little less control over what you do during the method invocation. However, you can subclass the `DynaActionForm` to override the reset or validate behavior.

The validation of the presentation data for a `DynaActionForm` is a little more complicated. We'll need to wait until we talk about the Struts Validator components before covering this topic.

## Configuring Dynamic ActionForms

To use the `DynaActionForm` in your Struts application, first you need to add a form-bean element to the configuration file, just as with regular `ActionForms`.

 In early beta releases of Struts 1.1, the form-bean section required that you set the dynamic attribute to true when using dynamic `ActionForms`. This is no longer necessary, as the framework will determine whether the class specified in the type attribute is a descendant of the `DynaActionForm` class.

When it comes to the configuration file, the difference between a regular `ActionForm` and a `DynaActionForm` is that you must include one or more form-property elements in order for the dynamic form to have properties. The `DynaActionForm` uses a java.util.Map internally to store the property key/ value pairs. The form-property elements are loaded into the Map and become the properties that get populated by the framework.

 The attributes for the form-bean and form-property were discussed in Chapter 4.

An example of configuring a DynaActionForm in the Struts configuration file is shown in Example 7-6.

*Example 7-6. A DynaActionForm must be specified in the Struts configuration file*

```
<form-beans>
  <form-bean
    name="loginForm"
    type="org.apache.struts.action.DynaActionForm">

    <!-- Specify the dynamic properties of the form -->
    <form-property
      name="email"
      type="java.lang.String "/>
    <form-property
      name="password"
      type="java.lang.String "/>

    <!-- You can also set the initial value of a property -->
    <form-property
      initial="false"
      name="rememberMe"
      type="java.lang.Boolean "/>
  </form-bean>
</form-beans>
```

The declarative properties are what make the ActionForm dynamic. At runtime, the framework creates an instance of the DynaActionForm class and makes it possible to set and get the configured property values. To add new properties, you only need to modify the configuration file; no source code needs to be changed. This provides immense power and flexibility.

As Chapter 4 outlined, the form-property element also allows you to specify the initial value for each property. The framework sets the property to that value when the application is started. The initial value also is used when the reset( ) method is called to reset the values back to their original states.

Unlike with the ActionForm class, where the default behavior for reset( ) does nothing, the reset( ) method in the DynaActionForm class resets all the properties back to their initial values. If you don't include the initial attribute for a property, it will be assigned a default value based on the Java programming language's conventions: numbers will be reset to zero (0) and properties of type Object will be reset to null.

The type attribute expects a fully qualified Java class name. Therefore, you will need to use the wrapper classes for primitives (for example, java.lang.Boolean for a boolean property type, java.lang.Integer for an int property, and so on). However, as was explained previously in this chapter, you should try to use only String properties, even with a DynaActionForm.

## Performing Validation with the DynaActionForm

The DynaActionForm doesn't provide any default behavior for the validate() method. Unless you subclass the DynaActionForm class and override the validate() method, there's no easy way to validate using the DynaActionForm. Fortunately, the framework comes to your aid again with a feature called the Struts Validator.

The Struts Validator was created by David Winterfeldt and is now in the main Struts distribution. The Validator is a framework that was intended to work with Struts from the beginning. It supports basic validation rules such as checking for required fields, email, date and time fields, and many others. One of the biggest benefits is that it provides many of the validation rules that web applications need to perform. It is also very easy to create your own validation rules. The Struts Validator will be covered in Chapter 11.

# Looking Ahead to JavaServer Faces

JavaServer Faces (JSF) is designed to provide a standard set of JSP tags and Java classes that will make it easier to build Java server application GUIs. One of the problems that JSF is trying to address is that the Servlet and JSP technologies don't provide specific enough APIs for creating the client GUI, and developers have to rely on HTML components and one of several alternatives to facilitate style and behavioral changes to all of the views. The mechanism to manage all of this eventually takes on a life of its own and overshadows the business of the application. Instead of performing maintenance on business operations and logic, more and more time is needed to manage the presentation controls.

JSF plans to fix this by creating a standard way to define complex HTML forms and other GUI elements. This will enable developers to focus their attention on a single component framework.

The first release of the framework includes the following design goals:

1. Create a standard GUI component framework, which can be leveraged by development tools to make it easier for tool users to both create high-quality GUIs and manage the GUIs' connections to application behavior.

2. Define a set of simple, lightweight Java base classes for GUI components, component state, and input events. These classes will address GUI lifecycle issues, notably managing a component's persistent state for the lifetime of its page.

3. Provide a set of common GUI components, including the standard HTML form input elements. These components will be derived from the simple set of base classes (outlined in #2) that can be used to define new components.

4. Provide a JavaBeans model for dispatching events from client-side GUI controls to server- side application behavior.

5. Define APIs for input validation, including support for client-side validation.

6. Specify a model for internationalization and localization of the GUI.

7. Automate the generation of appropriate output for the target client, taking into account all available client configuration data (browser version, etc.).

8. Automate the generation of output containing required hooks for supporting accessibility.

## What Does JSF Have to Do with Struts?

JSF and Struts should fit together quite well, and developers eventually will be able to supplement or substitute the Struts custom tag libraries with JSF components. The rest of the Struts framework (both model and controller components) will remain relatively unaffected by the JSF architecture.

 JSF also will include an event model, but the architecture will be designed so that developers can choose to use the GUI components with or without the event mechanism.

Because there currently is no final public specification for JSF, it's hard to be specific on exactly how the two will tie into each other. However, Craig McClanahan, the founder of the Struts framework, is now also one of the specification leads for the JSF JSR. We can look closely at Craig's comments on JSF and Struts and know that he is speaking with subject-matter expertise. In fact, Struts 1.1 ships with an early look at how the two might fit together. If you look in the *contrib* folder under the Struts binary installation, you will find a directory named *struts-faces*. This directory contains a library which supports the use of JSF in a Struts-based application. There are also a couple examples that you can actually run in a container and see JSF work first hand. For more information on this library and JSF in general, see Chapter 18. You can find the JSF JSR online at *http://jcp.org/jsr/detail/127.jsp*.

# CHAPTER 8

# JSP Custom Tag Libraries

Support for custom actions (also called custom tags) within JSP was introduced in the JSP 1.1 specification. This feature allows developers to extend the available tags beyond what JSP alone provides for. The custom tags are grouped together into tag libraries, which can be reused across applications.

The Struts framework takes advantage of the tag library feature of JSP to include several different categories of tags that help to make the presentation layer more manageable and reusable. Using the Struts custom tag libraries, developers are able to interact with the rest of the framework without including Java code in the JSP pages.

This chapter provides an overview of the different categories of tags available in the Struts framework and how they can make developing applications even easier. This chapter is not meant to be an exhaustive reference for every tag that's part of the Struts tag libraries—that information can be found within the Struts user guide or JavaDocs. The real purpose of this chapter is to put forth the benefits of using the Struts tag libraries and to provide a few strategies that can help make the switch to using the tags less painful.

Finally, this chapter will touch upon several new specifications that were approved during 2003 that are intended to help standardize some of the more commonly used custom tags and tag usages. This, in turn, will make applications built using these tags even more portable across containers and frameworks.

## Custom Tags Overview

This section provides a brief overview of JSP custom tags and how they can add value to an application. They are explicitly tied to the JavaServer Pages technology and therefore are used only when building web applications based on JSP, such as those built using the Struts framework.

# What Is a Tag?

Before we talk specifically about JSP tags, it's important that you understand what a tag is in general terms. Keep in mind that this section refers to tags in general, not JSP custom tags or Struts tags. We'll discuss those shortly.

If you're familiar with HTML, you already should have a good understanding of the concept of a tag. There are two basic types of tags:

- Bodyless tags
- Tags with a body

Bodyless tags are tags that specify attributes but contain no content. They have the syntax:

```
<tagName attributeName="someValue" attributeName2="someValue2"/>
```

Bodyless tags are most often used to perform simple actions such as rendering HTML fields or displaying images. An example of a bodyless tag is:

```
<img src="images/struts-power.gif"/>
```

Tags can define certain predefined attributes, which supply information to the tag and can affect how the tag performs its duties. In the HTML img tag, for example, the src attribute supplies the tag with the path to a graphical image that will be rendered by the tag. The tag is generic—it knows nothing specific about the image ahead of time. It's designed to receive an image path using the src attribute and display that image at runtime.

Tags with a body have a start tag and a matching end tag, with some content between them. The syntax looks like:

```
<tagName attributeName="someValue" attributeName2="someValue2">
  <!-- The Tag body is between the start and end tags -->
</tagName>
```

Tags with a body are used to perform operations on the body content, such as iterating over a collection, formatting HTML output, and so on. Here's another example from HTML:

```
<html>
  <!-- The HTML body inside the start and end HTML tags -->
</html>
```

The end tag must always begin with a / character.

# What Is a JSP Custom Tag?

When parsing an HTML file, the browser determines how to process and handle the tags contained within the file based on a set of standards. The purpose of JSP custom tags is to give the developer the ability to extend the set of tags that can be used inside a JSP page. With ordinary HTML tags, the browser contains the logic to process the tag and render the output. With JSP custom tags, the functionality exists in a special Java class called the *tag handler*.

The tag handler is a Java class that carries out the specific behavior of the tag. It implements one of several custom tag interfaces, depending on the type of tag that you need to develop. The handler class has access to all of the JSP resources, such as the PageContext object and the request, response, and session objects. The tag also is populated with the attribute information, so it can customize its behavior based on the attribute values.

### Advantages of using custom tags

There are many benefits of using custom tags instead of scriptlets and Java code in your JSP pages:

- Tags are reusable, which saves precious development and testing time.
- Tags can be customized using attributes, either statically or dynamically.
- Tags have access to all of the objects available to the JSP page, including request, response, and output variables.
- Tags can be nested, which allows for more complex interactions within a JSP page.
- Tags simplify the readability of a JSP page.

In general, using JSP tags helps to further the concept of reuse, as the behavior is implemented in a single location, the tag handler; it's not replicated throughout multiple JSP pages.

## What Is a Tag Library?

A tag library is a set of JSP custom tags grouped together from a packaging perspective. Although it's not a requirement, the tags within a tag library should solve a similar type of problem. Because web applications can include multiple tag libraries, there's no need to place all of the tags into a single library.

You can see an example of how tags can be grouped logically by looking at the Jakarta Taglibs project at *http://jakarta.apache.org/taglibs*. Tag libraries are available for rendering dates and times, manipulating strings, and many other purposes. Notice that each tag library is focused on a single concept or task. The Jakarta Taglibs project will be discussed later in this chapter.

### Tag library components

A tag library is made up of the following components:

- Tag handler
- Tag library descriptor file

- The application deployment descriptor (*web.xml*) file
- The tag library declaration in the JSP page

## Tag handler

You've already been introduced to the tag handler. This is where the implementation of the tag is located. It's a Java class that gets invoked at runtime and that performs some predefined behavior.

## The TLD file

The *tag library descriptor* (TLD) file is an XML file that contains meta-information about the tags within a library. Information such as the tag name, the attributes that are required, and the tag handler class name are all contained in this file and read in by the JSP container.

## The web.xml file

We discussed web application deployment descriptors in Chapter 3. Within this descriptor, you must define what tag libraries are being used in the web application and which TLD files should be used to describe each tag library.

## The JSP page

Obviously, the JSP page is a key component. It contains the include directives for one or more tag libraries, as well as the needed calls to the tag libraries within the JSP page. There is essentially no limit to how many tag libraries or tag references you can have in a JSP page.

 There have been some reports of sluggishness in JSP containers when the number of tags in a single JSP page approaches 40–50. Vendors have a lot of freedom in terms of how they initialize and process custom tags; some are better than others. If this becomes a problem for your implementation, you might try to redesign the page to reduce the number of tags or combine some of the tags into a single handler. If that doesn't solve your problem, run your tags in a different container and evaluate the performance.

Attempting to cover all aspects of JSP custom tags is beyond the scope of this book. In fact, there are entire books written on the subject. A good source of information on custom tags and their use in applications is Hans Bergsten's *JavaServer Pages* (O'Reilly).

# Tag Libraries Included with Struts

The Struts framework provides a fairly rich set of framework components. It also includes a set of tag libraries that are designed to interact intimately with the rest of the framework. The custom tags provided by the Struts framework are grouped into four distinct libraries:

- HTML
- Bean
- Logic
- Tiles

There also is a fifth library, called the Nested tag library, that we'll talk about separately later in this chapter.

 Earlier versions of the Struts framework contained a tag library called Form. It was replaced with the HTML tag library several versions ago, but form tags still sometimes show up in the documentation or example applications.

The tags within a particular library perform similar or related functions. For example, the tags within the HTML tag library are used to render HTML presentation components inside HTML forms. There's a tag to generate a checkbox, another for a button, and yet another to generate a hyperlink.

## Using Tag Libraries with Struts Applications

There's nothing special about using the Struts tags—they are like any other JSP custom tags. You must include the TLD declarations for each tag library you use in every page in which you need to use them. If you need to use the HTML and Logic tag libraries in a JSP page, for example, insert the following two lines at the top of the JSP page:

```
<%@ taglib uri="/WEB-INF/struts-html.tld" prefix="html" %>
<%@ taglib uri="/WEB-INF/struts-logic.tld" prefix="logic" %>
```

Once these lines are included and your web application deployment descriptor contains the necessary taglib elements, you can use the HTML and Logic tags within your JSP page. Continuing with the previous example, you need to add the following lines to your *web.xml* file:

```
<taglib>
    <taglib-uri>/WEB-INF/struts-html.tld</taglib-uri>
    <taglib-location>/WEB-INF/struts-html.tld</taglib-location>
</taglib>
```

```
<taglib>
    <taglib-uri>/WEB-INF/struts-logic.tld</taglib-uri>
    <taglib-location>/WEB-INF/struts-logic.tld</taglib-location>
</taglib>
```

Based on the snippets above, you would also need to make sure that the TLD files that are included with Struts are placed in the *WEB-INF* directory. This is not the only location that they can reside, but is the most common.

For more information on configuring the deployment descriptor for the web application, see "Configuring the web.xml File for Struts" in Chapter 4.

# Using JavaBeans with Struts Tags

In many cases, you'll use the tags from the various tag libraries in conjunction with JavaBeans. The JavaBeans may be ActionForms, whose properties correspond to input fields in the HTML form. In other cases, however, the beans will be ordinary value objects from the model layer. These beans can be in any scope: page, request, session, or application.

There are three ways to access the properties of a JavaBean:

- Accessing simple properties
- Accessing nested properties
- Accessing indexed properties

## Accessing Simple Properties

Accessing simple bean properties works similarly to the JSP `<jsp:getProperty>` action. A reference to a property named "firstName" is converted into a method call to `getFirstName()` or `setFirstName(value)`, using the standard JavaBeans specification naming conventions for bean properties.

Struts uses the Java introspection APIs to identify the names of the actual property getter and setter methods, so your beans can provide customized method names through the use of a BeanInfo class. See the JavaBeans specification, available at *http://java.sun.com/products/javabeans*, for more information.

## Accessing Nested Properties

Nested references are used to access a property through a hierarchy of property names separated by periods (.), similar to the way that nested properties are accessed in JavaScript. For example, the following property reference:

```
property="user.address.city"
```

is translated into the equivalent Java expression:

```
getUser().getAddress().getCity()
```

If a nested reference is used in a setter (such as when an input form is processed), the property setter is called on the last property in the chain. For the above property reference, the equivalent Java expression would be:

```
getUser().getAddress().setCity(value)
```

Nested properties are very convenient to use with custom tags. They almost always are used with the property attributes of the supported tags.

## Accessing Indexed Properties

Subscripts can be used to access individual elements of properties whose values are actually arrays, or whose underlying JavaBeans offer indexed getter and setter methods. For example, the following property reference:

```
property="address[2]"
```

is translated into the equivalent Java expression:

```
getAddress(2);
```

while the same property reference in a setter would call the equivalent of:

```
setAddress(2, address)
```

As you can see from these examples, the subscripts used in indexed references are zero-relative (that is, the first element in an array is address[0]), just as is true in the Java language.

# Struts HTML Tags

The Struts HTML tag library contains tags used to create HTML input forms, as well as other tags generally useful in the creation of HTML-based user interfaces. For example, instead of using a regular HTML text-input field, you can use the text tag from this library.

These tags are designed to work very closely with the other components of the Struts framework, including ActionForms. You always should attempt to use one of these tags first, rather than using standard HTML. These tags' special knowledge of the rest of the Struts components makes it worthwhile to use them.

Most of the tags within this library must be nested inside of a Struts form tag. There are a few tags included in this library that address issues not necessarily related to forms or form widgets. Those tags also will be discussed briefly in this section. Although not every HTML tag will be discussed, Table 8-1 provides a complete list of the tags that are available in the HTML tag library.

*Table 8-1. Custom tags within the Struts HTML tag library*

| Tag name | Description |
| --- | --- |
| base | Renders an HTML base element |
| button | Renders a button input field |
| cancel | Renders a cancel button |
| checkbox | Renders a checkbox input field |
| errors | Conditionally renders a set of accumulated error messages |
| file | Renders a file select input field |
| form | Defines an HTML form element |
| frame | Renders an HTML frame element |
| hidden | Renders a hidden field |
| html | Renders an HTML html element |
| image | Renders an input tag of type "image" |
| img | Renders an HTML img tag |
| javascript | Renders JavaScript validation based on the validation rules loaded by the ValidatorPlugIn |
| link | Renders an HTML anchor or hyperlink |
| messages | Conditionally displays a set of accumulated messages |
| multibox | Renders multiple checkbox input fields |
| option | Renders a select option |
| options | Renders a collection of select options |
| optionsCollection | Renders a collection of select options |
| password | Renders a password input field |
| radio | Renders a radio button input field |
| reset | Renders a reset button input field |
| rewrite | Renders a URI |
| select | Renders a select element |
| submit | Renders a submit button |
| text | Renders an input field of type "text" |
| textarea | Renders a textarea input field |
| xhtml | Render HTML tags as XHTML |

As stated earlier, this chapter will not discuss every tag within the Struts framework; to do so would be redundant, as that material is covered thoroughly in the Struts JavaDocs. Instead, certain tags will be selected and discussed based on their importance, on how confusing they are to new developers, and on whether there are practical strategies for using the tags. If you need a reference to the complete set of available tags, the *Jakarta Struts Pocket Reference* (O'Reilly) includes information and examples on all of the Struts tags.

## The html Tag

The `html` tag renders an HTML `html` element. It allows you to include a locale attribute that will write out the user's locale, assuming one has been stored into the session:

```
<html:html locale="true">
  <!-- Body of the JSP page -->
</html:html>
```

 Starting with Struts 1.2, the `locale` attribute will be deprecated and replaced with the `lang` attribute. In Struts, the locale is tied to a user's `HttpSession` object. In 1.1 and earlier, using the `locale` attribute requires this session object to be created; however, not all applications use sessions, and it is undesirable for those that don't to use them. The `lang` attribute will achieve the same functionality without the need for a session.

Struts 1.1 added a new attribute to the `html` tag called `xhtml`. Set this attribute to `true` in order to render `xml:lang` and `xmlns` attributes on the generated `html` element. This also causes all other html tags to render as XHTML 1.0.

## The base Tag

This tag renders an HTML base element with an `href` attribute pointing to the absolute location of the enclosing JSP page. This tag is useful because it allows you to use relative URL references that are calculated based on the URL of the page itself, rather than the URL to which the most recent submit took place (which is what the browser normally would resolve relative references against). This tag must be placed within the HTML head element. The following is an example of using the base tag:

```
<html:html locale="true">
  <head>
    <html:base/>
    <title><bean:message key="title.login"/></title>
  </head>
</html:html>
```

The base tag example here would produce the following output when executed in the main page of the Storefront application:

```
<html lang="en">
  <head>
    <base href="http://localhost:8080/storefront/index.jsp">
    <title>Virtual Shopping with Struts</title>
  </head>
<html>
```

This tag is very important when using relative URLs for images in a JSP page. There are two attributes for the base tag: `target` and `server`. You can use the target attribute in order to specify a window target for this base reference. The server attribute is used to specify the server name, and overrides the value that comes from `request.getServerName( )`.

# The form Tag

The Struts form tag is one of the most important tags in the HTML tag library. Its purpose is to render a standard HTML form tag and to link the HTML form with an `ActionForm` configured for the application.

Each field in the HTML form should correspond to a property of the `ActionForm`. When an HTML field name and a property name match, the property from the `ActionForm` is used to populate the HTML field. When the HTML form is submitted, the framework will store the user's input into the `ActionForm`, again matching up the HTML field names to the property names.

All of the HTML custom tags that render HTML controls must be nested within the html tag. DynaActionForm and its subclasses function the same way with the form tag.

The form tag controls many important aspects of the page. Its attributes are shown in Table 8-2.

*Table 8-2. The form tag attributes*

| Name | Description |
|---|---|
| action | The URL to which this form will be submitted. |
| enctype | The content encoding to be used when submitting this form. |
| focus | The field name to which initial focus will be assigned for this page. |
| focusIndex | If the focus field is a field array, such as a radio button group, you can specify the index in the array to receive focus. |
| method | The HTTP method that will be used to submit this request. |
| name | The name of the ActionForm whose properties will be used to populate the input field values. |
| onreset | The JavaScript event handler executed if the form is reset. |
| onsubmit | The JavaScript event handler executed if the form is submitted. |
| scope | The scope of the ActionForm for this form. |
| style | The CSS styles to be applied to this HTML element. |
| styleClass | The CSS stylesheet class to be applied to this HTML element. |
| styleId | The identifier to be assigned to this HTML element. |
| target | The frame target to which this form is submitted. |
| type | The fully qualified class name of the ActionForm for this page. |

## The action attribute

The value for the action attribute is used to select the `ActionMapping` the page is assumed to be processing, from which we can identify the appropriate `ActionForm` and scope.

If extension mapping is being used (*.do*), the action value should be equal to the value of the path attribute of the corresponding action element, optionally followed by the correct extension suffix. An example of this is:

```
<html:form action="login.do" focus="accessNumber">
```

If path mapping is used instead, the action attribute value should be exactly equal to the value of the path attribute of the corresponding action element:

```
<html:form action="login" focus="accessNumber">
```

## The enctype attribute

Typically, you won't need to set the enctype attribute. However, if your form is performing file uploads, you should set the enctype attribute to `multipart/form-data`. You also must make sure the method attribute is set to `POST`, which is the default method if none is specified.

## The name attribute

The `name` attribute specifies the name of the request- or session-scope `ActionForm` whose properties will be used to populate the input field values. If no such bean is found, a new bean will be created and added to the appropriate scope, using the Java class name specified by the type attribute.

If no value is specified for the name attribute, it will be calculated by using the value of the action attribute to look up the corresponding `ActionMapping` element, from which the form bean name will be determined. In other words, if no `name` attribute is specified for the `form` tag, the tag will use the value from the `name` attribute in the action element from the configuration file. This is a very important point that confuses many new Struts developers. Let's look at an example. Suppose there is an action element configured like the following:

```
<action
  path="/signin"
  type="com.oreilly.struts.storefront.security.LoginAction"
  scope="request"
  name="loginForm"
  validate="true"
  input="/security/signin.jsp">
  <forward name="Success" path="/index.jsp" redirect="true"/>
  <forward name="Failure" path="/security/signin.jsp" redirect="true"/>
</action>
```

Now say you have a form tag that looks like this declared in a JSP page:

```
<html:form action="signin">
```

Because the name attribute is not specified in the form tag, the tag will look up the *signin* action from the configuration file. It will retrieve the value of the name attribute from the action element and use that to check for an ActionForm in either the request or session scope. In this case, the loginForm will be selected because it's the value for the name attribute in the action element.

### The scope attribute

The scope attribute defines where the tag should look for the ActionForm. Its value must be either request or session. If the scope attribute is not specified, it will be calculated by using the value of the action attribute to look up the corresponding ActionMapping element, from which we will select the specified form bean scope. This is similar to how the name attribute is determined if it's not specified in the form tag.

### The type attribute

The type attribute specifies the fully qualified class name of the ActionForm to be created if no such bean is found in the specified scope. If this attribute is not specified, it will be calculated by using the value of the action attribute to look up the corresponding ActionMapping element, from which we will select the specified form bean type.

## Using Multiple form Tags

As with standard HTML, you can include more than one form tag within a JSP page. Obviously, only one form can be submitted at a time, but that doesn't stop you from declaring multiple form tags. For example, you might have a form tag for a search area of the page. When the user presses the search button, that form is submitted along with the search criteria fields. In that same page, you might also have another form tag that performs a different function. When a button within that form is pressed, that form and its corresponding fields are submitted. Example 8-1 provides an example of what that might look like.

*Example 8-1. Using multiple form tags*

```
<html:html locale="true">
 <head>
   <html:base/>
 </head>

 <body>
 <!-
   <html:form action="searchAction">
    <!-- The search fields -->
    <html:submit styleClass="button" value="Go"/>
   </html:form>

   <html:form action="anotherAction">
```

*Example 8-1. Using multiple form tags (continued)*

```
    <!-- The other form fields -->
    <html:submit styleClass="button"/>
  </html:form>
 </body>
</html:html>
```

## The button and cancel Tags

These two tags render HTML input elements of type button, populated from the specified value or from the content of the tag body. These tags are valid only when nested inside a form tag body.

Stylesheets also can be used with these tags by supplying a value for the styleClass attribute. By default, the button label is set to the value "Click" and the cancel label is set to the value "Cancel". You can override this using the value attribute.

The button produced by the cancel tag has a special characteristic that causes the validate( ) method to be skipped when it's pressed. The RequestProcessor just calls the execute( ) method, without going through the validation routine.

## The checkbox Tag

This tag renders an HTML input element of type checkbox, populated from the specified value or the specified property of the bean associated with the current form. This tag is valid only when nested inside a form tag body.

The underlying property value associated with this field should be of type boolean, and any value you specify should correspond to one of the strings that indicate a true value ("true", "yes", or "on").

The browser will send values in the request only for those checkboxes that are checked. To correctly recognize unchecked checkboxes, the ActionForm bean associated with this form must include a statement setting the corresponding boolean property to false in the reset( ) method.

## The messages and errors Tags

These two tags are responsible for displaying a set of general-purpose messages or errors to the user. Messages correspond to ActionMessages, and errors to ActionErrors. The messages/errors are created either in the validate( ) method or by the exception-handling framework. If no messages or errors are present, nothing will be rendered.

When using the errors tag, the message bundle must include message keys for the following values:

errors.header

Text that will be rendered before the error messages list. Typically, this message text will end with `<ul>` to start the error messages list.

errors.footer

Text that will be rendered after the error messages list. Typically, this message text will begin with `</ul>` to end the error messages list.

For example, we might set the header and footer values to:

```
errors.header=<h3><font color="red">Validation Error</font></h3>You must correct the
following error(s) before proceeding:<ul>

errors.footer=</ul><hr>
```

When the errors are written out to the HTML page, they'll appear inside a bulleted list. Now that the Struts framework supports multiple MessageResources within the configuration file, you can specify which one should be used using the bundle attribute.

## JavaScript Event Handlers

Many of the HTML tags support JavaScript event handlers through the use of their attributes. For example, to configure an onClick handler for a supported tag, you need to include the function name in the onClick attribute for the tag. Table 8-3 lists the attributes for the supported event handlers.

*Table 8-3. Attributes for the supported JavaScript event handlers*

| Attribute | Description |
| --- | --- |
| onblur | Executed when this element loses input focus. |
| onchange | Executed when this element loses input focus and its value has changed. |
| onclick | Executed when this element receives a mouse click. |
| ondblclick | Executed when this element receives a mouse double-click. |
| onfocus | Executed when this element receives input focus. |
| onkeydown | Executed when this element has focus and a key is depressed. |
| onkeypress | Executed when this element has focus and a key is depressed and released. |
| onkeyup | Executed when this element has focus and a key is released. |
| onmousedown | Executed when this element is under the mouse pointer and a mouse button is depressed. |
| onmousemove | Executed when this element is under the mouse pointer and the pointer is moved. |
| onmouseout | Executed when this element is under the mouse pointer but the pointer is moved outside the element. |
| onmouseover | Executed when this element is not under the mouse pointer but the pointer is moved inside the element. |

*Table 8-5. Custom tags* (continued)

*Table 8-3. Attributes for the supported JavaScript event handlers (continued)*

| Attribute | Description |
|-----------|-------------|
| onmouseup | Executed when this element is under the mouse pointer and a mouse button is released. |
| onreset | Executed if the parent form is reset. |
| onsubmit | Executed if the parent form is submitted. |

## HTML Navigation Attributes

Many of the tags also support navigation using only the keyboard. This is done using the attributes listed in Table 8-4.

*Table 8-4. Attributes for the keyboard navigational support*

| Attribute | Description |
|-----------|-------------|
| acesskey | The keyboard character used to move focus immediately to this element. |
| tabindex | The tab order (ascending positive integers) for this element. |

## Logic Tags

The Logic tag library contains tags that are useful for managing conditional generation of output text, looping over object collections for repetitive generation of output text, and application flow management. Table 8-5 lists the tags available within the Logic tag library.

*Table 8-5. Custom tags within the Logic tag library*

| Tag name | Description |
|----------|-------------|
| empty | Evaluate the nested body content of this tag if the requested variable is either null or an empty string. |
| equal | Evaluate the nested body content of this tag if the requested variable is equal to the specified value. |
| forward | Forward control to the page specified by the `ActionForward` entry. |
| greaterEqual | Evaluate the nested body content of this tag if the requested variable is greater than or equal to the specified value. |
| greaterThan | Evaluate the nested body content of this tag if the requested variable is greater than the specified value. |
| iterate | Repeat the nested body content of this tag over a specified collection. |
| lessEqual | Evaluate the nested body content of this tag if the requested variable is less than or equal to the specified value. |
| lessThan | Evaluate the nested body content of this tag if the requested variable is less than the specified value. |
| match | Evaluate the nested body content of this tag if the specified value is an appropriate substring of the requested variable. |

*Table 8-5. Custom tags within the Logic tag library (continued)*

| Tag name | Description |
|---|---|
| messagesNotPresent | Generate the nested body content of this tag if the specified message is not present in this request. |
| messagesPresent | Generate the nested body content of this tag if the specified message is present in this request. |
| notEmpty | Evaluate the nested body content of this tag if the requested variable is neither null nor an empty string. |
| notEqual | Evaluate the nested body content of this tag if the requested variable is not equal to the specified value. |
| notMatch | Evaluate the nested body content of this tag if the specified value is not an appropriate substring of the requested variable. |
| notPresent | Generate the nested body content of this tag if the specified value is not present in this request. |
| present | Generate the nested body content of this tag if the specified value is present in this request. |
| redirect | Render an HTTP redirect. |

The tags within the Logic tag library can be divided into four separate categories based on how they are used:

- Value comparison
- Substring matching
- Redirecting and forwarding
- Collection utilities

This division into categories is done for the purpose of explanation. The tags are not packaged or arranged into these categories; they all belong to the Logic package.

## Value Comparison

The value-comparison tags print out the body of the tag if and only if the comparison evaluates to true. There are several different types of comparison tags that you can use, depending on your specific needs.

Each of the value-comparison tags takes a value and compares it to the value of a comparison attribute. If the value given can be successfully converted to a number, a number comparison is performed; otherwise, a string comparison is performed.

The comparison tags share the common attributes listed in Table 8-6.

*Table 8-6. Common attributes of the comparison tags*

| Name | Description |
|---|---|
| name | The name of a bean to use to compare against the value attribute. If the property attribute is used, the value is compared against the property of the bean, instead of the bean itself. |
| parameter | The name of a request parameter to compare the value attribute against. |

*Table 8-6. Common attributes of the comparison tags (continued)*

| Name | Description |
|------|-------------|
| property | The variable to be compared is the property (of the bean specified by the name attribute) specified by this attribute. The property reference can be simple, nested, and/or indexed. |
| scope | The scope within which to search for the bean named by the name attribute. All scopes will be searched if not specified. |
| value | The constant value to which the variable, specified by another attribute(s) of this tag, will be compared. |

A few examples will help solidify how these comparison tags can be used. To check whether a particular request parameter is present, you can use the Logic present tag:

```
<logic:present parameter="id">
   <!-- Print out the request parameter id value -->
</logic:present>
```

To check whether a collection is empty before iterating over it, you can use the notEmpty tag:

```
<logic:notEmpty name="userSummary" property="addresses">
   <!-- Iterate and print out the user's addresses -->
</logic:notEmpty>
```

Finally, here's how to compare a number value against a property within an ActionForm:

```
<logic:lessThan property="age" value="21">
   <!-- Display a message about the user's age -->
</logic:lessThan>
```

## Substring Matching

The substring-matching tags take all the same arguments as the value-comparison tags. You compare the string specified by the value attribute to any of the comparison values you give it, specified by cookie, header, parameter, property, or name. Matching tags also have an additional location attribute that informs the tag where to start matching from (either "start" or "end").

In this example, the matchTag is being used to determine whether the request parameter action begins with the string "processLogin":

```
<logic:matchTag parameter="action" value="processLogin" location="start">
   Processing Login....
</logic:matchTag>
```

If the location attribute is not specified, a match between the variable and the value may occur at any position within the variable string.

## Redirecting and Forwarding

The forward and redirect tags within the Logic tag library might have been better suited to the HTML tag library. However, the fact that they are in the Logic tag library doesn't make them any less valuable. In fact, combined with one of the other Logic tags, these two tags become extremely useful.

The redirect tag is responsible for sending a redirect to the client's browser, complete with URL-rewriting if the container supports it. Its attributes are consistent with the Struts HTML link tag. The base URL is calculated based on which of the following attributes you specify (you must specify exactly one of them):

forward

    Use the value of this attribute as the name of a global ActionForward to be looked up, and use the context-relative URI found there.

href

    Use the value of this attribute unchanged.

page

    Use the value of this attribute as a context-relative URI, and generate a server-relative URI by including the context path.

The forward tag is responsible for either redirecting or forwarding to a specified global ActionForward. The forward tag has one attribute, name, which is the logical name of the ActionForward from the configuration file.

## Collection Utilities

One of the most useful and most widely used tags within the Struts tag libraries is the iterate tag. The iterate tag is responsible for executing its body content once for every element inside the specified collection. It has one required attribute:

id

    The name of a page-scope JSP bean that will contain the current element during an iteration.

An example is the best way to understand how to use the iterate tag:

```
<logic:iterate id="address" name="userSummary" property="addresses">
  <!-- Print out the address obejct in a table -->
</logic:iterate>
```

Here, the iterate tag will get the collection of addresses by calling the getAddresses( ) method on the userSummary bean. During each iteration, an individual address will be assigned to the address variable. This variable can be used inside the body of the iterate tag as if you had assigned it directly. During the next iteration, the next address object will be assigned to the address variable. This continues until the entire collection of addresses has been traversed.

The iterate tag is very flexible in terms of where it gets the collection to iterate over. The attributes that control how the iterate tag performs this behavior are listed in Table 8-7.

*Table 8-7. Attributes of the iterate tag*

| Name | Description |
| --- | --- |
| collection | A runtime expression that evaluates to a collection (conforming to the requirements listed above) to be iterated over. |
| id | The name of a page-scope JSP bean that will contain the current element of the collection on each iteration, if it is not null. |
| indexed | The name of a page-scope JSP bean that will contain the current index of the collection on each iteration. |
| length | The maximum number of entries (from the underlying collection) to be iterated through on this page. This can be either an integer that directly expresses the desired value, or the name of a JSP bean (in any scope) of type java.lang.Integer that defines the desired value. If not present, there is no limit on the number of iterations performed. |
| name | The name of the JSP bean containing the collection to be iterated over (if property is not specified), or the JSP bean whose property getter returns the collection to be iterated over (if property is specified). |
| offset | The zero-relative index of the starting point at which entries from the underlying collection will be iterated through. This can be either an integer that directly expresses the desired value, or the name of a JSP bean (in any scope) of type java.lang.Integer that defines the desired value. If not present, zero is assumed (meaning that the collection will be iterated from the beginning). |
| property | The name of the property of the JSP bean specified by name whose getter returns the collection to be iterated. |
| scope | The bean scope within which to search for the bean named by the name property, or "any scope" if not specified. |
| type | The fully qualified class name of the element to be exposed through the JSP bean named from the id attribute. If not present, no type conversions will be performed. The elements of the collection must be assignment-compatible with this class, or a request-time ClassCastException will occur. |

## Messages and Errors

The messagesPresent and messagesNotPresent tags evaluate the body content, depending on whether an ActionMessages or ActionErrors object is present in the request scope. Table 8-8 lists the attributes of these two tags.

*Table 8-8. Attributes of the messagesPresent and messagesNotPresent tags*

| Name | Description |
| --- | --- |
| name | The parameter key to retrieve the message from request scope. |
| property | The name of the property for which messages should be retrieved. If not specified, all messages (regardless of property) are retrieved. |
| message | By default the tag will retrieve the request-scope bean it will iterate over from the Action. ERROR_KEY constant string, but if this attribute is set to true, the request-scope bean will be retrieved from the Action.MESSAGE_KEY constant string. Also, if this is set to true, any value assigned to the name attribute will be ignored. |

# Bean Tags

The tags that are part of the Bean tag library are used for accessing JavaBeans and their associated properties as well as for defining new beans that are accessible to the remainder of the page via scripting variables and page-scope attributes. Convenient mechanisms to create new beans based on the values of request cookies, headers, and parameters are also provided. Table 8-9 lists the tags within the Bean tag library.

*Table 8-9. Custom tags within the Bean tag library*

| Tag name | Description |
|---|---|
| cookie | Define a scripting variable based on the value(s) of the specified request cookie. |
| define | Define a scripting variable based on the value(s) of the specified bean property. |
| header | Define a scripting variable based on the value(s) of the specified request header. |
| include | Load the response from a dynamic application request and make it available as a bean. |
| message | Render an internationalized message string to the response. |
| page | Expose a specified item from the page context as a bean. |
| parameter | Define a scripting variable based on the value(s) of the specified request parameter. |
| resource | Load a web application resource and make it available as a bean. |
| size | Define a bean containing the number of elements in a `Collection` or `Map`. |
| struts | Expose a named Struts internal configuration object as a bean. |
| write | Render the value of the specified bean property. |

 Many of the tags in this tag library throw a JspException at runtime when they are used incorrectly (e.g., when you specify an invalid combination of tag attributes). JSP allows you to declare an "error page" in the `<%@ page %>` directive. If you want to process the actual exception that caused the problem, it is passed to the error page as a request attribute under key org.apache.struts.action.EXCEPTION.

## The define Tag

This tag retrieves a specified bean property and defines it as an attribute that is accessible to the remainder of the current page. No type conversion is performed on the returned property value unless it is a Java primitive type, in which case it is wrapped in the appropriate wrapper class (e.g., int is wrapped by java.lang.Integer). The property value is stored in the scope defined by the toScope variable.

## The header Tag

This tag retrieves the value of the specified request header and defines the result as a page-scope attribute of type String. If no header with the specified name can be located and no default value is specified in the value attribute, a request-time exception will be thrown. If the attribute multiple is set to any non-null value, the id attribute will contain the result of the call to HttpServletRequest.getHeaders() rather than a call to HttpServletRequest.getHeader().

## The include Tag

This tag performs an internal dispatch to the specified application component (or external URL) and makes the response data from that request available as a bean of type String. The value is stored into the id attribute. This tag has a function similar to that of the standard <jsp:include> tag, except that the response data is stored in a page-scope attribute instead of being written to the output stream. This allows you to position the output as needed.

If the current request is part of a session, the generated request for the include will also include the session ID.

The URL used to access the specified application component is calculated based on which of the following attributes you specify (you must specify exactly one of them):

forward
> Use the value of this attribute as the name of a global ActionForward to be looked up, and use the application-relative or context-relative URI found there.

href
> Use the value of this attribute unchanged (as this might link to a resource external to the application, the session identifier is not included).

page
> Use the value of this attribute as an application-relative URI to the desired resource. This value must start with a "/".

## The message Tag

The message tag is one of the most widely used tags within the Struts tag libraries. It retrieves an internationalized message for the specified locale, using the specified message key, and writes it to the output stream. You can supply up to five parametric replacements (such as "{0}").

The message key may be specified directly, using the key attribute, or indirectly, using the name and property attributes to obtain it from a bean. The bundle attribute allows you to specify the name of an application-scope bean under which a MessageResources object can be found. If no locale attribute is specified, the Locale will be retrieved from the session using the key Action.LOCALE_KEY.

The following is an example of the message tag:

```
<td><bean:message key="global.user.firstName"/>:</td>
```

## The parameter Tag

This tag retrieves the value of the specified request parameter and defines the result as a page-scope attribute of type String. If any non-null value is specified for the multiple attribute, the result will be a String[] obtained from calling getParameters() instead of getParameter().

## The resource Tag

This tag retrieves the value of the specified web application resource and makes it available as either an InputStream or a String, depending on the value of the input attribute. If the input attribute contains any non-null value, an InputStream will be created. Otherwise, the resource will be loaded as a String.

 This tag calls the getResourceAsStream() method using the name attribute. The name attribute must start with a /.

## The write Tag

The write tag is another important tag within the Bean tag library, and it gets a great deal of use. It retrieves the value of the specified bean property and renders it to the page output as a String. The write tag uses the following rules:

- If the format attribute is specified, the value will be formatted based on the format string and the default locale. The formatKey attribute can also be used. It should specify the name of a format string from the message resource bundle.

- The formatKey attribute is used to specify a format string from the resource bundle. The specific resource bundle and locale can also be specified. If the bundle and locale are not specified, the default resource bundle and current user locale will be used.

- Otherwise, the usual toString() conversions will be applied.

The following is an example of using the write tag:

```
<td>Hello <bean:write name="user" property="firstName"/></td>
```

 If the ignore attribute is set to true and the bean specified by the name and scope attributes is not found, the tag will not throw an exception. If not set, or set to false, a runtime exception will be thrown.

# Nested Tags

The Struts custom tag libraries provide a great deal of power and flexibility to the developer. The freedom to access properties of a bean at any level using nested properties is very powerful.

There are some restrictions in how this technique can be deployed, however. When attempting to nest one tag inside another, the inside tag has certain dependencies on the outside tag that may make it cumbersome or impossible to cleanly render the dynamic data. There are workarounds, but these usually involve using scriptlets with Java within the JSP page. "Nested" tags were created to solve this problem and to enrich the Struts tag libraries.

The Nested tag library was created by Arron Bates to make it easier to nest Struts tags inside one another and to match the ability of the model layer to nest beans inside one another. The nested tags have become so popular that they have been added to the core libraries.

Nested tags parallel the current tags supported by the Struts framework. For example, there are HTML nested tags, Logic nested tags, and Bean nested tags. There is no need for nested Template tags, so those don't exist. The major difference is that nesting is better supported in the nested versions.

The tags within the Nested tag library are used in the same way that the non-nested versions are. Minor differences exist to allow for tags to know when they are nested within one another and therefore can access properties of the parent tag. Other than these small differences, they are very similar.

You can find more information on the nested tags in the Struts API documents. Tutorials and more information on the nested tags are available at *http://www.keyboardmonkey.com/struts/index.html*.

# Other Useful Tag Libraries

The Struts custom tags aren't the only tag libraries that work with Struts applications. Although some of the Struts tags make it very easy to use certain facets of the framework, other tags can assist you in developing applications and help to reduce the development time for a project.

We will mention only two of the more popular locations at which you can find additional tag libraries, but many other sites and vendors provide free or low-cost tag libraries too. You should always check to see if the tag you need already exists or if there's one that's close enough for you to simply extend or modify.

## The Jakarta Taglibs Project

One of the best resources is another Jakarta project named Taglibs. The goal of the Taglibs project is to provide an open source repository for JSP custom tag libraries and web publishing tool extensions.

There are around 25 separate tag libraries in the Taglibs project, each of which provides some unique functionality that most web applications need to perform sooner or later. The tag libraries are free and provide the source code, which allows you to not only get a better understanding of how to develop JSP tags but also to modify or extend the tags as your application dictates.

There's no sense in listing the available tags, as new ones are added regularly. The best idea is to check the site itself. You can find the Taglibs project on the Jakarta site at *http://jakarta.apache.org/taglibs*.

## JSPTags.com

Another useful web site that contains many JSP tags is *http://jsptags.com*. This site has been around for several years and has many tag libraries that you can use for free. It's also a great resource for other web application information. Make sure to check this site as well before setting off to create your own tag. Somebody may have already created the tag you need, saving you the development and testing time—always a good thing.

# The JSP Standard Tag Library (JSTL)

The intent of the early JSP specification group members was to define a set of standard JSP tags within the specification. This would allow vendors to generate their own versions of the standard tags but also allow developers to count on this set of standard tags to be available in all compliant containers. However, due to time constraints, that feature of the early JSP specification was not included.

Since then, many vendors have created their own versions of commonly used tag libraries, but these versions are different enough that developers can't easily port their JSP pages from one container to another without having to modify the pages. JSR 52, the JSP Standard Tag Library (JSTL), aims to fix that problem.

JSR 52 defines a set of standard tags that should be present in any compliant container. The second version of the specification has been finalized and approved, and the group has released a reference implementation of the tag library.

The tags provided in the first release can be grouped into five distinct areas:

- Core tags
- Internationalization tags

- XML tags
- SQL tags
- Functions

## JSTL Core Tags

The core tags include those related to expressions, flow control, and a generic way to access URL-based resources whose content can then be included or processed within the JSP page. They include tags such as if, forEach, import, redirect, and many more.

## JSTL Internationalization Tags

The internationalization tags are divided into two groups: messaging and formatting.

The messaging tags assist page authors with creating messages that can be adapted to any locale available in the JSP container. They include tags such as bundle and message.

The formatting tags allow various data elements, such as numbers, currencies, dates, and times, to be formatted and parsed in a locale-sensitive manner. They include tags such as formatDate, parseNumber, and timeZone.

## JSTL XML Tags

The JSTL XML tag library includes tags that allow XML documents to be accessed. The tags are based on XPath. The XML tags use XPath as a local expression language.

## JSTL SQL Tags

The JSTL SQL tags allow direct access to JDBC resources. They are designed for quick prototyping and simple applications. For larger, more advanced applications, database operations should not be present in the presentation layer—they are normally performed in the model layer. This helps to ensure separation of responsibility.

The tags within the JSTL SQL library include tags for configuring the JDBC resource as well as for querying and updating the database.

## Functions

Functions allow developers to extend the capabilities of the JSP 2.0 expression language (EL), which is briefly mentioned in the next section. The JSTL functions are grouped together within the Functions tag library.

The Functions tag library contains two essential areas of interest; one if the length function for determining the size of collections. The second area of focus of the Functions tag library is providing the ability for String manipulation. Both of these capabilities was missing from the original specification.

## A New Expression Language

JSTL also introduce a new expression language (EL) to make it easier for page authors to access application data without forcing them to learn a full-fledged programming language like Java. The EL is part of JSR 152 (the JSP 1.3 specification), but it has been included with JSTL to ensure that a specification is available for the JSTL schedule. The two groups are working closely together so that the EL fulfills both sets of needs.

The JSTL tag libraries come in two versions. One version, known as the JSTL-RT, will continue to support expressions as they are used today. The second version, known as JSTL-EL, will support the new expression language. Both versions will be supported.

For more information on the EL, refer to the JSTL 1.1 specification, which can be downloaded from *http://jcp.org/jsr/detail/52.jsp*.

## JSTL Requirements

JSTL requires a servlet container that supports the Servlet 2.3 specification and Version 1.2 of the JSP specification. If you are using a container that doesn't support these specifications, you will not be able to use JSTL. Tomcat is one container that supports both, but there are many more. Make sure to check with your vendor before attempting to use JSTL.

## JSTL and Struts

The Struts Bean and Logic tag libraries may eventually be phased out in favor of the JSTL tags. There already have been changes within Struts to better support JSTL and EL. In the next several versions of the Struts framework, look for more changes to help ease that migration.

It should be obvious from looking at the tags included with JSTL that not all of the Struts tags are being replaced. The tags within the HTML tag library in particular will be around for some time.

# CHAPTER 9

# Extending the Struts Framework

One of the biggest advantages of using a framework is the ability to extend and customize it based on the needs of the application. The Struts framework is no exception—it provides several very important extension points for developers. This chapter takes a quick glance at some of those extension points and discusses the benefits (as well as a few downsides) of extending the framework.

## What Are Extension Points?

Think of a framework as a house that comes with part of the structure already complete, but gives you the option to modify certain characteristics, such as the wallpaper and paint colors. If the default characteristics already suit your needs, you don't have to change anything. If you like the paint job, for example, that's one less thing to worry about.

This is similar to how a framework functions, and that's a big advantage when building applications. If functionality that suits the needs of your application is present in the framework, you don't have to worry about that aspect of the application. This, in turn, frees up developers to focus on the core application rather than the infrastructure.

This is not a perfect analogy, but the point is that a good framework should provide much of the infrastructure—the foundation and the plumbing, for example. The most important aspect of a framework, however, is that it should provide extension points throughout.

Framework extension points, also referred to as "hooks," allow you to extend the framework in specific places to adapt it to meet the application's requirements. Where and how a framework provides these hooks is very important. If they're provided incorrectly or in the wrong locations, it becomes very hard for an application to adapt the framework, which makes the framework less useful. If you extend the framework in places where there are no extensions points or in ways that the framework authors never intended, upgrading the application to newer versions of the framework becomes problematic. The rest of this chapter focuses on where the Struts framework provides these extension points and how you can take advantage of them to build out specialized functionality for your application.

# General Extension Points

This section discusses some extension points that affect the overall framework, not necessarily one particular layer. Arguably the most important of these is the PlugIn mechanism.

## Using the PlugIn Mechanism

The Struts framework provides a mechanism to allow components to be plugged in and loaded dynamically. This feature was added in Version 1.1 and is supported through the use of the org.apache.struts.action.PlugIn interface. Any Java class can function as a plug-in, as long as it implements the PlugIn interface.

A plug-in is simply any Java class that you need to initialize when the Struts application starts up, and destroy when the application shuts down.

The PlugIn interface contains two methods, as shown in Example 9-1.

*Example 9-1. The org.apache.struts.action.PlugIn interface*

```
public interface PlugIn {
  /**
   * Notification that the specified module is being started.
   */
  public void init(ActionServlet servlet, ModuleConfig config)
        throws ServletException;

  /**
   * Notification that the module is being shut down.
   */
  public void destroy();
}
```

During startup of a Struts application, the ActionServlet calls the init( ) method for each PlugIn that is configured; the framework supports configuration of one or more PlugIns for each application. Initialization routines that your plug- in needs to perform should be done during the init( ) method. This is a good time to initialize a database connection or establish a connection to a remote system, for example.[*]

---

[*] You also can initialize a database connection through the use of a datasource.

The second method that your plug-in must implement is the destroy( ) method. The framework calls this method when the application is being shut down. You should perform any necessary cleanup during this time. For example, this is the perfect time to close database connections, remote sockets, or any other resources that the plug-in is using.

Let's provide a concrete example of how to use the Struts framework's PlugIn mechanism. Suppose that your application needs the ability to communicate with an EJB tier. One of the first things you must do before that can occur is to get a reference to the Java Naming and Directory Interface (JNDI) service. JNDI enables clients to access various naming and directory services, such as datasources, JavaMail sessions, and EJB home factories. Example 9-2 illustrates a simple example of acquiring an InitialContext for a JNDI service using the Struts PlugIn mechanism.

*Example 9-2. An example of using the Struts PlugIn mechanism*

```
package com.oreilly.struts.storefront.framework.ejb;

import java.util.Hashtable;
import javax.naming.InitialContext;
import javax.naming.Context;
import org.apache.struts.action.ActionServlet;
import org.apache.struts.config.ModuleConfig;
import org.apache.struts.action.PlugIn;
import javax.servlet.ServletException;

public class JNDIConnectorPlugin implements PlugIn {
  private String jndiFactoryClass;
  private String jndiURL;
  private Context initCtx = null;

  public JNDIConnectorPlugin() {
    super();
  }

  public void init(ActionServlet servlet, ModuleConfig config)
    throws ServletException{
      // Get the host and port where the JNDI service is running
      jndiFactoryClass = servlet.getInitParameter("jndi-factory-class");
      jndiURL = servlet.getInitParameter("jndi-url");

      try{
        Hashtable props = new Hashtable();
        // The EJB spec also allows these to be read from the jndi.properties file
        props.put( Context.INITIAL_CONTEXT_FACTORY, jndiFactoryClass );
        props.put( Context.PROVIDER_URL, jndiURL );
        initCtx = new InitialContext(props);
      }catch( Exception ex ){
        throw new ServletException( ex );
      }
      // Store the JNDI Context into the ServletContext
```

*Example 9-2. An example of using the Struts PlugIn mechanism (continued)*

```
    servlet.getServletContext().setAttribute( "Storefront.InitCtx", initCtx );
  }

public void destroy(){
  try{
    if ( initCtx != null ){
      initCtx.close();
      initCtx = null;
      // No need to remove from ServletContext because app is being shut down
    }
  }catch( Exception ex ){
    ex.printStackTrace();
  }
 }
}
```

When the framework calls the init() method of the JNDIConnectorPlugin class, the plug-in creates an InitialContext object and stores it into the ServletContext. This allows the JNDI InitialContext to be used by the entire application, when needed.

This is just a simple example; there are many possible uses for the PlugIn mechanism. For example, the Validator framework, which we'll discuss in Chapter 11, uses the PlugIn mechanism to initialize the validation rules for an application.

### Adding the plug-in to the configuration file

The plug-in must be declared in the Struts configuration file in order for the framework to be aware of it and initialize it at startup. It's specified in the configuration file using the plug-in element:

```
<plug-in
    className="com.oreilly.struts.storefront.framework.ejb.JNDIConnectorPlugin"/>
```

You also can pass properties to your PlugIn class by using the set-property element.

> If more than one plug-in element is specified, they will be initialized in the order in which they are listed in the configuration file.

For more information on configuring the plug-in element or passing properties to an instance, see "The Struts Configuration File" in Chapter 4.

## Extending the Struts Configuration Classes

One of the biggest changes to Version 1.1 of the Struts framework is the org.apache.struts.config package. This package contains all of the classes that are used as in-memory representations of the information stored in the Struts configuration file. They represent everything from Action configurations to PlugIn configurations.

If you look back at Chapter 4, you'll see that most of the configuration elements in the Struts configuration file allow you to supply a fully qualified Java class name for the configuration class through the className attribute. This gives you the freedom to customize the configuration element and pass additional information.

For example, suppose that you want to pass an additional parameter to your Action classes. By default, the ActionMapping class, which extends ActionConfig from the config package, is used. To pass an additional parameter called ssl-required that controls whether HTTP or HTTPS is used, you can extend the ActionMapping class and configure this extension through the className attribute. The ability to extend the Struts configuration elements through this mechanism makes the framework extremely extensible and flexible enough to meet just about any application need.

# Controller Extension Points

The next set of possible extension points is within the controller layer. Some of these have been mentioned briefly in previous chapters, but they're repeated here for completeness.

## Extending the ActionServlet Class

In earlier versions of the Struts framework, it was almost a given that an application needed to extend the ActionServlet class because most of the controller functionality, excluding the Action class behavior, was present in this class. With Struts 1.1, this is no longer true. However, there are still a few good reasons why you might need to extend the ActionServlet class.

As was pointed out in Chapter 5, the initialization routines that are invoked when a Struts application is first launched reside in the ActionServlet class. If you need to modify the way the framework initializes itself, this is one of the places to do so. To extend the ActionServlet class, just create a subclass of org.apache. struts.action. ActionServlet. You can then override the method or methods that you need to function differently. Once this is done, you need to modify the deployment descriptor so that the Struts application will use your custom ActionServlet:

```
<servlet>
<servlet-name>storefront</servlet-name>
<servlet-class>
  com.oreilly.struts.storefront.framework.ExtendedActionServlet
</servlet-class>
</servlet>
```

Most of the runtime request-processing behavior has been moved to the Request-Processor class in Struts 1.1. If you need to customize the manner in which your Struts application processes a request, see the next section.

# Extending the RequestProcessor Class

If you need to override functionality within the RequestProcessor class, you must let the framework know that it should use your customized version rather than the default. You can make the framework aware of your specialized RequestProcessor by modifying the configuration file for the Struts application. If your configuration file doesn't already have a controller element within it, you'll need to add one (there are several attributes that can be configured within the controller element—see Chapter 4 for more details):

```
<controller
    contentType="text/html;charset=UTF-8"
    debug="3"
    locale="true"
    nocache="true"
    processorClass="com.oreilly.struts.framework.CustomRequestProcessor"/>
```

The processorClass attribute allows you to specify the fully qualified Java class name of your specialized RequestProcessor. The Struts framework will create an instance of your specialized RequestProcessor at startup and use it to process all of the requests for the application. Because each application module can have its own Struts configuration file, you can specify a different RequestProcessor for each module.

## Using the processPreprocess( ) method

There are many methods that can be overridden within the RequestProcessor class. One of the methods that was designed with extension in mind is the processPreprocess( ) method. This method is called for each request. By default, it does nothing with the requests, but you can use this method in various ways to change the default request-processing behavior. The processPreprocess( ) method looks like this:

```
protected boolean processPreprocess( HttpServletRequest request,
                                     HttpServletResponse response ){
    return (true);
}
```

This method is called early in the request-processing stage, before the ActionForm is called and before the execute( ) method is called on the Action object. By default, the processPreprocess( ) method returns true, which tells the RequestProcessor to continue processing the request. However, you can override this method and perform some type of conditional logic, and if the request should not be processed any further, you can return false. When processPreprocess( ) returns false, the RequestProcessor stops processing the request and simply returns from the doPost( ) or doGet( ) call. Consequently, it's up to you to programmatically forward or redirect the request within the processPreprocess( ) method.

Example 9-3 illustrates this approach. This example checks to see whether the request is from a local host. If so, it returns true and the request continues. If the request is from any other host, the request is redirected to the unauthorized access page and the method returns false.

*Example 9-3. Using the processPreprocess() method*

```java
protected boolean processPreprocess( HttpServletRequest request,
                                     HttpServletResponse response ){

  boolean continueProcessing = true;

  // Get the name of the remote host and log it
  String remoteHost = request.getRemoteHost();
  log.info( "Request from host: " + remoteHost );

  // Make sure the host is from one that you expect
  if ( remoteHost == null || !remoteHost.startsWith( "127.") ){
    // Not the localhost, so don't allow the host to access the site
    continueProcessing = false;

    ForwardConfig config = appConfig.findForwardConfig("Unauthorized");
    try{
      response.sendRedirect( config.getPath() );
    }catch( Exception ex ){
      log.error( "Problem sending redirect from processPreprocess()" );
    }
  }
  return continueProcessing;
}
```

The most important thing to note in this example is that even though the processPreprocess() method is returning false, it's still up to the method to take care of redirecting the request. Returning false just lets the RequestProcessor know that it doesn't need to continue. The controller doesn't do anything with the request; that's the responsibility of the processPreprocess() method.

 The manner in which Example 9-3 specifies the path in the sendRedirect() method prevents us from having to hardcode the URI of the *unauthorized_access.jsp* resource. This way, if the actual page for the forward changes, this method will not have to be modified.

There are other ways that you can perform the same logic without using the processPreprocess() method. One alternative is to use a servlet filter (part of the Servlet 2.3 API). Filters allow you to inspect the request before it ever reaches the Struts controller. However, there are two problems to be aware of with filters.

First, because filters are part of the 2.3 API, you will not be able to use them if you are using a servlet container that supports only 2.2. Second, because the filter inspects the request very early in the processing stage, filters don't have easy access to the Struts API. This makes it hard to look up ActionForwards or anything else that you might normally use in the processPreprocess( ) method. In fact, because the Struts controller hasn't even seen the request at the time the filter inspects it, the controller hasn't had a chance to select the proper application module.

# Extending the Base Action Class

There have been several places in previous chapters where I've mentioned a technique of creating a base Action that extends the Struts Action class and then using it as a superclass for other actions. One of the reasons for doing this is that in many applications, there is common logic that must be implemented by most of the Action classes. Letting this Action superclass contain most of this code eliminates the redundancy and keeps the size and complexity of the other action classes manageable. Example 9-4 provides a very simple version of a base Action class that performs this type of behavior.

*Example 9-4. A base Action class*

```
import java.util.Collection;
import java.util.LinkedList;
import java.util.List;
import java.util.Locale;
import java.util.Iterator;
import javax.servlet.http.*;
import org.apache.struts.action.*;
// Non Struts Imports
import com.oreilly.struts.storefront.framework.util.IConstants;
import com.oreilly.struts.storefront.framework.exceptions.*;
import com.oreilly.struts.storefront.framework.UserContainer;
import com.oreilly.struts.storefront.service.IStorefrontService;

/**
 * An abstract Action class that all Storefront Action classes can extend.
 */
abstract public class StorefrontBaseAction extends Action {
  /**
   * The default execute() method that all actions must implement.
   */
  public ActionForward execute( ActionMapping mapping,
                                ActionForm form,
                                HttpServletRequest request,
                                HttpServletResponse response ) throws Exception{

    // It just calls a worker method that contains the real execute logic
    return executeAction( mapping,form,request,response,getUserContainer(request));
  }

  /**
   * The actual do work method that must be overridden by the subclasses.
   */
  abstract public ActionForward executeAction( ActionMapping mapping,
                                               ActionForm form,
```

*Example 9-4. A base Action class (continued)*

```
                                        HttpServletRequest request,
                                        HttpServletResponse response,
                                        UserContainer userContainer )
    throws Exception;

// This super Action is also a good place to put common utility methods

public boolean isLoggedIn( HttpServletRequest request ){
  UserContainer container = getUserContainer(request);
  return ( container != null && container.getUserView() != null );
}

/**
 * Retrieve the UserContainer for the user tied to the request.
 */
protected UserContainer getUserContainer(HttpServletRequest request) {
  HttpSession session = request.getSession();
  UserContainer userContainer =
    (UserContainer)session.getAttribute(IConstants.USER_CONTAINER_KEY);

  // Create a UserContainer if one doesn't exist already
  if(userContainer == null) {
    userContainer = new UserContainer();
    userContainer.setLocale(request.getLocale());
    session.setAttribute(IConstants.USER_CONTAINER_KEY, userContainer);
  }
  return userContainer;
}
}
```

The StorefrontBaseAction class shown in Example 9-4 illustrates how you can use a base Action to perform repetitive behavior so that all of the subclasses need not perform it themselves.

Suppose, for example, that all of your Action classes needed to obtain the User-Container for the current user and use some information within it (e.g., user ID or security permissions). One approach is to force all of the Action classes to obtain the UserContainer on their own, handle the situation when there isn't one, and so on. An alternate, more manageable approach is to put that behavior in a super Action and pass the UserContainer to the subclasses.

As Example 9-4 shows, the StorefrontBaseAction implements the execute() method, but inside that method, it gets an instance of a UserContainer and passes it as an argument to the executeAction() method. Each subclass implements the abstract executeAction() method and has the UserContainer passed in, instantiated, and guaranteed not to be null. This is only a trivial example of what you can do. Any behavior that all actions need to perform is a candidate for being implemented in the Action superclass, so that when the time comes to modify the implementation, only the behavior in the superclass needs to change.

# Extending View Components

There generally is less reason or need to extend components located within the view layer than there is to extend components in the controller layer. Typically, views are written exclusively for an application. For example, it's unlikely that a JSP page written for one application will be used within a different application. This is not always the case, but differences between look-and-feel and content make such reuse improbable. The one area within the Struts view layer where extensions often are created, however, is in the JSP tag libraries.

## Extending Struts Custom Tags

The custom tags provided by the Struts framework can be reused across applications and application domains. Therefore, it makes sense that customization and extensions are more likely with these components than with JSP pages. Because the tag handlers are regular Java classes, specialization is achieved through subclassing.

Although you can extend any tag, the HTML tag library is the one that you'll most likely need to customize (mainly because the custom tags within this library have the greatest impact on the view content). Regardless of which tags you extend, you'll need to create your own tag library to hold your tag extensions.

You could modify the Struts tag libraries and include your new tag class, but that would make upgrading to newer versions of the Struts framework much harder. You're better off creating your own tag library that contains just your application's tags.

Once you've created a *.tld* file for your extensions and registered it with the web application deployment descriptor, you are free to use your tags just as you would any others.

## Extending Model Components

Because the Struts framework doesn't provide a great deal of components for the model layer, extensions to these components are better discussed in other Java programming books. However, there are two classes that might be placed into the category of extensible model components. They aren't the best representations of what a model component is, but they are responsible for holding model state.

## The UserContainer and ApplicationContainer Classes

I've mentioned the UserContainer and ApplicationContainer classes in previous chapters without defining exactly what they are. These two classes are not part of the Struts framework—I created them as part of the example Storefront application. The purpose of these two classes is to store user and application-specific information in instances of these classes, rather than in the HttpSession and ServletContext objects, respectively.

One of the problems with storing data in the HttpSession is that the interface to store and retrieve data from the session object is not strongly typed. In other words, the interface for any data is:

```
public void setAttribute( someString, someObject );
public Object getAttribute( someString );
```

The client must be aware of the key at which the data is stored in order to put an object into or retrieve an object from storage. For example, to store and then retrieve a set of permissions using the HttpSession, the methods would look like this:

```
public void setAttribute( permissionsKey, permissionsSet );
public Object getAttribute( permissionsKey );
```

The programmer would also need to explicitly cast the return value from the getAttribute( ) method. Some programmers prefer a more strongly typed interface instead:

```
userContainer.setPermissions( permissions );
userContainer.getPermissions();
```

Here, the client doesn't have to worry about what key the object is being stored under or how it's being stored. It can be an HttpSession object or some other data store; the client unaware of the store method because it's not forced to use the methods of the HttpSession directly.

There's nothing really complicated about the UserContainer class itself. It's an ordinary JavaBean that contains instance variables, along with public getters and setters for the properties. Example 9-5 illustrates a basic UserContainer class.

*Example 9-5. A basic UserContainer class*

```
package com.oreilly.struts.storefront.framework;
import java.util.Locale;
import javax.servlet.http.HttpSessionBindingListener;
import javax.servlet.http.HttpSessionBindingEvent;
import com.oreilly.struts.storefront.customer.view.UserView;

/**
 * Used to store information about a specific user. This class is used
 * so that the information is not scattered throughout the HttpSession.
 * Only this object is stored in the session for the user. This class
 * implements the HttpSessionBindingListener interface so that it can
 * be notified of session timeout and perform the proper cleanup.
 */
public class UserContainer implements HttpSessionBindingListener, Serializable {

  // The user's shopping cart
  private ShoppingCart cart = null;
```

*Example 9-5. A basic UserContainer class (continued)*

```java
// Data about the user that is cached
private UserView userView = null;

/**
 * The Locale object for the user. Although Struts stores a Locale for
 * each user in the session, the locale is also maintained here.
 */
private Locale locale;

public UserContainer() {
  super();
  initialize();
}

public ShoppingCart getCart() {
  return cart;
}

public void setCart(ShoppingCart newCart) {
  cart = newCart;
}

public void setLocale(Locale aLocale) {
  locale = aLocale;
}

public Locale getLocale() {
  return locale;
}

/**
 * The container calls this method when it is being unbound from the
 * session.
 */
public void valueUnbound(HttpSessionBindingEvent event) {
  // Perform resource cleanup
  cleanUp();
}

/**
 * The container calls this method when it is being bound to the
 * session.
 */
public void valueBound(HttpSessionBindingEvent event) {
  // Don't need to do anything, but still have to implement the
  // interface method.
}

public UserView getUserView() {
  return userView;
}
```

*Example 9-5. A basic UserContainer class  (continued)*

```
public void setUserView(UserView newView) {
  userView = newView;
}

/**
 * Initialize all of the required resources
 */
private void initialize() {
  // Create a new shopping cart for this user
  cart = new ShoppingCart();
}

/**
 * Clean up any open resources. The shopping cart is left intact
 * intentionally.
 */
public void cleanUp() {
  setUserView( null );
}
}
```

One thing to notice is that the UserContainer class in Example 9-5 implements the HttpSessionBindingListener interface. The methods of this interface allow the UserContainer to be notified when it is bound to and unbound from the session. This allows it to perform any necessary cleanup on the object. An instance of the UserContainer is created for each new user at the time the user enters the application. The UserContainer object itself is stored in the session, and it must have the duration of the session. If the user exits and re-enters the site, a new UserContainer typically is created for that user. The UserContainer also implements the Serializable interface. This is necessary in case the container needs to passivate or transfer the session's contents in a cluster.

The ApplicationContainer is used for a similar purpose, but at the application level, not the session level. It's useful for storing or caching information that is needed by all users across the application. Things such as selection lists, configuration properties, and other non-client-specific data that you need to get once and hold on to are candidates for the ApplicationContainer class. This class is created when the application is first started and destroyed when the application exits.

# Downsides to Extending the Framework

There are a few downsides to customizing or extending a framework. Although I've suggested that customization is a forecasted goal of using a framework, as with other things in software development, there are trade-offs.

When extending a framework, one of the biggest issues that you may face is what to do when newer versions of the framework are made available. Unless the framework developers paid careful attention to backward compatibility, your application may no longer work correctly with a newer version of the framework. The Struts framework, for example, underwent some significant changes to its APIs between Versions 1.0 and 1.1. In particular, the perform( ) method is no longer the controller's preferred method for invoking the Action; instead, it uses the execute( ) method. Fortunately, the developers working on the Struts framework were careful and ensured that the new functionality was compatible with applications built using earlier versions.

You should take that same care when building your applications. If, for example, you override methods of the Struts framework to achieve specialized behavior, it's not out of the realm of possibility that the method will be deprecated or removed in future Struts versions. In fact, several comments in the framework source indicate that certain portions of the Struts framework eventually will be retired. Although it's nearly impossible to protect your application from all potential changes, it's best that you go into developing it with your eyes wide open. Using a framework, even one that is as good and as complete as Struts, is not a silver bullet. You will have the same upgrade issues whether you build your own framework or use one provided by another source.

# CHAPTER 10

# Exception Handling

Throwing exceptions is Java's way of informing dependent clients that something abnormal occurred during the processing of a method. The client is notified of the type of problem by an instance of a specific exception being thrown, and it's entirely up to the client what course of action to take when an exception occurs. In some cases, the client may even choose not to take any action, which causes the JVM to continue to search for a handler for the exception.

Handling exceptions within your Struts applications is not much different. When an abnormal condition occurs, an exception is thrown to the calling client to notify it of the abnormality. What is different for web applications, and specifically the Struts framework, is what action is taken on behalf of the client and how these exceptions are reported back to the end user.

This chapter looks at how you can properly use the Java exception-handling mechanism within your Struts applications to help make your applications more robust and allow them to gracefully respond when things do not go as expected. Special attention is given to the differences between performing the exception handling programmatically and using the new declarative feature added to the Struts framework in Version 1.1.

## Java Exception Handling

Before we dive into how best to handle exceptions in the Struts framework, you should have a picture in your mind of what actually occurs when a method throws an exception. An understanding of the processes taking place in the JVM when an exception occurs may enlighten you as to the importance of throwing exceptions for the right reason, as well as the importance of throwing the right exceptions. Because there is additional overhead for the JVM to handle an exception, you should always take care to use exceptions correctly.

# Java Exceptions

In Java, exceptions are objects that are created when an abnormal condition, often referred to as an *exception condition*, occurs during the execution of an application. When a Java application throws an exception, it creates an object that is a descendant of java.lang.Throwable. The Throwable class has two direct subclasses: java.lang.Error and java.lang.Exception. Figure 10-1 shows a partial hierarchy tree for the Throwable class.

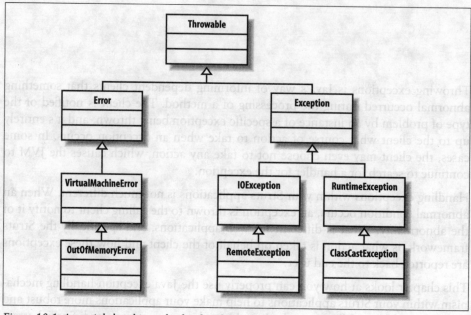

*Figure 10-1. A partial class hierarchy for the Throwable class*

Space does not permit all of the descendants of the Throwable class to be shown, as there are more than 100 direct and indirect subclasses in the core Java library alone. Normally, members of the Exception branches of the tree are thrown to indicate abnormal conditions that can usually be handled by the application. All of the exceptions your Struts application creates and throws should be subclasses of the Exception class. The other branch of Throwable, the Error class and its descendants, is reserved for more serious problems that occur during an application's lifecycle. For example, if there's no more memory available for an application, an OutOfMemoryError will occur, and there's typically nothing a client can do about it. Therefore, clients generally don't worry about handling the subclasses of Error. In most cases, it's the JVM itself that throws instances of Error or its subclasses.

# The Method Invocation Stack

The JVM uses a *method invocation stack*, also referred to as a *call stack*, to keep track of the succession of method invocations of each thread. The stack holds local information about each method that has been called, going all the way back to the original `main( )` method of the application. When each new method is invoked, a new stack frame is pushed onto the top of the stack, and the new method becomes the executing method. The local state of each method is also saved with each stack frame. Figure 10-2 illustrates an example Java call stack.

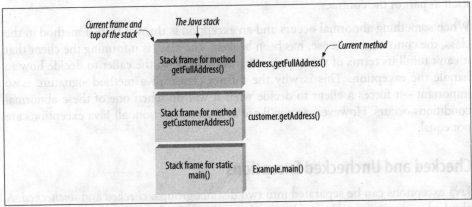

*Figure 10-2. An example of a Java method invocation stack*

When a Java method completes normally, the JVM pops the current method's stack frame from the stack and continues processing in the previous method where it left off. When an exception condition occurs, however, the JVM must find a suitable exception handler. It first checks to see if the current method catches the exception or one of its parent exceptions. If so, execution will continue in that catch clause. If the current method doesn't provide a catch clause to handle the exception raised, the JVM will start popping method frames off the call stack until it finds a handler for the exception or one of its parent exceptions. Eventually, if it pops all the way back to the main( ) method and still doesn't find a handler for the exception, the thread will terminate. If that thread is the main thread and there are no other non-daemon threads running, the application itself will terminate. If the JVM does find an exception handler along the way, that method frame will become the top of the stack and execution will continue from there.

It's important to know how the JVM handles exceptions because there is plenty going on underneath the hood when exceptions occur in your applications. It can be a lot of work for the JVM to locate an exception handler for a particular exception, especially if the handler is located far down the call stack. It's very important that you provide sufficient exception handlers at the appropriate levels. If you let exceptions go, they are likely to halt your application.

# What About the throws Clause?

When determining the method signatures for classes that are part of an application, you should give as much attention to deciding which exceptions the methods will throw as to what the parameters are and what the return type is.

You might have heard of the concept "design by contract." The idea behind this principle is that the set of public methods that a class exposes represents a virtual contract between a client and the class itself. The client has certain obligations in the way in which it invokes the method, and there may also be requirements on the class itself as part of the contract.

When something abnormal occurs and an exception is thrown from a method in the class, the contract, in a sense, has been broken. The class is informing the client that it can't fulfill its terms of the contract. It's entirely up to the caller to decide how to handle the exception. This is why the throws clause of a method signature is so important—it forces a client to decide what it will do when one of these abnormal conditions occurs. However, as you'll see in the next section, all Java exceptions are not equal.

## Checked and Unchecked Exceptions

Java exceptions can be separated into two distinct groups: *checked* and *unchecked*. A checked exception signals an abnormal condition that the client must handle. All checked exceptions must either be caught and handled within the calling method or be declared in the throws clause following the method signature. This is why they are called "checked." The compiler and the JVM will verify that all checked exceptions that can occur in a method are handled. The compiler and JVM don't care if unchecked exceptions are ignored, because these are exceptions that the client usually cannot handle anyway. Unchecked exceptions, such as java.lang. ClassCastException, are typically the result of incorrect logic or programming errors.

The determination of whether an exception is checked or unchecked is based simply on its location in the exception hierarchy. All classes that are descendants of the java.lang.Exception class, except for subclasses of RuntimeException, are checked exceptions; the compiler will ensure that they are either handled by the method or listed in the throws clause. RuntimeException and its descendants are unchecked exceptions, and the compiler will not complain about these not being listed in a throws clause for a method or being handled in a try/catch block. This is why they are referred to as "unchecked."

# Performance Impact of Exception Handling

In general, wrapping your Java code with try/catch blocks doesn't have a significant performance impact on your applications. Only when exceptions actually occur is there a negative performance impact, which is due to the lookup the JVM must perform to locate the proper handler for the exception. If the catch block for the exception is located in the same method, the impact is not so bad. However, the further down the call stack the JVM has to go to find the exception handler, the greater the impact becomes.

This is why you should use a try/catch block only for error conditions. You should never use exceptions for things such as controlling program flow. The following use of a try/catch block is probably fine, but it's getting very close to improper use of exception handling:

```
Double basePrice = null;
String basePriceStr = request.getParameter( "BASE_PRICE_AMOUNT" );

// Use a try/catch to make sure the value is a number
try{
    basePrice = Double.valueOf( basePriceStr );
}catch( NumberFormatException ex ){
    // The value could not be converted to a valid Double; set the default
    basePrice = ApplicationDefaults.DEFAULT_BASE_PRICE;
}
```

The previous code fragment shows a try/catch block determining an error condition and taking corrective action. The error condition is an invalid price value, and the corrective action is to assign a default value. There are other ways to determine whether a string is a valid Double value, but using this approach is fairly popular. Fortunately, the exception handler is located in the same method, and the JVM doesn't incur a large penalty for this occurrence.

Of course, rules are always somewhat subjective, and what is a valid reason to one developer may not be to another. You should be aware of the drawbacks and avoid using try/catch blocks other than for actual error conditions.

## System Versus Application Exceptions

Exceptions can be further classified into either *system exceptions* or *application exceptions*. System exceptions are more serious in nature. These are typically low-level problems that aren't related to the application logic and from which end users are not expected to recover. In many cases, system exceptions are unchecked, and your application isn't supposed to catch them because they are either non-programming errors or are so severe that nothing can be done about them.

Application exceptions are errors that occur because of a violation of a business rule or some other condition in the application logic. For example, you might throw an application exception when a user attempts to log in to the application but the account has been locked. This isn't a catastrophic error, but it is a problem that needs to be reported and handled.

Within Struts applications (and web applications in general), there are essentially two approaches you can take when an exception occurs. If the exception is an application exception from which the end user may be able to recover, you typically want to return control back to the input page and display a user-friendly statement of the problem and some action that can be taken to resolve it. Continuing with the locked account example, you could throw an AccountLockedException back to the action class, which would forward control back to the login page and inform the user that the account is locked.

If the thrown exception is a low-level exception such as a RemoteException, the only meaningful action the application can take is to display a system error page. There's nothing the user can do to fix the problem. It may be a programming error or some type of network issue, but the point is that you don't want to let the user see the stack trace of the exception. Instead, forward to a system error page that's more user-friendly to look at and optionally informs the user to notify the system administrator. The exception should also be logged to aid the developer in determining the root cause of the problem.

Later in this chapter, you'll see examples of how to return control back to the input page and show a localized message to the user. You will also learn ways of dealing with system errors by forwarding control to a system error page, all of which will add value to the application and to the user experience.

# Using Chained Exceptions

It's often suitable to catch a particular type of exception and rethrow a different one. This is sometimes necessary because a client might not know or care to handle the original exception. For example, say that a client invokes an action on a Struts application to upload an image file to a database. Let's further assume the Action class calls an update method whose signature looks like the following:

```
public void updateImageFile( String imagePath ) throws UploadException;
```

When the method is called with an image to upload and a problem occurs, an UploadException will be thrown. However, the underlying problem will be more specific—for example, the filesystem is full or the database already has the image, depending on the destination of the image upload. The original exception thrown may be IOException or SQLException, but the user doesn't need to know or care about this level of detail; all he needs to know is that the update function failed. Although the end user doesn't care about the specific exception thrown, the system administrator or the developers who will be assigned the task of debugging and fixing the problem do. That's why you don't want to throw away the root cause of the problem when you rethrow a different exception.

Prior to Version 1.4, Java didn't provide a built-in mechanism to wrap the original exception with a new one. Developers were left to their own devices to solve the problem. Most homegrown solutions looked something like the exception class in Example 10-1.

*Example 10-1. An exception class that supports chained exceptions*

```java
import java.io.PrintStream;
import java.io.PrintWriter;
/**
 * This is the common superclass for all application exceptions. This
 * class and its subclasses support the chained exception facility that allows
 * a root cause Throwable to be wrapped by this class or one of its
 * descendants.
 */
public class BaseException extends Exception {
  protected Throwable rootCause = null;

  protected BaseException( Throwable rootCause ) {
    this.rootCause = rootCause;
  }

  public void setRootCause(Throwable anException) {
    rootCause = anException;
  }

  public Throwable getRootCause() {
    return rootCause;
  }

  public void printStackTrace() {
    printStackTrace(System.err);
  }

  public void printStackTrace(PrintStream outStream) {
    printStackTrace(new PrintWriter(outStream));
  }

  public void printStackTrace(PrintWriter writer) {
    super.printStackTrace(writer);

    if ( getRootCause() != null ) {
      getRootCause().printStackTrace(writer);
    }
    writer.flush();
  }
}
```

The exception class in Example 10-1 allows you to wrap the original Throwable with an instance of this exception class or any of its descendants. The nice thing about this feature is that it allows you to abstract out the ugly details of lower-level exceptions, while at the same time keeping those details available so they can be printed out to a log and used by developers. Because these exceptions can be chained together endlessly, this concept is commonly referred to as *exception chaining*.

Exception chaining is an excellent way of preventing lower-layer abstractions, such as JDBC access, from propagating outward to an end user. The end user doesn't care about the lower-layer problem, and abstracting the problem to a higher-level exception will keep him from seeing many of the details.

Another benefit of using a higher-layer exception class is that the API of the upper layer is not tied nor coupled to the details of the implementation. Continuing our earlier example, suppose that a filesystem is initially used to store the images, and therefore the throws clause of the updateImageFile( ) method declares that it throws an IOException. If later the implementation changes to use JDBC instead, the throws clause and the clients invoking the method must be changed to declare or catch a SQLException. By using a higher level of abstraction, the client only needs to be concerned about the UploadException, regardless of the underlying implementation.

## Dealing with Multiple Exceptions

A slight variation on the exception chaining idea is the concept of throwing multiple exceptions from a method. For example, say a user is filling out a form that has several price fields that must fall between some minimum and maximum values. Let's further assume the price values can be validated only on the backend and not within an ActionForm.

Unless your application can throw multiple exceptions from a method, the user will see only one exception at a time. This approach will work, but will probably become very annoying for end users, who will have to fix one field and then resubmit only to receive the next error. It would be easier for users if all of the errors were displayed and could be fixed at the same time. Unfortunately, a Java method can throw only a single instance of Throwable.

One solution to dealing with multiple exceptions is to allow an exception class to have a primary exception while supporting a collection of other exceptions. Each exception can be treated the same, but the primary exception is used when only a single exception occurs, and the client can check the exception collection to see if there are more. Example 10-2 illustrates what the BaseException class from Example 10-1 would look like with this feature added to it.

*Example 10-2. An exception class that supports multiple nested exceptions*

```
package com.oreilly.struts.framework.exceptions;

import java.util.List;
import java.util.ArrayList;
import java.io.PrintStream;
import java.io.PrintWriter;
/**
 * This is the common superclass for all application exceptions. This
 * class and its subclasses support the chained exception facility that allows
 * a root cause Throwable to be wrapped by this class or one of its
```

*Example 10-2. An exception class that supports multiple nested exceptions (continued)*

```
 *  descendants. This class also supports multiple exceptions via the
 *  exceptionList field.
 */
public class BaseException extends Exception{

  protected Throwable rootCause = null;
  private List exceptions = new ArrayList();

  public BaseException(){
    super();
  }

  public BaseException( Throwable rootCause ) {
    this.rootCause = rootCause;
  }

  public List getExceptions() {
    return exceptions;
  }

  public void addException( BaseException ex ){
    exceptions.add( ex );
  }

  public void setRootCause(Throwable anException) {
    rootCause = anException;
  }

  public Throwable getRootCause() {
    return rootCause;
  }

  public void printStackTrace() {
    printStackTrace(System.err);
  }

  public void printStackTrace(PrintStream outStream) {
    printStackTrace(new PrintWriter(outStream));
  }

  public void printStackTrace(PrintWriter writer) {
    super.printStackTrace(writer);

    if ( getRootCause() != null ) {
      getRootCause().printStackTrace(writer);
    }
    writer.flush();
  }
}
```

Notice in Example 10-2 that a java.util.List has been added to the class. If more than one exception occurs during the processing of a method, the additional exceptions can be added and returned to the client. If the client wants to deal with only a single exception, it doesn't have to retrieve the additional ones.

# Exception Handling Provided by Struts

Prior to Version 1.1, the Struts framework provided very minimal exception handling for applications—it was left to you to extend the framework with your own exception-handling capabilities. This encouraged each development group to approach a solution from a different direction and made it difficult to discuss common solutions.

In Version 1.1, Struts added a small but effective exception-handling framework for your applications. The approach that the Struts designers took follows the EJB and Servlet specifications for handling security, allowing developers to use a declarative and/or a programmatic approach.

---

### Using the AppException Class

The `org.apache.struts.util.ModuleException` class is included with the Struts framework. This class is a wrapper around an `ActionError` and extends `java.lang.Exception`. It provides the ability to throw exceptions in a Struts application like:

```
throw new ModuleException("error.password.mismatch");
```

where the argument to the `ModuleException` constructor is a resource bundle key. The framework will automatically create `ActionError` objects from these exceptions and store them in the appropriate scope. You can extend the `ModuleException` class with application-specific exceptions for your application.

One problem with using this class, however, is that it couples your application, and specifically your exception-handling code, to the Struts framework. It relies on classes that are specific to the Struts framework, which is problematic if you are using an application tier such as EJB. You don't want to couple your entire application to Struts if you can avoid it. If you are building a small web application where you will never need to replace Struts with something else and you are not worried about coupling your model components to Struts, the `ModuleException` can add value. Otherwise, you might be better off avoiding its use.

---

## Declarative Versus Programmatic Exception Handling

*Declarative* exception handling is accomplished by expressing an application's exception-handling policy, including which exceptions are thrown and how they are to be handled, in a text file (typically using XML) that is completely external to the application code. This approach makes it easier to modify the exception-handling logic without major recompilation of the code.

---

*Programmatic* exception handling is the opposite. It is the traditional method, involving writing application-specific, intra-method code to handle the exceptions, rather than simply modifying an external configuration file. However, it is quite a bit more complex within a Struts application.

As with other Struts configuration options, the declarative mappings are done in the Struts configuration file. As you saw in Chapter 4, you can specify the exceptions that may occur and what to do if they occur, both at a global level and for a specific action mapping. For a discussion of the parameters available for the exception-handling elements, refer back to Chapter 4.

Example 10-3 shows a partial Struts configuration file that declares three different exceptions that may be thrown from the *login* action.

*Example 10-3. A Struts configuration file that uses declarative exception handling*

```
<?xml version="1.0" encoding="UTF-8" ?>

<!DOCTYPE struts-config PUBLIC
        "-//Apache Software Foundation//DTD Struts Configuration 1.1//EN"
        "http://jakarta.apache.org/struts/dtds/struts-config_1_1.dtd">

<struts-config>
  <action-mappings>
   <action
     path="/login"
     type="com.oreilly.struts.storefront.security.LoginAction"
     name="loginForm"
     scope="request"
     input="/login.jsp">
     <!--The following exceptions can be thrown during the login action -->
     <exception
       key="security.error.changepassword"
       path="/changePassword.jsp"
       type="com.oreilly.struts.framework.exceptions.ExpiredPasswordException"/>
     <exception
       key=" security.error.loginfailed"
       type="com.oreilly.struts.framework.exceptions.InvalidLoginException"
       path="/login.jsp"/>
     <exception
       key="security.error.accountlocked"
       type="com.oreilly.struts.framework.exceptions.AccountLockedException"
       path="/accountLocked.jsp"/>
   </action>
  </action-mappings>
</struts-config>
```

The exception element that is defined either in the action mapping or in the global exceptions section specifies the path to which to forward when one of the specified exceptions occurs during the corresponding action invocation. For example, if an ExpiredPasswordException is thrown during the *login* action, the controller will forward control to the *changePassword.jsp* page. Likewise, if an Account-LockedException is thrown, control will be forwarded to the *accountLocked.jsp* page.

Whenever an exception is not programmatically handled in the Action class, the RequestProcessor gets a chance to see if there is an exception element configured for that specific exception type. If there is, control is forwarded to the resource specified in the path attribute of the exception element. Example 10-4 shows the processException( ) method from the RequestProcessor class.

*Example 10-4. The processException( ) method from the Struts RequestProcessor*

```
protected ActionForward processException(HttpServletRequest request,
                                         HttpServletResponse response,
                                         Exception exception,
                                         ActionForm form,
                                         ActionMapping mapping)
    throws IOException, ServletException {

    // Is there a defined handler for this exception?
    ExceptionConfig config = mapping.findException(exception.getClass());
    if (config == null) {
        log.warn(getInternal().getMessage("unhandledException",
                                          exception.getClass()));
        if (exception instanceof IOException) {
            throw (IOException) exception;
        } else if (exception instanceof ServletException) {
            throw (ServletException) exception;
        } else {
            throw new ServletException(exception);
        }
    }

    // Use the configured exception handling
    try {
        ExceptionHandler handler = (ExceptionHandler)
        RequestUtils.applicationInstance(config.getHandler());
        return (handler.execute(exception, config, mapping, form,
                                request, response));
    } catch (Exception e) {
        throw new ServletException(e);
    }

}
```

Notice that an ExceptionConfig object may be returned from the findException( ) method at the beginning of the processException( ) method. The ExceptionConfig object is an in-memory representation of the exception element specified in the configuration file. If the findException( ) method doesn't find an exception element for the specific type of exception that occurred, the exception is thrown back to the client without going through a Struts exception handler. Unless the exception is an IOException or one of its subclasses, the exception will be wrapped by a ServletException instance and rethrown.

If there is an exception element specified in the action mapping for the specific type of exception that occurs, an ExceptionConfig object is returned from the findException( ) method. The getHandler( ) method is then called on the ExceptionConfig object, and the handler retrieved is used to process the exception.

The Struts framework has a default exception-handler class that is used to process the exceptions if you don't configure one of your own. The default handler class is org.apache.struts.action.ExceptionHandler. The execute( ) method of this handler creates an ActionError, stores it into the proper scope, and returns an ActionForward object that is associated with the path attribute specified in the exception element. To summarize, if you declare an exception element inside an action element, the default exception handler will create and store an ActionError into the specified scope and give control to the resource specified in the path attribute.

As you saw back in Chapter 4, the exception element also allows you to override the exception handler's behavior if you want a different behavior when an exception occurs. You can do this by specifying a fully qualified Java class that extends the org. apache.struts.action.ExceptionHandler class in the exception's handler attribute. This class will override the execute( ) method of ExceptionHandler in order to perform the specialized behavior. For example, your application exceptions could extend the BaseException class shown in Example 10-5.

*Example 10-5. An exception class that supports a message key and arguments*

```
package com.oreilly.struts.framework.exceptions;

import java.util.List;
import java.util.ArrayList;
import java.io.PrintStream;
import java.io.PrintWriter;
/**
 * This is the common superclass for all application exceptions. This
 * class and its subclasses support the chained exception facility that allows
 * a root cause Throwable to be wrapped by this class or one of its
 * descendants. This class also supports multiple exceptions via the
 * exceptionList field.
 */
public class BaseException extends Exception{

  protected Throwable rootCause = null;
  private List exceptions = new ArrayList();
  private String messageKey = null;
  private Object[] messageArgs = null;

  public BaseException(){
    super();
  }

  public BaseException( Throwable rootCause ) {
    this.rootCause = rootCause;
```

```
  }

  public List getExceptions() {
    return exceptions;
  }

  public void addException( BaseException ex ){
    exceptions.add( ex );
  }

  public void setMessageKey( String key ){
    this.messageKey = key;
  }

  public String getMessageKey(){
    return messageKey;
  }

  public void setMessageArgs( Object[] args ){
    this.messageArgs = args;
  }

  public Object[] getMessageArgs(){
    return messageArgs;
  }

  public void setRootCause(Throwable anException) {
    rootCause = anException;
  }

  public Throwable getRootCause() {
    return rootCause;
  }

  public void printStackTrace() {
    printStackTrace(System.err);
  }

  public void printStackTrace(PrintStream outStream) {
    printStackTrace(new PrintWriter(outStream));
  }

  public void printStackTrace(PrintWriter writer) {
    super.printStackTrace(writer);

    if ( getRootCause() != null ) {
      getRootCause().printStackTrace(writer);
    }
    writer.flush();
  }
}
```

The `BaseException` class in Example 10-5 contains a `messageKey` that can be used as a key in the Struts resource bundle. This key can be passed into the constructor of the `ActionError` class, and the Struts framework will match it to a message in the Struts resource bundle. This class also contains an object array that the creator of the exception can populate. These objects can then be used to substitute into a message from the bundle that contains substitution parameters based on the `MessageFormat` class. A message in the bundle might look like this:

```
global.error.invalid.price=The price must be between {0} and {1}.
```

When creating an `ActionError` object, you can pass an array of objects as the second parameter, and each object will be substituted into the parameters enclosed by the braces. The 0th element in the array will be inserted into the {0} position, the object at index 1 will be inserted into the {1} position, and so on. Chapter 12 covers this topic in more detail.

Example 10-6 illustrates how to extend the default exception-handler class and provide specialized behavior for substituting the arguments from the exception into the `ActionError` constructor.

*Example 10-6. A specialized exception handler*

```
package com.oreilly.struts.chapter10examples;

import javax.servlet.ServletException;
import javax.servlet.http.HttpServletRequest;
import javax.servlet.http.HttpServletResponse;
import org.apache.struts.action.ExceptionHandler;
import org.apache.struts.action.ActionForm;
import org.apache.struts.action.ActionError;
import org.apache.struts.util.AppException;
import org.apache.struts.action.ActionForward;
import org.apache.struts.action.ActionMapping;
import org.apache.struts.config.ExceptionConfig;

import com.oreilly.struts.framework.exceptions.BaseException;

public class SpecialExceptionHandler extends ExceptionHandler {

  protected ActionForward execute(Exception ex,
                                  ExceptionConfig config,
                                  ActionMapping mapping,
                                  ActionForm formInstance,
                                  HttpServletRequest request,
                                  HttpServletResponse response)
    throws ServletException {
    ActionForward forward = null;
    ActionError error = null;
    String property = null;

    /* Get the path for the forward either from the exception element
     * or from the input attribute.
     */
```

*Example 10-6. A specialized exception handler (continued)*

```
      String path = null;
      if (config.getPath() != null) {
       path = config.getPath();
      }else{
       path = mapping.getInput();
      }
      // Construct the forward object
      forward = new ActionForward(path);

      /* Figure out what type of exception has been thrown. The Struts
       * AppException is not being used in this example.
       */
      if( ex instanceof BaseException) {
       // This is the specialized behavior
       BaseException baseException = (BaseException)ex;
       String messageKey = baseException.getMessageKey();
       Object[] exArgs = baseException.getMessageArgs();
       if ( exArgs != null && exArgs.length > 0 ){
        // If there were args provided, use them in the ActionError
        error = new ActionError( messageKey, exArgs );
       }else{
        // Create an ActionError without any arguments
        error = new ActionError( messageKey );
       }
      }else{
       error = new ActionError(config.getKey());
       property = error.getKey();
      }

      // Store the ActionError into the proper scope
      // The storeException method is defined in the parent class
      storeException(request, property, error, forward, config.getScope());

      return forward;
   }
}
```

The specialized behavior that you perform in your handler class is up to you. The behavior shown in Example 10-6 makes the error messages more informative by inserting arguments into the ActionError.

For further information on how to install a custom exception handler, see "The Struts Configuration DTD" in Chapter 4.

There are plenty of other instances where you might need to override the default behavior. The default exception handler provided by the Struts framework doesn't support an exception object that stores multiple exceptions. If your application needs to support this behavior, you'll need to create your own ExceptionHandler class.

In most cases, the Struts exception handler is sufficient. Only when you need specialized exception handling that can't be obtained from the Struts exception handler should you bother to create your own. Figure 10-3 illustrates a sequence diagram for the Struts default exception-handling mechanism.

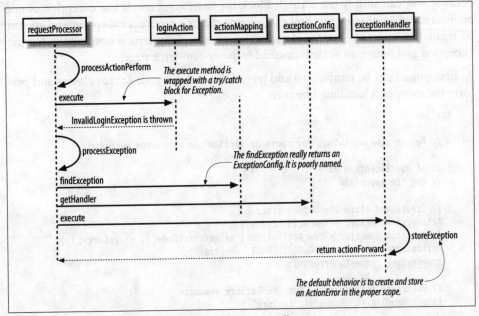

*Figure 10-3. A sequence diagram for Struts exception handling*

Using the Struts declarative exception-handling mechanism does not preclude you from also using a programmatic approach. In fact, they can work quite well together. Your Action classes will get the first opportunity to handle any specific exceptions and only if an exception is not caught and handled by the Action instance will it be caught by the processActionPerform() method in the RequestProcessor class. The RequestProcessor will then use the declarative exception-handling mechanism to process the error. The next section discusses how to handle exceptions using a programmatic approach.

## Using Programmatic Exception Handling

The alternate approach to the declarative exception handling provided by Struts is to build the application-specific exception handling into the code itself. This means that you will have to extend the framework with behavior specific to your application.

As mentioned earlier in this chapter, there are two basic courses of action when an exception is thrown within an Action class. If the exception is an application exception, the course of action is to log the exception, create and store an ActionError into the appropriate scope, and forward control to the appropriate ActionForward. Recall from the discussion of declarative exception handling that this is the same behavior that the Struts default exception handler performs.

In the case of the Storefront application, application exceptions would all be descendants of BaseException; it's easy to detect when an application exception occurs because you can simply use a catch block for BaseException. If the exception is not an instance of BaseException, you can assume that it's a system exception and should be treated as such. The course of action for system exceptions is normally to log the exception and return an ActionForward for the system error page.

At first, you might be tempted to add try/catch blocks in your Action classes and perform the exception handling like this:

```
try{

  // Peform some work that may cause an application or system exception

}catch( BaseException ex ){
  // Log the exception

  // Create and store the action error
  ActionErrors errors = new ActionErrors();
  ActionError newError = new ActionError( ex.getErrorCode(), ex.getArgs() );
  errors.add( ActionErrors.GLOBAL_ERROR, newError );
  saveErrors( request, errors );

  // Return an ActionForward for the Failure resource
  return mapping.findForward( "Failure" )

}catch( Throwable ex ){
  // Log the exception

  // Create and store the action error
  ActionError newError = new ActionError( "error.systemfailure" );
  ActionErrors errors = new ActionErrors();
  errors.add( ActionErrors.GLOBAL_ERROR, newError );
  saveErrors( request, errors );

  // Return an ActionForward for the system error resource
  return mapping.findForward( IConstants.SYSTEM_FAILURE_PAGE );
}
```

The problem with this approach is that you end up having the same redundant code inside almost every Action class. Eliminating this redundancy is one of the benefits of using the declarative approach. However, if you don't want to use the declarative approach, or if you can't because you're using an earlier version of Struts, there's an alternate approach that doesn't involve so much redundancy.

In Chapter 5, you saw how the use of an abstract base Action like the StorefrontBaseAction class can reduce the redundancy inside the Action classes for other issues. You can also push the programmatic exception-handling functionality up to the abstract class, so you don't need to have it in all of your Action classes. To do this, you will need to implement the additional executeAction() method. The executeAction() method is introduced by the StorefrontBaseAction class and is an implementation of the Template design pattern. Example 10-7 shows the execute() method of the StorefrontBaseAction class.

*Example 10-7. The execute() method of the StorefrontBaseAction*

```
public ActionForward execute(ActionMapping mapping,
                             ActionForm form,
                             HttpServletRequest request,
                             HttpServletResponse response)
    throws Exception {
  ActionForward forwardPage = null;
  try{
    UserContainer userContainer = getUserContainer( request );

    // Inform the specific action instance to do its thing
    forwardPage = executeAction(mapping, form, request, response, userContainer);
  }catch (BaseException ex){
    // Log the application exception using your logging framework
    // Call the generic exception handler routine
    forwardPage = processExceptions( request, mapping, ex );
  }catch (Throwable ex){
    // Log the system exception using your logging framework

    // Make the exception available to the system error page
    request.setAttribute( Action.EXCEPTION_KEY, ex );

    // Treat all other exceptions as system errors
    forwardPage = mapping.findForward( IConstants.SYSTEM_FAILURE_KEY );
  }
  return forwardPage;
}
```

The execute() method invokes the executeAction() method, which all Action subclasses must override, and wraps the invocation with the appropriate try/catch blocks.

The StorefrontBaseAction class is abstract and provides an abstract version of the executeAction() method, which is shown here:

```
abstract public ActionForward executeAction( ActionMapping mapping,
                             ActionForm form,
                             HttpServletRequest request,
                             HttpServletResponse response,
                             UserContainer userContainer )

    throws BaseException;
```

When any application exception occurs, as long as it extends StorefrontBaseAction, it will be caught in the try/catch block inside the execute() method. The subclasses don't have to worry about providing a catch block unless they plan to provide further specialized behavior for the exception.

The execute( ) method passes the exception, along with the request and mapping objects, to the processExceptions( ) method shown in Example 10-8.

*Example 10-8. The processExceptions( ) method in the StorefrontBaseAction*

```
protected ActionForward processExceptions( HttpServletRequest request,
                                           ActionMapping mapping,
                                           BaseException ex ){
  ActionErrors errors = new ActionErrors();
  ActionForward forward = null;

  // Get the locale for the user
  Locale locale = getUserContainer( request ).getLocale();
  if (locale == null){
    // If it hasn't been configured, get the default for the environment
    locale = Locale.getDefault();
  }

  processBaseException(errors, (FieldException) ex, locale);

  // Either return to the input resource or a configured failure forward
  String inputStr = mapping.getInput();
  String failureForward = mapping.findForward(IConstants.FAILURE_KEY);

  if ( inputStr != null) {
    forward = new ActionForward( inputStr );
  }else if (failureForward != null){
    forward = failureForward;
  }

  // See if this exception contains a list of subexceptions
  List exceptions = ex.getExceptions();
  if (exceptions != null && !exceptions.isEmpty() ){
    int size = exceptions.size();
    Iterator iter = exceptions.iterator();

    while( iter.hasNext() ){
      // All subexceptions must be BaseExceptions
      BaseException subException = (BaseException)iter.next();
      processBaseException(errors, subException, locale);
    }
  }

  // Tell the Struts framework to save the errors into the request
  saveErrors( request, errors );

  // Return the ActionForward
  return forward;
}
```

The processExceptions() method seems quite complex, but it's really not that bad. Here are the steps that the method performs:

1. Obtain the locale for the user.

2. Call the processBaseException() method to process the top-level exception.

3. If there are any subexceptions, process each one.

4. Save all of the ActionErrors that were created.

5. Return control back to either the resource identified in the input attribute of the action or a "Failure" ActionForward that has been configured for the action.

The processBaseException() method is where the ActionError objects are created. This method is shown in Example 10-9.

*Example 10-9. The processBaseException() method of the StorefrontBaseAction class*

```
protected void processBaseException( ActionErrors errors,
                                     BaseException ex,
                                     Locale locale) {

  // Holds the reference to the ActionError to be added
  ActionError newActionError = null;

  // The errorCode is the key to the resource bundle
  String errorCode = ex.getMessageKey();
  /**
   * If there are extra arguments to be used by the MessageFormat object,
   * insert them into the argList. The arguments are context sensitive
   * arguments for the exception; there may be 0 or more.
   */
  Object[] args = ex.getMessageArgs();

  /**
   * In an application that had to support I18N, you might want to
   * format each value in the argument array based on its type and the
   * user locale. For example, if there is a Date object in the array, it
   * would need to be formatted for each locale.
   */

  // Now construct an instance of the ActionError class
  if ( args != null && args.length > 0 ){
    // Use the arguments that were provided in the exception
    newActionError = new ActionError( errorCode, args );
  }else{
    newActionError = new ActionError( errorCode );
  }

  errors.add( ActionErrors.GLOBAL_ERROR, newActionError );
}
```

The processBaseException() method is responsible for creating the ActionError object. It uses the messageKey field to look up a bundle message, and if any arguments are included, it includes those in the ActionError constructor as well.

As you can see, adding programmatic exception handling to your applications definitely requires more work than using the default behavior provided by the Struts framework. It also makes maintenance more difficult if you drastically change your exception hierarchy or change how you want to handle certain exceptions. However, if you are using an earlier version of Struts, this may be your only choice. You may have to extend these examples for your own applications, but they show a well-designed approach that you can build upon.

Within the EJB and Servlet specifications, programmatic security is frowned upon because it's too easy to couple your application to the physical security environment. With exception handling, it's unlikely that you'll need to change the exceptions that are thrown based on the target environment. Therefore, there isn't the same stigma associated with programmatic exception handling as there is with programmatic security. It is true, though, that if you can take advantage of declarative exception handling, your application will be easier to maintain than if you have the same functionality in your source code. An application will almost always be modified over time, and new exceptions will need to be thrown and caught. The more you can specify declaratively, the easier time you'll have maintaining it.

# Tying Up the Loose Ends

Before we leave the topic of exception handling, there are several special cases that we should discuss. Each one of these is unique, and you may or may not need them in your applications.

## Handling Remote Exceptions

Remote Java objects are allowed to throw instances of java.rmi.RemoteException. In fact, every EJB method that is exposed to a remote client must declare that it throws RemoteException. Dealing with RemoteExceptions is very similar to handling system exceptions except that they are not descendants of either java.lang.Error or java.lang.RuntimeException.

Often, the application will not be able to recover from a RemoteException and will have to display the system error page. If you're using EJB and you get a RemoteException, you can attempt to recover by acquiring a new remote reference, but there's probably some type of programming or environment error that will prevent the end user from continuing. Whether you're using a programmatic or a declarative approach, you'll likely want to log the exception, create and store an ActionError object, and then forward to the system error page. You can also define the exception-handling behavior to forward the user back to the previous page and give her the choice of trying again. If some type of network blip caused the remote exception, it may be possible for the user to continue to use the application.

# Exceptions in Custom Tags

JSP custom tags usually throw JSPException objects or one of their descendants. Prior to the JavaServer Pages 1.2 specification, the JSPException class didn't support exception chaining, and because Struts was introduced before the 1.2 specification, several places inside the Struts custom tag libraries still disregard the original exception when a JSPException is created.

However, the Struts tags do usually store the exception in the request scope under the key Globals.EXCEPTION_KEY, which maps to a literal string of org.apache.struts. action.Action.EXCEPTION. If you need to get access to the root cause, you can probably use this key to retrieve the exception object.

Version 1.2 of the JSP specification modified the JSPException to support exception chaining; however, the Struts developers will probably choose to leave the current tags alone for backward compatibility and will take advantage of this new functionality only for future tags. However, in the custom tags that you create, you should use the rootCause field in the JSPException class when you rethrow exceptions as different types.

## The TryCatchFinally interface

The JSP 1.2 specification also introduced a new interface called TryCatchFinally. This interface, which is referred to as a "mix-in" interface, can be implemented by a tag handler in addition to one of the other tag interfaces.

The TryCatchFinally interface provides two methods:

```
public void doCatch(Throwable);
public void doFinally();
```

The container calls the doCatch() method if the tag body or one of the doStartEnd(), doEndTag(), doInitBody(), or doAfterBody() methods throws a Throwable. The doCatch() method can rethrow the same or a different exception after handling the error.

The container calls the doFinally() method after the doEndTag() or after the doCatch() method when an exception condition occurs.

The TryCatchFinally interface allows for better exception handling in custom tags. It is very important to allow limited resources that are being used by custom tags to be released. Without this interface, there's no guarantee that the container will provide the tag with an opportunity to release the resources being used by the tags.

## Internationalized Exception Handling

Chapter 12 covers internationalization in detail, but it's relevant to say a few words here about how exception handling and internationalization are connected. While throwing exceptions in Java, developers often do something like the following:

```
// Detect some problem and throw an exception
throw new InvalidLoginException( "An exception has occurred." );
```

The problem with hardcoding the string into the exception is that it's useful only for developers from the same locale. It might be difficult for developers or system administrators from different locales to use the log files where these exceptions are logged. Instead of hardcoding the messages for the exceptions, it may be better to get the message from a resource bundle. Obviously, exceptions that are thrown from third-party packages are not within your control, just as stack traces are hard to localize. Many organizations don't worry about localizing the exception messages, which is fine as long as no one from locales other than your own will ever need to use the information.

# Conclusion

The new declarative exception handling is a great addition to the Struts framework and one that should certainly save developers time, during both initial development and maintenance. Whenever possible, you should make a serious effort to take advantage of the declarative exception-handling features rather than attempting to write your own. The good news remains, however, that if you do need to create your own customized exception handling, the freedom and flexibility for you to do so exists in the framework.

# CHAPTER 11

# The Validator Framework

The Struts framework allows input validation to occur inside the `ActionForm`. To perform validation on data passed to a Struts application, developers must code special validation logic inside each `ActionForm` class. Although this approach works, it has some serious limitations. This chapter introduces David Winterfeldt's Validator framework, which was created specifically to work with the Struts components and to help overcome some of these limitations.

The Validator allows you to declaratively configure validation routines for a Struts application without programming special validation logic. The Validator has become so popular and widely used by Struts developers that it has been added to the list of Jakarta projects and to the main Struts distribution.

## The Need for a Validation Framework

Chapter 7 discussed how to provide validation logic inside the `ActionForm` class. The solution presented there requires you to write a separate piece of validation logic for each property that you need to validate. If an error is detected, you have to manually create an `ActionError` object and add it to the `ActionErrors` collection. Although this solution works, there are a few problems with the approach.

The first problem is that coding validation logic within each `ActionForm` places redundant validation logic throughout your application. Within a single web application, the type of validation that needs to occur across HTML forms is very similar. The need to validate required fields, dates, times, and numbers, for example, typically occurs in many places throughout an application. Most nontrivial applications have multiple HTML forms that accept user input that must be validated. Even if you use a single `ActionForm` for your entire application, you might still end up duplicating the validation logic for the various properties.

The second major problem is one of maintenance. If you need to modify or enhance the validation that occurs for an ActionForm, the source code must be recompiled. This makes it very difficult to configure an application.

The Validator framework allows you to move all the validation logic completely outside of the ActionForm and declaratively configure it for an application through external XML files. No validation logic is necessary in the ActionForm, which makes your application easier to develop and maintain. The other great benefit of the Validator is that it's very extensible. It provides many standard validation routines out of the box, but if you require additional validation rules, the framework is easy to extend and provides the ability to plug in your own rules (again without needing to modify your application).

# Installing and Configuring the Validator

The Validator framework is now part of the Jakarta Commons project. It's included with the Struts main distribution, but you can also get the latest version from the Commons download page at *http://jakarta.apache.org/commons/*. Unless you need the source code or the absolute latest version, you'll find all the necessary files included with the Struts 1.1 distribution.

## Required Packages

The Validator depends on several other packages to function properly, and the most important of these is the Jakarta ORO package. The ORO package contains functionality for regular expressions, performing substitutions, and text splitting, among other utilities. The libraries were originally developed by ORO, Inc. and donated to the Apache Software Foundation. Earlier versions of the Validator framework depended on a different regular expression package, called Regexp, which is also a Jakarta project. However, ORO was considered the more complete of the two, and the Validator that is included with Struts 1.1 now depends on the ORO package.

Other packages required by the Validator are Commons BeansUtils, Commons Logging, Commons Collections, and Digester. All of the dependent packages for the Validator are included in the Struts 1.1 download. The *commons-validator.jar* and *jakarta-oro.jar* files need to be placed into the *WEB-INF/lib* directory for your web application. The other dependent JAR files must also be present, but they should already be there due to Struts framework requirements.

## Configuring the Validation Rules

As mentioned earlier, the Validator framework allows the validation rules for an application to be declaratively configured. This means that they are specified externally to the application source. There are two important configuration files for the Validator framework: *validation-rules.xml* and *validation.xml*.

## The validation-rules.xml file

The *validation-rules.xml* configuration file contains a global set of validation rules that can be used out of the box by your application. This file is application-neutral and can be used by any Struts application. You should need to modify this file only if you plan to modify or extend the default set of rules.

 If you do need to extend the default rules, you might be better off putting your custom rules in a different XML file, so as to keep them separate from the default ones. This will help when it comes time to upgrade to a newer version of the Validator framework.

The *validator-rules_1_1.dtd* describes the syntax of the *validation-rules.xml* file. The root element is the form-validation element, which requires one or more global elements:

```
<!ELEMENT form-validation (global+)>
<!ELEMENT global (validator+)>
```

Each validator element describes one unique validation rule. The following fragment from the *validation-rules.xml* file is the definition for the required validation rule:

```
<validator
  name="required"
  classname="org.apache.struts.util.StrutsValidator"
  method="validateRequired"
  methodParams="java.lang.Object,
    org.apache.commons.validator.ValidatorAction,
    org.apache.commons.validator.Field,
    org.apache.struts.action.ActionErrors,
    javax.servlet.http.HttpServletRequest"
  msg="errors.required">
</validator>
```

 The validator element also allows a javascript subelement, but for the sake of brevity it is not shown here. The JavaScript support in the Validator framework is discussed later in the chapter.

The validator element supports seven attributes, as shown here:

```
<!ATTLIST validator name          CDATA #REQUIRED
                    classname     CDATA #REQUIRED
                    method        CDATA #REQUIRED
                    methodParams  CDATA #REQUIRED
                    msg           CDATA #REQUIRED
                    depends       CDATA #IMPLIED
                    jsFunctionName CDATA #IMPLIED>
```

The name attribute assigns a logical name to the validation rule. It is used to reference the rule from other rules within this file and from the application-specific validation file discussed in the next section. The name must be unique.

The classname and method attributes define the class and method that contain the logic for the validation rule. For example, as shown in the earlier code fragment, the validateRequired() method in the StrutsValidator class will be invoked for the required validation rule. The methodParams attribute is a comma-delimited list of parameters for the method defined in the method attribute.

The msg attribute is a key from the resource bundle. The Validator framework uses this value to look up a message from the Struts resource bundle when a validation error occurs. By default, the Validator framework uses the following values:

```
errors.required={0} is required.
errors.minlength={0} cannot be less than {1} characters.
errors.maxlength={0} cannot be greater than {1} characters.
errors.invalid={0} is invalid.
errors.byte={0} must be a byte.
errors.short={0} must be a short.
errors.integer={0} must be an integer.
errors.long={0} must be a long.
errors.float={0} must be a float.
errors.double={0} must be a double.
errors.date={0} is not a date.
errors.range={0} is not in the range {1} through {2}.
errors.creditcard={0} is not a valid credit card number.
errors.email={0} is an invalid email address
```

You should add these to your application's resource bundle, or change the key values in the *validation-rules.xml* file if you plan to use alternate messages.

The depends attribute is used to specify other validation rules that should be called before the rule specifying it. The depends attribute is illustrated in the minLength validation rule here:

```
<validator
  name="minLength"
  classname="org.apache.struts.util.StrutsValidator"
  method="validateMinLength"
  methodParams="java.lang.Object,
    org.apache.commons.validator.ValidatorAction,
    org.apache.commons.validator.Field,
    org.apache.struts.action.ActionErrors,
    javax.servlet.http.HttpServletRequest"
  depends="required"
  msg="errors.minlength">
</validator>
```

Before the minLength validation rule is called, the required rule will be invoked. You can also set up a rule to depend on multiple rules by separating the rules in the depends attribute with a comma:

```
depends="required,integer"
```

If a rule that is specified in the depends attribute fails validation, the next rule will not be called. For example, in the minLength validation rule shown previously, the validateMinLength( ) method will not be invoked if the required validation rule fails. This should stand to reason, because there's no sense in checking the length of a value if no value is present.

> The final attribute supported by the validator element is the jsFunctionName attribute. This optional attribute allows you to specify the name of the JavaScript function. By default, the Validator action name is used.

The Validator framework is fairly generic. It contains very basic, atomic rules that can be used by any application. As you'll see later in this chapter, it's this generic quality that allows it to be used with non-Struts applications as well. The org. apache.commons.Validator.GenericValidator class implements the generic rules as a set of public static methods. Table 11-1 lists the set of validation rules available in the GenericValidator class.

*Table 11-1. Validation rules in the GenericValidator class*

| Method name | Description |
| --- | --- |
| isBlankOrNull | Checks if the field isn't null and the length of the field is greater than zero, not including whitespace. |
| isByte | Checks if the value can safely be converted to a byte primitive. |
| isCreditCard | Checks if the field is a valid credit card number. |
| isDate | Checks if the field is a valid date. |
| isDouble | Checks if the value can safely be converted to a double primitive. |
| isEmail | Checks if the field is a valid email address. |
| isFloat | Checks if the value can safely be converted to a float primitive. |
| isInRange | Checks if the value is within a minimum and maximum range. |
| isInt | Checks if the value can safely be converted to an int primitive. |
| isLong | Checks if the value can safely be converted to a long primitive. |
| isShort | Checks if the value can safely be converted to a short primitive. |
| matchRegex p | Checks if the value matches the regular expression. |
| maxLength | Checks if the value's length is less than or equal to the maximum. |
| minLength | Checks if the value's length is greater than or equal to the minimum. |

Because the validation rules in the GenericValidator are so fine-grained, the Struts developers added a utility class to the Struts framework called org.apache.struts. util.StrutsValidator, which defines a set of higher-level methods that are coupled to the Struts framework but make it easier to use the Validator with Struts. They are listed here without descriptions because the names are similar enough to the ones from Table 11-1 to indicate their functionality.

- validateByte
- validateCreditCard
- validateDate

- validateDouble
- validateEmail
- validateFloat
- validateInteger
- validateLong
- validateMask
- validateMinLength
- validateMaxLength
- validateRange
- validateRequired
- validateShort

The `StrutsValidator` class contains the concrete validation logic used by Struts. This class and the methods listed above are declaratively configured in the *validation-rules.xml* file. When one of these methods is invoked and the validation fails, an `ActionError` is automatically created and added to the `ActionErrors` object. These errors are stored in the request and made available to the view components.

## The validation.xml file

The second configuration file that is required by the Validator framework is the *validation.xml* file. This file is application-specific; it describes which validation rules from the *validation-rules.xml* file are used by a particular `ActionForm`. This is what is meant by declaratively configured—you don't have to put code inside of the `ActionForm` class. The validation logic is associated with one or more `ActionForm` classes through this external file.

The *validation.xml* file is governed by the *validation_1_1.dtd*. The outermost element is the form-validation element, which can contain two child elements, global and formset. The global element can be present zero or more times, while the formset element can be present one or more times:

```
<!ELEMENT form-validation (global*, formset+)>
```

The global element allows you to configure constant elements that can be used throughout the rest of the file:

```
<!ELEMENT global (constant*)>
```

This is analogous to how you might define a constant in a Java file and then use it throughout the class. The following fragment shows a global fragment that defines two constants:

```
<global>
 <constant>
  <constant-name>phone</constant-name>
```

```
    <constant-value>^\(?(\d{3})\)?[-| ]?(\d{3})[-| ]?(\d{4})$</constant-value>
  </constant>
  <constant>
    <constant-name>zip</constant-name>
    <constant-value>^\d{5}(-\d{4})?$</constant-value>
  </constant>
</global>
```

This fragment includes two constants, phone and zip, although you can include as many as you need. These constants are available to the elements within the formset section. You can reuse them many times within the formset simply by referring to them by name.

This is best illustrated with an example. Example 11-1 shows a simple *validation.xml* file.

*Example 11-1. A simple validation.xml file*

```
<form-validation>
 <global>
  <constant>
   <constant-name>phone</constant-name>
   <constant-value>^\(?(\d{3})\)?[-| ]?(\d{3})[-| ]?(\d{4})$</constant-value>
  </constant>
 </global>
 <formset>
  <form name="checkoutForm">
   <field
    property="phone"
    depends="required,mask">
    <arg0 key="registrationForm.firstname.displayname"/>
    <var>
     <var-name>mask</var-name>
     <var-value>${phone}</var-value>
    </var>
   </field>
  </form>
 </formset>
</form-validation>
```

In Example 11-1, the phone constant that's declared in the global section is used in the var element to help validate the phone property.

The formset element can contain two child elements, constant and form. The constant element has the same format as the one in the global section. It can be present zero or more times. The form element can be present one or more times within the formset element:

```
<!ELEMENT formset (constant*, form+)>
```

The formset element supports two attributes that deal with I18N, language and country:

```
<!ATTLIST formset language CDATA #IMPLIED
                  country  CDATA #IMPLIED>
```

If you don't have any I18N requirements for your validation routines and want to use the default locale, you can leave out these attributes. The section "Internationalizing the Validation" later in this chapter discusses this topic in more detail.

The `form` element defines a set of fields to be validated. The `name` corresponds to the identifier the application assigns to the form. In the case of the Struts framework, this is the `name` attribute from the `form-beans` section.

The `form` element defines a set of fields that are to be validated. It contains a single attribute `name`, which should match one of the `name` attributes from the `form-beans` section of the Struts configuration file.

The `form` element can contain one or more `field` elements:

```
<!ELEMENT form (field+)>
```

The `field` element corresponds to a specific property of a JavaBean that needs to be validated. In a Struts application, this JavaBean is an `ActionForm`. In Example 11-1, the sole `field` element for the `checkoutForm` corresponds to the phone property in an `ActionForm` called `checkoutForm` in the `form-beans` section of the Struts configuration file. The `field` element supports several attributes, which are listed in Table 11-2.

Table 11-2. The attributes of the field element

| Attribute | Description |
| --- | --- |
| property | The property name of the JavaBean (or `ActionForm`) to be validated. |
| depends | The comma-delimited list of validation rules to apply against this field. For the field to succeed, all the validators must succeed. |
| page | The JavaBean corresponding to this form may include a page property. Only fields with a page attribute value that is equal to or less than the value of the page property on the form JavaBean are processed. This is useful when using a "wizard" approach to completing a large form, to ensure that a page is not skipped. |
| indexedListProperty | The method name that will return an array or a `Collection` used to retrieve the list and then loop through the list, performing the validations for this field. |

Both the `ValidatorActionForm` and `DynaValidatorActionForm` match on the action mapping rather than the form name. That is, instead of matching on the form name in the `name` attribute of the `form` element, you can use the `path` attribute of the `action` element. This allows the same form to be used for different action mappings, where each action mapping may depend on only certain form fields to be validated and the others to be left alone.

The `field` element contains several child elements:

```
<!ELEMENT field (msg?, arg0?, arg1?, arg2?, arg3?, var*)>
```

The `msg` child element allows you to specify an alternate message for a `field` element. The validation rule can use this value instead of the default message declared with the rule. The value for the msg element must be a key from the application resource bundle. For example:

```
<field property="phone" depends="required,mask">
  <msg name="mask" key="phone.invalidformat"/>
  <arg0 key="registrationForm.firstname.displayname"/>
  <var>
    <var-name>mask</var-name>
    <var-value>${phone}</var-value>
  </var>
</field>
```

The msg element supports three attributes:

```
<!ATTLIST msg name      CDATA #IMPLIED
              key       CDATA #IMPLIED
              resource CDATA #IMPLIED >
```

The name attribute specifies the rule with which the msg should be used. The value should be one of the rules specified in the *validation-rules.xml* file or in the global section.

The key attribute specifies a key from the resource bundle that should be added to the ActionError if validation fails. If you want to specify a literal message, rather than using the resource bundle, you can set the resource attribute to false. In this case, the key attribute is taken as a literal string.

The field element allows up to four additional elements to be included. These elements, named arg0, arg1, arg2, and arg3, are used to pass additional values to the message, either from the resource bundle or from the var or constant elements. The arg0 element defines the first replacement value, arg1 defines the second replacement value, and so on. Each arg element supports three attributes, name, key, and resource, which are the same as the attributes of the msg element described earlier.

Example 11-1 included elements for arg0 and arg1 like this:

```
<field property="phone" depends="required,mask,minLength">
  <arg0 key="registrationForm.firstname.displayname"/>
  <arg1 name="minlength" key="${var:minLength}" resource="false"/>
  <var>
    <var-name>mask</var-name>
    <var-value>${phone}</var-value>
  </var>
  <var>
    <var-name>minLength</var-name>
    <var-value>5</var-value>
  </var>
</field>
```

The last of the field child elements is the var element, as seen in Example 11-1 and in the previous fragment. The var element can set parameters that a field element may need to pass to one of its validation rules, such as the minimum and maximum values in a range validation. These parameters may also be referenced by one of the arg elements using a shell syntax: ${var:var-name}.

In Example 11-1, the substituted value for the phone constant is passed into the mask validation rule so that it can be used to check whether the property value conforms to the proper phone mask. The field element can have zero or more var elements.

Once you have the two XML resource files configured for your application, you need to place them in the *WEB-INF* directory. They will be referenced within the Struts configuration file, as described in the next section.

## Plugging in the Validator

Each Struts application needs to know that the Validator framework is being employed. As discussed in Chapter 9, you can use the PlugIn mechanism to hook the Validator framework into a Struts application.

Earlier versions of the Validator used an extra servlet to inform the Struts application that the Validator components were present. The ValidatorServlet has been deprecated and should not be used.

The following fragment illustrates how to set up the Validator as a plug-in:

```
<plug-in className="org.apache.struts.validator.ValidatorPlugIn">
  <set-property
    property="pathnames"
    value="/WEB-INF/validator-rules.xml,/WEB-INF/validator.xml"/>
</plug-in>
```

There was some confusion in one of the earlier beta releases for the Validator that used multiple set-property elements. That is no longer supported—you should use a single set-property element that specifies multiple Validator resource files, separated by commas. Also notice that the property value is the plural pathnames.

The Struts framework will call the init( ) method in the ValidatorPlugIn class when the application starts up. During this method, the Validator resources from the XML files are loaded into memory so that they will be available to the application. Before calling the init( ) method, however, the pathnames property value is passed to the ValidatorPlugIn instance. This is how the ValidatorPlugIn finds out which Validator resources to load. For more information on how the PlugIn mechanism works, see "Using the PlugIn Mechanism" in Chapter 9.

## Using an ActionForm with the Validator

You can't use the standard Struts ActionForm class with the Validator. Instead, you need to use a subclass of the ActionForm class that is specifically designed to work with the Validator framework. There are two root subclasses to select from, depending on whether you are planning to use dynamic ActionForms. Figure 11-1 shows the ActionForm and its descendants, to help you visualize the hierarchy.

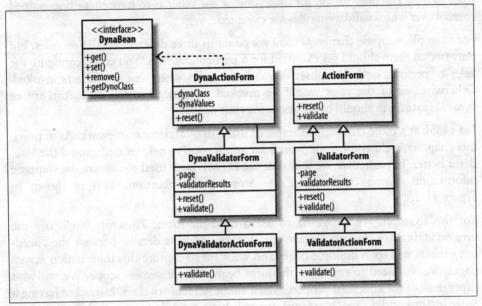

Figure 11-1. The ActionForm class hierarchy

If you are using dynamic ActionForms, you should use the DynaValidatorForm branch of the hierarchy. If you are using standard ActionForms, you can use the ValidatorForm or one of its descendants instead.

 Whether you use dynamic or regular ActionForms, the manner in which you configure the Validator is the same. Just be sure that whichever ActionForm subclass you choose, you configure the form-bean section of the Struts configuration file using the fully qualified class name. See "The form-beans element" in Chapter 4 for more details.

Dynamic or standard is only the first decision that you have to make when choosing the proper ActionForm subclass. Notice that in both the dynamic and standard branch of the ActionForm hierarchy in Figure 11-1, there are two versions of ValidatorForm. The parent class is called ValidatorForm, or DynaValidatorForm for the dynamic branch.

Each of these has a subclass that contains the name Action in its title. The subclass of the ValidatorForm is called ValidatorActionForm, and the subclass of the DynaValidatorForm is called DynaValidatorActionForm. The purpose of the two different versions is to allow you to associate the validation with the form-bean definition or the action definition. The ValidatorActionForm and DynaValidatorActionForm classes pass the path attribute from the action element into the Validator, and the Validator uses the action's name to look up the validation rules. If you use the ValidatorForm or DynaValidatorForm, the name of the ActionForm is used to look up the set of validation rules to use. The only reason for using one or the other is to have more fine-grained control over which validation rules are executed.

For example, suppose that an ActionForm contains three different validation rules, but only two of them should get executed for a particular action. You could configure the rules to perform only the subset of validation rules when that action gets invoked. Otherwise, all of the rules would be invoked. In general, using ValidatorForm or DynaValidatorForm should be sufficient for your needs.

Let's look at a more complete example of using the Validator framework. As in previous chapters, we'll employ the Storefront application to help us understand the Validator better. In particular, we'll look at the HTML form used to capture the shipping information during checkout of the Storefront application. This is shown in Figure 11-2.

For this example, we are going to use a dynamic form. Therefore, we'll use the DynaValidatorForm class to capture the shipping address details. Because the checkout process will span multiple pages and we want to capture this information across pages, we will need to configure the form bean to have session scope. We will also capture all of the checkout properties in a single ActionForm class. Instead of having a ShippingForm and a CreditCardForm, we will have a single form called CheckoutForm that captures all of the information.

In our Struts configuration file, we set up the checkoutForm as shown here:

```
<form-bean
  name="checkoutForm"
  type="org.apache.struts.validator.DynaValidatorForm">
  <form-property name="firstName" type="java.lang.String"/>
  <form-property name="lastName" type="java.lang.String"/>
  <form-property name="address" type="java.lang.String"/>
  <form-property name="city" type="java.lang.String"/>
  <form-property name="state" type="java.lang.String"/>
  <form-property name="postalCode" type="java.lang.String"/>
  <form-property name="country" type="java.lang.String"/>
  <form-property name="phone" type="java.lang.String"/>
</form-bean>
```

The type attribute specifies the exact ActionForm subclass.

 In early beta releases of Struts 1.1, the form-bean section required that you set the dynamic attribute to true when using dynamic ActionForms. This is no longer necessary, as the framework will determine whether the class specified in the type attribute is a descendant of the DynaActionForm class.

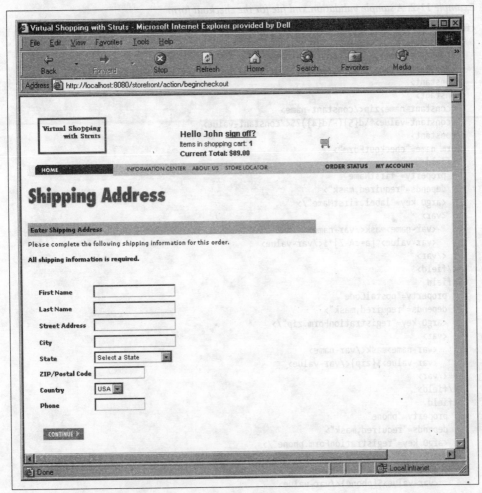

*Figure 11-2. Capturing the shipping address information*

The next step is to edit the application-specific validation logic, which is done in the *validation.xml* file. You must declare a validation rule for each property in the form that you need to validate. In some cases, you might need to specify multiple rules. In Figure 11-2, for example, the phone field is required, and it must fit a specific format. These are two separate rules that both must evaluate to true, or the validation for the form will fail. The entire *validation.xml* file is not shown because it's too large and most of it is redundant. The section shown in Example 11-2 will help you understand how things are connected.

*Example 11-2. A sample validation.xml file for the checkout form*

```xml
<formset>
  <constant>
    <constant-name>phone</constant-name>
    <constant-value>^\(?(\d{3})\)?[-| ]?(\d{3})[-| ]?(\d{4})$</constant-value>
  </constant>
  <constant>
    <constant-name>zip</constant-name>
    <constant-value>^\d{5}(-\d{4})?$</constant-value>
  </constant>
  <form name="checkoutForm">
    <field
      property="firstName"
      depends="required,mask">
      <arg0 key="label.firstName"/>
      <var>
        <var-name>mask</var-name>
        <var-value>^[a-zA-Z]*$</var-value>
      </var>
    </field>
    <field
      property="postalCode"
      depends="required,mask">
      <arg0 key="registrationForm.zip"/>
      <var>
        <var-name>mask</var-name>
        <var-value>${zip}</var-value>
      </var>
    </field>
    <field
      property="phone"
      depends="required,mask">
      <arg0 key="registrationForm.phone"/>
      <var>
        <var-name>mask</var-name>
        <var-value>${phone}</var-value>
      </var>
    </field>
  </form>
</formset>
</form-validation>
```

Now that we have everything configured for the Storefront, it's time to run the example. The nice thing about using a declarative approach versus a programmatic one is that once you have everything configured, you're ready to go. The absence of programming makes the declarative approach much simpler. This is especially true for the Validator framework. There's nothing to code, as long as the default validation rules satisfy your requirements.

When we submit the shipping address page with no information in the fields, the validation rules kick in. The result is shown in Figure 11-3.

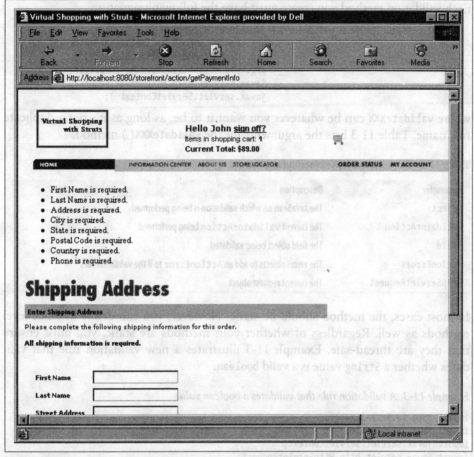

*Figure 11-3. The shipping address page using the Validator framework*

# Creating Your Own Validation Rules

The Validator framework is preconfigured with many of the most common rules that you're likely to need for your Struts applications. If your application has validation requirements that are not met by the default rules, you have complete freedom to create your own. There are several steps that you must follow, however, to create your own customized rules:

1. Create a Java class that contains the validation methods.
2. Edit the *validation-rules.xml* file or create your own version. If you do create a new validation resource file, be sure to add it to the list of resource files in the Validator plug-in.
3. Use the new validation rules in the *validation.xml* file for your application.

Each validation method you create must have the following signature:

```
public static boolean validateXXX( java.lang.Object,
                                   org.apache.commons.validator.ValidatorAction,
                                   org.apache.commons.validator.Field,
                                   org.apache.struts.action.ActionErrors,
                                   javax.servlet.http.HttpServletRequest,
                                   javax.servlet.ServletContext );
```

where validateXXX can be whatever you want it to be, as long as it's not a duplicate rule name. Table 11-3 lists the arguments for the validateXXX( ) method.

*Table 11-3. The validateXXX( ) method arguments*

| Parameter | Description |
| --- | --- |
| Object | The JavaBean on which validation is being performed |
| ValidatorAction | The current ValidatorAction being performed |
| Field | The field object being validated |
| ActionErrors | The errors objects to add an ActionError to if the validation fails |
| HttpServletRequest | The current request object |

In most cases, the method should be static. However, you can define instance-level methods as well. Regardless of whether your methods are static, you must ensure that they are thread-safe. Example 11-3 illustrates a new validation rule that validates whether a String value is a valid boolean.

*Example 11-3. A validation rule that validates a boolean value*

```
import java.io.Serializable;
import java.util.Locale;
import javax.servlet.ServletContext;
import javax.servlet.http.HttpServletRequest;
import org.apache.commons.validator.Field;
import org.apache.commons.validator.GenericTypeValidator;
import org.apache.commons.validator.GenericValidator;
import org.apache.commons.validator.ValidatorAction;
import org.apache.commons.validator.ValidatorUtil;
import org.apache.struts.action.ActionErrors;
import org.apache.struts.util.StrutsValidatorUtil;

public class NewValidator implements Serializable {
    /**
     * A validate routine that ensures the value is either true or false.
     */
    public static boolean validateBoolean( Object bean, ValidatorAction va,
        Field field, ActionErrors errors, HttpServletRequest request ) {

        String value = null;
        // The boolean value is stored as a String
```

```
   if (field.getProperty() != null && field.getProperty().length() > 0){
     value = ValidatorUtil.getValueAsString(bean, field.getProperty() );
   }


   Boolean result = Boolean.valueOf(value);
   if ( result == null ){
     errors.add( field.getKey(),
               StrutsValidatorUtil.getActionError(request, va, field));
   }

   // Return true if the value was successfully converted, false otherwise
   return (errors.empty());
  }
}
```

The next step is to add this new rule to the *validation-rules.xml* file, or to a new file
to keep your customized rules separate. The validator element for the vali-
dateBoolean rule should look something like:

```
<validator name="boolean"
   classname="NewValidator"
   method="validateBoolean"
   methodParams="java.lang.Object,
     org.apache.commons.validator.ValidatorAction,
     org.apache.commons.validator.Field,
     org.apache.struts.action.ActionErrors,
     javax.servlet.http.HttpServletRequest"
   msg="errors.boolean">
```

The final step is to use the new validation rule in the *validation.xml* file. This involves
creating a field element that matches a boolean property on an ActionForm:

```
<field property="sendEmailConfirmation" depends="boolean">
   <arg0 key="label.emailconfirmation"/>
</field>
```

# The Validator and JSP Custom Tags

Several JSP custom tags included within the Struts tag libraries can be used with the
Validator framework. One of the tags is used to generate dynamic JavaScript based
on the validation rules. The other tags are part of the core Struts framework and are
used both with and without the Validator.

The tags listed in Table 11-4 are generic and can be used with or without the Validator framework, but they all come in handy when using it.

*Table 11-4. JSP custom tags that can be used with the Validator*

| Tag name | Description |
|---|---|
| Errors | Displays any validation errors found during processing |
| ErrorsExist | Determines if there were any validation errors |
| Messages | Displays any messages found during processing |
| MessagesExist | Determines if there were any messages during processing |

The tags in Table 11-4 allow JSP pages to detect and obtain access to messages or errors that were detected in the Struts application. These tags were discussed in more detail in Chapter 8.

# Using JavaScript with the Validator

The Validator framework is also capable of generating JavaScript for your Struts application using the same framework as for server-side validation. This is accomplished by using a set of JSP custom tags designed specifically for this purpose.

### Configuring the validation-rules.xml file for JavaScript

The Validator custom tag called JavascriptValidator is used to generate client-side validation based on a javascript attribute being present within the validator element. Before the JSP custom tag can be used, there must be a javascript element for the validation rule. The following code fragment illustrates the required validation rule that includes a javascript element:

```
<validator
  name="required"
  classname="org.apache.struts.util.StrutsValidator"
  method="validateRequired"
  methodParams="java.lang.Object,
    org.apache.commons.validator.ValidatorAction,
    org.apache.commons.validator.Field,
    org.apache.struts.action.ActionErrors,
    javax.servlet.http.HttpServletRequest"
  msg="errors.required">
<javascript><![CDATA[
  function validateRequired(form) {
    var bValid = true;
    var focusField = null;
    var i = 0;
    var fields = new Array();
    oRequired = new required();

    for (x in oRequired) {
      if ((form[oRequired[x][0]].type == 'text' ||
          form[oRequired[x][0]].type ==   'textarea' ||
          form[oRequired[x][0]].type == 'select-one' ||
          form[oRequired[x][0]].type == 'radio' ||
```

```
        form[oRequired[x][0]].type == 'password') &&
        form[oRequired[x][0]].value == '') {
         if (i == 0)
           focusField = form[oRequired[x][0]];
           fields[i++] = oRequired[x][1];
         bValid = false;
        }
       }

      if (fields.length > 0) {
        focusField.focus();
        alert(fields.join('\n'));
      }
      return bValid;
    }]]>
   </javascript>
  </validator>
```

When the `JavascriptValidator` tag is included in the JSP page, the text from the javascript element is written to the JSP page to provide client-side validation. When the user submits the form, the client-side validation is executed, and any validation rules that fail present messages to the user.

You will need to include the javascript tag with the name of the `ActionForm` that it's going to validate against:

```
<html:javascript formName="checkoutForm"/>
```

The `formName` attribute is used to look up the set of validation rules to include as JavaScript in the page. You will have to add an onsubmit event handler for the form manually:

```
<html:form action="getPaymentInfo" onsubmit="return validateCheckoutForm(this);">
```

When the form is submitted, the `validateCheckoutForm()` JavaScript function will be invoked. The validation rules will be executed, and if one or more rules fail, the form will not be submitted. The javascript tag generates a function with the name `validateXXX()`, where XXX is the name of the `ActionForm`. Thus, if your `ActionForm` is called `checkoutForm`, the javascript tag will create a JavaScript function called `validateCheckoutForm()` that executes the validation logic. This is why the `onsubmit()` event handler called the `validateCheckoutForm()` function.

 By default, the `JavascriptValidator` tag generates both static and dynamic JavaScript functions. If you would like to include a separate file that contains static JavaScript functions to take advantage of browser caching or to better organize your application, you can use the `dynamicJavascript` and `staticJavascript` attributes. By default, both of these are set to true. You can set the `staticJavascript` attribute to false in your form and include a separate JavaScript page with the `dynamicJavascript` attribute set to false and the `staticJavascript` attribute set to true. See the documentation for the `JavascriptValidator` tag for more information.

# Internationalizing the Validation

The Validator framework uses the application resource bundles to generate error messages for both client-side and server-side validation. Thus, from an I18N perspective, much of the work for displaying language-specific messages to the user is included within the framework.

It was mentioned earlier that the formset element in the *validation.xml* file supports attributes related to internationalization. Those attributes are language, country, and variant. As you know, these attributes correspond to the java.util.Locale class. If you don't specify these attributes, the default Locale is used.

If your application has I18N validation requirements, you will need to create separate formset elements, one for each Locale that you need to support for each form that you need to validate. For example, if your application has to support validation for a form called registrationForm for both the default locale and the French locale, the *validation.xml* file should contain two formset elements—one for the default locale and the other for the French locale. This is shown in the following fragment:

```
<formset>
  <form name="registrationForm">
    <field
      property="firstName"
      depends="required,mask,minLength">
      <arg0 key="registrationForm.firstname.displayname"/>
      <var>
        <var-name>mask</var-name>
        <var-value>^\w+$</var-value>
      </var>
      <var>
        <var-name>minLength</var-name>
        <var-value>5</var-value>
      </var>
    </field>
  </form>
</formset>
<formset language="fr">
  <form name="registrationForm">
    <field
      property="firstName"
      depends="required,mask,minLength">
      <arg0 key="registrationForm.firstname.displayname"/>
      <var>
        <var-name>mask</var-name>
        <var-value>^\w+$</var-value>
      </var>
    </field>
  </form>
</formset>
```

# Using the Validator Outside of Struts

Although the Validator was originally designed to work with the Struts framework, it can be used to perform generic validation on any JavaBean. There are several steps that must be performed before the framework can be used outside of Struts.

Although the Validator is not dependent on the Struts framework, a considerable amount of work has been done inside of Struts to make it easier to use the Validator. This behavior will need to be replicated for your application if you plan to use the Validator without Struts.

The package dependencies are exactly the same for Struts and non-Struts applications. The ORO, Commons Logging, Commons BeanUtils, Commons Collections, and Digester packages are all required. You will also need an XML parser that conforms to the SAX 2.0 specification. You will not need to include the Struts framework, however.

Functions for loading and initializing the XML Validator resources are the first behaviors to replicate. These are the two XML files that are used to configure the rules for the Validator. When the Validator framework is used in conjunction with Struts, the org.apache.struts.Validator.ValidatorPlugIn class performs this duty. However, because the ValidatorPlugIn is dependent on Struts, you will need to create an alternate approach for initializing the appropriate Validator resources. To do this, you can create a simple Java class that performs the same behavior as the ValidatorPlugIn but doesn't have a dependency on the Struts framework. A simple example is provided in Example 11-4.

*Example 11-4. Using the Validator outside of Struts*

```java
import java.util.*;
import java.io.*;
import org.apache.commons.validator.ValidatorResources;
import org.apache.commons.validator.ValidatorResourcesInitializer;

public class ValidatorLoader{

  private final static String RESOURCE_DELIM = ",";
  protected ValidatorResources resources = null;
  private String pathnames = null;

  public ValidatorLoader() throws IOException {
    loadPathnames();
    initResources();
  }

  public ValidatorResources getResources(){
    return resources;
  }
}
```

*Example 11-4. Using the Validator outside of Struts (continued)*

```java
  public String getPathnames() {
    return pathnames;
  }

  public void setPathnames(String pathnames) {
    this.pathnames = pathnames;
  }

  protected void loadPathnames(){
    // Set a default just in case
    String paths = "validation-rules.xml,validation.xml";
    InputStream stream = null;

    try{
      // Load some properties file
      stream = this.getClass().getResourceAsStream( "validator.properties" );
      if ( stream != null ){
        Properties props = new Properties();
        props.load( stream );
        // Get the pathnames string from the properties file
        paths = props.getProperty( "validator-pathnames" );
      }
    }catch( IOException ex ){
      ex.printStackTrace();
    }
    setPathnames( paths );
  }

  protected void initResources() throws IOException {
    resources = new ValidatorResources();

    if (getPathnames() != null && getPathnames().length() > 0) {
      StringTokenizer st = new StringTokenizer(getPathnames(), RESOURCE_DELIM);
      while (st.hasMoreTokens()) {
        String validatorRules = st.nextToken();
        validatorRules = validatorRules.trim();

        InputStream input = null;
        BufferedInputStream bis = null;
        input = getClass().getResourceAsStream(validatorRules);

        if (input != null){
          bis = new BufferedInputStream(input);

          try {
            // pass in false so resources aren't processed
            // until last file is loaded
            ValidatorResourcesInitializer.initialize(resources, bis, false);
          }catch (Exception ex){
            ex.printStackTrace();
          }
        }
```

*Example 11-4. Using the Validator outside of Struts (continued)*

```
      }
      // process resources
      resources.process();
    }
  }
}
```

The work being done in the `ValidatorLoader` from Example 11-4 is very similar to what the `ValidatorPlugIn` does—it loads and initializes an instance of the `ValidatorResources` class. The object is an in-memory representation of the validation rules for an application. This example uses the `getResourceAsStream()` method to find and load a properties file that contains the list of Validator resource files.

Once you create and initialize an instance of the `ValidatorResources` class, you will need to cache it somewhere. In a Struts application, it's cached in the `ServletContext`. Your application can hang onto this object, or you can wrap the resource inside of a Singleton.

## Modifying the validation-rules.xml File

In the earlier section "Creating Your Own Validation Rules," you saw how to extend the Validator framework with your own customized rules. You'll have to do this here as well, but the method signatures will be different. The method signature in Example 11-3 included parameters that are part of the Servlet and Struts APIs. You will need to use different arguments to keep from being coupled to the Servlet API or the Struts framework.

First, the `methodParams` attribute needs to be modified to support the alternate arguments to the validation method. The following is a fragment for a rule called currency:

```
<global>
 <validator name="currency"
   classname="com.oreilly.struts.storefront.Validator"
   methodParams="java.lang.Object,org.apache.commons.validator.Field,java.util.List"
   method="isCurrency"
   msg="Value is not a valid Currency Amount."/>
</global>
```

Once the validation rule itself is set up, you need to use it in the application-specific validation file:

```
<form-validation>
 <global>
 </global>
 <formset>
  <form name="checkoutForm">
   <field property="paymentAmount" depends="required,currency">
    <arg0 key="registrationForm.paymentamount.invalid"/>
```

```
      </field>
    </formset>
  </form-validation>
```

Somewhere in the application, you must obtain access to the `ValidatorResources` object instance that was initialized in Example 11-4 and use it to validate the Java-Bean:

```
ValidatorResources resources = // Get instance of the ValidatorResources
Validator validator = new Validator(resources, "checkoutForm");

validator.addResource(Validator.BEAN_KEY, bean);
validator.addResource("java.util.List", lErrors);

try {
  // Execute the validation rules
  validator.validate();
} catch ( ValidatorException ex ) {
  // Log the validation exception
  log.warn( "A validation exception occured", ex );
}
```

Although the Validator framework is designed for use with or without Struts, some work is required before it's ready to use outside of the Struts framework. However, with a little up-front sweat, you can save yourself plenty of work downstream in the development cycle.

# CHAPTER 12

# Internationalization and Struts

Companies can no longer afford to think only about local marketplaces. Since the mid to late 1990s, the business world has been overrun with ideas about a world economy—all you have to do is look at what's happening in Europe with the Euro. Businesses and even countries are realizing that they can't just think about their traditional markets and at the same time continue to grow revenue and be successful; they must start thinking globally and attempt to bring in global customers for their products and services.

With the explosion of the World Wide Web in the mid-1990s, companies conducting business on the Internet began to find out that providing access to their products and services via a web site was an ideal way of attracting new customers from all over the world. One of the key reasons is 24/7 access. Regardless of the time zone the business or the customers are in, the Web allows a customer to shop and purchase goods and services at any time of the day or night. Traditional business hours are irrelevant on the Web. What unlimited access can mean to companies and their revenue is enormous. However, for the software developers that have to build and maintain the applications to support global customers, the task can be daunting.

This chapter focuses on what it takes to make a Struts application available to customers from around the world, regardless of their language or geographical location. As is often the case in software development, planning ahead is the most important thing you can do to help ensure success. After reading this chapter, you should be able to build Struts applications that make it possible to support a broad range of customers.

## What Is Internationalization?

Traditionally, software developers have focused on building applications that solve an immediate business problem. While doing so, it's easy and sometimes necessary to make assumptions about the user's language or country of residence. In many cases, these assumptions are valid and there's never a question of who the audience will be. However, if you have ever had to re-engineer an application because these assumptions weren't correct, you know how hard it can be to go back and correct the application design after the fact.

*Internationalization* (I18N), simply stated, is the process of designing your software ahead of time to support multiple languages and regions, so that you don't have to go back and re-engineer your applications every time a new language or country needs to be supported. An application that is said to support internationalization has the following characteristics:

- Additional languages can be supported without requiring code changes.
- Text elements, messages, and images are stored externally to the source code.
- Culturally dependent data such as dates and times, decimal values, and currencies are formatted correctly for the user's language and geographic location.
- Nonstandard character sets are supported.
- The application can quickly be adapted to new languages and/or regions.

When you internationalize an application, you can't afford to pick and choose which options you want to support. You must implement all of them or the process breaks down. If a user visits your web site and all of the text, images, and buttons are in the correct language but the numbers and currency are not formatted correctly, it will make for an unpleasant user experience.

Ensuring that the application can support multiple languages and regions is only the first step. You still must create localized versions of the application for each specific language and/or region that you want to support. Fortunately, here's where the benefits of I18N on the Java platform pay off. For applications that have been properly internationalized, all of the work to support a new language or country is external to the source code.

A *locale* is a region (usually geographic, but not necessarily so) that shares customs, culture, and language. Applications that are written for a single locale are commonly referred to as *myopic*. *Localization* (L10N) is the process of adapting your application, which has been properly internationalized, to a specific locale. For applications where I18N support hadn't been planned or built in, this usually means changes to text, images, and messages that are embedded within the source code. After the changes are applied, the source code may need to be recompiled. Imagine doing this time and time again for each new locale you have to support!

According to Richard Gillam from the Unicode Technology Group, which designed much of the I18N support in the Java libraries, "Internationalization is not a feature." Users will expect that the products they use will work for them in their native languages. Things can go wrong, and users get unhappy when assumptions that you make are incorrect. Start planning early for I18N support in your applications. Even if it doesn't look like you're going to need it, if you do you'll be that much further ahead, and it won't hinder development as long as you do it right from the start.

Not every application needs I18N support, and some developers and development organizations frown on adding in functionality that isn't part of the requirements. However, even if your application has no requirements to support more than a single locale, there are still benefits that you can gain from including some aspects of I18N. For example, by using resource bundles for all of your static text, you can save development and, more importantly, maintenance time. We'll see how this is true later in the chapter.

# Support for I18N in Java

Java provides a rich set of I18N features in the core library. This section briefly discusses a few of those core features. The I18N support in the Struts framework relies heavily on these components, and understanding how the Java I18N components cooperate with each other will help you understand how to internationalize your Struts applications.

The topic of internationalization is too broad to cover in depth in this book. A more complete discussion of the topic can be found in the book *Java Internationalization* by Andy Deitsch and David Czarnecki (O'Reilly).

## The Locale Class

The java.util.Locale class is undeniably the most important I18N class in the Java library. Almost all of the support for internationalization and localization in or around the Java language relies on this class.

The Locale class provides Java with instances of the locale concept mentioned earlier. A particular instance of the Locale represents a unique language and region. When a class in the Java library modifies its functionality during runtime based on a Locale object, it's said to be *locale-sensitive*. For example, the java.text.DateFormat is locale-sensitive because it will format a date differently depending on a particular Locale object.

The Locale objects don't do any of the I18N formatting or parsing work. They are used as identifiers by the locale-sensitive classes. When you acquire an instance of the DateFormat class, you can pass in a Locale object for the United States. The DateFormat class does all of the locale-sensitive parsing and formatting; it relies on the Locale only to identify the proper format.

Be careful when using the java.text.Format class or any of its descendants, including DateFormat, NumberFormat, and SimpleDateFormat, because they are not thread-safe. The thread-safety problem exists because an instance of the Calendar class is stored as a member variable and accessed during the parse( ) and format( ) method invocations. You will need to use a separate instance for each thread or synchronize access externally. Don't store a single instance in somewhere like the application scope and allow multiple client threads to access it. You can, however, store instances in the users' sessions and use different instances for each user to help ensure thread-safety. The thread-safety problem includes all versions of Java, including 1.4. The API documentation for the Format classes has been updated to indicate the known design issue.

When you create a Locale object, you typically specify the language and country code. The following code fragment illustrates the creation of two Locale objects, one for the U.S. and the other for Great Britain:

```
Locale usLocale = new Locale("en", "US");
Locale gbLocale = new Locale("en", "GB");
```

The first argument in the constructor is the language code. The language code consists of two lowercase letters and must conform to the ISO-639 specification. You can find a complete listing of the available language codes at *http://www.unicode.org/unicode/onlinedat/languages.html*.

The second argument is the country code. It consists of two uppercase letters that must conform to the ISO-3166 specification. The list of available country codes is available at *http://www.unicode.org/unicode/onlinedat/countries.html*.

The Locale class provides several static convenience constants that allow you to acquire an instance of the most-often-used locales. For example, to get an instance of a Japanese locale, you could use either of these:

```
Locale locale1 = Locale.JAPAN;
Locale locale2 = new Locale("ja", "JP");
```

### The default locale

The JVM will query the operating system when it's first started and set a default locale for the environment. You can obtain the information for this default locale by calling the getDefault( ) method on the Locale class:

```
Locale defaultLocale = Locale.getDefault();
```

The web container will normally use the default locale for its local environment, while using the one passed from the client in the HttpServletRequest to display locale-sensitive information back to the end user.

## Determining the user's locale

In the last section, you saw how to create Locale objects in Java by passing in the language and country code to the Locale constructor. Within web applications, including those built using the Struts framework, you rarely have to create your own locale instances because the container does it for you. The ServletRequest interface contains two methods that can be called to retrieve the locale preferences of a client:

```
public java.util.Locale getLocale();
public java.util.Enumeration getLocales();
```

Both of these methods use the Accept-Language header that is part of each client request sent to the servlet container.

Because the web server doesn't keep a long-term connection open with a browser, the client locale preference is sent to the servlet container with each request. Although the user's locale information may be sent with each request, Struts will, by default, retrieve the information only once and store it into the user's session. The Locale object, if stored into the session, is stored with a key of Globals.LOCALE_KEY, which translates to the string org.apache.struts.action.LOCALE.

 You can configure whether Struts stores the user's locale into the session by setting the locale attribute in the controller element within the Struts application configuration file. If you don't provide a value for the locale attribute, it defaults to true. See Chapter 4 for more information on configuring the locale.

Calling the getLocale() method on the HttpServletRequest object returns the preferred locale of the client, while the getLocales() method returns an Enumeration of preferred locales in decreasing order of preference. If a client doesn't have a preferred locale configured, the servlet container will return its default locale. Example 12-1 illustrates how to determine this information using a servlet.

*Example 12-1. Determining the user's locale information in a servlet*

```java
import java.io.IOException;
import java.io.PrintWriter;
import java.util.Enumeration;
import java.util.Locale;
import javax.servlet.ServletConfig;
import javax.servlet.ServletException;
import javax.servlet.http.HttpServlet;
import javax.servlet.http.HttpServletRequest;
import javax.servlet.http.HttpServletResponse;

/**
 * Prints out information about a user's preferred locales
 */
public class LocaleServlet extends HttpServlet {
  private static final String CONTENT_TYPE = "text/html";
```

*Example 12-1. Determining the user's locale information in a servlet (continued)*

```java
/**
 * Initialize the servlet
 */
public void init(ServletConfig config) throws ServletException {
  super.init(config);
}

/**
 * Process the HTTP Get request
 */
public void doGet(HttpServletRequest request, HttpServletResponse response)
throws ServletException, IOException {
  response.setContentType(CONTENT_TYPE);
  PrintWriter out = response.getWriter();

  out.println("<html>");
  out.println("<head><title>The Example Locale Servlet</title></head>");
  out.println("<body>");

  // Retrieve and print out the user's preferred locale
  Locale preferredLocale = request.getLocale();
  out.println("<p>The user's preffered Locale is " + preferredLocale + "</p>");

  // Retrieve all of the supported locales of the user
  out.println("<p>A list of preferred Locales in descreasing order</p>");
  Enumeration allUserSupportedLocales = request.getLocales();
  out.println("<ul>");
  while( allUserSupportedLocales.hasMoreElements() ){
    Locale supportedLocale = (Locale)allUserSupportedLocales.nextElement();
    StringBuffer buf = new StringBuffer();
    buf.append("<li>");
    buf.append("Locale: ");
    buf.append( supportedLocale );
    buf.append( " - " );
    buf.append( supportedLocale.getDisplayName() );
    buf.append("</li>");
    // Print out the line for a single Locale
    out.println( buf.toString() );
  }
  out.println("</ul>");

  // Get the container's default locale
  Locale servletContainerLocale = Locale.getDefault();
  out.println("<p>The container's Locale " + servletContainerLocale + "</p>");
  out.println("</body></html>");
  }
}
```

When you execute the servlet in Example 12-1, you should see output similar to the browser output in Figure 12-1.

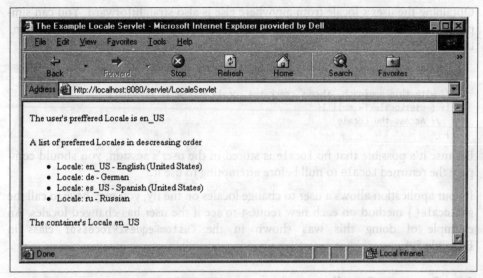

*Figure 12-1. Browser output from Example 12-1*

The output may be different if you have different locales configured for your system. Most web browsers allow you to configure the locales you prefer to support. With Microsoft Internet Explorer, for example, you can edit the languages in the Tools → Internet Options pulldown menu.

etting the user's locale within the Struts framework is easy. There are, in fact, several ways of getting the stored Locale for the user, depending on where you are trying to access it. If you are within an Action class, for example, you can simply call the getLocale() method defined in the Struts base Action class. The following fragment shows the getLocale() method:

```
protected Locale getLocale(HttpServletRequest request) {
    HttpSession session = request.getSession();
    Locale locale = (Locale) session.getAttribute(Globals.LOCALE_KEY);
    if (locale == null) {
        locale = defaultLocale;
    }
    return (locale);

}
```

You will need to pass the request object to this method because it will need to use the HttpSession to obtain the locale.

The getLocale() method will always return an instance of the Locale, even if one isn't stored in the session for the user. The method will return the defaultLocale if necessary. The defaultLocale property is stored as a static member variable that every Action subclass has access to:

```
protected static Locale defaultLocale = Locale.getDefault();
```

Obtaining the user's locale from anywhere else is also straightforward. You can simply get it directly from the session as the getLocale( ) method does, using the Action. LOCALE_KEY:

```
Locale userLocale = (Locale)session.getAttribute(Globals.LOCALE_KEY);

// With this approach, always check the Locale to see if it's null
if ( userLocale != null ){
  // Access the Locale
}
```

Because it's possible that no Locale is stored in the user's session, you should compare the returned Locale to null before attempting to use it.

If your application allows a user to change locales on the fly, you may have to call the getLocale( ) method on each new request to see if the user has changed locales. An example of doing this was shown in the CustomRequestProcessor class in Example 5-4.

## Java Resource Bundles

The java.util.ResourceBundle class provides the ability to group together a set of resources for a given locale. The resources are usually textual elements such as field and button labels and status messages, but they can also be items such as image names, error messages, and page titles.

The Struts framework does not use the ResourceBundle class provided by the core language. Instead, it provides similar functionality with the classes within its framework. The org.apache.struts.util.MessageResources class and its only concrete subclass, org.apache.struts.util.PropertyMessageResources, are used to perform parallel functionality to that of the ResourceBundle hierarchy. If you understand the fundamentals of the ResourceBundle in the code library, you basically understand how the version within the Struts framework operates.

 In retrospect, the MessageResources class should at least have been a subclass of the Java ResourceBundle.

You'll see an example of creating a resource bundle for a Struts application later in this chapter in the section "The Struts Resource Bundle."

## The MessageFormat Class

The Java ResourceBundle and the Struts MessageResources class allow for both static and dynamic text. Static text is used for elements such as field and button labels where the localized strings are used exactly as they are in the bundle—in other words, when the text for the message is known ahead of time. With dynamic text, part of the message may not be known until runtime. To help make the difference clearer, let's look at an example.

Suppose you need to display a message to the user informing him that the name and phone input fields are required in order to save. One approach would be to add entries like these to the resource bundle:

```
error.requiredfield.name=The Name field is required to save.
error.requiredfield.phone=The Phone field is required to save.

// other resource messages
```

This approach works fine, but what if there were hundreds of required fields? You would need a resource message for each required field, and the resource bundle would become very large and difficult to maintain. Note, however, that the only difference between the two messages is the name of the field that is required.

A much easier and more maintainable approach is to use the functionality of the java.text.MessageFormat class. This allows you to do something like this:

```
error.requiredfield=The {0} field is required to save.
label.phone=Phone
label.name=Name
```

The values that are not known until runtime are substituted in the message by a set of braces and an integer value. The integer inside the braces is used as an index into an Object[] that is passed in with the format() message of the MessageFormat class. Example 12-2 provides an example of this.

*Example 12-2. Using the MessageFormat class to format messages with variable text*

```
import java.util.ResourceBundle;
import java.util.Locale;
import java.text.MessageFormat;

public class FormatExample {
  public static void main(String[] args) {
    // Load the resource bundle
    ResourceBundle bundle = ResourceBundle.getBundle( "ApplicationResources" );

    // Get the message template
    String requiredFieldMessage = bundle.getString( "error.requiredfield" );

    // Create a String array of size one to hold the arguments
    String[] messageArgs = new String[1];

    // Get the "Name" field from the bundle and load it in as an argument
    messageArgs[0] = bundle.getString( "label.name" );

    // Format the message using the message and the arguments
    String formattedNameMessage =
      MessageFormat.format( requiredFieldMessage, messageArgs );
```

```
    System.out.println( formattedNameMessage );

    // Get the "Phone" field from the bundle and load it in as an argument
    messageArgs[0] = bundle.getString( "label.phone" );

    // Format the message using the message and the arguments
    String formattedPhoneMessage =
      MessageFormat.format( requiredFieldMessage, messageArgs );

    System.out.println( formattedPhoneMessage );
  }
}
```

Messages that contain variable data are known as *compound messages*. Using compound messages allows you to substitute application-specific data into messages from the resource bundle at runtime. It can also reduce the number of messages that your application requires in the resource bundle, which can decrease the amount of time that it takes to translate to other locales.

Using compound messages in your resource bundles can make translation a little harder because the text contains substitution values that are not known until runtime. Also, human translators must take into account where the variable text goes in the localized message, because the substitution values may need to be in different positions in the message for different languages.

The Struts framework includes the capabilities of the MessageFormat class but encapsulates the functionality behind the components within the framework.

## Multilingual Support

Most of us cringe at the thought of supporting user groups that are in one of several possible locales. In many cases, however, once an application has been installed and localized, it's like any other single-locale application. The users that access the application are either all from the same locale or are from locales similar enough that the language and cultural differences are insignificant.

*Multilingual* applications, on the other hand, take internationalization to the next level by allowing users from different locales to access the same application. This means that the application has to be flexible enough to detect the user's locale and format everything based on that locale. This is much harder to do than just localizing an application.

The discussion of building multilingual applications is so large that it can't be covered satisfactorily in this book. For the remainder of this chapter, we'll stick with just the everyday internationalization problems that you'll face, and not focus on multilingual support.

# Internationalizing Your Struts Applications

The internationalization support provided by the Struts framework focuses almost exclusively on the presentation of text and images for the application. Functionality such as accepting input from nontraditional languages is not covered within the Struts framework.

As you've already seen, depending on your Struts configuration settings, the framework can determine the preferred locale for a user and store it into the user's session. Once the user's locale has been determined, Struts can use this locale to look up text and other resources from the resource bundles. The resource bundles are essential components in the Struts framework.

## The Struts Resource Bundle

As you saw in Chapter 4, each of your application modules can be configured with one or more resource bundles. The information within each bundle is available to actions, action forms, JSP pages, and custom tags alike.

### Creating a Struts resource bundle

Resource bundles that you create must follow the conventions of the `PropertyResourceBundle` class from the Java core library. That is, you need to create a text file for your resource bundle that has a *.properties* extension and that adheres to the guidelines discussed in the JavaDoc for the `java.util.Properties` class. The most important of these guidelines is that the format of the messages within this file is:

```
key=value
```

Example 12-3 displays a properties file called *StorefrontMessageResources.properties* that can be loaded by the Struts framework.

*Example 12-3. A simple Struts resource bundle*

```
global.title=Virtual Shopping with Struts
global.error.invalidlogin=The login was unsuccessful! Please try again.
global.required={0} is a required value.

label.featuredproducts=This Weeks Featured Products
label.email=Email Address
label.password=Password
label.returning
label.firstName=First Name
label.lastName=Last Name
label.address=Address
label.city=City
label.state=State
label.postalCode=Postal Code
label.zip=Zip
label.country=Country
```

*Example 12-3. A simple Struts resource bundle (continued)*

```
label.phone=Phone

button.add=Add Me
button.delete=Delete
button.checkout=Checkout
button.saveorder=Save Order

errors.required={0} is required.
errors.minlength={0} can not be less than {1} characters.
errors.maxlength={0} can not be greater than {1} characters.
errors.invalid={0} is invalid.
errors.byte={0} must be a byte.
errors.short={0} must be a short.
errors.integer={0} must be an integer.
errors.long={0} must be a long.
errors.float={0} must be a float.
errors.double={0} must be a double.
errors.date={0} is not a date.
errors.range={0} is not in the range {1} through {2}.
errors.creditcard={0} is not a valid credit card number.
errors.email={0} is not a valid e-mail address.
```

You must be sure to name the message resource file with the extension *.properties*, or the Struts framework will not be able to load it.

Notice that the keys used in Example 12-3 are separated by a period (.). We could have used other characters in the keys, or we could have used a single-word key like labelPhone=Phone. Using namespacing in your keys is a great way to organize the localized text to make maintenance easier and to prevent name collisions. This is similar to how Java classes use package names.

You have to be careful, however, when using characters other than the period as a separator. The colon (:), for example, can be used instead of the equals sign (=) to separate the key and the value, and it will cause problems if you use it within your keys. If you don't want to use the period character in your keys, you can safely use the underscore or the hyphen character. Spaces are not a good choice, as they will also cause problems.

## Resource bundle naming guidelines

The naming of the resource bundle is critical to it working properly. All resource bundles have a base name that you select. In Example 12-3, the name StorefrontMessageResources was used as a base name. If you needed to provide an additional localized resource bundle for the French language and the country Canada, you would create a properties file called *StorefrontResouces_fr_CA.properties* with the appropriate localized resources.

When the Struts framework searches for a message from one of the bundles, it looks for a bundle that is the closest match, based on the base name and the locale. If no locale is provided, it will use the default locale. Only when it fails to find a resource bundle with a specific language and country code as part of the name will it default to the base resource bundle. The base resource bundle is the one without any language or country code in its name.

 You should always provide a base resource bundle. If a user with a locale that you don't support visits your site, the application will select the base bundle for that user.

### The resource bundle and the classpath

The resource bundle needs to be placed in a location where it can be found and loaded. This means that the same class loader that loads the web application must also be able to locate and load the resource bundle. For web applications, the appropriate location is the *WEB-INF/classes* directory.

If you provide a package name for the resource bundle, it must reside in the correct package as well. For example, if you name your resource bundle *com.oreilly.struts. StorefrontResources.properties*, you must place it into the *WEB-INF/classes/com/ oreilly/struts* directory.

## Accessing the Resource Bundle

The resource bundles for a Struts application are loaded at startup, and each bundle is represented in memory by an instance of the org.apache.struts.util. MessageResources class (actually by its concrete subclass, PropertyMessageResources).

Each MessageResources instance is stored in the ServletContext when the application is initialized and can be accessed from just about any component within the servlet container. However, you'll more typically use a combination of the custom tags and the ActionMessage or ActionError classes to access the resources, rather than calling methods on the MessageResources class directly. In fact, if you use a combination of the declarative exception handling discussed in Chapter 10 and the Validator framework from Chapter 11, it's possible that you won't have to create ActionMessage or ActionError instances at all; the framework will do it for you automatically.

If you need to create an ActionMessage or ActionError manually, however, you can. From the validate( ) method of an ActionForm, it would look something like this:

```
public ActionErrors validate(ActionMapping mapping, HttpServletRequest request){

  ActionErrors errors = new ActionErrors();

  if(getEmail() == null || getEmail().length() < 1) {
    errors.add(ActionErrors.GLOBAL_ERROR,
```

```
                new ActionError("security.error.email.required"));
    }

    if(getPassword() == null || getPassword().length() < 1) {
      errors.add(ActionErrors.GLOBAL_ERROR,
                new ActionError("security.error.password.required"));
    }
    return errors;
  }
```

The String argument passed into the constructor of the ActionError class must be a
key in the resource bundle. The ActionMessage and ActionError classes have several
constructors, most of which allow you to pass in substitution arguments, for when
your messages are compound messages, as explained earlier in this chapter. You can
also create ActionMessages and ActionErrors from an Action class. The following is a
small fragment from the Storefront LoginAction class:

```
// Log in through the security service
IStorefrontService serviceImpl = getStorefrontService();

String errorMsg = null;
UserView userView = null;
try{
   // Attempt to authenticate the user
   userView = serviceImpl.authenticate(email, password);
}catch( InvalidLoginException ex ){
   ActionErrors errors = new ActionErrors();
   ActionError newError = new ActionError("error.security.invalidlogin");
   errors.add( ActionErrors.GLOBAL_ERROR, newError );
   saveErrors( request, errors );
   return mapping.findForward( IConstants.FAILURE_KEY );
}catch( ExpiredPasswordException ex ){
   ActionErrors errors = new ActionErrors();
   ActionError newError = new ActionError("error.security.passwordexpired");
   errors.add( ActionErrors.GLOBAL_ERROR, newError );
   saveErrors( request, errors );
   return mapping.findForward( IConstants.FAILURE_KEY );
}catch (AccountLockedException ex){
   ActionErrors errors = new ActionErrors();
   ActionError newError = new ActionError("error.security.accountlocked");
   errors.add( ActionErrors.GLOBAL_ERROR, newError );
   saveErrors( request, errors );
   return mapping.findForward( IConstants.FAILURE_KEY );
}
```

This fragment is another reason why the declarative exception-handling feature of
Struts is so attractive. Look at the amount of work that we did here. With declarative exception handling, all of this would be defined within the Struts configuration
file.

## The Bean tag library's MessageTag class

The Struts framework contains several custom tags that can be used in conjunction with the MessageResources for an application. One of the most important, however, is the Message tag that is part of the Bean tag library.

This custom tag retrieves a message string from one of the bundles for an application. It supports optional parametric replacement if the JSP page requires it. All you need to do is provide the key from the bundle and specify which application bundle to use, and the tag will write out the information to the JSP page. For example, the following JSP fragment uses the MessageTag to write out the title of the HTML page:

```
<head>
    <title><bean:message key="global.title"/></title>
</head>
```

You'll use this tag quite often within your Struts applications.

# Setting the Character Set

Supporting character sets other than the typical U.S. default ISO-8859-1 is a little tricky. There are several steps that you must perform before your environment will be prepared to support them. First, you need to configure the application server and/or servlet container to support the character-encoding scheme that you want to use. For example, for Unicode you would tell the container to interpret input as UTF-8. Check with the vendor's documentation, as each one will be configured differently. You can also set up a servlet filter to do this, but this requires a container that supports the 2.3 Servlet API.

Next, the contentType property within the controller element in the Struts configuration file needs to be set correctly. Set it to text/html;charset=UTF-8 for HTML Unicode support. You can also specify this in the JSP pages by putting the following line at the top of each page:

```
<%@ page contentType="text/html; charset=utf-8" %>
```

and this line in the HTML head section:

```
<head>
<META HTTP-EQUIV="Content-Type" CONTENT="text/html; charset=UTF-8">
</head>
```

Another option is to set the content type and encoding scheme in the response object, like this:

```
response.setContentType("text/html; charset=UTF-8");
```

However, you might have to do this in several different places, making maintenance and customization more difficult.

You may also have to tell the browser to always send URLs as UTF-8. There's usually a checkbox or option to do this—in IE 5.5, it's in the advanced options section.

There are two final steps to ensure that your application can fully support Unicode. The first is to make sure your database is configured for Unicode. This is usually the default, but you should verify that this is the case. Second, if you're using the JRE rather than the SDK, use the I18N version and not the U.S. version.

# Exception Handling and Internationalization

Exception handling was covered in detail in Chapter 10, and as you saw, there are I18N issues that need to be considered when building an exception-handling framework for your application.

Unless you plan to localize the exception messages that are thrown, you need to isolate the exception messages and be sure that they are never shown to the end user. The one thing that is more frustrating for an end user than getting an exception message or stack trace printed out on the screen is getting one that is not in that user's native language.

As Chapter 10 pointed out, exceptions should be caught and localized messages should be displayed to the user. This can be accomplished by using the Struts message resource bundle and the ActionError class. You should never display a Java exception to the end user. Even when there's a system failure that can't be recovered from, you should still have a system error page that is localized for the user.

# CHAPTER 13

# Struts and Enterprise JavaBeans

As you've seen so far, you can use Struts to build both the controller and the view components of an MVC-based application. Struts isn't a framework for business logic or data access, so it doesn't play a key role in the model component. This means that business logic (other than presentation validation) would be out of place in an action or form class. It also means that choosing to use Struts in an application shouldn't place any constraints on the design of the model. The separation of responsibilities in a layered architecture means that your Struts classes shouldn't care about how your model is implemented. Likewise, the model shouldn't care (or even know) that the controller and view are built using Struts.

Up to this point, the example applications presented in this book have used the web tier to provide everything needed from the middle tier, including the business logic and database access. With this approach, the application model has consisted simply of regular Java classes deployed in the web container. These classes have had complete responsibility for servicing requests from the action classes that depend on the application model. This architecture is common among web applications, and it works well as long as the requirements in areas such as security, scalability, and transaction complexity stay within the limits of what a web container can do. Trying to do everything within the web tier can prove to be a challenge when these requirements, which aren't necessarily as high a priority in the design of a web container as they are in other container types, become too stringent.

The alternative to building the model into the web tier is to use a true application tier, such as a J2EE application server. With this approach, the web tier provides the controller and view, and the application tier supplies the business data and its associated rules. Such a design is appropriate when the scalability, security, and transactional needs of an enterprise application require a more robust container. This situation is what we want to consider in this chapter. While it's true that the development of your Struts classes can be independent of the model implementation, this does require some effort on your part. This chapter covers some of the issues you need to consider when developing an interface between your Struts actions and an application tier. In particular, the focus here is on interfacing to a model built using Enterprise JavaBeans (EJB).

---

### To EJB or Not to EJB?

As the J2EE architecture grew in significance for enterprise application development, it was often assumed that an application that didn't include EJB wasn't a J2EE application at all. The rush was on to build enterprise-strength systems backed by EJB containers and all they had to offer. For carefully designed applications that required the type of infrastructure inherent with EJB, the technology provided a standards-based approach that led to many successful deployments. However, the focus on the EJB portion of J2EE also led to its use in applications that could have been better served by more lightweight approaches. This, along with some developers' disappointment with the pace of EJB's evolution, has led to a backlash against using EJB at all. Developers fall on both sides of this issue, with some in the Struts community being quite vocal in their criticism of EJB. The more moderate opinion is that EJB offers value where its strengths are truly needed, but can be costly both in performance and complexity otherwise.

This chapter won't attempt to argue the pros and cons of EJB. That topic falls outside the scope of this book. Instead, we'll simply presume that you've been asked to build a Struts- based web tier that needs to interface with an EJB application tier. With that as a starting point, the main concerns will be to identify the key issues and come up with an effective approach for addressing them.

---

## Implementing the Storefront Service Using EJB

Even though this chapter is specific to EJB, the intent is still to keep the focus on Struts. With that in mind, the discussion of EJB implementation details will be kept to a minimum. EJB is a complex topic, but the nature of several design patterns geared toward the interaction between EJBs and their clients makes this an easier task than you might first think. After all, an overriding goal of this chapter is to demonstrate how to design an application so that your Struts classes aren't impacted by the choice to use an EJB implementation of the model. You already have a head start on some of the central issues here, having seen how the model component of a web application can be hidden behind a service interface. In particular, you've seen through the Storefront example how easy it is to swap a debug model with a full implementation that accesses a database when this design approach is followed.

Throughout this chapter, the Storefront example will be used to illustrate how an EJB application tier can be used with a Struts application. If it weren't for the remote nature of accessing an EJB from a client application, this implementation choice

---

wouldn't make any difference to you. However, the distributed aspects of EJB must be taken into account when your web-tier classes access this type of model. What you'll see in the remainder of this chapter are some recommendations on how best to implement the code needed to interface with the application tier. Key to this discussion is an approach for isolating the code that handles what's unique about EJB so that your action classes aren't affected.

## A Quick EJB Overview

The EJB specification defines three types of beans: entity, session, and message-driven. Each type of bean has a different purpose within an EJB application.

*Entity beans* provide transactional access to persistent data and are most often used to represent rows stored in one or more related tables in a database. For example, you might implement CustomerBean, ItemBean, and OrderBean entity classes, among others, to support the Storefront application. These entity beans would incorporate the functionality provided by the corresponding business object classes in the example application. When entity beans are used, they take on the primary role of supplying the application model. They are expected to provide both the required data persistence operations and the business logic that governs the data they represent. Because the model should be reusable across applications in an enterprise, entity beans need to be independent of the types of clients that ultimately access the application tier.

*Session beans* are often described as extensions of the client applications they serve. They can implement business logic themselves, but more often their role is to coordinate the work of other classes (entity beans, in particular). They are more closely tied to their clients, so the precaution of keeping entity beans reusable doesn't apply to session beans to the same extent. The application tier is primarily considered to be the application model, but session beans are also referred to as "controllers" because of the coordination they do. This is especially true when session-bean methods are used to implement transactions that touch multiple business objects.

 Session beans can be implemented as either stateless or stateful. A *stateless* session bean maintains no state specific to its client, so a single instance can efficiently be shared among many clients by the EJB container. A *stateful* bean instance, on the other hand, is assigned to a specific client so that state can be maintained across multiple calls. Holding state in the application tier can simplify the client application logic, but it makes it more difficult to scale to a large number of clients. Typical web applications maintain their client state in the user session, and possibly the database, instead of making use of stateful session beans. For this reason, we'll focus on stateless beans for our examples here.

The EJB 2.0 specification added *message-driven beans* as the third bean type so that EJB could be integrated with the Java Message Service (JMS). Message-driven beans differ from the other two types in that they respond asynchronously to requests instead of being called directly by a client application. The container invokes a message-driven bean whenever a JMS message that meets the selection criteria of the bean is received. For example, in a more complex version of the Storefront application, a message-driven bean could be used to respond to a notification that an item is being backordered. The bean could be responsible for emailing any customers that had orders already in place for the item. Message-driven beans have no direct interaction with client applications, so they are even less dependent on the client than entity beans are.

## The Session Façade

The first step in designing an interface to the application tier is to identify the entry points exposed to a client application. Message-driven beans aren't called directly, so they don't come into play here. However, a typical EJB application can include a number of session and entity beans. As already pointed out, standard practice is to insulate entity beans from the details of the client so that they can be reused in other applications. If your Struts actions were to interact with entity beans directly, the web tier would quickly become coupled to the object model implemented by the application tier. This tight coupling, combined with the distributed nature of EJB, would lead to a number of issues:

- Changes in the EJB object model would require corresponding changes in the web tier.

- Action classes often would be required to execute multiple remote calls to the application server to satisfy the business logic needs of a request.

- The business logic and transaction-management code needed to orchestrate multiple calls would have to exist in the web tier.

To avoid these issues, the interface exposed to the clients of the application tier is almost always limited to session beans. This approach is commonly referred to as either "session wraps entity" or a "session façade." There are quite a few advantages to this design. When a client application makes a single call to a session-bean method to perform a required operation, the session bean can easily execute the request as a single transaction, and the implementation details can be hidden. This session-bean method might need to access a number of entity beans, or even other session beans, to satisfy the request. No matter what the flow of control is on the application server, the complexity is hidden from the client. Because session beans become the only clients of the entity beans when using a session façade, there's little chance of the entities becoming tied to any particular type of external client.

Even though the discussion here assumes that the business objects are implemented as entity beans, this doesn't have to be the case in an EJB application. The same concerns and advantages that support using a session façade apply when other implementations are used. Just as some Java developers don't like EJB, not all EJB developers like entity beans. Because the session façade hides the object model from the client, entity beans can be replaced with another approach, such as Java data objects (JDOs) or regular data access objects (DAOs), without impacting the interface exposed to the client.

## The Business Interface

When using a session façade, you must first define the details of the interface between the web and application tiers. You might have some questions about which side should be the primary driver of this contract between the two tiers. Early in the development of the Storefront example, the IStoreFrontService interface was introduced to define the application-tier functionality required to support the presentation needs of the application. In particular, the presentation layer relies on the supporting service to authenticate users and to provide product descriptions needed to build the online catalog. Taking a user-centered view of the application, it's easy to see how the service-layer requirements can be driven by the web tier. After all, if a certain view is to be built, the model functionality to support it has to exist. However, one of the main reasons to implement an enterprise's business logic within EJBs is to allow those business rules and the supporting data to be used to across multiple applications. This includes providing support for clients other than those associated with web applications. This isn't a problem, because the division of responsibility between session and entity beans helps to protect the reusability of business logic.

Because session beans are treated as extensions of the clients they serve, there's nothing wrong with defining a session façade that's specific to a particular client application. As long as your entity and message-driven beans remain independent of the client, it's reasonable to implement a session-bean interface in response to the requirements set forth by a specific client. If multiple client views of the model are required, multiple façades can be implemented to support them.

The façade presented by a session bean can support either local or remote clients. Local clients of a session or entity bean can only be other EJBs deployed within the same container. These clients are tightly coupled to the beans they access, but they offer performance advantages when calls need to be made between EJBs. This is because these method calls use pass-by-reference semantics instead of being treated as remote calls between distributed components. Session beans are often local clients of entity beans, but it's less common for them to have local clients of their own to support. Our web-tier components obviously aren't EJBs running within the application tier, so we care only about remote clients for our purposes here. What we need to do, then, is define the remote interface for our session façade.

Every session bean that supports remote clients must have a corresponding remote interface that extends the javax.ejb.EJBObject interface. This interface determines the business methods that are exposed by the session bean. It might seem strange, but you'll almost never see a method explicitly declared in a remote interface. This is because of an EJB design pattern known as the *business interface*.

 In addition to its remote interface, a session bean supporting remote clients must have a home interface that extends javax.ejb.EJBHome, an implementation class, and one or more XML deployment descriptors. Unlike the remote interface, which declares the bean's business methods, the home interface defines factory-like methods for creating session-bean references. By definition, the bean's methods are implemented by the implementation class. The deployment descriptors identify and configure a bean for use within a particular EJB container. We'll define each piece for our example as we go along.

When you think of a class and an interface with which it's associated, you would normally expect that the class would explicitly implement that interface. This isn't true with remote (or local) interfaces in EJB. Instead, the container creates an intermediate object (often referred to as an EJBObject) to implement the remote interface. This object intercepts calls made by clients of the bean, then delegates them to the implementation class after performing any operations (such as security or transaction management) that might be required. Instead of the Java compiler verifying that the bean class implements each of the business methods declared by the remote interface, that responsibility falls to the deployment tools provided by the container. Even a bean class that compiles without any errors will fail at deployment if there's a mismatch between it and its remote interface.

If you declared a session bean to implement its remote interface, you'd be guaranteed that the compiler would catch any problems with its business-method declarations. The problem is that you'd also have to provide dummy implementations of the non-business methods declared by javax.ejb.EJBObject. These methods would never be called (they're called only on the intermediate object created by the container), but they would have to be there to satisfy the compiler. Instead of taking this approach, most EJB developers create a second interface, known as the business interface, that declares the business methods that need to be exposed. Declaring the remote interface to extend this interface and the bean class to implement it exposes the required methods, so the compiler can verify that the bean implements them. This pattern provides a convenient starting point for defining our client access mechanism.

The use of a business interface also prevents programmers from accidentally passing or returning a *this* reference to an instance of a bean class that has been declared to implement its remote interface. This topic is beyond the scope of this book, but the short explanation is that the EJB container can manage bean instances properly only when they're referred to using only their remote (or local) interfaces. A bean reference can't be returned in place of its remote interface if the bean class implements only its business interface.

Returning to the IStorefrontService interface that eventually must be satisfied by our implementation, recall that it contains methods related to both user authentication and the product catalog. Even when using a session façade, you would likely separate these responsibilities into separate session beans. This would reduce the complexity of the session beans involved and simplify their maintenance. However, given that EJB design isn't our focus here, our first simplification will be to assume that our façade will consist of a single Storefront session bean. You probably wouldn't do this in a real application, but once you know how to interface with a single session bean, applying the same technique to multiple session beans is straightforward. A suitable business interface for the Storefront session bean is shown in Example 13-1.

*Example 13-1. The business interface for the Storefront session bean*

```
package com.oreilly.struts.storefront.service;

import java.rmi.RemoteException;
import java.util.List;
import com.oreilly.struts.storefront.catalog.view.ItemDetailView;
import com.oreilly.struts.storefront.customer.view.UserView;
import com.oreilly.struts.storefront.framework.exceptions.*;

/**
 * The business interface for the Storefront session bean
 */
public interface IStorefront {

  public UserView authenticate( String email, String password )
    throws InvalidLoginException, ExpiredPasswordException,
      AccountLockedException, DatastoreException, RemoteException;

  public List getFeaturedItems() throws DatastoreException, RemoteException;

  public ItemDetailView getItemDetailView( String itemId )
    throws DatastoreException, RemoteException;
}
```

The first thing to notice about the IStorefront interface is that its methods don't exactly match those declared by IStorefrontService. First of all, our business interface doesn't include the logout( ) and destroy( ) methods found in the service interface. The reason for this is that those methods represent web-tier functionality, not true business logic that needs to move to the application tier. Also, every method in IStorefront is declared to throw RemoteException, which is not part of the declarations in IStorefrontService. All business methods exposed to a remote client of an EJB must be declared to throw RemoteException, which is used to report communication failures specific to remote method execution. This is the one aspect of a remote interface that can't be hidden by the business interface. Without this restriction, this interface could be made to look very much like our service interface. Once we cover how our example session bean will be implemented, we'll discuss how these mismatches between the interfaces can be handled.

It's also important to notice that our business interface is referencing the view classes already created to support the service interface. The same Data Transfer Object (DTO) pattern introduced in Chapter 7 applies to an EJB-based model. Instead of exposing the actual business object implementation classes or many fine-grained methods to access their properties, you can use simple JavaBean classes to communicate the state of the model to the client. We declared our BaseView superclass to be Serializable so that the view classes could be referenced in a remote interface. DTO classes tend to consist of simple data types, so this constraint should be a minor one.

With our business interface defined, Example 13-2 shows the trivial remote interface declaration we'll need to eventually deploy our session bean.

*Example 13-2. The remote interface for the Storefront session bean*

```
package com.oreilly.struts.storefront.service;

import javax.ejb.EJBObject;

public interface Storefront extends EJBObject, IStorefront {
 /**
  * The remote interface for the Storefront session bean. All methods are
  * declared in the IStorefront business interface.
  */
}
```

## Stateless Session Bean Implementation

Without getting into anything too elaborate, we next want to come up with an implementation of our session façade. We'll make a few decisions here to simplify things, but the result will be all we need to illustrate how to interface the web and application tiers. It will also be good enough for you to deploy in an EJB container and use to test your Struts interface.

If you were given the task of implementing the application tier of the Storefront application using EJB, you probably would produce a design consisting of both session and entity beans. You could represent the model components using entity beans, and you'd likely have a number of session beans to provide the functionality for security, catalog, and order operations. The session beans would provide the workflow functionality required from process business objects, and the entity beans would serve as the corresponding entity business objects.

We've already made the decision to use only a single session bean for the example. The session façade makes our next simplification easy as well. Because we've isolated the interface between our two tiers into a façade, any division of responsibilities between session and entity beans is of no concern to us as Struts developers. The web tier sees only session-bean methods and DTO classes, so nothing else about the implementation will affect the web components. Given that, we'll implement our façade using a single stateless session bean that does not require any other EJBs.

 If you're starting with an EJB implementation that includes entity beans, you might want to use XDoclet (available from *http://www.sourceforge.net/projects/xdoclet/*) to automatically generate Struts ActionForms from these beans. For more complex EJB implementations than what we're looking at here, XDoclet also provides an automated means of generating the various interfaces and deployment descriptors required for a bean. This code generation is performed based on special JavaDoc tags that you include in your EJB implementation classes.

Because we're not using entity beans, we can make use of the same ORM approach and entity business object classes already used by the StorefrontServiceImpl class. In fact, our implementation will look very much like that class, with the exception of the callback methods required by the javax.ejb.SessionBean interface. This is shown in Example 13-3.

*Example 13-3. The Storefront session bean*

```
package com.oreilly.struts.storefront.service;

import java.sql.Timestamp;
import java.util.ArrayList;
import java.util.Iterator;
import java.util.List;
import javax.ejb.CreateException;
import javax.ejb.EJBException;
import javax.ejb.SessionBean;
import javax.ejb.SessionContext;
import org.odmg.*;
import ojb.odmg.*;
import com.oreilly.struts.storefront.businessobjects.CustomerBO;
import com.oreilly.struts.storefront.businessobjects.ItemBO;
```

*Example 13-3. The Storefront session bean (continued)*

```java
import com.oreilly.struts.storefront.catalog.view.ItemDetailView;
import com.oreilly.struts.storefront.catalog.view.ItemSummaryView;
import com.oreilly.struts.storefront.customer.view.UserView;
import com.oreilly.struts.storefront.framework.exceptions.AccountLockedException;
import com.oreilly.struts.storefront.framework.exceptions.DatastoreException;
import com.oreilly.struts.storefront.framework.exceptions.ExpiredPasswordException;
import com.oreilly.struts.storefront.framework.exceptions.InvalidLoginException;

/**
 * This is a simple Session Bean implementation of the Storefront service
 */
public class StorefrontBean implements SessionBean, IStorefront {
  private SessionContext ctx;
  private Implementation odmg = null;
  private Database db = null;

  public UserView authenticate( String email, String password )
   throws InvalidLoginException, ExpiredPasswordException,
     AccountLockedException, DatastoreException {

     // Query the database for a user that matches the credentials
     List results = null;
     try{
       OQLQuery query = odmg.newOQLQuery();
       // Set the OQL select statement
       String queryStr = "select customer from " + CustomerBO.class.getName();
       queryStr += " where email = $1 and password = $2";
       query.create(queryStr);

       // Bind the input parameters
       query.bind( email );
       query.bind( password );

       // Retrieve the results
       results = (List)query.execute();
     }catch( Exception ex ){
       ex.printStackTrace();
       throw DatastoreException.datastoreError(ex);
     }

     // If no results were found, must be an invalid login attempt
     if ( results.isEmpty() ){
       throw new InvalidLoginException();
     }

     // Should only be a single customer that matches the parameters
     CustomerBO customer  = (CustomerBO)results.get(0);

     // Make sure the account is not locked
     String accountStatusCode = customer.getAccountStatus();
     if ( accountStatusCode != null && accountStatusCode.equals( "L" ) ){
       throw new AccountLockedException();
     }
```

*Example 13-3. The Storefront session bean (continued)*

```
        // Populate the value object from the Customer business object
        UserView userView = new UserView();
        userView.setId( customer.getId().toString() );
        userView.setFirstName( customer.getFirstName() );
        userView.setLastName( customer.getLastName() );
        userView.setEmailAddress( customer.getEmail() );
        userView.setCreditStatus( customer.getCreditStatus() );

        return userView;
    }

    public List getFeaturedItems() throws DatastoreException {
        List results = null;
        try{
            OQLQuery query = odmg.newOQLQuery();
            // Set the OQL select statement
            query.create( "select featuredItems from " + ItemBO.class.getName() );
            results = (List)query.execute();
        }catch( Exception ex ){
            ex.printStackTrace();
            throw DatastoreException.datastoreError(ex);
        }
        List items = new ArrayList();
        Iterator iter = results.iterator();
        while (iter.hasNext()){
            ItemBO itemBO = (ItemBO)iter.next();
            ItemSummaryView newView = new ItemSummaryView();
            newView.setId( itemBO.getId().toString() );
            newView.setName( itemBO.getDisplayLabel() );
            newView.setUnitPrice( itemBO.getBasePrice() );
            newView.setSmallImageURL( itemBO.getSmallImageURL() );
            newView.setProductFeature( itemBO.getFeature1() );
            items.add( newView );
        }
        return items;
    }

    public ItemDetailView getItemDetailView( String itemId )
    throws DatastoreException {
        List results = null;
        try{
            OQLQuery query = odmg.newOQLQuery();

            // Set the OQL select statement
            String queryStr = "select item from " + ItemBO.class.getName();
            queryStr += " where id = $1";
            query.create(queryStr);
            query.bind(itemId);

            // Execute the query
            results = (List)query.execute();
        }catch( Exception ex ){
```

*Example 13-3. The Storefront session bean (continued)*

```
          ex.printStackTrace();
          throw DatastoreException.datastoreError(ex);
        }

        //
        if (results.isEmpty() ){
          throw DatastoreException.objectNotFound();
        }

        ItemBO itemBO = (ItemBO)results.get(0);

        // Build a ValueObject for the Item
        ItemDetailView view = new ItemDetailView();
        view.setId( itemBO.getId().toString() );
        view.setDescription( itemBO.getDescription() );
        view.setLargeImageURL( itemBO.getLargeImageURL() );
        view.setName( itemBO.getDisplayLabel() );
        view.setProductFeature( itemBO.getFeature1() );
        view.setUnitPrice( itemBO.getBasePrice() );
        view.setTimeCreated( new Timestamp(System.currentTimeMillis() ));
        view.setModelNumber( itemBO.getModelNumber() );
        return view;
}

/**
 * Opens the database and prepares it for transactions.
 */
private void init() throws DatastoreException {
  // Get odmg facade instance
  odmg = OJB.getInstance();
  db = odmg.newDatabase();
  // Open database
  try{
    db.open("repository.xml", Database.OPEN_READ_WRITE);
  }catch( ODMGException ex ){
    throw DatastoreException.datastoreError(ex);
  }
}

public void ejbCreate() throws CreateException {
  try {
    init();
  }catch ( DatastoreException e ) {
    throw new CreateException(e.getMessage());
  }
}

public void ejbRemove() {
  try {
    if (db != null) {
      db.close();
    }
```

*Example 13-3. The Storefront session bean (continued)*

```
    }catch ( ODMGException e ) {}
}

public void setSessionContext( SessionContext assignedContext ) {
    ctx = assignedContext;
}

public void ejbActivate() {
    // Nothing to do for a stateless bean
}

public void ejbPassivate() {
    // Nothing to do for a stateless bean
}

}
```

In our StorefrontBean class, the business method implementations are unchanged from the StorefrontServiceImpl versions. Only the management of the database connection needed to be modified. Whenever the EJB container creates a new instance of this bean, the ejbCreate( ) callback method is invoked and a database connection is established. This connection is closed in the corresponding ejbRemove( ) method that is called prior to the instance being destroyed. The container never passivates stateless session beans, so do-nothing implementations are supplied for the ejbPassivate( ) and ejbActivate( ) methods of the SessionBean interface. If we needed more than one session bean in our example, we'd move these two methods into an adapter class and extend all our concrete implementation classes from it.

A more correct EJB approach would be to open the database connection using a javax.sql.DataSource connection factory obtained from a JNDI lookup. This allows the container to manage connection pooling and transaction enlistment for you automatically. Again, this doesn't affect our interface, so we can continue to use this simple implementation.

Our session bean now has a remote interface and an implementation class. That leaves the home interface, which is always simple in the case of a stateless session bean. All we need is a single create( ) method, as shown in Example 13-4.

*Example 13-4. The home interface for the Storefront session bean*

```
package com.oreilly.struts.storefront.service;

import java.rmi.RemoteException;
import javax.ejb.CreateException;
import javax.ejb.EJBHome;
```

```
/**
 * The home interface for the Storefront session bean.
 */
public interface StorefrontHome extends EJBHome {
  public Storefront create() throws CreateException, RemoteException;
}
```

## JBoss Deployment

We need to select an EJB container and create the required XML deployment descriptors before we can deploy and use our session bean. The open source JBoss application server fits our requirements perfectly. This full-featured J2EE implementation, complete with EJB support, is a favorite among open source developers. You can download the software for free from *http://www.jboss.org*.

With our minimal implementation, we don't need anything complicated as far as deployment information for our session bean. Example 13-5 shows the standard *ejb-jar.xml* descriptor for our bean. For the most part, this file simply identifies the home and remote interfaces and the implementation class. It also declares that all of the business methods are nontransactional (because they're read-only methods).

*Example 13-5. The ejb-jar.xml deployment descriptor for the Storefront session bean*

```
<?xml version="1.0" encoding="UTF-8"?>
<!DOCTYPE ejb-jar PUBLIC "-//Sun Microsystems, Inc.//DTD Enterprise JavaBeans 2.0// EN"
"http://java.sun.com/dtd/ejb-jar_2_0.dtd">

<ejb-jar >

    <description>
        Generic deployment information for the Storefront session bean
    </description>
    <display-name>Storefront Session Bean</display-name>

    <enterprise-beans>
      <session >
        <ejb-name>Storefront</ejb-name>
        <home>com.oreilly.struts.storefront.service.StorefrontHome</home>
        <remote>com.oreilly.struts.storefront.service.Storefront</remote>
        <ejb-class>com.oreilly.struts.storefront.service.StorefrontBean</ejb-class>
        <session-type>Stateless</session-type>
        <transaction-type>Container</transaction-type>
      </session>
    </enterprise-beans>

    <assembly-descriptor >
      <container-transaction >
        <method >
          <ejb-name>Storefront</ejb-name>
          <method-name>*</method-name>
        </method>
```

```
            <trans-attribute>NotSupported</trans-attribute>
        </container-transaction>
    </assembly-descriptor>

</ejb-jar>
```

In addition to the *ejb-jar.xml* file, most containers require one or more vendor-specific descriptors as part of a bean's deployment information. In this case, all we need to do is associate a JNDI name with our bean. Example 13-6 shows how this is done with JBoss. The fully qualified name of the bean's remote interface was chosen as the JNDI name. It's also common to use the home interface name.

*Example 13-6. The JBoss deployment descriptor for the Storefront session bean*

```
<?xml version="1.0" encoding="UTF-8"?>
<!DOCTYPE jboss PUBLIC "-//JBoss//DTD JBOSS//EN"
 "http://www.jboss.org/j2ee/dtd/jboss.dtd">

<jboss>

    <enterprise-beans>
        <session>
            <ejb-name>Storefront</ejb-name>
            <jndi-name>com.oreilly.struts.storefront.service.Storefront</jndi-name>
        </session>
    </enterprise-beans>

</jboss>
```

Deployment of an EJB requires packaging it into a Java archive (JAR) file. The deployment JAR file for our session bean needs to include the following files:

- The home and remote interface class files
- The bean implementation class file
- The two deployment descriptors (these files must be placed in a *META-INF* directory)
- The *OJB.properties* file and the various repository XML files used by the ORM framework
- The business object and DTO class files referenced by the Storefront bean

Once you've created this JAR file, you can deploy the bean by copying the file to the *server/default/deploy* directory underneath your JBoss installation. You can place the JAR files for your JDBC driver and the OJB classes in the *server/default/lib* directory. At this point, you can start JBoss and verify that you have everything in place to execute the application tier.

# Interfacing Struts to EJB

It's now time to turn our attention back to the client side of our session façade. In this section, we'll first cover how to satisfy the requirements of our service interface with our session-bean implementation. We'll then look at how to better manage the JNDI lookups and home and remote interface management inherent in being a remote client to an EJB.

## Using a Business Delegate

As you saw when we defined the business interface for the Storefront session bean, we still have some work to do to match it up to the Storefront service interface. Our business interface doesn't include all the methods of IStorefrontService, and the methods that are declared include RemoteException in their throws clauses. We'll address these differences by going back to the Business Delegate pattern introduced in Chapter 6. Recall that the purpose of this pattern is to hide the business-service implementation from the client application.

We'll start out with a fairly straightforward Business Delegate implementation and then cover some specific ways to improve it. An initial implementation is shown in Example 13-7.

*Example 13-7. A business delegate for the Storefront session bean*

```
package com.oreilly.struts.storefront.service;

import java.rmi.RemoteException;
import java.util.Hashtable;
import java.util.List;
import javax.ejb.CreateException;
import javax.naming.Context;
import javax.naming.InitialContext;
import javax.naming.NamingException;
import javax.rmi.PortableRemoteObject;
import com.oreilly.struts.storefront.catalog.view.ItemDetailView;
import com.oreilly.struts.storefront.customer.view.UserView;
import com.oreilly.struts.storefront.framework.exceptions.*;

/**
 * This class is a business delegate that supports the implementation of the
 * IStorefrontService interface using the Storefront session bean.
 */
public class StorefrontEJBDelegate implements IStorefrontService {

  private IStorefront storefront;

  public StorefrontEJBDelegate() {
    init();
  }
```

*Example 13-7. A business delegate for the Storefront session bean (continued)*

```java
  private void init() {
    try {
      Hashtable props = new Hashtable();
      props.put(Context.INITIAL_CONTEXT_FACTORY,
        "org.jnp.interfaces.NamingContextFactory");
      props.put(Context.PROVIDER_URL, "localhost");

      InitialContext ic = new InitialContext(props);
      Object home = ic.lookup("com.oreilly.struts.storefront.service.Storefront");

      StorefrontHome sfHome = (StorefrontHome)
        PortableRemoteObject.narrow(home, StorefrontHome.class);
      storefront = sfHome.create();
    }
    catch (NamingException e) {
      throw new RuntimeException(e.getMessage());
    }
    catch (CreateException e) {
      throw new RuntimeException(e.getMessage());
    }
    catch (RemoteException e) {
      throw new RuntimeException(e.getMessage());
    }
  }

  public UserView authenticate( String email, String password )
   throws InvalidLoginException, ExpiredPasswordException,
     AccountLockedException, DatastoreException {
    try {
      return storefront.authenticate(email, password);
    }
    catch (RemoteException e) {
      throw DatastoreException.datastoreError(e);
    }
  }

  public List getFeaturedItems() throws DatastoreException {
    try {
      return storefront.getFeaturedItems();
    }
    catch (RemoteException e) {
      throw DatastoreException.datastoreError(e);
    }
  }
  public ItemDetailView getItemDetailView( String itemId )
   throws DatastoreException {
    try {
      return storefront.getItemDetailView(itemId);
    }
    catch (RemoteException e) {
      throw DatastoreException.datastoreError(e);
```

```
    }
  }

  public void logout( String email ) {
    // Do nothing for this example
  }

  public void destroy() {
    // Do nothing for this example
  }
}
```

When an instance of the StorefrontEJBDelegate class is created, its init() method is called to obtain a remote reference to the Storefront session bean. This method performs the required JNDI lookup using the naming service implementation provided by JBoss. As written, the delegate assumes that the naming service is running on the local machine. Later, we'll look at how to externalize the details of the JNDI lookup that must be performed by a delegate. Once a remote reference is obtained, the delegate holds it as part of its state. This field is declared to be of the business interface type because we need it only for accessing business methods. Even though the storefront field isn't declared to be of the session bean's remote interface type, the required handling of RemoteException makes it clear that our delegate is accessing a remote object.

Other than what is required to obtain a remote reference, most of the code in our delegate does nothing more than relay business method calls to the session-bean implementation. The logout() and destroy() methods have no counterparts in the application tier, so those implementations don't include session-bean calls. If we needed to do something in these methods, that code could either be implemented directly in the StorefrontEJBDelegate methods or in another web-tier component that could be called by the delegate.

## Exception handling

The exception handling found in this implementation of the StorefrontEJBDelegate class is worth noting. In addition to hiding the details of JNDI lookups, a business delegate used with a session bean should also hide the EJB-specific exceptions that come with being a remote client. In the business methods of the delegate, any RemoteException that gets thrown from a session-bean call is caught and reported to the client using a DatastoreException. Hiding the remote nature of the model implementation addresses the mismatch in declared exceptions between our business interface and the IStorefrontService declarations.

If the inclusion of RemoteException in our business interface had been the only difference between this and the service interface, it might have been tempting to simply add this exception to IStorefrontService and continue forward. However, this would have unnecessarily cluttered the contract for whatever service implementation might be used with implementation details.

The only reason our delegate uses a DatastoreException to respond to a RemoteException is to leave the service interface unaffected by the implementation approach. If this self-imposed constraint were relaxed so that changes to IStorefrontService were acceptable, a better approach would be to declare an exception class whose sole purpose is to report exceptions from a delegate in a generic fashion. For example, if we were to declare an application exception named ServiceDelegateException, we could throw that when a RemoteException occurred. Instead of throwing a RuntimeException to report a failure in obtaining a remote reference, the init() method could also be updated to make use of ServiceDelegateException. This new exception would be a more accurate indication of the type of error that occurred than using a DatastoreException. Furthermore, adding this new exception to our IStorefrontService declarations still wouldn't expose the fact that the implementation is based on EJB.

## Swapping the implementation

All that's left to do is to swap the current Storefront service implementation with the delegate we have created. The framework put into place with the Storefront-ServiceFactory in Chapter 6 makes this easy to do. We simply need to change the class specified for our service implementation in the *web.xml* file to the following:

```
<init-param>
    <param-name>storefront-service-class</param-name>
    <param-value>
        com.oreilly.struts.storefront.service.StorefrontEJBDelegate
    </param-value>
</init-param>
```

With this change made, an action will be creating a delegate instance whenever it calls the getStorefrontService() method implemented in the StorefrontBaseAction. This method should be called only once during a request, to avoid the unnecessary overhead of creating additional remote references. However, even taking care to use the same delegate throughout a request leaves us with an implementation that isn't very efficient. The next section covers some ways to improve our use of JNDI and home interfaces.

Don't forget that you'll need to copy the JBoss client JARs to the *lib* directory for your web application before using your delegate. You'll also need the home and remote interface class files for the Storefront session bean in the *classes* directory.

## Managing EJB Home and Remote References

Implementing a business delegate clearly isolates and minimizes the dependencies between the web and application tiers. We were able to implement our Storefront session bean using a business interface that isn't tied to any particular client type. We also were able to leave our Struts action classes untouched when switching to this implementation of our model. We do have a couple of problems to address, though, to turn this into a solution you would want to use in a real application. Most importantly, we need to improve how we're obtaining our home interface references. We also should get rid of the hardcoded parameters used by our JNDI lookup.

Performing a JNDI lookup to obtain a home interface reference is an expensive (slow) operation. We couldn't do much about this overhead if we actually needed a new home reference for each request, but that's not the case. An EJB home is a factory object that is valid throughout the lifetime of the client application. There is no state in this object that prevents it from being used across requests or client threads. Our delegate would be significantly improved if the home reference it needed were cached within the web tier after being requested the first time.

As with any design problem, there is more than one technique we should consider for caching our home reference. We're basically talking about application-scope data in the web tier, so modifying the delegate to store the reference in the ServletContext after doing the required JNDI lookup is a potential solution. This would prevent any additional lookups, but it would require us to make the ServletContext available to our delegate through its constructor. This one change would ripple out to our service factory, because it currently instantiates an IStorefrontService implementation using its no-argument constructor. It would be preferable to choose a solution without such a strong tie to HTTP constructs. A more flexible approach is to apply the EJBHomeFactory pattern as a way to cache the references we need.

### Implementing an EJBHomeFactory

The EJBHomeFactory pattern is defined in *EJB Design Patterns* by Floyd Marinescu (Wiley & Sons). Implementing this pattern allows you to create and cache any EJB home reference needed by your application. Because it's not dependent on the ServletContext, you can reuse this technique in non-web applications. Example 13-8 shows the implementation of this pattern that we'll use for the Storefront application.

*Example 13-8. An EJBHomeFactory implementation*

```
package com.oreilly.struts.storefront.framework.ejb;

import java.io.InputStream;
import java.io.IOException;
import java.util.*;
import javax.ejb.*;
import javax.naming.*;
import javax.rmi.PortableRemoteObject;

/**
 * This class implements the EJBHomeFactory pattern. It performs JNDI
 * lookups to locate EJB homes and caches the results for subsequent calls.
 */
public class EJBHomeFactory {
  private Map homes;
  private static EJBHomeFactory singleton;
  private Context ctx;

  private EJBHomeFactory() throws NamingException {
    homes = Collections.synchronizedMap(new HashMap());
    try {
      // Load the properties file from the classpath root
      InputStream inputStream = getClass().getResourceAsStream(
        "/jndi.properties" );
      if ( inputStream != null) {
        Properties jndiParams = new Properties();
        jndiParams.load( inputStream );

        Hashtable props = new Hashtable();
        props.put(Context.INITIAL_CONTEXT_FACTORY,
        jndiParams.get(Context.INITIAL_CONTEXT_FACTORY));
        props.put(Context.PROVIDER_URL, jndiParams.get(Context.PROVIDER_URL));
        ctx = new InitialContext(props);
      }
      else {
        // Use default provider
        ctx = new InitialContext();
      }
    } catch( IOException ex ){
      // Use default provider
      ctx = new InitialContext();
    }
  }

  /**
   * Get the Singleton instance of the class.
   */
  public static EJBHomeFactory getInstance() throws NamingException {
    if (singleton == null) {
      singleton = new EJBHomeFactory();
    }
    return singleton;
  }
```

*Example 13-8. An EJBHomeFactory implementation (continued)*

```
/**
 * Specify the JNDI name and class for the desired home interface.
 */
public EJBHome lookupHome(String jndiName, Class homeClass)
  throws NamingException {
  EJBHome home = (EJBHome)homes.get(homeClass);
  if (home == null) {
    home = (EJBHome)PortableRemoteObject.narrow(ctx.lookup(
      jndiName), homeClass);
    // Cache the home for repeated use
    homes.put(homeClass, home);
  }
  return home;
  }
}
```

The getInstance method of EJBHomeFactory differs from most Singleton implementations in that it isn't declared to be synchronized. As discussed in *EJB Design Patterns*, using a synchronized method here would degrade performance without providing any significant benefit in return. If multiple instances of EJBHomeFactory are instantiated due to simultaneous calls to getInstance during initialization, some redundant home references will likely be created, but no harm will be done.

Notice that our EJBHomeFactory class accepts the JNDI name and class for the home interface it is requested to locate. If we needed to access more than one session bean in the application tier, we would simply implement a delegate class for each session bean and use our factory to locate the corresponding home interface. Besides the performance improvements the caching of homes gives us, all the ugly narrowing and exception handling that goes along with looking up these references is kept in one place.

The EJBHomeFactory constructor also takes care of externalizing the provider and factory parameters we need to access the naming service. A standard approach for doing this is to use a *jndi.properties* file that includes entries like the following:

```
java.naming.factory.initial=org.jnp.interfaces.NamingContextFactory
java.naming.provider.url=localhost
```

If you call the no-argument constructor for the InitialContext class, the classpath is searched for a *jndi.properties* file. If this file is found, its entries are used to initialize the naming context. In our example, the factory class explicitly loads this file from the classpath. Otherwise, classloader priorities within the web server could prevent these settings from being picked up before the default values defined for the server.

The JNDIConnectorPlugin example in Chapter 9 demonstrated how the naming service parameters could be read from the *web.xml* file and stored in the ServletContext. We're not using that approach here because we want to keep our factory independent of the web tier.

## Using an EJBHomeFactory in a business delegate

Our business delegate can be simplified now that we have a standard approach for locating the home interface. We can change the implementation of the init( ) method to the following:

```
private void init() {
  try {
    StorefrontHome sfHome = (StorefrontHome)EJBHomeFactory.getInstance().
      lookupHome("com.oreilly.struts.storefront.service.Storefront",
      StorefrontHome.class);
    storefront = sfHome.create();
  }
  catch (NamingException e) {
    throw new RuntimeException(e.getMessage());
  }
  catch (CreateException e) {
    throw new RuntimeException(e.getMessage());
  }
  catch (RemoteException e) {
    throw new RuntimeException(e.getMessage());
  }
}
```

## What about the remote references?

In our implementation, a remote reference to the session bean is created for each request. This isn't a problem from a performance standpoint, because the overhead attached to creating a remote reference pales in comparison with that associated with the home. However, this doesn't mean that you can't cache remote references if you want. In fact, if you're interfacing with a stateful session bean, you can't keep creating new remote references across requests, because you won't be calling the same bean instance each time.

You can avoid creating a new remote reference for each request by caching a business delegate instance in the session. Unlike with homes, you can't cache a remote reference as application-scope data. Even for stateless session beans, a remote reference holds information tied to the client thread that created it, so you can't share it across user sessions. If you cache the business delegate, there are some important changes to make—the user session could be serialized and restored by the web container, and a remote reference isn't required to be serializable. For a stateless session bean, you need to be able to create a new remote reference in the event of an error or a restart of the EJB container being accessed. For a stateful session bean, you need to hold an EJB handle in your delegate instead of a remote reference, so that you can always maintain a way to access the same bean.

In addition to the coverage in *EJB Design Patterns*, you can find more information on the patterns discussed in this chapter in *Core J2EE Patterns* by Deepak Alur, John Crupi, and Dan Malks (Prentice Hall).

# Using Dynamic Proxies

In this section, we'll look at one last example of something you might want to implement within your business delegate. Our current implementation works well for the Storefront application, but delegates tend to become cluttered with redundant-looking methods if they have to support an interface with more than a few methods. We declared only three methods for our overly simple Storefront model, but even they follow a somewhat monotonous pattern. With the exception of the logout() and destroy() methods, each business method in the delegate is implemented by calling the method with the same name on the session bean and catching a RemoteException to replace it with a DatastoreException. A dynamic proxy offers a way to get rid of this redundancy.

If you ever find yourself performing the same additional steps as part of delegating a set of method calls to another object, you should consider introducing a dynamic proxy. This concept is a little difficult to grasp if you've never worked with one before, but its use can do away with a lot of repetitive code. Basically, a dynamic proxy is an object created at runtime using reflection that implements one or more interfaces you specify. The implementation of the interface methods consists of calling the invoke() method of an object you also specify. This invoke() method is declared by the java.lang.reflect.InvocationHandler interface, which must be explicitly implemented by the object used to construct the proxy. The proxy passes parameters to the invoke() method that identify the interface method that was called and the arguments that were passed to it. This idea is always easiest to explain by example, so Example 13-9 shows a replacement for our business delegate that can be used with a dynamic proxy.

*Example 13-9. Dynamic proxy implementation of the Storefront service*

```
package com.oreilly.struts.storefront.service;

import java.lang.reflect.*;
import java.rmi.RemoteException;
import java.util.*;
import javax.ejb.CreateException;
import javax.naming.*;
import javax.rmi.PortableRemoteObject;
import com.oreilly.struts.storefront.catalog.view.ItemDetailView;
import com.oreilly.struts.storefront.customer.view.UserView;
import com.oreilly.struts.storefront.framework.ejb.EJBHomeFactory;
import com.oreilly.struts.storefront.framework.exceptions.*;

/**
 * This class is a dynamic proxy implementation of the IStorefrontService
 * interface. It implements two of the IStorefrontService methods itself and
 * delegates the others to the methods declared by the IStorefront business
 * interface with the same name.
 */
public class DynamicStorefrontEJBDelegate implements InvocationHandler {
```

*Example 13-9. Dynamic proxy implementation of the Storefront service (continued)*

```java
private IStorefront storefront;
private Map storefrontMethodMap;

public DynamicStorefrontEJBDelegate() {
  init();
}

private void init() {
  try {
    // Get the remote reference to the session bean
    StorefrontHome sfHome = (StorefrontHome)EJBHomeFactory.getInstance().
      lookupHome("com.oreilly.struts.storefront.service.Storefront",
      StorefrontHome.class);
    storefront = sfHome.create();

    // Store the business interface methods for later lookups
    storefrontMethodMap = new HashMap();
    Method[] storefrontMethods = IStorefront.class.getMethods();
    for (int i=0; i<storefrontMethods.length; i++) {
      storefrontMethodMap.put(storefrontMethods[i].getName(),
        storefrontMethods[i]);
    }
  }
  catch (NamingException e) {
    throw new RuntimeException(e.getMessage());
  }
  catch (CreateException e) {
    throw new RuntimeException(e.getMessage());
  }
  catch (RemoteException e) {
    throw new RuntimeException(e.getMessage());
  }
}

public void logout(String email) {
  // Do nothing for this example
}

public void destroy() {
  // Do nothing for this example
}

public Object invoke(Object proxy, Method method, Object[] args )
  throws Throwable{
  try {
    // Check for the two methods implemented by this class
    if (method.getName().equals("logout")) {
      logout((String)args[0]);
      return null;
    }
    else if (method.getName().equals("destroy")) {
      destroy();
```

*Example 13-9. Dynamic proxy implementation of the Storefront service (continued)*

```
          return null;
        }
      else {
        // This method should match a method implemented by the
        // session bean that has the same name and argument list
        Method storefrontMethod = (Method)storefrontMethodMap.get(
          method.getName());
        if (storefrontMethod != null) {
          // Call the method on the remote interface
          return storefrontMethod.invoke( storefront, args );
        }
        else {
          throw new NoSuchMethodException("The Storefront does not implement "
            + method.getName());
        }
      }
    } catch( InvocationTargetException ex ) {
      if (ex.getTargetException() instanceof RemoteException) {
        // RemoteException isn't declared by the IStorefront method that was
        // called, so we have to catch it and throw something that is
        throw DatastoreException.datastoreError(ex.getTargetException());
      }
      else {
        throw ex.getTargetException();
      }
    }
  }
}
```

The intent behind DynamicStorefrontEJBDelegate is for a dynamic proxy that is created as an implementation of the IStorefrontService interface to delegate all those calls to the invoke() method declared here. Notice that this delegate class is not declared to implement IStorefrontService. In fact, the only business methods from IStorefrontService that appear in this class are the logout() and destroy() methods that aren't implemented by our session bean.

To use the dynamic proxy–based delegate, we need to modify our approach for obtaining an implementation of the service interface from the factory. Rather than devising something elegant for a small part of this example, we'll just hardcode the new approach we need. This is shown in the following version of the createService() method of StorefrontServiceFactory:

```
public IStorefrontService createService(){
  Class[] serviceInterface = new Class[] { IStorefrontService.class };
  IStorefrontService proxy = (IStorefrontService)Proxy.newProxyInstance(
    Thread.currentThread().getContextClassLoader(), serviceInterface,
    new DynamicStorefrontEJBDelegate() );
  return proxy;
}
```

When an action class asks for an implementation of the service interface, the factory now creates a dynamic proxy that implements this interface using an instance of `DynamicStorefrontEJBDelegate`. When the action makes a call on the service interface, the call goes to the proxy and is transformed into a call on the delegate's `invoke( )` method. The `invoke( )` method checks the name of the method that was called and either calls the `logout( )` or `destroy( )` method implemented in the class or delegates it to the session-bean method with the same name. This sequence of calls is illustrated in Figure 13-1. The trapping and replacement of `RemoteException` when our business delegate calls a session-bean method are now handled in a single place. This single `invoke( )` method can handle all of the methods exposed by the session-bean business interface without modification.

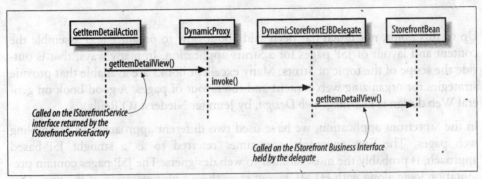

Figure 13-1. Sequence diagram for retrieving item detail through a dynamic proxy

A dynamic proxy is an appealing technique for minimizing method clutter in a business delegate, but there's a price to pay. When considering an approach such as this that relies heavily on reflection, you need to weigh the slower runtime performance that will result against the improved maintainability of your code.

# Conclusion

Not all web applications require the sophistication and complexity of an EJB container. The well-documented benefits of using an EJB server must be evaluated seriously against the added development and management complications for each project. Don't just assume that you have to use EJB for the model portion of a Struts application. However, if you do decide that EJB is appropriate, it doesn't have to impact the rest of the code. There are approaches that you can take to limit the coupling of your application to EJB and make it much easier to use.

# CHAPTER 14
# Using Tiles

Up to this point, not much has been said about how to organize and assemble the content and layout of JSP pages for a Struts application. In many ways, that is outside the scope of the topic of Struts. Many excellent books are available that provide strategies for organizing web content and the layout of pages. A good book on general Web design is *Learning Web Design*, by Jennifer Niederst (O'Reilly).

In the Storefront application, we have used two different approaches to assembling web pages. The first approach, sometimes referred to as a straight JSP-based approach, is probably the most familiar to web designers. The JSP pages contain presentation logic along with HTML layout tags; there's no separation of the two. This approach is typically used for smaller, less complicated web applications.

The second approach uses the JSP include directive. It's used by developers for larger web applications, or after they realize how repetitive the first approach can be. If you have spent much time maintaining web applications, you know how frustrating it can be to update a site's look and feel. Using the JSP include directive allows for more reuse, which reduces the total development and maintenance costs.

A third approach, which is introduced in this chapter, describes a far better way to reduce the amount of redundant code a web application contains and, at the same time, allows you to separate the content from the layout better than the first two approaches.

## Understanding Templates

Traditional GUI toolkits such as VisualWorks Smalltalk (*http://smalltalk.cincom.com/index.ssp*) or Java Swing all provide some type of layout manager that dictates how content should be displayed within the frame or window. For typical web sites, the layout can undergo many changes, both small and large, over its lifetime. Using layouts and layout managers can help to separate the different sections of the page from the layout so that they can be altered with minimal impact to the rest of the application. Unfortunately, the JSP technology does not natively provide any direct support for layouts or layout managers. This is why the template-based approach was invented. The concept of templates is not a new one—it has been around for many years, in one form or another.

To understand how templates can actually simplify a web site's layout, let's compare it with an approach that uses the JSP include mechanism. The current *index.jsp* page of the Storefront application is shown in Example 14-1.

*Example 14-1. The index.jsp page for the Storefront application*

```
<%@ taglib uri="/WEB-INF/struts-html.tld" prefix="html" %>
<%@ taglib uri="/WEB-INF/struts-logic.tld" prefix="logic" %>
<%@ taglib uri="/WEB-INF/struts-bean.tld" prefix="bean" %>

<html:html>
 <head>
 <title><bean:message key="global.title"/></title>
 <html:base/>
 <script language=javascript src="include/scripts.js"></script>
 <link rel="stylesheet" href="stylesheets/format_win_nav_main.css" type="text/css">
 </head>

 <body topmargin="0" leftmargin="0" bgcolor="#FFFFFF">

 <!-- Header information -->
 <%@ include file="include/head.inc"%>

 <!-- Menu bar -->
 <%@ include file="include/menubar.inc"%>

 <!-- Include the special offer -->
 <%@ include file="include/mainoffer.inc"%>

 <!-- Featured items header row -->
 <table width="645" cellpadding="0" cellspacing="0" border="0">
  <tr>
   <td width="21">
   <html:img height="1" alt="" page="/images/spacer.gif" width="1" border="0"/>
   </td>
   <td width="534">
   <html:img page="/images/week_picks.gif" altKey="label.featuredproducts"/>
   </td>
   <td width="1" bgcolor="#9E9EFF">
   <html:img height="1" alt="" page="/images/spacer.gif" width="1" border="0"/>
   </td>
   <td width="1"  bgcolor="#9E9EFF">
   <html:img height="1" alt="" page="/images/spacer.gif" width="1" border="0"/>
   </td>
   <td width="90" bgcolor="#9E9EFF" align="right">
   <html:img height="1" alt="" page="/images/spacer.gif" width="90" border="0"/>
   </td>
  </tr>
```

```
<tr>
<td>
<html:img height="1" alt="" page="/images/spacer.gif" width="21" border="0"/>
</td>
<td colspan="4" bgcolor="#9E9EFF">
<html:img height="1" alt="" page="/images/spacer.gif" width="1" border="0"/>
</td>
</tr>
</table>

<html:img height="10" alt="" page="/images/spacer.gif" width="1" border="0"/><br>

<!-- Include the featured items -->
<%@ include file="include/featureditems.inc"%>

<!-- Include the copyright statement -->
<%@ include file="include/copyright.inc"%>
</body>
</html:html>
```

Although the main page uses the JSP include directive, the layout is mixed with content in the page. For example, notice that the page specifies explicitly that the *head.inc* include file comes first, then the *menubar.inc* file, the *mainoffer.inc* file, and so on, right down to the *copyright.inc* include at the bottom of the page. For each page that we want to have this same layout, we need to add the same statements in exactly the same order. If a customer wants the menu along the left side instead of across the top, every page will have to be changed.

The Storefront application uses the JSP include mechanism rather than a straight JSP approach. Although the include mechanism is a step in the right direction because it does reduce redundancy (imagine if we included the copyright content in every page!), it's still less efficient than a template-based approach.

## What Is a Template?

A *template* is a JSP page that uses a JSP custom tag library to describe the layout of a page. The template acts as a definition for what the pages of an application will look like, without specifying the content. The content is inserted into the template page at runtime. One or more pages may use the same template.

The purpose of a template is to get a consistent look and feel within an application without having to hardcode that look and feel in every page. It makes sense that most of the pages will use the same template; however, it's not uncommon to have a different look and feel for a few pages within an application and therefore to require more than one template.

## Static Versus Dynamic Content

With JSP, there are two different kinds of content to include: static and dynamic. The include directive shown here:

```
<%@ include file="include/copyright.inc"%>
```

includes the source of the target page at translation/compile time. Therefore, it's not possible to include runtime content using the include directive. The JSP include directive treats a resource as a static object, and the context of the resource is included literally in the page.

In direct contrast, the include action shown here:

```
<jsp:include page="include/copyright.inc"/>
```

handles the resource as a dynamic object. The request is sent to the resource, and the result of the processing is included. Templates use a dynamic approach so that runtime expressions can be evaluated and included.

Example 14-2 illustrates a template for the Storefront application.

*Example 14-2. A basic template for the Storefront application*

```
<%@ taglib uri="/WEB-INF/struts-html.tld" prefix="html"%>
<%@ taglib uri="/WEB-INF/struts-bean.tld" prefix="bean"%>
<%@ taglib uri="/WEB-INF/struts-tiles.tld" prefix="tiles"%>

<html:html>
 <head>
  <title><bean:message key="global.title"/></title>
  <html:base/>
 </head>
 <body topmargin="0" leftmargin="0" bgcolor="#FFFFFF">

  <!-- Header page information -->
  <tiles:insert attribute="header"/>

  <!-- Menu bar -->
  <tiles:insert attribute="menubar"/>

  <!-- Main body information -->
  <tiles:insert attribute="body-content"/>

  <!-- Copyright information -->
  <tiles:insert attribute="copyright"/>
 </body>
</html:html>
```

Not many new concepts are introduced in the template file in Example 14-2. The first thing that you should notice is that we are using Struts custom tag libraries. The fact that we are using the Tiles tag library as well as the HTML and Bean libraries shouldn't be too shocking; the Tiles tag library is just like any other. We'll talk in detail about the Tiles tag library later in this chapter.

The rest of the page is a mixture of HTML layout tags. You should notice that there's no content included, only insert tags where content will be inserted at runtime. You should already be familiar with the Struts tags shown here, so we won't say anything about them. The insert tag performs a role similar to that of the JSP include directive. It's basically saying that somewhere there's a variable called header, for instance, and that the attribute value of "header" should be passed to the insert tag, and the content that is produced should be inserted right here. The same thing goes for the menubar, body-content, and copyright inserts. We'll explain shortly how the "real" content is substituted for these attributes at runtime.

Notice that this layout is very similar to the one shown in Example 14-1. The only difference is that instead of explicitly including the mainoffer and featureditem includes, as Example 14-1 does, the template file includes a body-content section. This allows us to reuse the template for any page that has this generic format. Once we figure out how to supply the page-specific body content, we can reuse this template over and over again. This one file can then control the layout of multiple pages. If we need to modify the layout of the site, this is the only file we need to change—that's the real power of using a template-based approach.

The last piece of the puzzle is how the header, menubar, body-content, and copyright sections are put together to form the rendered output. The important point to remember is that the JSP page shown in Example 14-2 is the template. You still need JSP pages that supply page-specific content used by the template. For example, if we rewrite the *index.jsp* page from Example 14-1 using the template from Example 14-2, it will look like the one in Example 14-3.

*Example 14-3. The index.jsp page for the Storefront application using a template*

```
<%@ taglib uri="/WEB-INF/struts-tiles.tld" prefix="tiles" %>

<tiles:insert page="/layouts/storefrontDefaultLayout.jsp" flush="true">
  <tiles:put name="header" value="/common/header.jsp" />
  <tiles:put name="menubar" value="/common/menubar.jsp" />
  <tiles:put name="body-content" value="/index-body.jsp" />
  <tiles:put name="copyright" value="/common/copyright.jsp" />
</tiles:insert>
```

The first thing to notice in Example 14-3 is that the Tiles tag library is included at the top. Every page (or *tile*) that needs to use the Tiles tag library must include it with this line:

```
<%@ taglib uri="/WEB-INF/struts-tiles.tld" prefix="tiles" %>
```

Two tags from the Tiles library are used in Example 14-3: insert and put. (The complete set of Tiles tags and their associated attributes are discussed later in this chapter.) You already saw the insert tag in Example 14-2, but it's performing a slightly different function in Example 14-3. Two attributes are being supplied to the insert tag: page and flush. The page attribute informs the tag that this JSP page is using a particular template (or *layout*, in the Tiles world). We are calling the template from Example 14-2 *storefrontDefaultLayout.jsp*. The flush attribute informs the controller to flush the page output stream before inserting content into the result page.

The put tag in Example 14-3 answers a question that we asked in the previous section: how does the page-specific content get supplied to the template? As you can see, the attributes for the put tag in this example are name and value. If you compare the values of the different name attributes, you'll see that they match up to the ones that the template file in Example 14-2 expects. When the *index.jsp* page from Example 14-3 is executed, the template file is processed and dynamically passed the *header.jsp*, *menubar.jsp*, *index-body.jsp*, and *copyright.jsp* files from the put tags:

```
<tiles:insert page="/layouts/storefrontDefaultLayout.jsp" flush="true">
  <tiles:put name="header" value="/common/header.jsp" />
  <tiles:put name="menubar" value="/common/menubar.jsp" />
  <tiles:put name="body-content" value="/index-body.jsp" />
  <tiles:put name="copyright" value="/common/copyright.jsp" />
</tiles:insert>
```

At runtime, the values of the put tags are dynamically substituted into the template file and processed. The resulting output is what gets displayed to the client.

To wrap up the discussion of templates, here is another page that uses the same template from Example 14-2 but supplies a different body-content. Example 14-4 shows the *itemdetail.jsp* page.

*Example 14-4. The itemdetail.jsp page for the Storefront application*

```
<%@ taglib uri="/WEB-INF/struts-tiles.tld" prefix="tiles" %>

<tiles:insert page="../layouts/storefrontDefaultLayout.jsp" flush="true">
  <tiles:put name="header" value="../common/header.jsp"/>
  <tiles:put name="menubar" value="../common/menubar.jsp"/>
  <tiles:put name="body-content" value="../catalog/itemdetail-body.jsp"/>
  <tiles:put name="copyright" value="../common/copyright.jsp"/>
</tiles:insert>
```

The only difference between the *index.jsp* page in Example 14-3 and the *itemdetail. jsp* page in Example 14-4 is the content supplied by the body-content attribute.

If you are still not convinced of the value of using templates, notice that the *index.jsp* and *itemdetail.jsp* pages in Examples 14-3 and 14-4 do not specify anything about how the content should be laid out. They both reference the *storefrontDefaultLayout. jsp* file, which has sole responsibility for displaying the content in a prescribed format. If we want to change the layout of the site, we have to modify only the *store-frontDefaultLayout.jsp* file.

# Installing and Configuring Tiles

Before you can use the Tiles framework, you must ensure that it's installed and properly configured within your web container. The Tiles framework is not dependent on any specific container. You will need to obtain the required files and ensure that they are placed into their proper directories within the web application.

## Downloading Tiles

The Tiles framework is included with the Struts distribution. It previously was included in the *contrib* folder, but it is now part of the core distribution. You also can find the latest source and binary distribution, as well as other useful information, at *http://www.lifl.fr/~dumoulin/tiles/index.html*.

## Installing the Required JARs and Misc Files

With earlier versions of Struts and Tiles, each was contained within its own JAR file. With Struts 1.1, Tiles components have now been integrated into *struts.jar*. As with all other things Struts, you will also need the standard commons JAR files installed in the WEB-INF/lib directory.

You will also need to install the Tiles TLD file, *struts-tiles.tld*, in the *WEB-INF* directory for the application.

 Don't add the *struts.jar* file to the classpath of your servlet container in an attempt to avoid placing it in the *WEB-INF/lib* directory of each individual web application. Doing so may cause `ClassNotFoundExceptions` to be thrown.

You should put the *tiles-config_1_1.dtd* file in the *WEB-INF* directory, too. This DTD is used to validate Tiles definition files, which we'll discuss later in this chapter.

## Adding the Tiles Tag Library

As with any other JSP tag library, you must add the Tiles library to the web application deployment descriptor before you can use it. Add the following taglib element to the *web.xml* file:

```
<taglib>
    <taglib-uri>/WEB-INF/struts-tiles.tld</taglib-uri>
    <taglib-location>/WEB-INF/struts-tiles.tld</taglib-location>
</taglib>
```

There should already be taglib elements present if you are using any of the standard Struts tag libraries. Each page that needs to use the Tiles tag library must include the following line at the top:

```
<%@ taglib uri="/WEB-INF/struts-tiles.tld" prefix="tiles" %>
```

## Configuring Tiles to Work with Struts

The Tiles framework can be used with or without Struts. Depending on how you use it, there are several options for configuring it for a web application. Because this book is about Struts, we'll focus on how to use it within a Struts application.

 With earlier versions of the Tiles framework, you had to configure a special ActionServlet called ActionComponentServlet in the *web.xml* file. It was also necessary to configure a special RequestProcessor in the Struts controller element. This is no longer true—a Tiles plug-in is now available that will take care of all the initialization.

The Tiles plug-in is really necessary only if you are planning on using Tiles definitions. It is possible to use the Tiles libraries with Struts without configuring the plug-in. However, it doesn't hurt to configure it, and it may save you time later if you decide to use definitions.

To add the Tiles plug-in to a Struts application, add the following plug-in element to the Struts configuration file:

```
<plug-in className="org.apache.struts.tiles.TilesPlugin" >
    <set-property property="definitions-config" value="/WEB-INF/struts-tiles-defs.xml" />
    <set-property property="definitions-debug" value="2" />
    <set-property property="definitions-parser-details" value="2" />
    <set-property property="definitions-parser-validate" value="true" />
    <set-property property="moduleAware" value="true" />
</plug-in>
```

Within the plug-in element, you can specify one or more set-property elements to pass additional parameters to the Plugin class. The definitions-config initialization parameter specifies the XML file or files containing Tile definitions. If multiple filenames are used, they must be comma-separated.

### The definitions-debug property

The definitions-debug parameter specifies the debug level. The allowed values are:

0   No debug information is written out.

1   Partial debug information is provided.

2   Full debug information is provided.

The default value is 0.

### The definitions-parser-details property

The definitions-parser-details parameter indicates the required level of debugging information while the definition files are being parsed. This value is passed to the Commons Digester. The allowed values are the same as those for the definitions-debug parameter. The default value is 0.

### The definitions-parser-validate property

The definitions-parser-validate parameter specifies whether the parser should validate the Tiles configuration file. The allowed values are true and false. The default is true.

### The moduleAware property

The moduleAware parameter specifies that a factory is created for each Struts module in the application.

### The definitions-factory-class property

There is an additional parameter, not shown, called definitions-factory-class. You can create a custom definitions factory and supply the class name here. The default is org.apache.struts.tiles.xmlDefinition.I18NfactorySet.

# Using Tiles

The Tiles framework provides a templating mechanism that allows you to separate the responsibilities of layout from those of content. As with the templates described earlier in this chapter, you have the ability to establish a layout and dynamically insert the contents of your pages into that layout at runtime. This is a powerful mechanism if you need to customize your site based on such things as internationalization, user preferences, or just the typical look-and-feel changes that occur in every web application sooner or later. The Tiles framework provides the following features:

- Template capabilities
- Dynamic page construction and loading
- Screen definitions
- Support for tile and layout reuse
- Support for internationalization
- Support for multiple channels

There has been a Template tag library within the Struts framework for quite some time. These tags allow you to use a very basic templating approach to assemble your JSP pages in a web application. Although these tags are helpful in separating the content for a web application from its prescribed layout, the Tiles framework goes much further and actually provides a superset of the Template tag library's behavior, as well as many other features.

 The Tiles framework was previously called Components, but the name was changed because that term is so overused. The Tiles documentation and source code still make reference to the old name in some places. Cedric Dumoulin created the Tiles framework to extend the concept of templates and provide developers with more flexibility and freedom when creating web applications built with JSP technology.

The content for the web applications is still driven by JSP pages and JavaBeans. However, the layout is specified within a separate JSP page or, as we'll see later, in an XML file.

## What Is a Tile?

A *tile* is an area or region within a web page. A page can consist of just one region or be broken up into several regions. Figure 14-1 illustrates an example from the Storefront application.

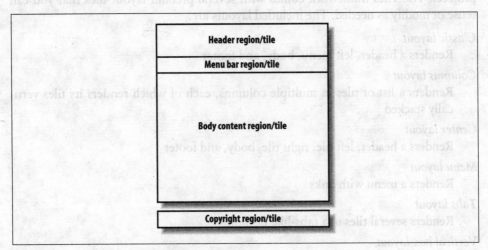

*Figure 14-1. The regions of the Storefront application*

A JSP page is typically made of several regions, or tiles. There's nothing too special about the page, other than the fact that it's designed to be used with the Tiles framework and makes use of the Tiles tag library.

The most important aspect of a tile is that it is reusable. This is true for layouts as well as body content. Unlike most JSP pages, tile components are reused within an application and possibly across different applications. Other than that, there's nothing that complicated about a tile. In fact, most of the examples we've seen so far can be classified as tiles, including Examples 14-2 through 14-4.

## Using a Layout Tile

In the Tiles world, a *layout* is what we have been referring to as a template. A layout serves the exact same purpose as a template—that is, to assemble a group of tiles to specify the format of a page. Example 14-2 is, in fact, a Tiles layout. The syntax between Tiles and a template library like the one included with Struts is almost identical.

 The Tiles framework provides a superset of the functionality included with the standard Struts template tags defined by David Geary, but it takes the concept of templates even further by providing additional functionality.

Layouts also are considered tiles. JSP pages and even entire applications can reuse layouts, and it's common to build a library of layouts that are used in many different projects. The Tiles framework comes with several prebuilt layout tiles that you can reuse or modify as needed. The included layouts are:

*Classic layout*
Renders a header, left menu, body, and footer

*Columns layout*
Renders a list of tiles in multiple columns, each of which renders its tiles vertically stacked

*Center layout*
Renders a header, left tile, right tile, body, and footer

*Menu layout*
Renders a menu with links

*Tabs layout*
Renders several tiles in a tabs-like fashion

*Vertical box layout*
Renders a list of tiles in a vertical column

Because one of the main goals of Tiles is reusability, you can reuse these layouts within your application with little or no modifications. You also have the freedom to customize the layouts in any way you need.

## Passing Parameters to the Layout

The layout tile shown in Example 14-2 is generic. It doesn't know anything about the *itemdetail.jsp* content or any of the other pages, for that matter. This is intentional, as it allows us to reuse this layout for many pages. Instead of being hardcoded within the layout page, the content is supplied or "passed" as parameters to the layout page at runtime. Let's look at the *signin.jsp* tile for the Storefront application, shown in Example 14-5.

*Example 14-5. The signin.jsp tile for the Storefront application*

```
<%@ taglib uri="/WEB-INF/struts-tiles.tld" prefix="tiles" %>

<tiles:insert page="../layouts/storefrontDefaultLayout.jsp" flush="true">
  <tiles:put name="header" value="../common/header.jsp"/>
  <tiles:put name="menubar" value="../common/menubar.jsp"/>
  <tiles:put name="body-content" value="../security/signin-body.jsp"/>
  <tiles:put name="copyright" value="../common/copyright.jsp"/>
</tiles:insert>
```

The purpose of the put tags in Example 14-5 is to supply the layout tile, which is specified in the enclosing insert tag, with content. The values of the name attributes in Example 14-5 (as in the other tiles shown in Examples 14-3 and 14-4) must match the ones that the layout tile is expecting.

The insert tag optionally can include an ignore attribute that will cause the tag to not write out anything when it can't find a value for an expected attribute. By default, a runtime exception is thrown when an attribute has not been supplied.

# The Tiles Tag Library

This section introduces the JSP custom tags used by the Tiles framework. Table 14-1 lists the tags available to the framework. The tags are very similar to the ones provided in any template-based framework, but with more functionality.

*Table 14-1. Tags within the Tiles tag library*

| Tag name | Description |
| --- | --- |
| add | Add an element to the surrounding list. |
| definition | Create a tile component definition. |

*Table 14-1. Tags within the Tiles tag library (continued)*

| Tag name | Description |
|---|---|
| get | Get the content from request scope that was put there by a put tag. |
| getAsString | Render the value of the specified tile/component/template attribute to the current Jsp-Writer. |
| importAttribute | Import a tile's attribute into the specified context. |
| initComponentDefinitions | Initialize a tile definitions factory. |
| insert | Insert a tiles component. |
| put | Put an attribute into a tile context. |
| putList | Declare a list that will be passed as an attribute. |
| useAttribute | Use an attribute value inside a page. |

# The insert Tag

The insert tag is responsible for inserting content into a page. In a layout tile, the insert tag prescribes where the content will go using attribute values. In a regular, non-layout tile, the insert tag is used to retrieve a layout and allow content to be passed to the layout using put tags. Table 14-2 lists the attributes for the insert tag.

*Table 14-2. Attributes for the insert tag*

| Attribute name | Description |
|---|---|
| attribute | The name of an attribute in the current tile/component context. The value of this attribute is passed to the name attribute. |
| beanName | The name of the bean used as a value. The bean is retrieved from the specified context, if any. Otherwise, the pageContext.findAttribute( ) method is used. If the beanProperty attribute is also specified, retrieve the value from the corresponding bean property.<br><br>If the bean (or bean property value) is an instance of one of the Attribute classes (Direct, Instance, etc.), the insertion is done according to the class type. Otherwise, the toString( ) method is called on the bean, and the returned String is passed to the name attribute. |
| beanProperty | The name of the bean property. If specified, the value is retrieved from this property. |
| beanScope | The context scope the bean can be found within. If not specified, the pageContext.findAttribute( )method is used. The scope can be any JSP scope, component, or template. In the two latter cases, the bean is searched in the tile/component/template context. |
| component | A string representing the URI of a tile or template. The template, page, and component attributes have exactly the same behavior. |
| controllerUrl | The URL of a controller called immediately before the page is inserted. The URL usually denotes a Struts action. The controller (action) is used to prepare data to be rendered by the inserted tile.<br><br>Only one of controllerUrl or controllerClass should be used. |

*Table 14-2. Attributes for the insert tag (continued)*

| Attribute name | Description |
|---|---|
| controllerClass | The class type of a controller called immediately before the page is inserted. The controller is used to prepare data to be rendered by the inserted tile. |
| | Only one of `controllerUrl` or `controllerClass` should be used. The class must implement or extend one of the following: `org.apache.struts.tiles.Controller`, `org.apache.struts.tiles.ControllerSupport`, or `org.apache.struts.action.Action`. |
| definition | The name of the definition to insert. Definitions are defined in a centralized file. For now, only definitions from a factory can be inserted with this attribute. To insert a definition defined with the `definition` tag, use beanName="". |
| flush | `true` or `false`. If `true`, the current page output stream is flushed before tile insertion. |
| ignore | If this attribute is set to `true` and the attribute specified by the name does not exist, simply return without writing anything. The default value is `false`, which will cause a runtime exception to be thrown. |
| name | The name of an entity to insert. The search is done in this order: `definition`, `attribute`, then `page`. |
| page | A string representing the URI of a tile or template. The `template`, `page`, and `component` attributes have exactly the same behavior. |
| role | If the user is in the specified role, the tag is taken into account; otherwise, the tag is skipped and the content is not written out. |
| template | A string representing the URI of a tile or template. The `template`, `page`, and `component` attributes have exactly the same behavior. |

Several examples of the insert tag were shown earlier in this chapter.

# The definition Tag

The `definition` tag is used to create a tile (template) definition as a bean. The newly created bean will be saved under the specified id, in the requested scope. The definition tag has the same syntax as the insert tag. The new definition can extend a definition described in the definition factory (XML file) and may overload any previously defined parameters. Table 14-3 lists the attributes supported by the definition tag.

*Table 14-3. Attributes for the definition tag*

| Attribute name | Description |
|---|---|
| extends | The name of a parent definition that is used to initialize this new definition. The parent definition is searched in the definitions factory. |
| id | The name under which the newly created definition bean will be saved. This attribute is required. |
| page | URL of the template/component to insert. Same as `template`. |
| role | The role to check before inserting this definition. If the role is not defined for the current user, the definition is not inserted. Checking is done at insertion time, not during the definition process. |

*Table 14-3. Attributes for the definition tag  (continued)*

| Attribute name | Description |
|---|---|
| scope | The variable scope in which the newly defined bean will be created. If not specified, the bean will be created in page scope. |
| template | A string representing the URL of a tile/component/template (a JSP page). |

The following fragment illustrates how to use the definition tag in a JSP page:

```
<tiles:definition
  id="storefront.default"
  page="/layouts/storefrontDefaultLayout.jsp"
  scope="request">
    <tiles:put name="header" value="/common/header.jsp" />
    <tiles:put name="menubar" value="/common/menubar.jsp" />
    <tiles:put name="copyright" value="/common/copyright.jsp" />
</tiles:definition>
```

A complete example is shown later, in the "Declaring Definitions in a JSP Page" section of this chapter.

## The put Tag

The put tag is used to pass attributes to a tile component. This tag can be used only inside the insert or definition tags. The value (or content) of the put tag is specified using the value attribute or the tag body. It is also possible to specify the type of the value:

string
> Content is literally translated.

page *or* template
> Content is included from specified URL.

definition
> Content comes from specified definition (from factory). Name is used as definition name.

If the type attribute is used, it is taken into account by the get or insert tags inside the inserted tile. If the type attribute is not specified, the content is untyped, unless it comes from a typed bean.

 Setting direct="true" is equivalent to setting type="string".

Table 14-4 lists the attributes for the put tag.

*Table 14-4. Attributes for the put tag*

| Attribute name | Description |
| --- | --- |
| beanName | The name of the bean used to retrieve the value. The bean is retrieved from the specified context, if any. Otherwise, the `pageContext.findAttribute()` method is used. If `beanProperty` is specified, retrieve the value from the corresponding bean property. |
| beanProperty | The property name in the bean. If specified, the value is retrieved from this property. |
| beanScope | The scope used to search for the bean. If not specified, the `pageContext.findAttribute()` method is used. The scope can be any JSP scope, "tile", "component", or "template". In the three later cases, the bean is searched in the tile/component/template context. |
| content | Content that's put into tile scope. This attribute is equivalent to the `value` attribute and was added for compatibility with the JSP template tags. |
| direct | How the content is handled: `true` means content is printed directly; `false` means content is included. `false` is the default. This is another way to specify content type. If `direct="true"`, content is "string"; if `direct="false"`, content is "page". This attribute was added for compatibility with the JSP template tags. |
| name | The name of the attribute. |
| role | If the user is in the specified role, the tag is taken into account. Otherwise, the tag is skipped and the content is not written out. |
| type | The content type. Valid values are "string", "page", "template", or "definition". |
| value | The attribute value—can be a `String` or an `Object`. The value can come from a direct assignment (value="aValue") or from a bean. One of `value`, `content`, or `beanName` must be present. |

# The putList Tag

The `putList` tag creates a list that will be passed as an attribute to a tile. The list elements are added using the `add` tag. This tag can be used only inside the `insert` or `definition` tag. Table 14-5 lists the attribute for the `putList` tag.

*Table 14-5. Attribute for the putList tag*

| Attribute name | Description |
| --- | --- |
| name | The name of the List. This attribute is required. |

# The add Tag

The `add` tag adds an element to the surrounding list. This tag can be used only inside the `putList` tag. The value can come from a direct assignment (value="aValue") or from a bean. One of `value` or `beanName` must be specified. Table 14-6 lists the attributes for the add tag.

*Table 14-6. Attributes for the add tag*

| Attribute name | Description |
| --- | --- |
| beanName | The name of the bean used to retrieve the value. The bean is retrieved from the specified context, if any. Otherwise, the pageContext.findAttribute() method is used. If beanProperty is specified, retrieve the value from the corresponding bean property. |
| beanProperty | The bean property name. If specified, the value is retrieved from this property. |
| beanScope | The scope used to search for the bean. If not specified, the pageContext. findAttribute() method is used. The scope can be any JSP scope, "component", or "template". In the two latter cases, the bean is searched in the tile/component/template context. |
| content | The value is the same as the value attribute. This attribute was added for compatibility with the JSP template tags. |
| direct | How the content is handled: true means content is printed directly; false means content is included. false is the default. |
| role | If the user is in the specified role, the tag is taken into account; otherwise, the tag is ignored (skipped). The role isn't taken into account if the add tag is used in a definition. |
| type | The content type: "string", "page", "template", or "definition". If the type attribute is not specified, content is *untyped*, unless it comes from a typed bean. |
| value | The value to be added. Can be a String or Object. |

## The get Tag

The get tag retrieves content from the tile context and includes it in the page. Table 14-7 lists the attributes for the get tag.

*Table 14-7. Attributes for the get tag*

| Attribute name | Description |
| --- | --- |
| flush | true or false. If true, the current page output stream is flushed before tile insertion. |
| ignore | If this attribute is set to true and the attribute specified by the name does not exist, simply return without writing anything. The default value is false, which will cause a runtime exception to be thrown. |
| name | The name of the content to get from the tile scope. This attribute is required. |
| role | If the user is in the specified role, the tag is taken into account; otherwise, the tag is ignored. |

## The getAsString Tag

The getAsString tag retrieves the value of the specified tile attribute property and renders it to the current JspWriter as a String. The usual toString() conversion is applied to the value. If the named value is not found, a JSPException will be thrown. Table 14-8 lists the attributes for the getAsString tag.

*Table 14-8. Attributes for the getAsString tag*

| Attribute name | Description |
|---|---|
| ignore | If this attribute is set to `true` and the attribute specified by the name does not exist, simply return without writing anything. The default value is `false`, which will cause a runtime exception to be thrown. |
| name | The attribute name. This attribute is required. |
| role | If the user is in the specified role, the tag is taken into account; otherwise, the tag is ignored. |

## The useAttribute Tag

The `useAttribute` tag declares a Java variable and an attribute in the specified scope, using the tile's attribute value. The variable and attribute will have the name specified by id, or the original name if not specified. Table 14-9 lists the attributes for the useAttribute tag.

*Table 14-9. Attributes for the useAttribute tag*

| Attribute name | Description |
|---|---|
| classname | The class of the declared variable. |
| id | The declared attribute and variable name. |
| ignore | If this attribute is set to `true` and the attribute specified by the name does not exist, simply return without error. The default value is `false`, which will cause a runtime exception to be thrown. |
| name | The tile's attribute name. This attribute is required. |
| scope | The scope of the declared attribute. Defaults to "page". |

## The importAttribute Tag

The `importAttribute` tag imports the attribute from the tile to the requested scope. The name and scope attributes are optional. If not specified, all tile attributes are imported in page scope. Once imported, an attribute can be used like any other bean from the JSP context. Table 14-10 lists the attributes for the importAttribute tag.

*Table 14-10. Attributes for the importAttribute tag*

| Attribute name | Description |
|---|---|
| ignore | If this attribute is set to `true` and the attribute specified by the name does not exist, simply return without error. The default value is `false`, which will cause a runtime exception to be thrown. |
| name | The tile's attribute name. If not specified, all attributes are imported. |
| scope | The scope into which the attribute is imported. Defaults to "page". |

## The initComponentDefinitions Tag

The `initComponentDefinitions` tag initializes the definitions factory. Table 14-11 lists the attributes for the tag.

*Table 14-11. Attributes for the initComponentDefinitions tag*

| Attribute name | Description |
| --- | --- |
| classname | If specified, the classname attribute of the factory to create and initialize. |
| file | The definition file's name. This attribute is required. |

# Using Definitions

So far, we've seen that using Tiles can add value to an application because you're able to organize the layout of a page into a single resource, the layout JSP page. This can save development time and, more importantly, the time it takes to change the layout for an application. However, there is a problem with the approach used in the Storefront application shown earlier. In each of the non-layout tiles, there is redundant code that specifies what content to use for the header, menubar, and copyright content—the same attributes are being passed in every page. This may not always be the case, but in general, these values will be constant throughout an application. For instance, the same copyright is typically shown on every page.

It's redundant to have to specify these in every tile. Ideally, we could declare these attributes in one place, and the tiles could include just the page-specific attributes where needed. *Tiles definitions* provide just such functionality. A definition allows you to statically specify the attributes that are used by a template, which in turn allows you to specify only the page-specific attributes in your tiles. Definitions enable you to:

- Centralize declaration of page description
- Avoid repetitive declaration of nearly identical pages (by using definition inheritance)
- Avoid creation of intermediate components used to pass parameters
- Specify the name of a definition as a forward in the Struts configuration file
- Specify the name of a definition as component parameters
- Overload definition attributes
- Use a different copy of a component, depending on the locale (I18N)
- Use a different copy of a component, depending on a key (this might be used to show different layouts depending on the client type)

Definitions can be declared in a JSP page or an XML file. Either way, you should strive to keep the definitions in a central place. If you are planning on using a JSP page to specify your definitions, put all the definitions for your application in a single page. Don't spread your definitions throughout your site, as that will only make maintenance more difficult.

# Declaring Definitions in a JSP Page

As previously mentioned, there are two locations in which you can specify definitions: a JSP page or an XML file. We'll discuss the JSP page approach first.

To use the JSP approach, create a JSP page and declare all of your definitions in that file. For the Storefront application, we've created a file called *storefront-defs.jsp* and put the default definition in it, as Example 14-6 shows.

*Example 14-6. Declaring tiles definitions in a JSP page*

```
<%@ taglib uri="/WEB-INF/struts-tiles.tld" prefix="tiles" %>

<tiles:definition
  id="storefront.default"
  page="/layouts/storefrontDefaultLayout.jsp"
  scope="request">
    <tiles:put name="header" value="/common/header.jsp" />
    <tiles:put name="menubar" value="/common/menubar.jsp" />
    <tiles:put name="copyright" value="/common/copyright.jsp" />
</tiles:definition>
```

The definition in Example 14-6 uses the same layout tile used earlier. The common files that were spread through the various tiles are now located in the definition file. This makes changing their values much easier. For instance, if we wanted to specify a different copyright page, the only place to change it would be in the definition file; we would not have to modify every JSP page.

The definition tag syntax looks very similar to the syntax for the insert tags shown earlier. We just need to provide an id attribute and switch the path attribute to the page attribute. Also, the default scope for the definition tag is page. It was set to request scope here to give it a little broader scope.

To take advantage of the definition, the tile components need to be able to access it. Because we have given the definition request scope and it will exist only for the lifetime of a request, we need a way to include the definition in the various JSP pages. Fortunately, we already know how to include a JSP page in another page using the JSP include directive. Example 14-7 shows what the *signin.jsp* page looks like using the JSP definition file.

*Example 14-7. The signin.jsp page using a tile definition*

```
<%@ taglib uri="/WEB-INF/struts-tiles.tld" prefix="tiles" %>

<%@include file="../common/storefront-defs.jsp" %>

<tiles:insert definition="storefront.default">
  <tiles:put name="body-content" value="/index.jsp"/>
</tiles:insert>
```

With this approach, the tile components have to insert only the page-specific content. Compare Example 14-7 to Example 14-5. Notice that the *signin.jsp* file using the definition needs to provide only the page-specific content, the *sign-body.jsp* file.

## Declaring Definitions in a Configuration File

You also have the option of declaring definitions in a centralized XML file. Whether you use the JSP or the XML alternative really depends on your requirements. With the XML approach, you won't need to use the include directive shown earlier.

### Creating a definition configuration file

To use the XML approach, create an XML file that follows the syntax of the *tiles-config.dtd* file. The definition XML file should be placed in the *WEB-INF* directory, as with the other application meta-information. The DTD should also be placed in the *WEB-INF* directory. Example 14-8 shows an example of a definition XML file.

*Example 14-8. The Storefront definition XML file*

```
<!DOCTYPE tiles-definitions PUBLIC
 "-//Apache Software Foundation//DTD Tiles Configuration//EN"
 "http://jakarta.apache.org/struts/dtds/tiles-config.dtd">

<tiles-definitions>
 <definition name="storefront.default" path="/layouts/storefrontDefaultLayout.jsp">
  <put name="header" value="/common/header.jsp" />
  <put name="menubar" value="/common/menubar.jsp" />
  <put name="copyright" value="/common/copyright.jsp" />
 </definition>
</tiles-definitions>
```

There's not much difference between the definition format specified in the JSP file in Example 14-6 and the XML file in Example 14-8. The XML file uses a slightly different syntax, but it's still very similar.

The two formats are just similar enough to cause problems. Notice that in the JSP definition, you use the put tag:

```
<tiles:put
 name="body-content"
 value="../security/signin-body.jsp"/>
```

but in the XML definition, you use the put element:

```
<put
 name="header"
 value="/common/header.jsp" />
```

Make sure that you don't get these two confused, as this can be a difficult bug to track down.

Each definition should have a unique name. JSP tags and pages use the name to retrieve the definition. It can't be used as a URL, however; it's only a logical name for the definition.

## Extending Tile Definitions

One of the most powerful features of tile definitions is the ability to create new definitions by extending existing ones. All attributes and properties of the parent definition are inherited, and you can override any attribute or property. To extend a definition, add the extends attribute. Example 14-9 shows an example of a definition named storefront.custom extending the storefront.default definition.

*Example 14-9. Definitions can extend other definitions*

```
<tiles-definitions>
 <definition name="storefront.default" path="/layouts/storefrontDefaultLayout.jsp">
  <put name="header" value="/common/header.jsp" />
  <put name="menubar" value="/common/menubar.jsp" />
  <put name="copyright" value="/common/copyright.jsp" />
 </definition>
</tiles-definitions>

<tiles-definitions>
 <definition name="storefront.custom" extends="storefront.default">
  <put name="copyright" value="/common/new-copyright.jsp" />
 </definition>
</tiles-definitions>
```

In Example 14-9, all of the attributes in the storefront.default definition are inherited. However, the storefront.customer definition overrides the value for the copyright attribute with an alternate copyright page. This is a very powerful feature. If you have multiple child definitions all extending a root definition, changing a value in the root definition changes it for all the children. Thus, you can change the layout in the root definition and have it changed for all child definitions.

## Using Definitions as Forwards in Struts

Tiles definitions can also be used as Struts forwards, instead of actual URLs. To use definitions in this manner, you first create the definitions:

```
<tiles-definitions>
  <definition name="storefront.default"
              path="/layouts/storefrontDefaultLayout.jsp">
    <put name="header" value="/common/header.jsp" />
    <put name="menubar" value="/common/menubar.jsp" />
    <put name="copyright" value="/common/copyright.jsp" />
  </definition>

  <definition name="storefront.superuser.main" extends="storefront.default">
```

```
        <put name="header" value="/common/super_header.jsp" />
        <put name="menubar" value="/common/super_menubar.jsp" />
        <put name="copyright" value="/common/copyright.jsp" />
    </definition>
</tiles-definitions>
```

This fragment shows two definitions, the standard default definition and a second one that defines the layout for a "superuser." A superuser might be someone that frequents the site and places many orders, and such a user might be given more options on the menu bar to facilitate faster ordering.

In the Struts configuration file, we need to define the forwards that use these definitions:

```
<global-forwards>
    <forward name="Super_Success" path="storefront.superuser.main" />
</global-forwards>
```

You can then use the `Super_Success` forward to send the user to the `storefront.superuser.main` definition just as you would for any other forward.

## Internationalization Support with Tiles

Although the Struts framework provides certain I18N capabilities that can be used with Tiles, Tiles also provides the ability to select a particular tile based on the user's locale. To support this feature in your application, you need to create a different Tiles definition file for each locale that you need to support. For example, if you need to support a set of definitions for the U.S. locale and a separate set for the German locale, you must create two separate definition files:

- *tiles-tutorial-defs_en.xml*
- *tiles-tutorial-defs_de.xml*

The suffix naming conventions follow the ones set by the `java.util.ResourceBundle`, which is also used by the resource bundles for Struts. When a request for a definition is made, the correct definition is determined by the included locale.

 As with regular Java resource bundles, you should always provide a base definition that is used when no locale is provided or when an unsupported locale is used. No language or country suffix is appended to the name of the Tiles base definition file.

Once you have created the locale-specific definition files and placed them in the *WEB-INF* directory, the only other necessary step is to ensure that a `Locale` is stored in the user's `HttpSession`. The Tiles framework depends on the same `Locale` instance that Struts uses to determine which definition file to use. You will need to ensure that the Struts framework is storing the user's `Locale` in the session. This is accomplished by setting the locale attribute to true in the controller element. See "The Struts Configuration DTD" in Chapter 4 for more information on the controller element.

That's all there is to it. Note that you should still rely on the Struts resource bundle for locale-sensitive resources such as text, messages, and images. The I18N support in Tiles should be used for differences in layout based on the locale. Struts and Tiles work very well together to provide complete I18N support.

# CHAPTER 15

# Logging in a Struts Application

As dedicated and knowledgeable Java programmers, we always want to believe that the software we create will stand up to the utmost scrutiny. However, as human beings, we'll all fallible, so it's never a good practice to believe that our software contains no defects. The important thing is to use every means available to try to eliminate the defects, or at least reduce them to an acceptable amount.

Generating log messages that tell you what the application is doing can help you locate any defects that are present in your software. However, logging is important for other reasons as well. For example, security and auditing might depend on logging to provide information to the system administrators about what the authorized and, more importantly, unauthorized users of the application are doing. By providing real-time information about potential security attacks on the application, logging can give a much-needed edge to the system administrators and allow for quicker reactions to attacks. Finally, good logging practices can also play a role in solving some tricky performance problems. Knowing how many times a certain page or method is executed is helpful when tracking down why the application isn't performing up to expectations.

This chapter takes a close look at how the use of logging in your Struts application can help you identify defects before the application gets into production, or, if your software is already being used in production, how logging can help you to quickly identify problems with the software and arrive at solutions.

## Logging in a Web Application

The importance of logging has been evident to experienced developers for many years. Arguably, logging can be as important a part of your framework as exception handling or even security, both of which may rely on logging functionality to help carry out their responsibilities. Without logging, application maintenance can become a nightmare for the developers. We all know that all "real" applications periodically go through maintenance cycles.

Still, you may wonder whether logging in web applications is as necessary and important as logging in other types of applications. Because web applications can sometimes be smaller and less complex than their enterprise counterparts, you might think that logging is less important in these applications. However, with nontrivial web applications, this is not the case—logging is just as critical there as it is in an enterprise application.

## System Versus Application Logging

Log messages can be arbitrarily broken down into two categories: *system* messages and *application* messages. System messages have to do with the internal operation of the application, rather than something specific to a user or data—for example, a system message might indicate that the application is unable to send an email because the SMTP host is not responding. On the other hand, an application message might indicate that the user "Jane Doe" tried to submit a purchase order that was above her company's credit limit.

The system message in the first case might be logged with a priority of "error," whereas the application message might only get a priority of "info." We can then set up the logging environment so that "error" messages generate an email or a pager message to the system administrators for immediate attention, while "info" messages go into a file for later auditing.

The different types and categories of log messages are typically used for different purposes across organizations. Although many applications may log messages with the priority of "error," what's an error to one organization may just be a warning to another. There's not a great deal of consistency across organizations, and there may never be—organizations have different priorities, and what's critical to one may not necessarily be critical to another.

In this chapter, we generalize the discussion of system versus application messages. Because views of what's considered an error differ, there's no general way to specify what's an error, a warning, or just general information for your particular application. That's a decision that you, your development team, and your product-management group will have to make. We'll keep our discussion at a higher level and not focus on these issues.

# Using the Servlet Container for Logging

The Servlet specification requires that every servlet container allow developers to log events to the container log file. Although the name and location of the log file are container-dependent, the manner in which these events are logged is dictated by the specification and is portable across web containers.

The `javax.servlet.ServletContext` class contains two methods that can be used for logging messages to the container's log:

```
public void log( String msg );
public void log( String msg, Throwable throwable );
```

You can use either of these methods by obtaining the `ServletContext` and passing the appropriate arguments. Example 15-1 illustrates how this can be done using a Struts Action.

*Example 15-1. The LoginAction using the ServletContext to log messages*

```java
public class LoginAction extends StorefrontBaseAction {

  public ActionForward execute( ActionMapping mapping,
                                ActionForm form,
                                HttpServletRequest request,
                                HttpServletResponse response )
  throws Exception{

    // Get the user's login name and password. They should have already been
    // validated by the ActionForm.
    String email = ((LoginForm)form).getEmail();
    String password = ((LoginForm)form).getPassword();

    // Obtain the ServletContext
    ServletContext context = getServlet().getServletContext();

    // Log which user is trying to enter the site
    context.log( "Login email: " + email );

    // Log in through the security service
    IStorefrontService serviceImpl = getStorefrontService();
    UserView userView = serviceImpl.authenticate(email, password);

    // Log the UserView for auditing purposes
    context.log( userView.toString() );

    UserContainer existingContainer = null;
    HttpSession session = request.getSession(false);
    if ( session != null ){
      existingContainer = getUserContainer(request);
      session.invalidate();
    }else{
      existingContainer = new UserContainer();
    }

    // Create a new session for the user
    session = request.getSession(true);
    existingContainer.setUserView(userView);
    session.setAttribute(IConstants.USER_CONTAINER_KEY, existingContainer);

    return mapping.findForward(IConstants.SUCCESS_KEY);
  }
}
```

The LoginAction in Example 15-1 shows a very simple example of sending log messages to the container's log file. It calls the log( ) method and passes a literal string message that will be written to the log. As was mentioned earlier, the name and location of the log are dependent on which web container is being used.

Some web containers may assign a separate log file for each web application, while others may use just a single log file. If only one log file is used, messages from different web applications will end up in the same log file and generally will be prefixed with the web application name.

## Using Filters

Filters are a new feature of the 2.3 Java Servlet specification. Servlet filters allow you to inspect and/or transform the content of the HTTP request and response objects. Because of the manner in which filters are invoked by the servlet container, they can operate on dynamic as well as static content.

 Struts 1.1 supports both the 2.2 and 2.3 Servlet specifications. If you are not using a 2.3-compliant container, you will not be able to take advantage of servlet filters.

Using filters, servlet developers can perform the following tasks:

- Access a web resource before a request to it is invoked.
- Process a request for a resource before it is invoked.
- Modify the request headers and data by wrapping the request with a customized version of the request object.
- Modify the response headers and data by wrapping the response with a customized version of the response object.
- Intercept a method call on a resource after it has been performed.
- Perform actions on a servlet, or group of servlets, by one or more filters in a specified order.

Based on the tasks required by servlet developers, the Servlet specification describes several possible types of filters:

- Authentication filters
- Logging and auditing filters
- Image conversion filters
- Data compression filters
- Encryption filters
- Tokenizing filters
- Filters that trigger resource-access events

- XSLT filters that transform XML content
- MIME-type chain filters
- Filters that cache URLs and other information

All of these types of filters are interesting, but in this chapter we are interested in using filters for logging and auditing. With filters, it's possible to log messages using any data that is contained in the request and response objects. Because the filter is coupled tightly to the servlet container, you'll probably still need logging functionality elsewhere in your application. Using filters for logging is generally not sufficient for the entire application. However, filters are perfect for auditing or tracking a user's actions through the system.

If you need to get an idea of which parts of your site your users are frequenting or where certain user groups are going most often, filters may be an ideal solution. They might even be able to give you information about the specific data that the users are viewing most often. For example, say that you have an online catalog application and you are interested in knowing which catalogs the users are browsing most often. Because the request and response objects contain this information, you can easily track this information and store it into a database for further analysis.

## Creating a Filter

There are three basic steps for creating a filter:

1. Create a Java class that implements the javax.servlet.Filter interface and that contains a no-argument constructor.
2. Declare the filter in the web application deployment descriptor using the filter element.
3. Package the filter class along with the rest of the web application resources.

### Creating the filter class

The first step in creating a servlet filter is to create a new Java class (or use an existing one) and have it implement the javax.servlet.Filter interface. Java classes can implement multiple interfaces, so you don't necessarily have to create a new class. However, the class will eventually need to be loaded by the web container, so it shouldn't be one that is installed only on a backend system, like an EJB container.

The Filter interface has three methods that must be implemented by your class:

```
public void init(FilterConfig filterConfig) throws ServletException;

public void doFilter(ServletRequest request,
                     ServletResponse response,
                     FilterChain chain)
   throws IOException, ServletException;

public void destroy();
```

The web container calls the init( ) method when it's ready to put the filter into service. You can initialize any needed resources in this method. The destroy( ) method is the opposite of the init( ) method. The web container calls this method when it takes the filter out of service. At this point, you should clean up any open resources that the filter may be using, such as database connections.

Finally, the web container calls the doFilter( ) method every time a request is received and the container determines that the filter instance should be notified. This is where you should place whatever functionality the filter is designed to perform.

Example 15-2 shows an example filter class that could be used to log to the servlet log file or to initialize a third-party logging service.

*Example 15-2. A servlet filter class example*

```java
import java.io.IOException;
import javax.servlet.Filter;
import javax.servlet.FilterChain;
import javax.servlet.FilterConfig;
import javax.servlet.ServletRequest;
import javax.servlet.ServletContext;
import javax.servlet.ServletResponse;
import javax.servlet.ServletException;
/**
 * An example servlet filter class.
 */
public class LoggingFilter implements Filter{

    public final static String LOG_FILE_PARAM = "log_file_name";
    private FilterConfig filterConfig = null;
    private ServletContext servletContext = null;

    public void init( FilterConfig config ) throws ServletException {
        // Initialize any neccessary resources here
        this.filterConfig = config;
        this.servletContext = config.getServletContext();

        // You can get access to initialization parameters from web.xml
        // although this example doesn't really use it
        String logFileName = config.getInitParameter( LOG_FILE_PARAM );

        // You can log messages to the servlet log like this
        log( "Logging to file " + logFileName );

        // Maybe initialize a third-party logging framework like log4j
    }

    public void doFilter( ServletRequest request,
                          ServletResponse response,
                          FilterChain filterChain )
        throws IOException, ServletException {

        // Log a message here using the request data
```

*Example 15-2. A servlet filter class example (continued)*

```
      log( "doFilter called on LoggingFilter" );

    // All request and response headers are available to the filter
      log( "Request received from " + request.getRemoteHost() );

    // Call the next filter in the chain
      filterChain.doFilter( request, response );
  }

  public void destroy(){
    // Remove any resources to the logging framework here
      log( "LoggingFilter destroyed" );
  }

  protected void log( String message ) {
    getServletContext().log("LoggingFilter: " + message );
  }

  protected ServletContext getServletContext(){
    return this.servletContext;
  }
}
```

 Just as you must be careful with multiple threads in Java servlets, you must be careful not to violate any thread-safety practices with filters. The servlet container may send concurrent threads to a single instance of a filter class, and you must ensure that you don't do anything to cause problems between the threads. In other words, no client-specific data should be stored in instance variables. Local variables are fine, just as they are in Java servlets, because they are stored on the stack rather than the heap.

### Declaring the filter in the deployment descriptor

The second step in creating a servlet filter is to configure the proper elements in the deployment descriptor for the web application. As you learned in Chapter 4, the name of the deployment descriptor file for a web application is *web.xml*.

The first step in setting up the filter declaration in the web application's deployment descriptor is to create the actual `filter` elements. Chapter 4 describes the `filter` element in detail. The following deployment descriptor fragment illustrates how it looks using the `LoggingFilter` class from the previous section:

```
<filter>
  <filter-name>MyLoggingFilter</filter-name>
  <filter-class>LoggingFilter</filter-class>
  <init-param>
    <param-name>log_file_name</param-name>
    <param-value>log.out</param-value>
  </init-param>
</filter>
```

You can also optionally specify initialization parameters, icons, a description, and a display label. See Chapter 4 for more details on the attributes of the filter element.

Once the filter element is added, you need to add a filter-mapping element that will associate or link the specified filter to a servlet or static resource in the web application. Filters can be applied to a single servlet or to groups of servlets and static content, using two distinct mapping approaches. The following deployment descriptor fragment illustrates a filter mapping to a single servlet called MyExampleServlet:

```
<filter-mapping>
  <filter-name>MyLoggingFilter</filter-name>
  <servlet-name>MyExampleServlet</servlet-name>
</filter-mapping>
```

Every time the web container receives a request for the MyExampleServlet resource, the doFilter() method in the LoggingFilter class will be invoked. The following XML fragment illustrates how the example filter can be mapped to all requests sent to the web application:

```
<filter-mapping>
  <filter-name>MyLoggingFilter</filter-name>
  <url-pattern>/*</url-pattern>
</filter-mapping>
```

The filter mapping in this case will map all requests to the MyLoggingFilter because every request URI will match the "/*" URL pattern.

### Packaging the filter

The final step is to package the filter class with the rest of the resources of the web application. As with any other Java resource that is part of a web application, the filter class must be bundled with the WAR file and able to be loaded by the web application's class loader. In most cases, the filter class should be placed under the *WEB-INF/classes* directory for the web application. Filter classes may also be inserted into a JAR file and placed in the *WEB-INF/lib* directory.

## Using Event Listeners

Web application event listeners are Java classes that implement one or more of the servlet event-listener interfaces. Event listeners support event notifications for changes in state in the ServletContext and HttpSession objects. Event listeners that are bound to the ServletContext support changes at the application level, while those that are bound to the HttpSession objects are notified for state changes at the session level.

Multiple listeners can be set up for each event type, and the servlet developer may offer a preference regarding the notification order for the listeners based on event type.

Tables 15-1 and 15-2 list the event types and event-listener interfaces available to the servlet developer.

*Table 15-1. ServletContext application events and listener interfaces*

| Event type | Description | Listener interface |
|---|---|---|
| Lifecycle | The ServletContext is about to service the first request or is about to be shut down by the servlet container. | ServletContextListener |
| Attributes | Attributes on the ServletContext have been added, removed, or replaced. | ServletContextAttributesListener |

*Table 15-2. HttpSession application events and listener interfaces*

| Event type | Description | Listener interface |
|---|---|---|
| Lifecycle | An HttpSession object has been created, invalidated, or timed out. | HttpSessionListener |
| Attributes | Attributes on an HttpSession object have been added, removed, or replaced. | HttpSessionAttributesListener |

# Creating an Event Listener

The steps for creating an event listener are similar to those of creating filters. There are three primary steps to perform:

1. Create a Java class that implements the event-listener interface for which you are interested in receiving events. This class must contain a no-argument constructor.

2. Declare the event listener in the web application deployment descriptor using the listener element.

3. Package the event listener class along with the rest of the web application resources.

## Creating the event listener class

As when you create filters, the first step is to create a Java class that implements the appropriate listener interface. As an example, we'll create a Java class that implements the javax.servlet.ServletContextListener interface and is responsible for initializing the logging service when the web application is started. This class is illustrated in Example 15-3.

*Example 15-3. ServletContextListener interface*

```
import javax.servlet.ServletContext;
import javax.servlet.ServletContextEvent;
import javax.servlet.ServletContextListener;
/**
 * An example event listener class that
 * initializes a logging service.
```

*Example 15-3. ServletContextListener interface (continued)*

```java
*/
public class LoggingListener implements ServletContextListener{
  private ServletContext context = null;

  /**
   * Called by the container before the first request is
   * processed. This is a good time to initialize
   * the logging service.
   */
  public void contextInitialized( ServletContextEvent event ){
    this.context = event.getServletContext();

    // Initialize the logging service here

    // Log a message that the listener has started
    log( "LoggingListener initialized" );
  }

  /**
   * Called by the container when the ServletContext is about
   * ready to be removed. This is a good time to clean up
   * any open resources.
   */
  public void contextDestroyed( ServletContextEvent event ){
    // Clean up the logging service here

    // Log a message that the LoggingListener has been stopped
    log( "LoggingListener destroyed" );
  }

  /**
   * Log a message to the servlet context application log or
   * system out if the ServletContext is unavailable.
   */
  protected void log( String message ) {
    if (context != null){
      context.log("LoggingListener: " + message );
    }else{
      System.out.println("LoggingListener: " + message);
    }
  }
}
```

The event-listener class in Example 15-3 contains two methods that are invoked by the web container:

```java
public void contextInitialized( ServletContextEvent event );
public void contextDestroyed( ServletContextEvent event );
```

The web container calls the contextInitialized() method before the first request is processed. You should initialize any needed resources in this method. For example, this is an ideal location to initialize a logging service. The contextDestroyed()

method is called when the web application is taken out of service. This is where any open resources that the listener class is using should be closed.

Because there can be multiple event-listener classes for the same event, let's use another ServletContext event-listener class to make our example more realistic. Example 15-4 shows the DBConnectionPoolListener class. Both the LoggingListener and the DBConnectionPoolListener will receive event notifications when the ServletContext is initialized and destroyed.

*Example 15-4. The DBConnectionPoolListener class*

```
import javax.servlet.ServletContextListener;
import javax.servlet.ServletContextEvent;
/**
 * An example event listener class that
 * initializes the database connection pooling.
 */
public class DBConnectionPoolListener implements ServletContextListener{

  /**
   * Called by the container before the first request is
   * processed. This is a good time to initialize
   * the connection pooling service.
   */
  public void contextInitialized( ServletContextEvent event ){
    // Initialize the connection pooling here
  }

  /**
   * Called by the container when the ServletContext is about
   * ready to be removed. This is a good time to clean up
   * any open resources.
   */
  public void contextDestroyed( ServletContextEvent event ){
    // Shut down the connection pooling and open database connections
  }
}
```

Because both the LoggingListener and DBConnectionPoolListener are listening for the same type of application events, the servlet container will notify them in the order in which they are listed in the descriptor, based on the event type.

## Declaring the event listener in the deployment descriptor

The following web application deployment descriptor fragment shows you how to set up the event listeners:

```
<web-app>
  <listener>
    <listener-class>LoggingListener</listener-class>
  </listener>
```

```
<listener>
  <listener-class>DBConnectionPoolListener</listener-class>
</listener>

<servlet>
  <servlet-name>ExampleServlet</servlet-name>
  <servlet-class>ExampleServlet</servlet-class>
</servlet>

<servlet-mapping>
  <servlet-name>ExampleServlet</servlet-name>
  <url-pattern>/example</url-pattern>
</servlet-mapping>
</web-app>
```

The LoggingListener will be notified first, followed by the DBConnectionPoolListener instance. When the web application shuts down, the listeners are notified in reverse order. The HttpSession event listeners are notified prior to listeners for the application context.

### Packaging the event listener

The packaging of the event-listener classes follows the guidelines described in the previous section for filters. That is, the classes must either be in the *WEB-INF/classes* directory or be installed in a JAR file located in the *WEB-INF/lib* directory for the web application.

# Jakarta Commons Logging

The Commons Logging package is an open source Logging library that allows developers to use a common logging API, while maintaining the freedom to use many different third-party logging implementations. The Commons Logging API insulates the application and protects it from becoming coupled to a specific logging implementation. The API provides a small set of Java classes and interfaces that an application imports and relies upon but that has no implicit dependencies on any one logging product.

The Logging library allows developers to declaratively configure the logging implementation; the library will dynamically discover which implementation is being used. An application that uses the Commons Logging API does not have to be modified when the logging implementation is changed. This is the greatest benefit of such a package.

The Commons Logging package supports several logging implementations out of the box:

- log4j (*http://logging.apache.org/log4j*)
- JDK 1.4 Logging

- LogKit (*http://avalon.apache.org/logkit/*)
- SimpleLog (writes log messages to stdout and stderr)
- NoOpLog (log messages are ignored)

 The Commons Logging package includes only the SimpleLog and NoOpLog implementations; it does not contain the other third-party logging implementations. You will need to download those separately.

Another powerful feature of the Commons Logging package is that it is completely extensible. If you are using a logging package that is not yet supported, you can create an adapter to that implementation by extending the appropriate components, and your application can use the Commons Logging API.

## Installing the Commons Logging Package

You can download the latest source and binary code for the Commons Logging package at *http://jakarta.apache.org/commons/logging.html*. Struts 1.1 already includes *commons-logging.jar*, which is the only required binary file. Unless you want the absolute latest from the nightly build, the version included with the Struts framework should suit your needs. You should place the *commons-logging.jar* file into the *WEB-INF/lib* directory for the web application.

You will also need to decide on a logging implementation. The Commons Logging package includes an implementation called SimpleLog that writes log messages to stdout and stderr. If you don't want to worry about getting *log4j* working and are not using Java 1.4, the SimpleLog implementation is a good choice to get things started.

Once you decide on an implementation, you must configure the implementation class so that the Commons Logging factory component can discover it at application startup. There are many ways to do this, but the easiest is to create a properties file called *commons-logging.properties* that contains the class name of the logging implementation. The most important property key in this file is the org.apache.commons. logging.Log key, which is used to set the implementation class.

The following illustrates how to set up the Commons Logging package to use the SimpleLog implementation:

```
org.apache.commons.logging.Log=org.apache.commons.logging.impl.SimpleLog
```

At runtime, the logging component will search for the *commons-logging.properties* file and attempt to instantiate the fully qualified class name found there. The class name specified must be available to the web application class loader. The properties file should be placed in the *WEB-INF/classes* directory. To switch to *log4j*, all you need to do is switch the class name in the *commons-logging.properties* file, like this:

```
org.apache.commons.logging.Log=org.apache.commons.logging.impl.Log4JCategoryLog
```

Note that you still need to configure *log4j* for your environment, including creating a *log4j.properties* file. Each logging implementation may have different configuration requirements that must be satisfied.

## Using the Commons Logging API

Once the configuration steps are completed, your application is ready to use the Commons Logging API. You must include the following `import` statements in each class or component in which you wish to use the logging API:

```
import org.apache.commons.logging.Log;
import org.apache.commons.logging.LogFactory;
```

To get an instance of a log component to which you can send log messages, you need to use either of the getLog( ) factory methods on the org.apache.commons.logging. LogFactory class:

```
public static Log getLog(Class class);
public static Log getLog(String name)
```

Both getLog( ) methods return an object that implements the org.apache. commons. logging.Log interface. To create a Log instance to be used within the LoginAction class, for example, you could pass the class name to the getLog( ) method:

```
Log log = LogFactory.getLog( LoginAction.class );
```

The Log instance would then be available for use within the LoginAction class:

```
if (log.isInfoEnabled()){
  // Log which user is trying to enter the site
  log.info( "Login email: " + email );
}
```

The Log interface implements the logging methods that you can use to send log messages to the intended destination. The most important of these are:

- debug( )
- error( )
- fatal( )
- info( )
- trace( )
- warn( )

Each of these log methods has an overloaded version that takes a Throwable. There are also methods that allow you to determine whether debug is enabled, whether error is enabled, and so on. Checking to see if a particular logging level is enabled before attempting to log a message can improve the performance of your application. For example, if you have this code fragment:

```
StringBuffer buf = new StringBuffer();
buf.append( "Login Successful - " );
```

```
buf.append( "Name: " );
buf.append( userView.getFirstName() );
buf.append( " " );
buf.append( userView.getLastName() );
buf.append( " - " );
buf.append( "Email: " );
buf.append( userView.getEmailAddress() );

// Log the information for auditing purposes
log.debug( buf.toString() );
```

it would improve the performance of the application if the append statements were not all executed when the logging threshold was set to not log debug statements. You can use the isDebugEnabled( ) method for this:

```
if ( log.isDebugEnabled() ){
  StringBuffer buf = new StringBuffer();
  buf.append( "Login Successful - " );
  buf.append( "Name: " );
  buf.append( userView.getFirstName() );
  buf.append( " " );
  buf.append( userView.getLastName() );
  buf.append( " - " );
  buf.append( "Email: " );
  buf.append( userView.getEmailAddress() );

  // Log the UserView for auditing purposes
  log.debug( buf.toString() );
}
```

In this case, the application is not wasting time creating the StringBuffer only to have it not be used.

## Struts Framework and the Commons Logging Package

The Struts framework does perform some limited internal logging, and also uses the Commons Logging API. Thus, the Struts framework will use whichever logging implementation you configure for your application.

The Struts logs are a great way for you to see what's going on inside Struts as it processes requests, but other than for debugging purposes, there's no need for you to worry about them. In most production environments, the messages generated by the Struts framework should be disabled. The manner in which you disable the framework-specific log messages depends on which logging implementation you choose.

The rest of this chapter is devoted to one of the most popular logging implementations used by developers, *log4j*. Because it's also supported by the Commons Logging package, it's an excellent choice for your Struts application's logging needs.

# Using the log4j Package

You may have heard or read about the *log4j* library from other sources, but in case you haven't, let's briefly discuss the library's history here. Like Struts, *log4j* is an open source project that is part of the Jakarta set of projects. It's essentially a set of Java classes and interfaces that provides logging functionality to multiple types of output destinations. It has been around for several years and is constantly being refined and tuned for all types of Java development. In fact, *log4j* has been so successful that it has been ported to several other very popular languages, including C, C++, Python, and even .NET.

 At the time of this writing, *log4j* has released Version 1.2.8, which is its 22nd major public release. The next major version, 1.3, is in the works, but it won't be released for a while. Version 1.2 is backward compatible with earlier versions, so if you are using 1.1.3, this material will still be relevant for you.

Recently, the Apache Software Foundation has created a new Apache project called *Apache Logging Services*. According to the release, the new project is intended to provide "cross-language logging services." Log4j is a central theme to this project.

According to the creators of *log4j*, it was built with two central concepts in mind: speed and flexibility. One of the distinctive features of the logging framework is its notion of *inheritance* in categories, or loggers as they are now called. *log4j* supports a parent/child relationship between the configured loggers in the environment. For example, if we configured a logger for all the classes in the `com.oreilly.struts` package and another logger for all the classes in the `com.oreilly.struts.storefront` package, the first logger would be the parent of the second. This hierarchical structure gives us the flexibility to control what log messages are written out based on such things as the package structure.

You don't need to go this far if your requirements don't call for it. If you want, you can configure a single root logger for your entire environment. You can configure *log4j* for your specific needs, and you can change its behavior whenever you like by simply editing an external configuration file—you don't have to change the application's source code.

A discussion of *log4j* could fill a small book. I'll assume that you are familiar with the basic concepts and will cover only the essentials of how to integrate *log4j* with the Struts framework here. If you haven't yet become familiar with *log4j*, this is a good time to do so. For a more detailed discussion, you can download or view the documentation at the Jakarta *log4j* web site at *http://logging.apache.org/log4j*.

## Integrating log4j with Struts

To ensure that the *log4j* libraries are available to your Struts applications, you should place the *log4j* JAR file in the *WEB-INF/lib* directory for each web application that you deploy. Resist the temptation to put it inside the container-wide *lib* directory, even if you're deploying multiple web applications with *log4j*. If you do attempt to install it at the container level, you probably will encounter one or more Class-NotFoundException problems.

Based on the requirements set forth in the 2.3 Servlet specification, the web container should automatically load all JAR files in the *WEB-INF/lib* directory, including the *log4j* library. After this initial step is complete, you are free to use *log4j* as the logging implementation for the Commons Logging package.

 Keep in mind that the configuration of *log4j* is totally independent of the configuration of the logging implementation for the Commons Logging package. You still need to understand how to configure *log4j* (if that's the implementation you choose) and perform the necessary steps required by the *log4j* package.

## What Are Loggers?

The org.apache.log4j.Logger is the central class in the *log4j* toolkit. Other than configuration, most of the functionality is performed through this class. In earlier versions of the *log4j* project, the org.apache.log4j.Category class implemented this functionality. To promote backward compatibility, the Logger class extends the Category class. Although the methods in the Category class have not yet been deprecated, you should always go through the Logger class itself. Eventually, the Category class will be removed from the library.

When used with Struts, most of the *log4j* classes and interfaces (other than the configuration aspects of *log4j*) are encapsulated within the Commons Logging API.

## Configuring log4j Appenders

With *log4j*, you can send log messages to multiple destinations. *log4j* refers to a message destination as an *appender*. The *log4j* framework provides the following appenders for you to use out of the box:

- Console Appender
- File Appender
- Socket Appender
- Java Message Service (JMS) Appender
- NT Event Logger Appender
- Unix Syslog Appender

- Null Appender
- SMTP Appender
- Telnet Appender
- Asynchronous Appender

The *log4j* framework allows one or more appenders to be established for a logging environment. You can even send log messages to particular appenders, based on various conditions. The other nice feature of the appender architecture is that if none of these default appenders meets your application's requirements, you can create your own by extending the org.apache.log4j.AppenderSkeleton class.

## Understanding the log4j Log Levels

A log message in *log4j* can be assigned one of five different levels or priorities. The levels allow you to set a threshold for a particular logger and filter out any log messages that don't reach the threshold for which the Logger is configured. The five logging levels are:

- DEBUG
- INFO
- WARN
- ERROR
- FATAL

 An earlier version of *log4j* also defined the levels OFF and ALL; however, these seem to have been deprecated and probably should be avoided. If you set the threshold to DEBUG, you'll get the same results as using ALL, and OFF isn't really necessary because you can simply choose not to configure an appender for the environment, which will stop all logging from occurring.

There is a cascading effect that causes only levels equal to the threshold and higher to be logged. For example, if a threshold of WARN is configured, only messages with a level of WARN, ERROR, or FATAL will make it to an output destination.

## Initializing log4j

There are many properties that can be configured for the *log4j* toolkit. In fact, *log4j* is so flexible that all the configuration options can't be covered here. The best source of information is the *log4j* manual itself. You can find the manual online at *http://logging.apache.org/log4j/docs/documentation.html*, and it's also available locally when you download *log4j*.

Because *log4j* doesn't make any assumptions about the environment in which it is running, you need to configure the environment for your particular needs. In other words, no default appenders are configured out of the box.

There are various ways in which you can initialize the configuration properties for the *log4j* environment. We will focus on two related, but distinct, approaches here.

### Initializing using the log4j.properties file

The first approach is to create a file called *log4j.properties* that contains the necessary configuration elements for your logging needs. This file must follow the guidelines of the java.util.Properties format. One of these guidelines is that each property is in the format key=value.

Example 15-5 illustrates a very simple *log4j* configuration file that logs messages with a logging threshold of INFO to the console using an org.apache.log4j.ConsoleAppender.

*Example 15-5. j.properties file*

```
# A basic log4j configuration file that creates a single console appender

# Create a single console appender that logs INFO and higher
log4j.rootLogger=INFO, stdout

# Configure the stdout appender to go to the console
log4j.appender.stdout=org.apache.log4j.ConsoleAppender

# Configure the stdout appender to use the PatternLayout
log4j.appender.stdout.layout=org.apache.log4j.PatternLayout

# Pattern to output the caller's filename and line number.
log4j.appender.stdout.layout.ConversionPattern=%5p [%t] (%F:%L) - %m%n
```

The configuration file shown in Example 15-5 is a very simple example of setting up a single appender—in this case, the ConsoleAppender, which directs log messages to System.out.

This *log4j.properties* file must be installed in the *WEB-INF/classes* directory so that the *log4j* environment will be able to locate it and use it to configure the logging environment for the web application. If you have multiple web applications, you can have a separate *log4j.properties* file for each.

The *log4j* configuration file shown in Example 15-5 sends log messages to only a single destination, the console. However, you can configure the log messages to go to multiple locations and also have certain messages go to certain locations based on the level of the message and other parameters. Example 15-6 shows a simple example using two appenders.

*Example 15-6. j configuration file using two appenders*

```
# A sample log4j configuration file

# Create two appenders, one called stdout and the other called rolling
log4j.rootLogger=DEBUG, stdout, rolling

# Configure the stdout appender to go to the console
log4j.appender.stdout=org.apache.log4j.ConsoleAppender

# Configure the stdout appender to use the PatternLayout
log4j.appender.stdout.layout=org.apache.log4j.PatternLayout

# Pattern to output the caller's filename and line number
log4j.appender.stdout.layout.ConversionPattern=%5p [%t] (%F:%L) - %m%n

# Configure the rolling appender to be a RollingFileAppender
log4j.appender.rolling=org.apache.log4j.RollingFileAppender

# Configure the name of the logout for the rolling appender
log4j.appender.rolling.File=output.log

# Set up the maximum size of the rolling log file
log4j.appender.rolling.MaxFileSize=100KB

# Keep one backup file of the rolling appender
log4j.appender.rolling.MaxBackupIndex=1

# Configure the layout pattern and conversion pattern for the rolling appender
log4j.appender.rolling.layout=org.apache.log4j.PatternLayout
log4j.appender.rolling.layout.ConversionPattern=%d{ABSOLUTE} - %p %c - %m%n
```

The *log4j* configuration file in Example 15-6 creates one appender that logs messages to the console, just as in Example 15-5, and another appender that logs messages to a log file called *output.log*. Again, we won't try to cover all of the configuration settings for *log4j*; you can learn more from the *log4j* web site.

## Initializing using an XML file

The second approach to initializing the configuration properties for the *log4j* environment is to use an XML file. Example 15-7 illustrates an XML file that configures the same information as in Example 15-5.

*Example 15-7. j configuration file using an XML format*

```
<?xml version="1.0" encoding="UTF-8" ?>
<!DOCTYPE log4j:configuration SYSTEM "log4j.dtd">

<log4j:configuration xmlns:log4j=http://logging.apache.org/log4j'>

  <appender name="stdout" class="org.apache.log4j.ConsoleAppender">
    <layout class="org.apache.log4j.PatternLayout">
      <param name="ConversionPattern" value="%5p [%t] (%F:%L) - %m%n"/>
```

*Example 15-7. j configuration file using an XML format (continued)*

```
    </layout>
  </appender>

  <root>
    <priority value ="INFO" />
    <appender-ref ref="stdout" />
  </root>
</log4j:configuration>
```

You normally place this XML file in the *WEB-INF/classes* directory, just as with the *log4j.properties* file. However, you must set the log4j.configuration system property equal to the name of the file, so that the *log4j* environment knows which file to load. There's no default filename when using the XML format. (We didn't have to do this with the properties file because the name *log4j.properties* is part of the *log4j* default initialization. If it locates this file anywhere in the classpath, it will use it to initialize the *log4j* environment.)

There are various ways to set the log4j.configuration property, and the various containers may provide alternative methods. In Tomcat Version 4.0, for example, you can set a variable called CATALINA_OPTS in the *catalina.bat* file to provide this information to the logging environment. For example:

```
    set CATALINA_OPTS=-Dlog4j.configuration=log4j.xml
```

When you start up Tomcat, the *log4j* environment will then be able to locate the XML configuration file. Other containers may provide alternate methods for setting the value, but you can always set the value on the Java command line as a system property. You will probably need to modify the container's startup script using this approach, however:

```
    java -Dlog4j.configuration=log4j.xml
```

If the *log4j* environment is unable to find a valid configuration file, either properties-based or XML-based, you will see something similar to the following message when you first attempt to initialize the logging environment:

```
    log4j:WARN No appenders could be found for logger XXX.
    log4j:WARN Please initialize the log4j system properly.
```

The XXX in the first message will actually show the name of the logger for which no appenders were configured.

### Specifying a relative versus an absolute path

When you use a system property to configure the *log4j* configuration file within a web application, the file is relative to the web application by default. The following example tells *log4j* to search for a file called *log4j.xml* in the *WEB-INF/classes* directory for the web application:

```
    java -Dlog4j.configuration=log4j.xml
```

Most containers use a separate class loader for each web application, and some containers may not allow the web applications to know about classes or JARs loaded by the container itself. However, if you need to use an absolute path, you can specify one like this:

```
java -Dlog4j.configuration=file:/c:/dev/env/log4j.xml
```

Be careful when using an absolute path—because the configuration file is not relative to a web application, all web applications will share the same one.

Generally speaking, specifying a relative path is much more flexible than using an absolute path because you can't always guarantee the directory structure of all your target environments.

### Synchronization issues

There's one more issue that you should be aware of when logging to resources such as filesystems. Even though *log4j* is able to handle multiple client threads using the same appender (because all threads are synchronized), if you have multiple appenders writing to the same resource or file, you will have unpredictable results. In other words, there is no synchronization between appenders, even within the same JVM.

This really has nothing to do with a deficiency in the *log4j* design; it's just a case of not being able to easily synchronize multiple writers to a resource. The easiest way to solve this problem is to ensure that if you have multiple appenders or web applications logging to the filesystem, you don't allow them to log to the same file. If you do, you will probably experience synchronization-related issues.

## Log File Rollover

In a normal production environment, log files can grow quite large if not managed properly. If the logging threshold is set to DEBUG or INFO or if the files are not purged from time to time, the files can grow without bounds.

It's a good idea to periodically back up the log files and start again with an empty log file. For some production environments, this "rollover" period may be nightly; others may only need to perform this routine weekly. Unless you can shut down the application while you back up the log files, it's very cumbersome to back them up manually.

Fortunately, *log4j* provides a type of appender that automatically swaps the log file out with a new one while at the same time maintaining a backup of the old log file. The org.apache.log4j.DailyRollingFileAppender class provides the ability to log to a file and roll over or back up the log file while the application is still running. You can also specify the rollover frequency and the date pattern that will be used for the backup names. Having this functionality available out of the box makes *log4j* invaluable to any application that needs to roll over log files at user-defined intervals.

# Using Commons Logging in JSP Pages

We've covered how to use the Commons Logging API within Java components, but we haven't yet discussed how to use them in JSP pages. There are a number of ways to use the library within JSP pages, but we'll just cover the two easiest approaches here.

The first approach is to use the same three steps defined earlier, this time performing them in the JSP page itself:

1. Import the Commons Log and LogFactory classes.

2. Define and initialize a logger variable for the page.

3. Start logging.

Example 15-8 illustrates this approach in a basic JSP page.

*Example 15-8. Using Commons Logging in a JSP page*

```
<%@ page import="org.apache.commons.logging.Log" %>
<%@ page import="org.apache.commons.logging.LogFactory" %>

<%-- Get a reference to the logger for this class --%>
<% Log logger = LogFactory.getLog( this.getClass() ); %>

<% logger.debug( "This is a debug message from a jsp" ); %>

<html>
<head>
  <title>Using Commons Logging in a JSP page</title>
</head>

<body>
  <% logger.info( "This is another log message in the jsp" ); %>

  There should be two log messages in the log file.
</body>
</html>
```

You must have the Commons Logging environment configured properly for this to work, just as when using it in the Java classes. Any JSP page that is part of the web application will be able to use the logging utilities. Because most containers use a different class loader for each web application, any JSP page that is not part of the *log4j-*configured web application may not be able to use the logging utilities.

Although Example 15-8 shows just how easy it can be to use the Commons Logging API in your JSP pages, there are a few issues with this approach. The most obvious one is that your JSP pages will contain Java code. As mentioned several times in this book, many developers see this as something that should be avoided. Fortunately, there is another way.

The Jakarta Taglibs project contains a custom JSP tag library designed for *log4j* called the Log tag library. You can view information and download the tag library from the Jakarta Taglibs web site at *http://jakarta.apache.org/taglibs/doc/log-doc/intro.html*.

Just like any other custom tag library, you must properly configure it for your web application. This means putting the *log.tld* file into the *WEB-INF* directory and installing the Log tag JAR file into the *WEB-INF/lib* directory. You will also need to add the appropriate `taglib` element to your web application's deployment descriptor, similar to how you added the Struts tag libraries:

```
<taglib>
  <taglib-uri>/WEB-INF/log.tld</taglib-uri>
  <taglib-location>/WEB-INF/log.tld</taglib-location>
</taglib>
```

Once the Log custom tag is installed and configured for your web application, you can use it in your JSP pages as shown in Example 15-9.

*Example 15-9. An example JSP page using the Log tag*

```
<%@ taglib uri="/WEB-INF/log.tld" prefix="logger" %>

<logger:debug message="This is a debug message from a jsp using the Log tag" />

<html>
<head>
  <title>Using the Log Tag in a JSP page</title>
</head>

<body>

  <logger:info message="This is another message using the log4j tag" />

  There should be two log messages in the log4j log file.

</body>
</html>
```

Notice that the JSP page in Example 15-9 contains no Java code. Although it doesn't look too different from Example 15-8, this approach is much cleaner with a larger and more complex JSP page.

Another nice feature of the Log tag is that it gives you the ability to perform a dump of objects stored at the page, request, session, or application scope. This is very useful when you are in the middle of debugging your web application. Example 15-10 illustrates how easy this is to do.

*Example 15-10. Using the Log tag library to dump information*

```
<%@ taglib uri="/WEB-INF/log.tld" prefix="logger" %>

<html>
<head>
  <title>Using the Log Tag in a JSP page</title>
</head>

<body>

  <logger:dump scope="page"/>
  <logger:dump scope="request"/>
  <logger:dump scope="session"/>
  <logger:dump scope="application"/>

  The page, request, session, and application dumps should be in the log file.

</body>
</html>
```

Unfortunately, the Log tag doesn't yet work with the Commons Logging package. It depends on the *log4j* implementation. Still, it's a valuable tag if you need to provide additional debugging in your JSP pages.

# The Performance Impact of log4j

The potential performance impact of logging in an application is significant. For a typical production application, thousands or even hundreds of thousands of log messages can be logged every day, depending on the logging threshold that's configured. The consequences might be even worse if exception stack traces are logged due to errors in the application.

The *log4j* documentation states that much attention has been given to minimizing the performance impact of logging using *log4j*. Nothing is free, however, and there is an additional cost associated with generating log messages. The question is, does that cost outweigh the benefits gained from the additional logging information?

The time cost of creating a log message using *log4j* depends on several factors:

- The type of appender being used
- The *log4j* layout being used to format the messages
- The parameter construction time to create the log message
- The depth of the logger hierarchy and where the log threshold is assigned

The type of appender has much to do with how long it will take to create a log message. Logging a message using an SMTP appender will take a different amount of time than logging to the filesystem. On a typical machine using Java 1.3, logging a message to the filesystem will take anywhere from 20 microseconds to upwards of

300 microseconds, depending on which layout you use. While this is a very small number, over time it can add up.

Probably the most significant impact on logging is what information you attempt to log and how you format that information. *log4j* uses a subclass of org.apache.log4j. Layout to determine how the message should be formatted in the output destination. Using the SimpleLayout class is the fastest, as it logs only the log level and the message. On the other hand, the PatternLayout class allows for a great amount of flexibility in the format of the message; you can log all sorts of information, including the class creating the message, the line number, and even the Java thread that is generating the message. However, all of this additional information comes at a severe price in terms of performance. The *log4j* documentation contains several warning messages in the JavaDocs for the PatternLayout class stating that performance may suffer greatly if certain information is written out with the log message.

You must be very particular about what information you need in the log message. You should be able to get by with the class, the level, and the message. The other information is nice to have, but in most cases it's superfluous.

Creating the message that goes into the log statement can also impact the time and performance. Creating a message using values such as:

```
logger.debug("Session id is: " + sessId + " for user " + user.getFullName() );
```

can add significant time to logging. This isn't related to *log4j*, but rather to the cost associated with making Java method calls and concatenating the strings together before the actual log statement can be generated.

Finally, as mentioned earlier, loggers can be connected together in a parent/child relationship. Because the logging threshold can be assigned at any level, the *log4j* environment may have to search up the hierarchy to determine whether the log message should be written. If this hierarchy is very deep, this traversal can add significant time to the log statement creation.

Generally, in the development stages of your application, logging costs are less important. The performance of logging shouldn't matter that much while you're still developing and debugging the application; in fact, this is typically where you want as much logging as the application can generate. When it's time to go to QA or production, turn down the logging levels.

With other languages, the logging code might not ever make it into the compiled binaries. Preprocessors might remove the logging code to keep the binary size smaller and prevent the log messages from showing up. However, this is not necessary using *log4j*—you have the flexibility of controlling how much logging is done just by changing the configuration file. (Of course, the log statements are still present in the binary code once it's compiled.)

# Third-Party log4j Extensions

Several helpful third-party tools and utilities are available for *log4j*. Most of them are free and/or open source. For example, there are several Swing-based GUI applications that allow you to view and filter log messages dynamically, which is ideal for administrators in a production environment.

There are also several other types of appenders that other developers have created that might be helpful to you. You can find these third-party extensions in the *log4j* download area at *http://logging.apache.org/log4j/docs/download.html*. It's definitely worth the time to take a look and see what's there. The list of available extensions is constantly growing.

# Java 1.4 Logging API

Even if you aren't using Java 1.4, you've probably heard of it and the new features that it includes. One of the new features is the logging API now included with the core library. You may be wondering what the difference is between *log4j* and this new library, and whether you should be using that instead.

There are several similarities between *log4j* and the 1.4 logging implementation. However, there are also a few major differences. Let's look at the similarities first. Both *log4j* and the Java 1.4 logging implementation use a hierarchical namespace for the loggers. This allows you to configure loggers that basically align along your application's package structure, although this is not the only way to structure the loggers. They also both support multiple levels or priorities. The 1.4 logging implementation actually contains a few more levels than *log4j*, though you might not ever use the extra ones because they are so fine-grained.

The differences between the two implementations are generally not big enough to cause you to miss out on important functionality. However, it does appear that *log4j* offers more functionality for those that really need it. More importantly, *log4j* works with Java Versions 1.1 and above, while the 1.4 logging implementation works only with Version 1.4. There was talk about making it backward compatible, but that hasn't happened yet and may never happen. Also, there are currently many more appender types available for *log4j* than for Java 1.4, but this is not a major issue because the most important ones are present in Java 1.4.

Regardless of whether you use *log4j* or Java 1.4 as your logging implementation, you should leverage the Commons Logging API to protect your application from inevitable change. Coupling your application to any single third-party implementation is not recommended, in terms of logging or anything else.

# CHAPTER 16

# Packaging Your Struts Application

Contrary to what many developers might assume, designing and building an application is only half the battle. When the application is finished, it must then be packaged and deployed into the target environment. Many applications are built and packaged with the intent of being installed into a customer's production environment. For others, the target deployment environment is in-house. For web applications, fortunately, the work that has to be accomplished in either case is very similar.

Internal deployments may be less formal and less nerve-racking. However, they still should be taken seriously and conducted in an efficient and professional manner. Whether the customer is a "real" customer or another department within the organization, an unprofessional deployment can leave a bad impression. Formalizing the packaging and deployment process allows developers to focus on building a quality application and spend less time worrying whether the application will install and run correctly when it's finished. In fact, the best time to establish a formal deployment process is in the beginning stages of development. By doing this earlier, rather than later in the development cycle, you will have an opportunity to test and fine tune the entire process.

This chapter discusses the best practices for packaging and deploying a Struts application, including coverage of what it takes to automate the build process for your environment. Special attention is given to Ant, the Java-based build tool available from Jakarta.

## To Package or Not to Package

Applications need to be deployed to be useful. There's really no point in developing an application that never gets deployed, although this occurs more often than you might think. The need for deployment is obvious, but what about packaging? Does every Struts application have to be packaged before it gets deployed? The short answer is yes. In this chapter, though, we'll examine the long answer.

Before we get into the details of packaging and deploying Struts applications, let's define exactly what these two concepts mean in the context of web applications that are built using the Struts framework. Although the two concepts are closely related, they are not the same thing.

## What Is Packaging?

Packaging a Struts application involves gathering all the files and resources that are part of the application and bundling them together in a logical structure. Many different types of resources are usually included in a Struts application, and all of these need to be bundled with the application. Some of the more common types of resources that can be packaged with a Struts application are:

- HTML and/or XML files
- Images, audio, and video files
- Stylesheets
- JavaServer Pages
- Properties files
- Java utility classes
- Configuration files
- `Action` and `ActionForm` classes
- Third-party JARs

During the design stage, time and effort should be spent on deciding how you are going to structure the application. Not every detail needs to be figured out and resolved before construction begins, but you should understand the target environment's requirements and how these requirements will affect your packaging and deployment strategy. Ideally, you should decide on the principal package and directory structure for the application before construction gets underway. This will help to alleviate the normal miscommunication between developers and reduce the number of redundant resource files.

## What Is Deployment?

As the previous section mentioned, packaging and deployment are closely related, but involve different tasks. While packaging determines where the resource files will reside in the package structure and how those resources will be bundled, deployment deals with how the bundled application will be installed and configured inside a target web container.

There are two approaches that you can use when deploying a web application into a container. The first approach is to deploy the web application in a web archive (WAR) file. Most web containers install a WAR file and make it available for users, often without even requiring a restart of the container. This approach is convenient because once the WAR file is properly built, the rest of the work is handled by the container. One of the downsides of this approach, however, is that if a change is made to any file or resource within the web application, a new WAR file must be created and redeployed into the container. The details of how to deploy your Struts application as a WAR file are discussed later in the chapter.

The second approach to deploying a Struts application puts more work on the developer. It still involves packaging your application as a WAR file, but includes manually unpackaging the WAR file into a directory of the container. The exact location of the directory is container-dependent. In Tomcat and Resin, for example, the default web applications directory is *webapps*. In the WebLogic application server, you have to unpack the WAR file underneath the *applications* directory. (All three of these containers also allow you to specify alternate installation directories.)

When expanding the WAR file, you need to create a directory into which to unpack the files. The name of the directory is usually the name of the web application. So for example, if the web application was called Storefront and you wanted to install it into Tomcat, you could create a directory called *storefront* under the *webapps* directory and unpack the WAR file there.

The WAR file should not contain the *storefront* directory as part of its structure.

This deployment approach is referred to as an *exploded directory format*, because the WAR file is exploded back into its original structure within the container. The benefit of this approach over deploying the WAR file itself is that when there are changes, only the changed files need to be redeployed into the container. This is much easier when you're still developing or debugging the application, but you may not want to leave it like this for production.

When deploying a web application into production, it's a better approach to leave the WAR file packed because there's less chance of one or more files getting contaminated. Leaving it as a single WAR file forces you to replace the entire WAR file if changes need to be made, so there's no chance of a version of a file getting out of sync with the rest of the application.

## Deciding How to Package Your Application

Because Struts applications are web applications, most of the questions about how to package them are answered in the Servlet and JavaServer Pages specifications. A web application must follow a very strict set of guidelines and conventions that make the web application portable across other web containers.

Fortunately, packaging your Struts application in the WAR format solves much of the hassle regarding packaging. However, there are many questions that you will have to resolve. For example, you'll have to decide where all the JSP pages go and whether you should store your Struts Action and ActionForm classes together or in separate action and form packages. Although there are definitely best practices, there are no hard-and-fast rules for resolving issues such as these. Some of the solutions will depend on your organization's requirements and policies.

## Namespace Management

A namespace is simply a set of names that may or may not be associated. A namespace is normally used to prevent conflicts or collisions between similar entities and to allow clients to reference these entities by some logical name.

In software development, a namespace is a way to package classes, interfaces, and other types of information into a hierarchical structure. There are many examples of namespaces throughout the computer industry. The manner in which the Internet Domain Name System (DNS) works is a type of namespace. Within the *oreilly.com* domain, for instance, other IP addresses are linked together in a hierarchal fashion. All of this referencing helps prevent IP addresses from colliding. Another example, which is more closely related to software development, is the namespace that is used within JNDI. But by far the most familiar use of a namespace in Java development is for creating classes and interfaces that reside in a package.

As you know, Java applications are organized as sets of packages. Even when you don't specify a package explicitly, it's still part of a package.[*] The purpose of the package is to prevent name collisions and to help identify entities (in this case, Java classes) easily. When extending the Struts framework with your own classes and interfaces, you need to decide how best to package these components for your application. Not every application will contain the same classes and interfaces.

## JSP File Placement

For many developers, where you place the JSP pages may seem like an easy question to answer. Although you may have to decide which directory a particular JSP page belongs in, that's normally all that has to be decided. However, there are situations where more control may need to be placed on who and what has access to the JSP pages. One suggestion is to put the JSPs in a directory underneath the *WEB-INF* directory.

---

[*] Any Java class that doesn't have a package statement declared in the source file is considered to be part of the *default package*.

The purpose of this approach is threefold:

- It forces all requests to go through the ActionServlet class.
- It prevents users from bookmarking a page.
- It protects the *WEB-INF* directory and helps protect JSP pages from being called directly.

This alternate approach has gained some popularity, although not all of the containers currently support it. Although the 2.3 Servlet specification seems to indicate that something to this effect may be possible, different vendors may not agree in their interpretation of the specification—for example, in the past, the WebLogic developers have stated that they interpret section SRV.6.5 of the Servlet specification differently. WebLogic will return a 404 or 500 error code when you attempt to access a JSP page underneath the *WEB-INF* directory (although there has been some indication that WebLogic will make this option available in future versions of their container).

Even though some containers do support the above approach, you may not need to put the JSP pages underneath the *WEB-INF* directory. If you call Struts actions only from your web application and don't link to JSP pages directly (which is a requirement for Struts 1.1), this approach will not have much benefit for your applications. There are portable alternatives—for example, you can use the security-constraint element in the *web.xml* file. Just create the required directories for the JSP pages that you want to protect. In the Storefront example, suppose that users shouldn't be able to access the JSP pages underneath the *order* directory. A security-constraint element like this could then be added:

```
<security-constraint>
  <web-resource-collection>
    <web-resource-name>SecureOrderJSP</web-resource-name>
    <description>Protect the Order JSP Pages </description>
    <url-pattern>/order/*</url-pattern>
    <http-method>GET</http-method>
    <http-method>POST</http-method>
  </web-resource-collection>
  <auth-constraint>
    <role-name></role-name>
  </auth-constraint>
</security-constraint>
```

Figure 16-1 shows what happens when a client attempts to access a JSP page directly within the *order* directory.

When the security-constraint element is added to the *web.xml* file for the Storefront application, it says that no user without the proper authentication can access the order JSP pages. However, in this example, the role-name element was intentionally left blank and therefore will never match an actual role. You could also have specified that only users with an admin role could access the pages, and then never given

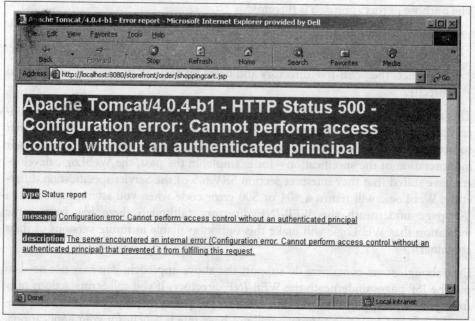

*Figure 16-1. A 500 error will occur when accessing a protected JSP*

that role to an actual user. The container would still be able to access these pages through forwards and includes.

You must be careful what you put in the url-pattern element, however. If you have resources such as images in subdirectories, they will not be available when the browser attempts to download them. Using the */order/\** pattern means that nothing under the *order* directory can be requested directly by the client; this includes images in subdirectories, and the browser will have difficulty receiving the images for a returned HTTP response message.

## Precompiling JavaServer Pages

If you are using JavaServer Pages as your Struts presentation technology, you are probably very familiar with the compilation process that the JSP container performs on the application's behalf. When the web container receives a request for a resource with an extension of *.jsp*, the JSP container is selected to process the request. If this is the first request for the JSP page or if the timestamp for the JSP page is newer than the existing servlet class, the page will normally be compiled.[*]

---

[*] Most containers have an option that disables detection so that pages that have changed will not be recompiled. This option is usually selected in a production environment because incremental changes should not be introduced in production. Also, allowing this to occur would amount to a security risk.

The JSP container uses a two-step process. First, the JSP page is translated from the JSP code into a Java source file. Each container may have its own implementation to translate the JSP page. The second step takes the Java source file and compiles it into a servlet class file using whichever Java compiler is installed for the JSP container.

Although just-in-time compilation is a nice feature while you are developing or debugging an application, you may not want to make the JSP source available in a deployment package. This is an issue of both security and licensing—although the JSP pages should contain only presentation logic, that's still intellectual property. If this is the case, you can precompile the JSP pages and not provide the JSP source code to customers. You'll have to distribute only the compiled bytecode, making it harder for the source code to be seen. Once the JSP pages are compiled into Java class files, you can even run them through an obfuscator to make it harder for them to be viewed through decompilation tools. Precompiling the JSP pages gives you more options for dealing with issues like these.

As always, though, there are some downsides to precompiling JSP pages. For one thing, you lose the ability to update or fix a problem quickly. Instead of just placing a new JSP file onto the server and letting the JSP container compile it when it's accessed, you must do the recompilation by hand and deploy the servlet class. Another downside is that when some containers detect a problem with a single JSP, they will stop processing the rest of the application's JSP pages. When this occurs, you must make sure that every JSP page compiles successfully before the container will deploy the web application. Developers may actually consider this a benefit rather than a disadvantage, but it can be problematic in production environments if you are trying to make a quick fix to a bug.

Unfortunately, there's no standard way to precompile the JSP pages. Each container has a different way of doing it. This section briefly discusses how to precompile pages using three of the available containers on the market: Tomcat, Resin, and WebLogic.

## Precompiling JSP pages with Tomcat

The JSP implementation in Tomcat, which is called Jasper (or Jasper 2 in Version 5.0), provides a reference implementation for the latest specification. It's packaged along with Catalina, the reference implementation of the latest Servlet specification, inside of Tomcat. The JSP-to-Java compiler is available as a separate program that can be executed from the command line. Its job is to convert a JSP page into a Java source file. From there, a standard Java compiler can convert the source code into bytecode.

The program is called *jspc.bat* (or *jspc.sh*, depending on which platform you're using) and is included in the Tomcat installation directory. Many options can be set to configure everything from the output directory to the package name of the Java source. There's even an option that will cause the compiler to create XML that can be added to the *web.xml* file for each JSP page that gets precompiled. You can do one page at a time or specify an entire web application.

However, as with many things in Java today, Ant is the preferred way of compiling a web application, including JSPs. The Tomcat documentation includes a sample Ant script that will use the *jspc* tool to precompile the JSPs. Check the Tomcat documentation for your particular version of Tomcat. For Tomcat Version 5.0, see the following link *http://jakarta.apache.org/tomcat/tomcat-5.0-doc/jasper-howto.html*.

### Precompiling JSP pages with Resin

To precompile JSP pages using Resin, you can use the *httpd.exe* command from the Resin *bin* directory, like this:

```
resin/bin/httpd –conf conf/resin.conf –compile <URL>
```

Here, the URL is a JSP resource within a web application installed in Resin.

You can also use the command-line version, like this:

```
resin/bin/httpd –e <URL>
```

With this approach, you can compile only a single JSP page at a time, although you could easily create a script that went through your entire web application. An easier way to configure this is to use Ant, as discussed later in this chapter.

 Resin 2.1.X had some issues with precompiling JSPs when they used tag libraries (which all Struts pages do). These issues have been resolved in Resin 3.0.

### Precompiling JSP pages with WebLogic

With WebLogic, there are two approaches to precompiling JSPs. The first approach is to manually execute the compiler from the command line. This approach is useful when debugging certain JSP problems.

To run the WebLogic JSP compiler from the command line, you must execute the following command:

```
java weblogic.jspc -options fileName
```

Just replace *fileName* with the JSP you need to compile. There are many options that can be added with the –options flag. For Version 7.0, you can view the list of options at *http://e-docs.bea.com/wls/docs70/jsp/reference.html*. For Version 8.0, *http://e-docs. bea.com/wls/docs81/jsp/reference.html* has the available options.

The second approach to precompiling JSPs with WebLogic is to allow the container to precompile the JSPs when an application is deployed or first started. To accomplish this, you need to add a <jsp-descriptor> element.

Using the `<jsp-descriptor>` element within the *weblogic.xml* deployment descriptor, you can set the precompile parameter to true.

```
<jsp-descriptor>
    <jsp-param>
        <param-name>
            precompile
        </param-name>
        <param-value>
            true
        </param-value>
    </jsp-param>
</jsp-descriptor>
```

When set, WebLogic will compile all of the JSPs when an application is deployed or redeployed.

However, WebLogic will not deploy the web application if any one of the JSP pages fails to compile. Once it detects an error compiling a page, all compilation stops and the web application will not be deployed until you fix whatever is causing the problem. After fixing it, you must restart WebLogic to start the process all over again.

One of the major drawbacks to using this option is that the server will precompile the JSPs every time it's started or the application is deployed. This can delay how fast the server is ready to accept incoming requests for the application. To avoid this problem, you can precompile the JSPs into *.class* files using the WebLogic JSP compiler and include them in the *WEB-INF/classes* directory of the WAR. You will also need to add the following `<jsp-descriptor>` elements in the WebLogic deployment descriptor.

```
<jsp-descriptor>
    <jsp-param>
        <param-name>precompile</param-name>
        <param-value>false</param-value>
    </jsp-param>
    <jsp-param>
        <param-name>pageCheckSeconds</param-name>
        <param-value>-1</param-value>
    </jsp-param>
</jsp-descriptor>
```

# Packaging EJB Resources with Struts

If you're communicating with EJBs in the middle tier, it might be necessary to package some of the EJB resources along with your web application package. Because the web tier acts as a client to the EJB server, certain resources are required to connect and communicate with the beans.

The beans' home and remote interfaces, for example, need to be packaged either in the *classes* directory or as a JAR file in the *lib* directory of the web application. Also, some of the JNDI classes need to be included so that clients can acquire home and remote objects. The actual client-side EJB stub classes are not required, however. This wasn't always the case, but the latest specification now describes a mechanism that allows these to be automatically downloaded when a request is made using an EJB remote interface.

In many cases, it's enough to put the EJB container JAR file in the *WEB-INF/lib* directory. For example, if you are using WebLogic, you can put the *weblogic. jar* file in the web tier, as it contains all of the necessary client-side resources. You will also need to include any Data Transfer Objects being referenced by the two tiers. They will need to be included on both sides.

# Packaging the Application as a WAR File

Packaging your web applications using the WAR format is very convenient. The structure is precise, and because it is specified so carefully, porting your applications across the various web containers is much easier. The next section describes the steps that you must perform to package your web application as a WAR file.

## Creating the WAR File

The first step in packaging your application as a WAR file is to create a root directory. In most cases, this directory will have the same name as your web application. For our example, we will create a directory called *storefront*.

After deciding how your JSP and HTML pages will be placed within your application, place them underneath the root directory in their appropriate subdirectories. For the Storefront example, our directory structure so far would look like Figure 16-2.

Figure 16-2 shows 11 subdirectories, 8 of which contain JSP pages for the application. The *images* directory contains images that are used globally throughout the application, the *stylesheets* directory stores cascading stylesheets for the application, and the *include* directory contains files that are included using either a static or dynamic include.

The next step in setting up the WAR file is to ensure that you have a *WEB-INF* directory underneath your root web application directory. The *WEB-INF* directory contains all of the resources that are used internally by the application. For example, the TLD files for your custom tag libraries reside in this directory, as does the web deployment descriptor. This is also where the Struts configuration files belong. No resource within this directory can be made public outside of the application.

Underneath the *WEB-INF* directory, create two subdirectories: one called *classes* and the other called *lib*. The *classes* directory should contain all of your utility and

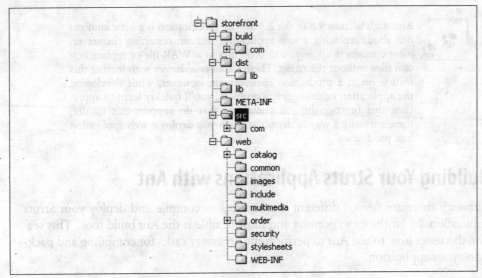

*Figure 16-2. The Storefront application directory structure*

servlet classes. The *lib* directory should contain the JAR files that the application depends on.

Once all of the resources for the web application are accounted for and are inside the appropriate directories, you need to use Java's archiving tool *jar* to package the directories and files. From a command line, change to the root directory of your web application and use the *jar* utility. You need to give the file a *.war* extension, like this:

```
jar cvf storefront.war .
```

Because you changed to the root directory, the *storefront* directory will not be included in the WAR file. This is fine, because you may want to call the root directory something else when it's installed. When you install the web application, if you plan to explode the WAR file, all you need to do is create a directory and un-*jar* the files, like this:

```
C:\tomcat\webapps>mkdir storefront
C:\tomcat\webapps>cp storefront.war storefront
C:\tomcat\webapps>cd storefront
C:\tomcat\webapps\storefront>jar xf storefront.war
```

The location where the WAR file gets expanded is container-dependent. If you plan to distribute the WAR file without exploding it, all you have to do is place it in the appropriate place for the container. You don't have to recreate the *storefront* directory, although you might want to delete the existing directory when deploying a newer version.

Although Section 9.8 of the 2.3 Servlet specification is a little ambiguous about replacing a web application without restarting the server, most containers allow you to drop in a new WAR file or replace certain files without restarting. There's always a danger with leaving this feature on in a production environment; however, while developing the application or debugging a problem, you'll quickly learn to appreciate this functionality. In containers that do support this feature, there's usually a way to disable it when you deploy a web application into production.

# Building Your Struts Applications with Ant

Although there are several different mechanisms to compile and deploy your Struts application, by far the most popular and most flexible is the Ant build tool.[*] This section discusses how to use Ant to perform the necessary tasks for compiling and packaging your application.

## What Is Ant?

Ant is a platform-independent build tool that can be configured to compile your Java source code files, build your deployment JAR and WAR files, unit-test your code, and create your project's JavaDoc documentation. It also has many other uses and can be expanded to perform new tasks of your own creation.

Ant is similar to the Unix *make* utility (also known as *gmake* in Linux and *nmake* in DOS/Windows). *make* utilities have been used for generations to manage projects for languages such as C and C++, but these utilities are platform-dependent because the rules they use are typically shell commands executed by the host operating system. Unlike *make*, Ant's rules (or tasks, in Ant terminology) are Java classes and can be run on any platform with a supported JVM.

## Installing and Configuring Ant

You can download Ant from the Jakarta web site at *http://ant.apache.org/*. The examples provided in this chapter were tested with Ant 1.6. Download the binary *zip* file (for Windows) or the *.tar.gz* file (for Unix) and uncompress the archive into your desired installation directory. You should also download the *optional.jar* file and install it in the *ANT_HOME/lib* directory. While it's not used in this project, the *optional.jar* file has many extra tasks that you may find useful in the future.

Ensure that the *ANT_HOME/bin* directory is added to your system PATH. Your installation may also require you to add the ANT_HOME environment variable, which should be set to the Ant installation directory. The Ant binary typically can

---

[*] Ant is an acronym for "Another Neat Tool."

determine what ANT_HOME should be, but if you get an error when trying to run Ant, set this environment variable. There is also a caveat when running Ant under Windows 95/98—do not install it in a directory with a long pathname, because the batch file used to run the installation script may not be able to handle the pathname. See the Ant installation documentation for more information.

# Getting Started

Ant reads its build commands from an XML file. By default, it looks for a file called *build.xml*, but you can give the file any name by using the -buildfile *file* option when running Ant. From a command prompt, change directories to the base project directory (in this example, it's *storefront*). In this directory, you should see the *build.xml* file.

The Ant build file consists of a project that has zero or more targets, each of which consists of zero or more tasks. The project element is defined at the top of the build file:

```
<project name="storefront" default="war" basedir=".">
```

Here, the project is named storefront and the default target to execute is the war target. The default target is what gets executed if you type *ant* at the command line without specifying a target. Because the project root directory is the same directory that the *build.xml* file is located in, "." is used to indicate the base directory property.

The build directory structure for the Storefront application is shown in Figure 16-3.

A target takes the form:

```
<target name="dostuff">
  <task1 param1="value1" param2="value2"/>
  <task2 param="value"/>
  ...
</target>
```

A target must have a name and may have several additional attributes that determine when and if the target actually gets executed. The target should contain zero or more tasks.

A task is an atomic unit of work in the Ant world. Each task is bound to a Java class file that Ant executes, passing to it any arguments or subelements defined with that

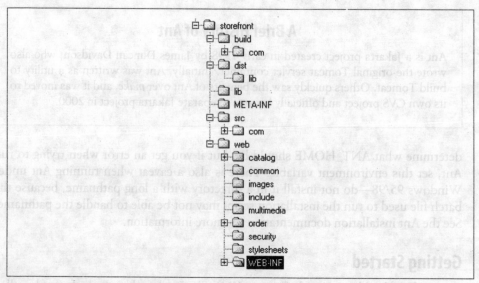

*Figure 16-3. The build structure for the Storefront application*

task. The Ant tool is extensible and allows you to create your own tasks. For this book and the Storefront example, the built-in tasks included with the Ant distribution are all you will need. If, however, you need to create a new task, you can do so by defining the task in the *build.xml* file, using the taskdef task to bind the task name to a Java class file. The Java class file must extend org.apache.tools.ant.Task and be located in the Ant classpath. There are several other requirements that are beyond the scope of this book, but details can be found in the Ant documentation.

Before you run Ant, you may have to change a few properties in the Storefront *build. xml* file to suit your development environment:

```
<property name="webserver.home"
    value="c:/tomcat"/>
<property name="webserver.deploy"
    value="${webserver.home}/webapps"/>
<property name="servlet.jar"
    value="${webserver.home}/common/lib/servlet.jar"/>
```

These three properties define where the servlet container is located, where its deployment directory is located, and where it keeps the servlet API classes. First, the webserver.home property is set to the root directory of the servlet container. In this case, the Tomcat 4.0 web server and servlet container are being used. The Storefront *build. xml* file supports several other containers, but they are commented out; you just need to uncomment the one that you want to use. Tomcat's deployment directory is the *webapps* directory found just under the Tomcat root directory. Tomcat keeps the servlet API classes in the *common/lib/servlet.jar* relative to the Tomcat root directory.

Lastly, we need to define the classpath that will be used during compilation of our project. Ant allows us to associate a set of files with a property name. In the following *build.xml* fragment, the list of all the JAR files necessary to compile the Storefront example is bound to the build.classpath property:

```
<path id="build.classpath">
  <pathelement location="${servlet.jar}"/>
  <pathelement location="${lib.dir}/commons-beanutils.jar"/>
  <pathelement location="${lib.dir}/commons-collections.jar"/>
  <pathelement location="${lib.dir}/commons-dbcp.jar"/>
  <pathelement location="${lib.dir}/commons-digester.jar"/>
  <pathelement location="${lib.dir}/commons-logging.jar"/>
  <pathelement location="${lib.dir}/commons-pool.jar"/>
  <pathelement location="${lib.dir}/commons-services.jar"/>
  <pathelement location="${lib.dir}/commons-validator.jar"/>
  <pathelement location="${lib.dir}/jdbc2_0-stdext.jar"/>
  <pathelement location="${lib.dir}/log4j.jar"/>
  <pathelement location="${lib.dir}/poolman.jar"/>
  <pathelement location="${lib.dir}/struts.jar"/>
  <pathelement location="${lib.dir}/tiles.jar"/>
  <pathelement path="${build.dir}"/>
</path>
```

We could have used include elements to define the build.classpath property in far fewer lines; however, it's much clearer to explicitly list each JAR file used during the build process so that nothing that might prevent a successful build is added or omitted.

Dereferencing the property name using the Ant syntax ${property} allows the tasks to use the build.classpath property.

## Compiling Java Source Files

The Java source files for the Storefront application are compiled using the Ant javac task. The compiling target, compile, depends on the prepare target:

```
<target name="compile" depends="prepare">
  <javac destdir="${build.dir}" deprecation="on">
    <classpath refid="build.classpath"/>
      <src path="${src.dir}"/>
  </javac>
</target>
```

A target may depend on zero or more other targets, using the following syntax:

```
<target name="final-jar" depends="jars, wars">
```

Specifying the depends attribute allows you to control the order in which Ant targets are executed. In this case, the compile target is not executed until the prepare target has been executed:

```
<target name="prepare">
  <tstamp/>
  <mkdir dir="${build.dir}"/>
  <mkdir dir="${dist.dir}/lib"/>
</target>
```

The prepare target generates timestamp values that can be turned into properties and attached to compilation products such as JAR and WAR files. For this small project, however, timestamps are not used. The prepare target also creates the necessary output subdirectories for our Java classes and WAR file.

The compile target instructs Ant to run the javac compiler on all the files within the source directory and send all the class files to the build directory. The deprecation option is on, so you'll get a detailed message if you accidentally include a deprecated method in one of the source files:

```
<target name="compile" depends="prepare">
  <javac destdir="${build.dir}" deprecation="on">
    <classpath refid="build.classpath"/>
      <src path="${src.dir}"/>
  </javac>
</target>
```

The javac task uses the build.classpath property shown in the previous section.

## Using Ant to Build the WAR File

The Ant war task builds the web archive. The war target used to build the web archive is shown here:

```
<target name="war" depends="compile">
  <echo>building war...</echo>
  <war warfile="${dist.dir}/lib/storefront.war"
       webxml="${web.dir}/WEB-INF/web.xml">
    <fileset dir="${web.dir}"/>
    <classes dir="${build.dir}"/>
    <classes dir="${lib.dir}">
      <include name="*.properties"/>
      <include name="poolman.xml"/>
    </classes>
    <lib dir="${lib.dir}">
      <include name="*.jar"/>
    </lib>
  </war>
</target>
```

As mentioned previously, the war target is the default target for the project. This means that when Ant is run from the command line without a target argument, the war target is executed. The war target runs only if the compile target has been run first. The war task requires you to define the name of the WAR file and the location of the *web.xml* file. All the other attributes are optional; if you are interested in seeing them, they are listed in the online Ant documentation (*http://ant.apache.org/manual/CoreTasks/war.html*). Another great reference on Ant is *Ant: The Definitive Guide* by Jesse Tilly and Eric Burke (O'Reilly).

The nested elements tell the war task where the contents of the WAR file are located. The fileset element defines the base web content of the WAR file. This element is used to declare where the HTML files, JSP pages, images, and so on are located. The classes element points to the Java class files that should be included in the *WEB-INF/classes* directory in the WAR file, and the lib element declares which files should be included in the *WEB-INF/lib* folder.

In the Storefront example, everything in the *web* subdirectory is included. The various subdirectories contain all of the necessary resources (HTML, JSP pages, images, etc.). All of the compiled classes in the *build* subdirectory are copied into the WAR file's *WEB-INF/classes* directory along with the properties files. All of the third-party JARs in the *lib* subdirectory are copied into the WAR's *WEB-INF/lib* directory. If the *lib* subdirectory contains any JARs that you don't want to be included, you can use the following snippet:

```
<lib dir="${lib.dir}">
    <include name="*.jar"/>
    <exclude name="dont_need.jar"/>
</lib>
```

Here, all the JARs in the *lib* directory except *dont_need.jar* will be copied into the WAR file's *WEB-INF/lib* directory.

The last and often the clearest option is to explicitly include each desired JAR file. While slightly more verbose, this method is immune to changes to the *lib* folder if other developers in the project start adding JARs indiscriminately. It is also much easier to see exactly what is going to be included in the WAR file.

## Cleaning Up

The final two targets are trivial but important. The clean target deletes the *build* directory, thus removing all of the Java class files:

```
<target name="clean">
    <delete dir="${build.dir}"/>
</target>

<target name="distclean">
    <antcall target="clean"/>
    <delete dir="${dist.dir}"/>
</target>
```

The distclean target reverts the project back to its pristine "distribution" state. That is, all build products—class files and the WAR file—are removed, so the project directory looks the same as it did when the project directory tree was first installed.

Note that the distclean target calls the clean target. While this isn't really necessary for this small project, it demonstrates more of the power of Ant by invoking another target via the antcall task. The antcall task can even call a target with arguments, but that is beyond the scope of this book.

You can download various plug-ins that allow you to use Ant inside of your specific IDE. For example, the AntRunner plug-in allows Ant to be used within the JBuilder IDE. For this and other plug-ins, see the external tools section of the Ant site at *http://ant.apache.org/external.html*.

# Creating an Automated Build Environment

Once you have put together a satisfactory build environment, you should go the extra step to automate it. This means that no human interaction is needed to execute new builds. It's very common for build frequencies to increase the closer you get to the end of a construction phase. You can, of course, just manually kick off builds when you need them, but a better and much more efficient approach is to use a scheduling mechanism to invoke your Ant build environment.

There are at least two scheduling mechanisms that you can employ, depending on your environment. In Unix, you can use the *cron* daemon, and on the Windows platform, you can take advantage of the Task Scheduler.

## Using cron to Invoke Ant

*cron* is a program that allows you to automate tasks by running user-defined programs at regular intervals. *cron* allows you to define both the program that is to be run and the exact time at which to run it. The *cron* program is a daemon program, which means that it runs in the background until it's needed. It wakes up every minute, checks to see if there are any scheduled tasks that need to be performed, and, after it runs the tasks, goes back to waiting.

The list of tasks for *cron* to execute comes from a file called a *cron* table, which is commonly referred to as *crontabs*. The *crontabs* is a schedule that lists the tasks to run and the date and time to run them.

Some system administrators may disable *cron* from running on a server in order to save processing power. In this case, you'll need to get permission to run *cron* programs. You can verify that *cron* is running and that you have permission to access it by typing *crontab -l* at the command prompt.

All you need to do is edit *crontabs* and add an entry that calls your *ant* program, which in turn will kick off the build. Check the Unix manpages for more information on using *cron*.

## Using Microsoft Task Scheduler

The Windows platform contains an application called Task Scheduler (or Scheduled Tasks in newer versions of the platform). This program performs the same function as *cron*, but for the Windows platform. It has a wizard that walks you through setting up a task that gets fired off at regular intervals. Figure 16-4 shows the main screen of the Scheduled Tasks application. A task has been created that will invoke a batch file that can in turn call Ant to perform a build for your environment.

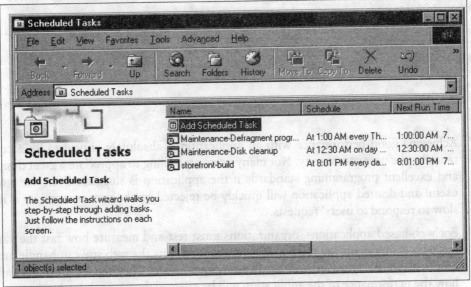

*Figure 16-4. The Scheduled Tasks application on the Windows platform*

The amount of control that you have over the time intervals is not as granular as it is on the Unix platform. However, it is sufficient enough to kick off daily builds at a certain time. See the Windows documentation for your specific version for more details.

 Part of automating your build environment is pulling the source files from the source code repository and compiling them. Most source control systems, such as Clear Case, CVS, and PVCS, have a command-line API to pull source files in a read-only mode in order to compile them. Using Java and Ant, this part of the automation process is pretty straightforward.

# Restarting Your Server Remotely

If your deployment server is located on a different server from the build environment (and it really should be), you will need to move the deployment files over and possibly restart the server. The easiest way to do this is with the Ant ftp and telnet tasks. You can even have Ant email you reports on the result of the latest build using the email task. See the Ant documentation for more information on these and other helpful tasks.

# CHAPTER 17

# Addressing Performance

Achieving good performance with an application is absolutely critical to its acceptance by the user community. Not many users are willing to appreciate a great design and excellent programming standards if the application is sluggish. Even the most useful and desired application will quickly be rejected by the user community if it's slow to respond to users' requests.

For web-based applications, organizations must test and measure how fast the various web components are, how many simultaneous hits the web site can handle, and how scalable the software and hardware resources are. They must also understand how the performance of the application will be affected during peak loads.

This chapter explores the performance implications of using the Struts framework and its associated technologies to build web applications, and how certain design and programming decisions will affect the overall performance of the application. A distinction is made between performance, load, and stress testing and the steps necessary to carry out each.

## What Is Good Performance?

Most developers have had the unfortunate experience of building a slow application. Obviously, developers don't set out to create slow applications, and there probably isn't a user group asking, "Could you please make the application run slower?" Too often, bad performance isn't discovered until the application is finished and installed into a production environment. But why does this happen?

The simple truth is that it happens because not enough attention is given to performance matters during design and construction. This is not to say that performance should be the primary focus at all times—if you focus on performance too exclusively or too soon, it may negatively affect the design and code. On the other hand, if you wait too long, you may find yourself with upset users complaining about poor performance, and you'll be left wondering what went wrong.

You may have heard the axiom "Test soon, test often." This is a good principle to follow to help ensure that you are not surprised at the end of construction with a poorly performing application. The sooner you can detect a performance problem, the more likely it is that you'll get a chance to fix it before the application goes into production. Another apt saying is "Don't leave any broken windows." This means that when you detect a problem, you should fix it and not let it linger. Picture a building with a broken window that's not immediately fixed. If people are led to believe that having one broken window in the building is acceptable, they will eventually decide that it's all right to have many broken windows. Before long, the building will be in shambles, and all the tenants will have moved out. If you find obvious performance problems during early tests, fix them.

So how do you measure the performance of a web application? What's considered acceptable or too slow? The answers to these questions are strictly related to the nonfunctional requirements of the application.* There are tangible and quantitative measurements that can be taken to help determine whether the application is able to meet the minimum requirements set out in the nonfunctional requirements.

The problem is that each application is different and therefore has different nonfunctional requirements. One application might need to have an average response time of 3.0 seconds and support 50 concurrent users, while another might have to support 500 simultaneous users. Performance testing is a little more nebulous than functional testing, where it's easy to see when the application fails to meet the design specifications.

According to Alberto Savoia, the Director of Software Research at Sun Microsystems's Laboratories, there are four behavioral laws that make web page performance critical to an organization's success:

*The Law of Stickiness*
> This law states that web users are sticky, but not loyal. If they find a web site that serves their needs, they tend to continue to use that site. If the web site begins to respond slowly and cause the users to wait, they will move to another site that fulfills their same needs. The point is to strive to keep the performance of the application strong in order to keep the users coming back.

*The Law of User Perspective*
> This law states that you should always measure the performance of your application from the user's point of view, not from your own. The point here is that, for example, while your environment may have a 100-MB network with an otherwise light load on it, the user may be using a modem with a much smaller bandwidth capability. Always keep in mind what the user's environment and network capabilities will be and test accordingly.

---

* The nonfunctional requirements are part of the analysis work that should be done for any nontrivial application. These requirements describe the broader issues of the application, such as availability, disaster recovery, package dependencies, hardware configuration, and, almost always, performance criteria.

*The Law of Responsibility*

This law states that the users don't care what or who is at fault for poor web site performance; they will always blame the application. The problem might be their ISP or another nonapplication issue, but most users will not be able to isolate the problem to that level and instead will blame the application or site. You must be aware of all the factors that may impact the performance of your application.

*The Law of Expectations*

This law states that users' satisfaction is based on their expectations, which are set by their personal experiences with other, similar web sites. When measuring the performance of your application, don't rely just on arbitrary numbers to indicate what's slow or fast; compare your results with those of your competitors.

These simple, common-sense laws explain the human-behavior aspects of web site performance. In general, however, slow is slow and fast is fast, and generalizations can be made across applications and business domains. But before we discuss how to detect whether performance problems exist in an application, a distinction must be made between the types of performance testing that should be conducted.

# Performance Versus Load Testing

There are many different types of software testing: functional, unit, integration, white box, black box, regression, and so on. Performance and load testing are among the most important types of testing, but they usually get the least amount of attention. There are two general reasons for this neglect. The first reason is that developers typically wait until the very end of the development cycle to start testing the performance of the application, and the end of the cycle is when you have the least amount of time for testing. It is true, however, that it's not always practical to conduct performance testing during every phase of development. Early phases tend to focus on the architecturally significant pieces, and there may not be enough of the application built to test its performance. You should, however, gather some preliminary performance measurements as early as possible.

Another reason that performance and load testing don't get much attention is that they're honestly hard to do. While there are many tools on the market, both free and commercial, it's not always easy to use these tools to detect problems. The tools must be able to simulate many simultaneous users of a system, but that involves understanding what virtual users are,* what the different threading models are, and how they affect performance and load. Also, you must be able to look at the results and determine whether or not they are acceptable. All of this can be overwhelming to

---

* Virtual users are simulated users that testing applications use to simulate the impact of multiple users on a system without requiring "real" users to sit around testing the application. A user session is recorded for each virtual user and can be played back as if a real user were using the application.

the average developer. This is part of what keeps developers from conducting the tests; they just don't understand the necessary steps, or how and where to get started. Many organizations house a separate team that is solely responsible for performance testing.

Although performance, load, and stress testing are related, they are not the same thing and are not carried out in exactly the same manner. *Performance testing* involves executing the functional behavior of the application and essentially timing how long it takes for each result to complete. The amount of time that a single task takes to finish is known as its *response time*. If you execute the method many times and then take the average, this is its average response time.

The average response time for the *signin* action in the Storefront application, for example, is roughly 250 milliseconds.* This result is for a single user. You should always conduct the initial performance testing using a single user to get a baseline. If there are performance bottlenecks for a single user of the system, you can bet that these problems will have an impact when multiple users start logging in. In general, the faster the response time is, the faster the application is. This end-to-end time can also be thought of as the *transaction time for the function being tested.*

*Based on the response time, you can come up with a rough throughput time. Throughput* defines the number of transactions that can occur in a set amount of time. The theoretical throughput that is calculated based on a single user will probably differ with real loads. Due to multiprocessing and other hardware and software features, applications can achieve a higher throughput by adding more hardware and software resources. This enables the application to process more transactions per time period, which increases the throughput numbers.

*Load testing* is analogous to volume testing. This type of testing is performed to see how the application will react to a higher user load on the system. During this type of testing, you can adjust the hardware and software configurations to determine which configuration gives the best throughput for a given user load. Load testing is usually hard to conduct because you are constantly going back and forth, adjusting configuration systems to see what gives you a higher throughput. No application can sustain an infinite user load. The idea is to try to maximize the number of concurrent users with an acceptable average response time.

Throughput is usually measured in *transactions per second* (tps), but it can also be measured per minute, per hour, and so on. Armed with response times and throughput numbers, you can make intelligent decisions about how the application should be configured to ensure the best performance and scalability for the users. You should share these numbers with the network engineers, so they'll understand how much network bandwidth the application might require.

---

* The tests were conducted on a Pentium III 750 MHz machine with 1 GB of memory and all tiers collocated on the same box.

*Stress testing* is the next logical extension. Stress testing is essentially load testing using peak loads. When conducting stress tests, you really are trying to stress the application to its limits to see how it reacts, how efficiently the memory is used, and what other types of problems will surface.

Stressing your application under a heavy simulated load offers many benefits. In particular, stress testing allows you to:

- Identify bottlenecks in the application under a large user load before they occur in the production environment.
- Control risks and costs by predicting scalability and performance limits.
- Increase uptime and availability of the application through proper resource planning.
- Avoid missing go-live dates due to unexpected performance and scalability problems.

Performance, load, and stress testing should be performed on an application to get the complete picture. They can point to parts of the application that might become bottlenecks, both under normal loads and as the number of users climbs.

# Performance- and Stress-Testing Tools

There is an abundant supply of performance- and stress-testing tools available on the market today. Some are quite inexpensive, while others are astronomically expensive. Commercial testing products tend to offer more plentiful features, but there's really no correlation between cost and quality when it comes to these types of tools. For most applications, you don't need to spend an arm and a leg on a testing tool when there are free or cheaper ones that will do the job. The best advice is to start out with one of the free or inexpensive tools and see if it meets the project's needs. If not, take a look at one of the more expensive commercial products to see what it has to offer. Table 17-1 lists several performance- and stress-testing tools.

*Table 17-1. Available performance- and stress-testing tools*

| Company | Product | URL |
|---|---|---|
| Apache Group | JMeter | *http://jakarta.apache.org/jmeter* |
| Mercury Interactive | LoadRunner | *http://www.mercuryinteractive.com/products/loadrunner* |
| RadView | WebLoad | *http://www.radview.com* |
| Empirix | e-Test Suite | *http://www.empirix.com* |
| Segue Software, Inc. | SilkPerformer | *http://www.segue.com* |
| Microsoft | WAS | *http://www.microsoft.com/technet/treeview/default.asp?url=/technet/ itsolutions/intranet/downloads/webstres.asp* |
| Apache Group | Flood | *http://httpd.apache.org/test/flood* |
| SourceForge | The Grinder | *http://grinder.sourceforge.net* |

# Testing the Storefront Application

The Storefront application represents a typical shopping-cart application that you might encounter on the Internet or may even have built before. A normal application of this type would connect to a database with tens of thousands or even hundreds of thousands of records.

 By default, the Storefront application uses a debug implementation and doesn't connect to a database. This was done so you didn't have to have a database installed just to run the example application.

There's no real point in going through the entire exercise of testing the Storefront application; the numbers wouldn't mean anything anyway. It would, however, be helpful to show how to get started and what steps must usually be taken to get performance numbers out of an application. The following are the general steps:

1. Understand the performance goals.
2. Establish the performance baselines for the application.
3. Run tests to collect performance data.
4. Analyze the data to detect where the problems are.
5. Make the necessary software and hardware changes to increase performance.
6. Repeat Steps 3 through 5 as necessary to reach the performance goals.

This section works through each of these steps. For this exercise, we are going to use a scaled-down version of the Mercury Interactive LoadRunner product, called Astra LoadTest. This is a feature-rich commercial product. A demo version that will support up to 10 virtual users is available for download at *http://www.svca.mercury-interactive.com/products/downloads.html*.

## Understand the Performance Goals

Before you begin testing, it's important to understand the performance goals of the application. The performance goals are normally specified in the nonfunctional requirements for an application, using the following units:

- Average transaction response time
- Transactions per second (tps)
- Hits per second

It's not absolutely critical that you know what the performance numbers need to be before starting to test the application, but it can help to have a set of expectations. Sooner or later, someone is going to ask you how the application performs. To be able to say "it's good" or "it stinks," you'll need to evaluate its performance relative to some set of goals.

## Establish a Performance Baseline

Once you're ready to start testing, the first thing you should do is establish a baseline. A baseline is a snapshot of your application's performance before anything has been done to it. It's always a good idea to get a performance baseline before you start changing code to improve the performance. Otherwise, how do you know whether you've made it better or worse?

### Taking a baseline

Most performance-testing tools allow you to record the interaction sequence between a browser and the web application. Although most tools also allow you to manually create the testing scripts, using the tools' automatic recording aspects is very convenient. Figure 17-1 illustrates the recording screen of the Astra LoadTest software.

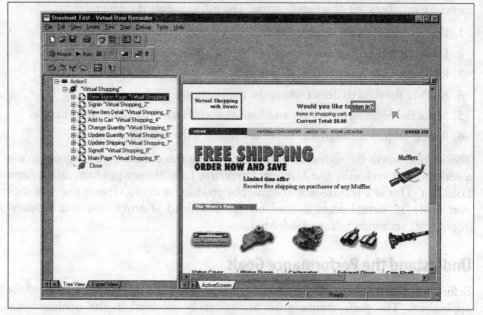

*Figure 17-1. The recording screen of the Astra LoadTest application*

With Astra, as with most other web testing tools, each interaction with the web application can be recorded as a separate transaction. In Figure 17-1, each element in the tree view on the left-hand side of the screen represents a separate transaction that can be played back and have its performance metrics recorded.

Once you start recording, all interaction between the client and the server is recorded, including request parameters and headers. You can then play back this recording and modify different parameters, such as the number of users executing the recording.

Once you have the necessary test scripts, you can establish the baseline. The baseline measurement is normally taken with a single user using the application. Depending on whether you are conducting performance tests or are concentrating on load testing, the number of virtual users can vary. It's typically a good idea to start with one user and scale upward. If the application is slow with a single user, it's likely to be slow with multiple users. Figure 17-2 shows the testing script from Figure 17-1 running against the Storefront application with a single user.

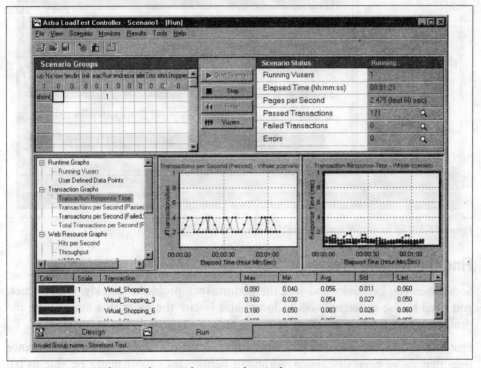

*Figure 17-2. Testing the Storefront application with a single user*

Once the testing scenario is complete, the software gives you a summary report of the performance of your application. The baseline report for the Storefront application with a single user is shown in Figure 17-3.

Once you have the baseline numbers, if you determine that the performance needs to improve, you can start to modify the application. Unfortunately, this is never easy. You have to know where the problems are in order to determine where to focus. There's not much point in speeding up the application in the places that it's already fast. You need to use the tools to help you determine where the bottlenecks are.

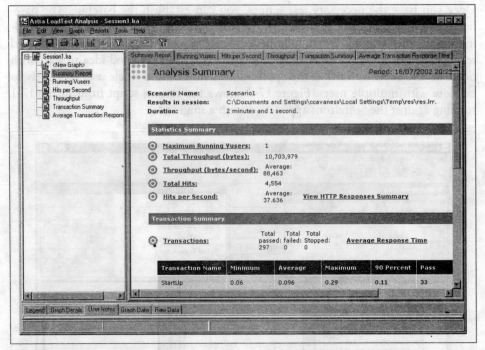

*Figure 17-3. The summary report for the Storefront application*

# Find the Trouble Areas

Sometimes you get lucky and find the performance problems quickly. Other times, you need to use different tools to locate and isolate the areas that are causing the problems. This is where profiling tools can help.

Profiling your application is somewhat different from conducting the performance tests that we've been discussing. Although performance tools might be able to tell you which web request took the longest to complete, they can't tell you which Java method took up the most time. This is the purpose of profilers.

Table 17-2 lists several profiling tools that can be useful in locating trouble areas of the application.

*Table 17-2. Commercially available profiling tools*

| Company | Product | URL |
| --- | --- | --- |
| Rational | Quantify | *http://www.rational.com* |
| Inprise | Optimizelt | *http://www.borland.com/optimizeit/* |
| Sitraka Software | JProbe | *http://www.sitraka.com* |

Profiling an application is similar to debugging. You see where the application spends most of its time, how many calls are made to a specific function, how many objects are created, how much memory is used, and so on. You start from a high level and work your way down to the methods that are causing the performance or scalability problems. Once you fix the problem areas, you run the tests again. This is repeated until all of the problems are resolved, or until you have to ship the product.

The performance tools can also help you determine where the problem areas are. In Figure 17-4, for instance, we see that the average transaction response time for one action seems much higher than those for the others.

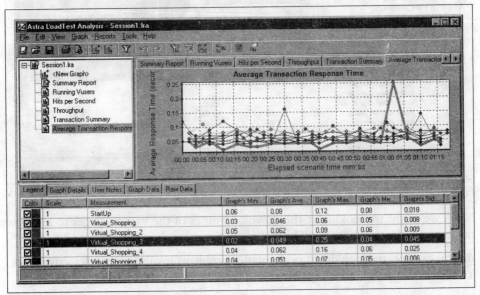

Figure 17-4. Higher average response times may indicate a problem

The numbers shown here are extraordinarily good. The worst response time for the Storefront application is 0.25 seconds. Most developers would kill to have a problem like that! That's because we aren't doing anything "real" in the application. It's an example application that doesn't really connect to a backend system with thousands of records to sift through. This brings up a good point, however. Just because one transaction is slower than the rest doesn't mean that it's slow. It might just be slow relative to other really fast transactions. Don't spend time speeding up something from very fast to super fast. Concentrate on the parts of the application that are truly slow. 0.25 seconds is very fast, and if this were a "real" application, we would ship it immediately.

The operation that shows the worst response time in Figure 17-4 is the "view item detail" action. With Astra, we can break the transaction down even further to see what's going on. Figure 17-5 breaks down the view item detail page into its constituent parts.

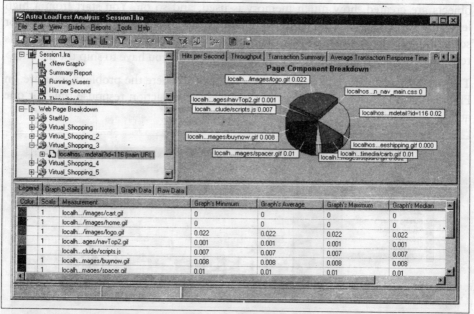

*Figure 17-5. The item detail page broken down into its parts*

Next, we might try looking at the download times of the various pages to see how the item detail page stacks up. The download times are shown in Figure 17-6.

As you can see, tracking down performance problems involves some detective work. You have to look behind every corner and leave no stone unturned.

## Make the Necessary Changes to Software and Hardware

Once you think you've found the problem and made the necessary changes, go back to the testing scripts once again. Keep doing this over and over until all of the performance issues are solved or it's time to ship the product. Because time is limited, it's vital that you plan your testing activities to cover the largest areas of the application and to focus on specific components that are known to cause performance or scalability problems.

There's usually not just one problem to fix—it's a constant back-and-forth process that could go on forever, except for the fact that you eventually have to ship the product. It's imperative that you concentrate on the biggest performance areas first.

## Performance and Scalability Gotchas

This section presents several well-known issues that may affect performance and scalability for your Struts applications. This section is not meant to be exhaustive, but rather to single out a few of the more serious concerns.

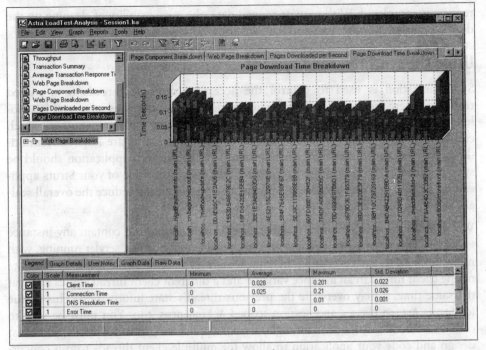

*Figure 17-6. Page download times of the Storefront application*

# Request Scope Versus Session

Memory is limited. You can purchase more memory for a machine, but at some point you'll stop receiving the same return on your investment. It's very common to store objects and data in the user's HttpSession. In some cases, this might be the only way to achieve a particular requirement. However, you must consider the effect that storing objects and data in the session has on an application.

The more information and objects that are stored in the session, the more you need to worry about scalability. Say that you store 0.5 MB worth of data for a single user. If the application were loaded with 1000 concurrent users, that would equal 500 MB (0.5 GB) worth of memory.

> Don't forget that there are other resources taking up memory, not just user sessions. There's application-scope data, the rest of the Struts framework, your application components, the container itself, the JVM, and so on. You must consider all of these factors.

As you can see, using the session to store data can quickly eat up memory. A better alternative is to use the HttpServletRequest to temporarily store data that can be used by other components and then reclaimed by the garbage collector when the request is completed. With request-scoped data, the responsibility of cleaning up the data is between the container and the JVM, not the application.

## Using the synchronized Keyword

Synchronization is used to control the access of multiple threads to a shared resource. There are many situations where synchronization makes sense and is absolutely necessary to keep multiple threads from interfering with one another, which can lead to significant application errors. Struts applications are inherently multi-threaded, and you might think that certain parts of the web application should be synchronized. However, using the synchronized keyword inside of your Struts applications can cause some significant performance problems and reduce the overall scalability of the applications.

We've all heard at one time or another that servlets should not contain any instance variables. This is because there may be only a single instance of a servlet running, with multiple client threads executing the same instance concurrently. If you store the state of one client thread in an instance variable and a different client thread comes along at the same time, it may overwrite the previous thread's state information. This is true for Struts Action classes and session-scoped ActionForms, too. You must be sure to code in a thread-safe manner throughout your application. In other words, you must design and code your application to allow for multiple client threads to run concurrently throughout the application without interfering with one another. If you need to control access to a shared resource, try to use a pool of resources instead of synchronizing on a single object. Also, keep in mind that the HttpSession is not synchronized. If you have multiple threads reading and writing to objects in the user's session, you may experience severe problems that are very difficult to track down. It's up to the programmer to protect shared resources stored in the user's session.

## Using java.util.Vector and java.util.Hashtable

You must also be careful which Java classes you use throughout your Struts applications, especially when it comes to selecting a collection class. The java.util. Vector and java.util.Hashtable classes, for example, are synchronized internally. If you are using Vector or Hashtable within your Struts applications, this may have the same effect as using the synchronized keyword explicitly.

You should avoid using these classes unless you are absolutely sure that you need to. Instead of using Vector, for example, you can use java.util.ArrayList. Instead of Hashtable, use the java.util.HashMap class. Both of these classes provide similar functionality without the synchronization overhead.

## Using Too Many Custom Tags

JSP custom tags are great at what they do. Using them instead of coding Java directly in your JSP pages is recommended by almost everyone who has used both approaches. You have to be careful, however, when using too many custom tags in a single JSP page. Some containers are not very efficient at pooling tag handlers, and some may generate poorly written Java code.

If your JSP pages are performing slowly, one possible solution is to move some of the code to another JSP page and use the JSP include mechanism. A second approach is to simply reduce the number of tags in the page, although this is less practical. If these solutions don't work, try a different container. Each container may deal with tags differently—while one may be slow with your application, another may be fast.

## Improperly Tuning the JVM

The JVM supports many different options for tuning and configuring its runtime parameters. Sometimes it's necessary to adjust these options to achieve better performance from your application.

The two most important options when trying to increase performance or scalability for your application are the -Xms(size) and -Xmx(size) options. The -Xms option allows you to set the initial size of the application heap. The -Xmx option allows you to set the maximum size for the heap.

The heap is the memory storage area for the application. The larger the storage area, the more memory the application can use. You might ask, "Why not just set it to the maximum size allowed by the physical memory?" The problem with that approach is that it becomes an area that the garbage collector has to clean up. The garbage collector in the JVM runs periodically and attempts to reclaim any unused memory.

The garbage collector has to search through all of the memory assigned to an application. Each time the garbage collector runs, the application will pause. The longer it takes for the garbage collector to do its job, the longer the users will have to wait during a collection cycle. It's very important to set the heap size correctly. Unfortunately, there's no general way to determine the correct heap size for an application. Each application is different, and each one creates and destroys objects at a different rate. The best that you can do is to set the values to standard starting points and make changes incrementally. You will eventually reach a point where performance or scalability gets worse as the values get higher. Lower the values again and leave them alone. In general, you should start with these values:

```
-Xms 256M
-Xmx 256M
```

 Many sources recommended setting the initial and maximum heap sizes to the same value, so that the JVM doesn't have to pause the application when it needs to acquire more memory. This, in turn, should help to improve performance.

The default minimum value is 2 MB, and the default maximum value is 64 MB. The letter after the number in the option can be:

- k or K for kilobytes
- m or M for megabytes

To see a list of other supported JVM options, type *java -X* on the command line. Assuming that your path is set up correctly for the Java executable, you should see something similar to Figure 17-7.

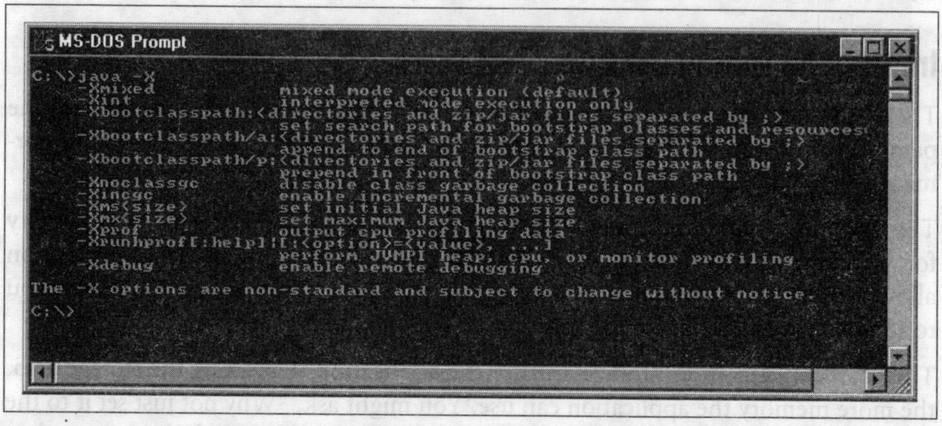

*Figure 17-7. Typing java -X displays the options available for the JVM*

## Using Too Many Remote Calls

When accessing remote components such as EJBs from your application, you may find that the overhead of network communication starts to cause performance problems. One thing to look at is the "granularity" of your remote calls. If you find that you are making many calls that retrieve a small amount of information on each page, try bundling a related set of calls into fewer remote invocations. For example, if you are displaying a product list, querying the products, and then requesting the details of each product as separate remote calls, this would be a good candidate for one aggregated call that returns all the product information and details at once. You can also improve the performance of an application that uses remote references by caching the remote reference. See Chapter 13 for more information.

## Using Too Many Graphics

When a web page contains graphics, they are downloaded separately from the HTML content. Each image may also require and use separate connections. Even when the performance problems are related to images, a user may have the impression that the entire application is slow. Don't use too many images, and especially stay away from large images. This is one sure way to improve the performance of your application.

# CHAPTER 18

# JavaServer Faces

Sooner or later, every software developer has the opportunity to build a rich client using Swing, Delphi, C++, or one of Microsoft's user interface (UI) programming languages. It quickly becomes obvious that the development of these applications is wholly different than working on an application intended to run within a web browser. The differences are many, but one of the biggest standouts is the lack of readily available UI components for web applications.

With the advent of MVC, the goal of separating application logic from the presentation of the business data has become a well-accepted design practice. While greatly improved development environments such the frameworks discussed throughout this book (along with technologies such as Java servlets and JSPs) have aided developers who build browser-based applications, other technologies are continually emerging. When building applications whose purpose is to solve a "real-world" business problem, your chance of beating your competitors to the marketplace is very closely tied to the ability to develop applications that are faster, better, and cheaper.

This chapter presents an overview of one of the next-generation technologies that is attracting much attention—largely because of its promise to do things faster, better, and maybe even cheaper. As with many other software development topics, entire books are being written on the topic, so we'll focus on how this new technology integrates with Struts and leave the details for another book.

## Struts and JavaServer Faces

You might be wondering, "What does JavaServer Faces have to do with Jakarta Struts?" The truth is, quite a bit. First and foremost, Craig McClanahan has a hand in both. As mentioned several times already, he is the creator of Struts and still participates as its steward, but he is also one of the technical leads on the JavaServer Faces JSR-127, along with Ed Burns. However, the key similarity between JSF is that both attempt to solve the same problem. That is, they are both Java frameworks for building web-based applications, with one big exception—JSF is an actual specification, along the lines of JDBC, JNDI, EJB and so forth. Like other Java specifications, Sun and the JSR committee provide a set of APIs that describe the contract between a client and a provider of the technology. With JSF, the actual implementation of the JSF specification is left to the vendor to implement.

 In many specifications, a reference implementation is provided with the API to help ensure adherence to the specification and compatibility between providers.

In contrast to JSF, Struts is based on a proprietary framework and API. Actions and forms built for use within a Struts application must be modified (or even rewritten) when switching to a different framework. There's also only one provider of Struts: Apache and the Struts development community. With JSF, there will be multiple implementations.

JSF's goal is to provide a way to build UIs (buttons, checkboxes and other widgets) that are client-independent. It does this by utilizing a rendering kit that contains client-dependent parts of the UI. The rendering kit detects the client in use and renders the widgets appropriately. JSF also supports the ability to create custom widgets, much like Java Swing. In fact, you can build completely new rendering kits if there are none available for your client type.

## Do We Really Need Another UI Framework?

An often asked and completely valid question is: "Do we really need a new UI framework?" In fact, many would argue that we have too many already! These questions do need to be asked, but one must keep an open mind when asking them. Contrary to how one group or another might try to market a framework (commercial or open source), no single framework can contain every feature that every application might demand; this holds true for all types of frameworks. The more important question is: "Does JSF bring anything new to the mix?"

## The Big-Picture Benefits of JSF

JSF does include several features currently found in existing UI frameworks. However, along with these features, it also includes things that can't be obtained from a single framework. Let's spell out several niceties of JSF and why you might consider using it by itself or in conjunction with the Struts framework.

The goal of JSF is to provide reusable server components for creating user interfaces. As such, it provides the following benefits for Java developers:

- An extensible UI component model
- An event handling model
- A pluggable rendering model
- A presentation validation framework (for both client and server side validation)

- A simple page navigational model
- Internationalization (I18N) support
- Integrated support for accessibility

These benefits alone make JSF as powerful, if not more so, than many of the UI frameworks available today. Add to that a standardization which guarantees that multiple vendors will provide implementations, and JSF starts to become a very attractive option.

# Overview of JSF Architecture

The architecture of JSF is not completely unlike other MVC architectures you've probably encountered when building web applications. In fact, some of its pieces should be quite familiar now that you've read this book. However, JFS adds functionality in several places where Struts is lacking, and it does so a way that separates interface from implementation. As stated earlier, this is an important (but often overlooked) quality.

Because it's built around the MVC concept, you might expect to see models, views, and controllers in JSF. And while these elements are all present in JSF, the web imposes some distinct limitations on the MVC model. Let's look at a simplified scenario of how a traditional MVC architecture works:

1. The view responds to user actions by invoking methods on the controller.

2. The controller interacts with the model and updates it.

3. The model creates and publishes events that views and controllers respond to by updating themselves.

Unfortunately, these steps don't work in the web world. Web browsers rarely sit and wait for an event to be published. Instead, they make a request for information and then expect that information to be returned—they are certainly not preconditioned to listen for events.

JSF's approach is to provide components to handle the controller aspects of the application. These include the FrontController (similar to the Struts ActionServlet), NavigationHandler, conversion and formatting components, ActionListeners to interpret the commands, and validate the presentation data. JSF also provides components for the view. These are implemented as client-specific rendering kits made up of renderers. These renderers know how to make items such as a buttons or text fields in a browser.

JSF contains these essential ingredients:

*Reusable UI Components*
  Components for buttons, text fields, and other visual elements.

*Renderers*
  For rendering data to the appropriate client type (e.g. HTML for web browsers).

*Validation and Conversion*

> Tools to convert and validate client-specific types to Java types (e.g., user-entered text to a Java Date).

*Component Tree*

> An in-memory representation of the user interface.

# The JSF Request/Response Lifecycle

A JSF application supports two types of requests and two types of responses:

*Faces request*

> A request sent from a previously generated JSF response.

*Non-Faces request*

> A request sent to an application component such as a servlet or JSP.

*Faces response*

> A response created by the rendering response phase of the JSF processing lifecycle.

*Non-Faces response*

> A response that was *not* created by the rendering response phone (e.g., a JSP that doesn't include JSF components).

According to the specification, these different requests and responses result in three possible lifecycles for a JSF application:

- Non-Faces request generates a Faces response
- Faces request generates a non-Faces response
- Faces request generates a Faces response (probably the most common)

Figure 18-1 illustrates the request/response lifecycle for the standard scenario.

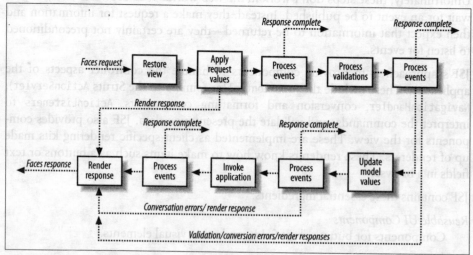

*Figure 18-1. The standard JSF request/response lifecycle*

As mentioned earlier, there are more similarities than differences between JSF and Struts. The low-level components within JSF sound a great deal like the components included with the Struts tag libraries. In fact, there's a great deal of overlap between these seemingly disparate technologies, and Craig McClanahan has publicly announced that he plans on a seamless integration of JSF and Struts. The goal is to allow you to replace the use of some of the Struts tags in your application with UI components of JSF, while continuing to utilize the Struts Controller and Action classes. You might imagine how a JSF Front controller could pass a request on to the Struts RequestProcessor to perform some business service on its behalf. This process is indicated in the "Invoke application" step in Figure 18-1.

# Installing and Running the Example Struts-Faces Application

In an effort to prove that JSF and Struts could work together, Craig McClanahan developed an integration library for Struts and JSF. Currently, there is code within the *contrib* folder of the Struts source download that provides early access to what the integration between Struts and JSF will look like. It's incomplete and probably not ready for production applications, but it's worthwhile to take a look so that you can see and understand what might be coming in future releases of Struts.

At the time of this writing, the version of the *struts-faces* library that ships with the 1.1 source download was based on the EA4 release of JSF. It's not compatible with the final release of the JSF API, which has recently occurred. This should be fixed in a future release of Struts. In the meantime you can find a version that works with the final JSF release at *http://cvs.apache.org/builds/jakarta-struts/nightly/struts-faces*.

After downloading the *struts-faces* library, unzip the contents. The download contains a *readme.txt* file that discusses many important issues and discusses how to install the library. There are two example JSF/Struts applications included; one with Tiles and one without. You can choose to build from the source or just utilize the WAR files that are included. However, even with the WAR files, you must perform some additional steps. These extra steps are necessary due to the beta nature of the JSF reference implementation and a license preventing JSF from being redistributed in an application until the implementation is final. When the reference implementation is made final (this should happen soon), the restrictions will be lifted and the *struts-faces* library will fall under the standard Sun licensing rules.

The extra steps necessary to run the application are as follows:

1. Extract the *struts-faces.war* file (located in the *struts-faces/webapps*) directory into a temp directory.

2. Download the JSF reference implementation from *http://java.sun.com/j2ee/ javaserverfaces* and extract it.

3. Copy the *jsf-api.jar* and *jsf-impl.jar* JAR files from the JSF reference implementation to the *WEB-INF/lib* of the temporary directory (where you expanded *struts-faces.war*).

4. JAR this "new" web application using the command jar `cvf ../struts-faces.war *`.

After you perform the extra steps, deploy the newly created *struts-faces.war* (which now should contain the two JSF JARs) into your favorite container, such as Tomcat. You can run the example application using the URL *http://localhost:8080/struts-faces*.

# Converting Existing Struts Applications to JSF

To convert an existing Struts application to use JSF within a Struts application, you will need to perform the following steps:

1. Add the *struts-faces.jar* file to your application's *WEB-INF/lib* directory.

2. Add the JARs for your particular JSF implementation to your application's *WEB-INF/lib* directory.

3. Configure the Web Application Deployment Descriptor (*web.xml*) to use the Faces Front Controller.

You can now modify your application's pages to use the JSF tag libraries.

# Further Reading

There are many new articles and several new web sites dedicated to the latest events and happenings in the JSF world. Table 18-1 lists several of the sites that have fresh content added regularly.

*Table 18-1. JSF informational web sites*

| Name | URL |
| --- | --- |
| JSFCentral | *http://www.jsfcentral.com* |
| James Holmes's JSF Page | *http://www.jamesholmes.com/JavaServerFaces* |
| Sun's own JSF Site | *http://java.sun.com/j2ee/javaserverfaces* |

These sites have tons of links and other resources that will help you to dig deep into JSF, and along with these sites, there are no fewer than 5 books coming out on JSF in 2004. It's obvious that JSF is going to be a key player in the UI framework space—but for now it's just a matter of waiting to see how effectively it's marketed and how quickly it's adopted by Java developers.

# Changes Since Struts 1.0

There have been many changes to the Struts framework between Versions 1.0 and 1.1. Although these changes were discussed throughout this book, this appendix consolidates them and highlights the most important of the new features. It does not attempt to list every change throughout the framework; as for any Struts release, your best bet for obtaining detailed information is to review the release notes at *http://jakarta. apache.org/struts/userGuide/release-notes.html.*

## ActionServlet and RequestProcessor

A new class called RequestProcessor was added to the framework in Struts 1.1. This class takes over much of the work that the ActionServlet class performed in previous versions. With 1.1, you can still configure the class name of the ActionServlet that you want to use for an application in the *web.xml* file, but the RequestProcessor now carries out much of the real request-processing work.

By default, applications use the org.apache.struts.action.RequestProcessor class to handle all incoming requests. You are not required to do anything if the default behavior suits your requirements. You can, however, choose to override the default implementation with one of your own. You can switch implementations by configuring the controller element in the Struts configuration file. See Chapter 4 for more details on configuring the controller element.

## Modifications to the Struts Action Class

The Struts base Action class has been modified with a new method called execute( ). This new method should be called instead of the perform( ) method. The main difference between the two is that the execute( ) method declares that it throws java. lang.Exception, whereas the earlier perform( ) method declared that it could throw IOException and ServletException. This change was necessary to facilitate the new declarative exception-handling feature that was added to Struts 1.1. As a result, the perform( ) method has been deprecated and should not be used in 1.1 applications.

# Changes to web.xml and struts-config.xml

There have been many changes to the two configuration files required by Struts applications. The *web.xml* file has had several initialization parameters removed; they are now supported by elements within the *struts-config.xml* file. The *web.xml* file also supports a few new parameters. The elements of both files are covered in Chapter 4 and will not be repeated here. You can check the Struts DTD to see exactly which elements are supported in a Struts configuration file. You will also need to update your Struts configuration file to use the latest DTD, which is called *struts-config_1_2.dtd*.

# Action Statics Changed

There were numerous constants declared in the Action class. Those static constants have been moved to a new class called org.apache.struts.Globals, shown in Example A-1.

*Example A-1. The new Globals class*

```
package org.apache.struts;

import java.io.Serializable;

public class Globals implements Serializable {

    public static final String ACTION_SERVLET_KEY =
        "org.apache.struts.action.ACTION_SERVLET";

    public static final String APPLICATION_KEY =
        "org.apache.struts.action.MODULE";

    public static final String CANCEL_KEY =
        "org.apache.struts.action.CANCEL";

    public static final String MODULE_KEY =
        "org.apache.struts.action.MODULE";

    public static final String DATA_SOURCE_KEY =
        "org.apache.struts.action.DATA_SOURCE";

    public static final String ERROR_KEY =
        "org.apache.struts.action.ERROR";

    public static final String EXCEPTION_KEY =
        "org.apache.struts.action.EXCEPTION";

    public static final String FORM_BEANS_KEY =
        "org.apache.struts.action.FORM_BEANS";

    public static final String FORWARDS_KEY =
```

```
    "org.apache.struts.action.FORWARDS";

public static final String LOCALE_KEY =
    "org.apache.struts.action.LOCALE";

public static final String MAPPING_KEY =
    "org.apache.struts.action.mapping.instance";

public static final String MAPPINGS_KEY =
    "org.apache.struts.action.MAPPINGS";

public static final String MESSAGE_KEY =
    "org.apache.struts.action.ACTION_MESSAGE";

public static final String MESSAGES_KEY =
    "org.apache.struts.action.MESSAGE";

public static final String MULTIPART_KEY =
    "org.apache.struts.action.mapping.multipartclass";

public static final String PLUG_INS_KEY =
    "org.apache.struts.action.PLUG_INS";

public static final String REQUEST_PROCESSOR_KEY =
    "org.apache.struts.action.REQUEST_PROCESSOR";

public static final String SERVLET_KEY =
    "org.apache.struts.action.SERVLET_MAPPING";

public static final String TRANSACTION_TOKEN_KEY =
    "org.apache.struts.action.TOKEN";

public static final String XHTML_KEY =
    "org.apache.struts.globals.XHTML";

}
```

# TagUtils and ModuleUtils

Many utility methods previously found in org.apache.struts.utils.RequestUtils and ResponseUtils have been moved to other, more appropriate classes. These changes are summarized in Table A-1.

*Table A-1. Methods previously in RequestUtils and/or ResponseUtils*

| Method name | Now located in |
| --- | --- |
| selectModule | ModuleUtils |
| getModuleName | ModuleUtils |
| getRequestModuleConfig | ModuleUtils |

| Method name | Now located in |
| --- | --- |
| getModuleConfig | ModuleUtils |
| getModulePrefixes | ModuleUtils |
| computeParameters | TagUtils |
| computeURL | TagUtils |
| getActionMappingName | TagUtils |
| getActionMappingURL | TagUtils |
| lookup | TagUtils |
| getScope | TagUtils |
| retrieveUserLocale | TagUtils |
| message | TagUtils |
| present | TagUtils |
| pageURL | TagUtils |
| saveException | TagUtils |
| getModuleConfig(PageContext) | TagUtils |
| getActionMessages | TagUtils |
| getActionErrors | TagUtils |
| encodeURL | TagUtils |
| isXhtml | TagUtils |
| filter | TagUtils |
| write | TagUtils |
| writePrevious | TagUtils |

# New Features of Struts 1.1

The new features in Version 1.1 of the Struts framework are covered in detail throughout this book. Descriptions of the most important ones are provided here.

## Declarative Exception Handling

Prior to 1.1, exception handling was left up to the application. There was no support for it in the core framework, and developers were left to their own devices to figure out how to handle exceptions within an application.

Starting with 1.1, exception handling is now part of the core framework. You can declaratively configure which exceptions actions can throw and what should happen when they occur. Chapter 10 covers exception handling in detail and includes details about this declarative methodology.

## Dynamic ActionForms

A new type of `ActionForm` class was added in 1.1, and broader support for it has been added throughout the entire framework. The `DynaActionForm` and its subclasses allow you to configure form-bean instances in the Struts configuration file. This saves development time because you are no longer required to create `ActionForm` classes.

 It's a little too general to say that you'll never need to create another `ActionForm` class—however, the number of them that you need to create should be drastically reduced.

See Chapter 7 for more information on this new feature.

## Plug-ins

The `PlugIn` feature was added to the Struts framework to provide a mechanism to notify and initialize services when the Struts application starts up and shuts down. There is a wide range of possibilities for this feature, and in fact, the Struts Validator and the Tiles library both take advantage the `PlugIn` mechanism. See Chapter 9 for more information on using plug-ins in your applications.

## Multiple Application Modules

The addition of application modules to the framework allows a single Struts application to support more than one Struts configuration file. This facilitates a project being divided into subprojects, each with its own configuration file. While this might sound more complicated, it allows better support for parallel development.

The support for multiple application modules is still undergoing some changes and modifications. At the time of this writing, you can use extension mapping only for the controller servlet, and it may be a while before the rest of the components have full support for this new feature.

## Nested Tags

Nested tags are a set of JSP custom tags that were added to the Struts framework to give developers better control over accessing properties from a JavaBeans object graph. Many JavaBeans objects contain nested JavaBeans objects that can be referenced by the parent bean. For example, a Customer object may hold a reference to an Address object. To better support the nested nature of these JavaBeans in the Struts views, the nested tags were created. The tags within the Nested tag library are discussed in Chapter 7.

# The Struts Validator

The Struts Validator is a validation framework that supports both Struts and non-Struts applications. It was designed with Struts in mind, though, and it has many nice features that are desirable for the types of applications typically built using Struts. Chapter 11 covers the Struts Validator in detail.

One thing worth mentioning as far as upgrading goes is earlier versions of the Validator framework relied on the RegExp package from Jakarta. This has been switched to Jakarta's ORO package. See Chapter 11 for more details on why this change was made and how it affects the configuration of the Validator.

# Change to Commons Logging

The entire Struts framework now relies on the Commons Logging library, which is an open source logging API from Jakarta. It provides a simple, consistent logging API that can be used within all applications and that allows different implementations to be plugged in dynamically. You will need the Commons Logging JARs, but these should already be included with the Struts framework. This change also required some configuration settings to be added. Chapter 15 covers the Commons Logging library as well as general logging in a Struts application.

# Removal of Admin Actions

Several "administrative" actions were included with previous versions of the Struts framework. These actions could be used for such things as reloading a Struts application (including the configuration settings) without shutting down the application. The ability to add new action mappings dynamically was also supported. These actions have been removed from the framework and are no longer available. If your application requires this functionality, you will have to provide it programmatically.

# Deprecation of the GenericDataSource

The org.apache.struts.util.GenericDataSource class has been deprecated. This class was never designed to be a full-scale data source implementation for large, high-availability applications. It was meant for smaller applications, and never had the advanced features found in the more mature data source products.

If you need a data source implementation, it's recommended that you use either one that is available with your container, or the one available in the Commons DBCP project at *http://jakarta.apache.org/commons/dbcp*.

# Dependency on Commons Projects

The Struts framework now has the following dependencies on packages from the Jakarta Commons project:

- Commons BeanUtils
- Commons Digester
- Commons Collections
- Commons Logging
- Commons FileUpdate
- Commons Lang

# Downloading and Installing Struts

This appendix provides instructions and helpful tips on installing the Struts framework. All attempts have been made to ensure that these instructions work with the latest available versions of the containers. If you encounter any problems, check the STRUTS-USER mailing list.

## The Binary Versus Source Distributions

There are two distribution methods for the Struts framework, source and binary. The source distribution gives you more control over the build package environment. However, this method is not for beginners. Unless you have a specific need (e.g., you need to insert a modified class file into the build), you should stick with the binary distribution. This section presents both methods.

### Building Struts from the Source Distribution

You can obtain the source packages of Struts and the rest of the Jakarta projects from *http://jakarta.apache.org/site/sourceindex.html*. Several different versions are usually available, so be sure to get the one that's appropriate for your needs. There is always a nightly build of Struts that includes the latest changes and fixes. In most situations, you'll want to go with the nightly build, but be aware that it may also include new bugs.

 When choosing a download, you have the option of selecting a ZIP file or a compressed TAR file. Choose the one that is appropriate for your operating system.

Once you have downloaded the appropriate version, extract the contents into a directory. The directory doesn't have to be empty, but it's easier if it is. The Struts source distribution file unpacks everything into a subdirectory called *jakarta-struts*.

Before you can build the source files, you will also need to download several prerequisite software packages (if they're not already installed in your environment). The following list describes the required software:

*Java SDK*

Version 1.2 or later. You can download the latest version from *http://java.sun.com/j2se*.

*Servlet container*

One that supports the 2.2 Servlet specification or later and the 1.1 JavaServer Pages specification or later.

*Ant build tool*

Version 1.5.4 or later. You can download the latest version from *http://ant.apache.org/*.

*Servlet API classes*

All servlet containers should contain the necessary files; just make sure the necessary JARs are in the classpath for the build tool.

*XML parser*

One that supports JAXP Version 1.1 or later. The Xerces parser is compatible and can be obtained from *http://xml.apache.org/xerces-j*.

*Xalan XSLT Processor*

Version 1.2 or later. Note that some problems have been reported with Version 2.0. The processor is used to convert the XML documentation files into HTML documentation files. The processor also includes the Xerces parser. You can download Xalan from *http://xml.apache.org/xalan-j/index.html*.

*JDBC 2.0 Optional package classes*

The Struts framework supports an implementation of `javax.sql.DataSource` and therefore requires the JDBC 2.0 Optional classes to be present. You can obtain the JDBC 2.0 classes from *http://java.sun.com/products/jdbc/download.html*.

You will also need to download the third-party packages listed in Table B-1 and extract the JAR files included with the packages. Each package has both a source and binary distribution available. Unless you are a true masochist, you should download the binary distributions of these packages.

*Table B-1. Third-party packages required for Struts compilation*

| Package name | URL |
| --- | --- |
| Commons BeanUtils | *http://jakarta.apache.org/commons/beanutils.html* |
| Commons Collections | *http://jakarta.apache.org/commons/collections.html* |
| Commons Digester | *http://jakarta.apache.org/commons/digester.html* |
| Commons Logging | *http://jakarta.apache.org/commons/logging.html* |
| Commons Pool | *http://jakarta.apache.org/commons/pool/index.html* |
| Commons FileUpload | *http://jakarta.apache.org/commons/fileupload* |

*Table B-1. Third-party packages required for Struts compilation (continued)*

| Package name | URL |
| --- | --- |
| Commons Lang | *http://jakarta.apache.org/commons/lang* |
| Commons DBCP | *http://jakarta.apache.org/commons/dbcp* |
| Commons Validator | *http://cvs.apache.org/viewcvs/jakarta-commons/validator* |
| Jakarta ORO | *http://jakarta.apache.org/oro* |

 The URL *http://jakarta.apache.org/commons/components.html* provides a nice summary of the different release schedules of the Commons components.

Extract the binary distributions of each of these packages and put the JAR files somewhere that you can easily reference them, as will need to in the next step. Each package is extracted into its own subdirectory. You can leave the JAR files there for easier reference.

The next step is to create a *build.properties* file that specifies environmental dependencies such as the location of the third-party JARs extracted in the previous step. The Struts source distribution provides a *build.properties.sample* file in the top-level source distribution directory. Open this file and rename it *build.properties*. You need to customize this file for your particular environment. The file paths are relative to the location of the properties file. For example, to reference the Commons BeanUtils JAR file that is located in a directory called *lib* one level up, you would need to change the properties file to look like this:

```
# The JAR file containing version 1.0 (or later) of the Beanutils package
# from the Jakarta Commons project.
commons-beanutils.jar=../lib/commons-beanutils-1.3/commons-beanutils.jar
```

Once you have all of the file paths set in the *build.properties* file, you are ready to turn the Struts source files into Struts binary files. Make sure Ant is installed and configured correctly, and make sure you downloaded the *xalan.jar* file and placed it in the *<ANT_HOME>/lib* directory (this is needed so that an Ant task can process the XML documentation files). You will need to be able to execute Ant from the command line in the top-level source directory.

Once you've completed these steps, go to the directory where the *build.properties* file is located and type:

```
ant dist
```

Messages will be spewed out in the console. When they finally stop, they should show that the build was successful, as in Figure B-1.

If the build is unsuccessful, you will get a failed message, usually with enough information to determine the cause. For example, if you forget to put the *xalan.jar* in the *<ANT_HOME>/lib* directory, the output will look similar to that in Figure B-2.

**MS-DOS Prompt**

```
static:
      [echo] Processing webapp upload
compile:
      [echo] Processing webapp upload
dist:
      [echo] Processing webapp upload
init:
      [echo] Processing webapp validator
prepare:
      [echo] Processing webapp validator
source:
      [echo] Processing webapp validator
libs:
struts:
      [echo] Processing webapp validator
static:
      [echo] Processing webapp validator
compile:
      [echo] Processing webapp validator
dist:
      [echo] Processing webapp validator
dist:
dist.source:
dist:
BUILD SUCCESSFUL
Total time: 22 seconds
C:\build-test\jakarta-struts>_
```

*Figure B-1. A success message is printed when complete*

Assuming that the build was successful, the Struts binaries and dependent files are copied to the *dist* directory underneath the top-level source distribution directory.

## Installing the Binary Distribution

Download the binary distribution and unpack it into a directory. The files are in a subdirectory called *jakarta-struts* within the distribution. As with the source distribution, you can download either a ZIP file or a compressed TAR file. You can obtain the binary distribution from *http://jakarta.apache.org/site/binindex.html*.

> If you built Struts from the source distribution, the binary files will already be unpacked into the *dist/lib* directory of the top-level source distribution directory.

The following steps need to be performed for a Struts application to work properly. Any necessary container-dependent modifications to these steps are discussed in the sections for the individual containers later in this appendix.

1. Copy all of the JAR files from the distribution's *lib* directory to the web application's *WEB- INF/lib* directory.

2. Copy all of the *.tld* files to the web application's *WEB-INF* directory.

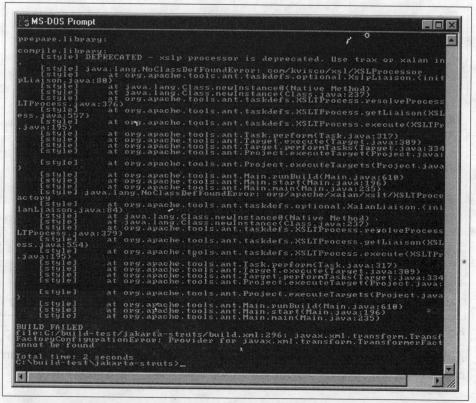

*Figure B-2. A stack trace is usually included in failed builds*

3. If you plan to use the Validator framework, copy the *validation-rules.xml* file to the *WEB- INF* directory. See Chapter 11 for more information on the configuration files required by the Struts Validator.

4. Create a web application deployment descriptor (*web.xml*) and copy it to the *WEB-INF* directory. See Chapter 4 for details on how to configure the *web.xml* file.

5. Create a *struts-config.xml* file and copy it to the *WEB-INF* directory. See Chapter 4 for details on how to configure the configuration file for Struts.

6. Create a properties file called *commons-logging.properties* and copy it to the *WEB-INF/ classes* directory. Put the following line in the file:

```
org.apache.commons.logging.Log=org.apache.commons.logging.impl.SimpleLog
```

7. Create a Struts resource bundle and copy it to the *WEB-INF/classes* directory. See Chapter 12 for how to format this bundle and Chapter 4 for how to configure the Struts configuration file to use this bundle.

That's really all there is to installing the Struts framework. You still have to build the necessary JSP pages and other framework components, such as Action and

---

ActionForm classes, but this is what is required to get the environment running. It's highly recommended that you play around with the example applications that are distributed with Struts. They are complete web applications, packaged as WAR files that you can copy to the container's *webapps* directory.

You have the option of using one of many different containers to run the Struts framework. In many cases, the steps just described should be followed exactly. However, not all containers are created equal, and some require modifications to the steps listed. The necessary modifications, if any, are described below.

## Tips on Installing Struts in Tomcat

Depending on which version of Tomcat you use, you may have to perform a few additional steps. Because Struts 1.1 requires a container to support the 2.2 Servlet specification and the 1.1 JavaServer Pages specification, the minimum version of Tomcat that will work is Tomcat 3.2. However, if possible, you should attempt to use the latest version of Tomcat (5.x), as it has many improvements that allow the Struts applications to perform better.

## Tips on Installing Struts in WebLogic

With earlier versions of WebLogic such as 5.1, you had to perform several non-intuitive steps in order to get Struts to work correctly. Some of these problems had to do with WebLogic unpacking only *.class* files and not other files such as JARs. However, no additional steps are necessary when using WebLogic 7.0 and 8.1.

## Tips on Installing Struts in WebSphere

If you have the latest patches applied, no extra steps are required. WSAD 5.1 includes support for Struts and comes ready-to-use with 1.1.

# APPENDIX C

# Resources

This appendix provides a list of resources that you can use to further your knowledge of Struts.

## The Struts Mailing Lists

By far the two best places to learn and ask questions about the Struts framework are the two mailing lists, STRUTS-USER and STRUTS-DEV. The user list currently has around 1,750 subscribers and has been growing at a rate of 50 to 100 new users a month for the past year or so.

The STRUTS-USER list is designed for Struts developers, both new and experienced alike. You definitely should consult the FAQ (*http://www.tuxedo.org/~esr/faqs/smart-questions.html*) before posting any questions. There's not much flaming on the list, but you will get pummeled if you don't think about the question you're asking before posting it.

The STRUTS-DEV mailing list is devoted to those working on the framework itself. Anyone can post on it, but you should not ask questions here about your application, or questions that can be better answered on the user list. In almost all cases, unless you are contributing to the development of the framework or bug fixes, or would like to get involved in this manner, you should be posting to the user list.

You can subscribe to either or both lists from *http://jakarta.apache.org/struts/index.html#Involved*. There are also several ways to search the lists (you can search through many Jakarta mailing lists, not just the ones for Struts). One option for searching the Struts mailing lists is to go to *http://www.mail-archive.com/index.php?hunt=struts* and select whether you want to search through the DEV or the USER list.

Another way to search is to use the *eyebrowse* feature from the Apache Software Foundation (*http://nagoya.apache.org/eyebrowse*). You can search through all of the Apache mailing lists here as well.

# The Struts Resource Web Page

There are many interesting and informative links on the main Struts site. One of the best is the Struts Resource Page (*http://jakarta.apache.org/struts/resources/index.html*). The list is divided by category (tutorials, articles, books, etc.). You could easily spend a solid month following all of these links.

# Tiles Site

The creator of the Tiles library, Cedric Dumoulin, also maintains his own site at *http://www.lifl.fr/~dumoulin/tiles/*. You can find tutorials and general information on Tiles at this site, and you can also download the latest version of the library.

# Nested Tags Site

The Nested tag libraries were released in November 2001 and added to the core Struts framework several months later. The creator of the libraries, Arron Bates, maintains a site where you can find great tutorials and tons of information on the nested tags. The URL for his site is *http://www.keyboardmonkey.com/next/index.jsp*.

# The Struts Console

Several Struts GUI tools are available and more are created every day, but one of the best and most widely used is the Struts Console, an application briefly discussed in Chapter 4 and available for download at *http://www.jamesholmes.com/struts*.

# Easy Struts Project

The Easy Struts Project, hosted on SourceForge, provides tools and plug-ins for various IDEs in order to increase productivity when building Struts applications. There are plug-ins for JBuilder, Eclipse, and other popular IDEs. You can find more information on the Easy Struts Project at *http://easystruts.sourceforge.net*.

We'd like to hear your suggestions for improving our indexes. Send email to *index@oreilly.com*.

## D

DAO (Data Access Object) pattern, 153, 155–166

data model, storefront application (example), 148–151
 diagram, 148

data persistence, 141

data source
 alternative implementations, 85
 configuring within a Struts configuration file, 85

data transfer objects (see DTOs)

Database Connection Pool (DBCP), 84

database tables, 154

DataSource connection factory, 309

data-source element, 84

DataSource interface, 83

data-sources element, 83–85

DBConnectionPoolListener class, 358

DBCP, 85

DBCP (Database Connection Pool), 84

declarative exception handling, 47, 242–249

Decorator pattern, 15

default application, 106

default exception-handler class, 245
 extending (example), 247
 multiple exceptions, 248

default initialization, 107

default locale, 284

define tag, custom tag (Bean tag library), 212

definition tag, custom tag (Tiles tag library), 337

deploying web applications, 376

deployment descriptor, 67
 complete example of storefront application, 80
 declaring the event listener in, 358
 declaring the filter in, 354
 defined, 69
 format, 70

deployment information, servlet containers, 69

design by contract, 236

design model, 137

design-stage artifacts, 138

development issues
 building an interface between Struts actions and an application tier, 297
 redundant code in a web application, 324
 Struts actions interacting directly with entity beans, 300

Digester component, 100

directories
 guidelines for Struts applications, 68
 structure for the storefront web application, 68
 subdirectories and, 67

DispatchAction class, 45
 defined, 124
 example of shopping-cart functionality, 124–128

distributed application, DTOs in, 50

distributions (binary versus source)
 binary, building Struts from, 425–427
 source, building Struts from, 422–425

DOCTYPE element, 100

Document Type Definition (see DTD)

doGet( ) method, ActionServlet class, 105

doPost( ) method, ActionServlet class, 105

DTD (Document Type Definition), 70, 71
 DOCTYPE element, 100
 Struts configuration DTD, 83

DTOs (data transfer objects), 50
 and ActionForms, difference between, 57
 banking, 51
 in a distributed application, 50
 pattern, 173
 EJB-based models, and, 304
 UserView class, storefront application (example), 118

Dumoulin, Cedric, 333, 429

DynaActionForm class, 57, 86, 188–191
 configuring, 189
 form tag, and, 202
 performing validation with, 191

dynamic action forms, 86

dynamic content
 rendering, 167
 versus static content, 327

dynamic proxies, 320–323
 implementation of the storefront service, 320–323
 sequence diagram for retrieving item detail through a dynamic proxy, 323

DynamicStorefrontEJBDelegate, 322

DynaValidatorActionForm class, 264, 267

DynaValidatorForm class, 267

## E

EAR files, 69

EAServer, 4

Easy Struts Project, 429

## H

HashMap, 119
header tag, custom tag (Bean tag library), 212
heap sizes, setting, 407
helper class, 43
Holmes, James, 101
home interface for the storefront session bean, 309
home reference, caching, 316
hooks, 219
Host, HTTP request header field, 23
HTML (Hypertext Markup Language)
  documents as view components, 170
  hardcoding limitations, 4
html tag, custom tag (HTML tag library), 201
HTML tag library, 58, 199–207
  custom tags, 200–207
    base tag, 201
    button tag, 205
    cancel tag, 205
    checkbox tag, 205
    errors tag, 205
    form tag, 202–205
    html tag, 201
    messages tag, 205
HTTP
  methods
    GET, 22
    POST, 22
  request, 22
    header fields, 23
  request/response
    model (diagram), 21
    phase, 20–25
  response
    header, using Telnet to inspect, 32
    message (example), 25
    status code categories, 23
  versus HTTPS, 25
HttpServlet class, 43
HttpServletRequest interface, 26, 27
HttpServletResponse class
  sendRedirect( ) method, 28
HttpSession class, 26
  application events and listener interfaces, 356
Hypertext Markup Language (see HTML), 4

## I

I18N (see internationalization)
IAuthentication interface
  banking application (example), 37–40
  storefront application (example), 157
impedance mismatch, 141
importAttribute tag, custom tag (Tiles tag library), 341
include tag, custom tag (Bean tag library), 213
IncludeAction class, 123
indexed properties, accessing in JavaBeans, 199
index.jsp file
  itemdetail.jsp file, and, 329
  JSP include mechanism versus templates, 325
  using a template, 328
inheritance in categories in the logging framework, 363
init( ) method, example of overriding methods, 107
initComponentDefinitions tag, custom tag (Tiles tag library), 341
initialization
  ActionServlet, of the (diagram), 109
  custom, 107
  default, 107
  parameters, 69
    config, 74
    declaring, 74
    web.xml using Struts 1.1, for, 75
  process overview, 108
init-param element, 71
insert tag, custom tag (Tiles tag library), 336
installing the Struts framework, 422–427
interaction diagrams, 138
interfacing Struts to EJB, 312–323
internationalization, 4, 61, 184
  character sets, setting, 295
  characteristics of applications supporting, 282
  defined, 281
  exception handling, 256, 296
  Java support, 283–290
  locale
    default, 284
    determining the user's locale information in a servlet (example), 285
  Locale class, 283–288

# T

## About the Author

**Chuck Cavaness** is a Senior Technologist at the S1 Corporation (*http://www.s1.com*). His expertise spans server-side Java, distributed object computing, and application servers. Chuck is the most recent moderator for the "Java in the Enterprise" discussion forum hosted by *JavaWorld*. He spent several years writing Smalltalk and CORBA applications, and he has taught courses in object-oriented programming at Georgia Tech. He's written articles for *JavaWorld* and InformIt.com. He has also been the technical editor for many J2EE books, including *Using JavaServer Pages and Servlets* (Que, 2000) and *Special Edition Using Java 2 Enterprise Edition* (Que, 2001). Chuck earned his degree in computer science from Georgia Tech. His current interests focus on building enterprise applications for the banking and financial services arena.

Chuck is the coauthor of *Special Edition Using Enterprise JavaBeans 2.0* (Que, 2001) and *Special Edition Using Java 2 Standard Edition* (Que, 2000).

## Colophon

Our look is the result of reader comments, our own experimentation, and feedback from distribution channels. Distinctive covers complement our distinctive approach to technical topics, breathing personality and life into potentially dry subjects.

The animal on the cover of *Programming Jakarta Struts*, Second Edition is a Percheron draft horse. This breed originated in the province of Le Perche in northwestern France. Purebreds are predominantly black or gray, and some have white markings on their heads and feet. They weigh an average of 2000 pounds and are usually 16 to 17 hands (64 to 68 inches) high. Percherons adapt well to many climates and are extremely versatile: their ruggedness and power makes them ideal for hauling heavy loads, their placid nature makes them easy to handle, and their natural grace and beauty complement the finest horse-drawn carriages. They can be ridden, and some have even been made into jumpers.

In 732 A.D., Arabian horses abandoned by the Moors after the Battle of Tours were bred with native Flemish stock, producing the first Percherons. When the Crusaders invaded ten centuries later, more Arabian blood was added to the breed. However, the number of Percherons dwindled during the French Revolution, as horse breeding was suppressed. After the revolution, the new French government revived the breed by establishing a stud program for army mounts, using two Arabian sires at Le Pin, Normandy. In 1832 a foal named Jean Le Blanc was born in Le Perche, and all current Percheron bloodlines trace directly back to this horse.

Le Perche has since exported purebred stock worldwide, and an official Breed Association registers Percherons to ensure that the line remains genetically pure. The breed was most popular after World War I, when farmers from both Britain and the United States became familiar with them while serving in the armed forces. A 1930

U.S. census showed that registered Percherons outnumbered other draft horses by a margin of three to one, but after World War II, the farm tractor nearly replaced the breed entirely. However, it was kept alive by many farmers, especially those in Amish communities. Today, Percherons continue to work on farms and often perform in competition at livestock fairs. They are also used used to provide recreational hay, sleigh, and carriage rides.

Philip Dangler was the production editor and copyeditor for *Programming Jakarta Struts*, Second Edition. Mary Brady, Emily Quill, and Darren Kelly provided quality control. Julie Hawks wrote the index.

Emma Colby designed the cover of this book, based on a series design by Edie Freedman. The cover image is a 19th-century engraving from the Dover Pictorial Archive. Emma Colby produced the cover layout with QuarkXPress 4.1 using Adobe's ITC Garamond font.

Melanie Wang designed the interior layout, based on a series design by David Futato. This book was converted to FrameMaker 5.5.6 by Andrew Savikas with a format conversion tool created by Erik Ray, Jason McIntosh, Neil Walls, and Mike Sierra that uses Perl and XML technologies. The text font is Linotype Birka; the heading font is Adobe Myriad Condensed; and the code font is LucasFont's TheSans Mono Condensed. The illustrations that appear in the book were produced by Robert Romano and Jessamyn Read using Macromedia FreeHand 9 and Adobe Photoshop 6. The tip and warning icons were drawn by Christopher Bing. This colophon was written by Philip Dangler.

## SHROFF / O'Reilly Reprints

### TITLES AT REDUCED PRICES

| ISBN | Title | Author | Price |
|------|-------|--------|-------|
| 8173663661 | .NET Framework Essentials, 324 Pages | Thai | 75.00 |
| 8173664277 | Access Cookbook for 97, 2000 & 2002 (B / CD-ROM), 724 Pages | Getz | 100.00 |
| 8173662231 | ActionScriprt: The Definitive Guide, 726 Pages | Moock | 150.00 |
| 8173662886 | Building Oracle XML Applications (B / CD-ROM), ... Pages | Muench | 100.00 |
| 8173664250 | Building Wireless Community Networks, 144 Pages | Flickenger | 50.00 |
| 8173662584 | Cascading Style Sheets: The Definitive Guide, 476 Pages | Meyer | 75.00 |
| 8173662878 | Developing ASP Components 2/ed, 864 Pages | Powers | 100.00 |
| 817366272X | DHCP for Windows 2000, 288 Pages | Alcott | 75.00 |
| 8173663599 | Exim: The Mail Transport Agent, 638 Pages | Hazel | 75.00 |
| 8173660573 | Java Threads, 2/ed, 336 Pages | Oaks | 100.00 |
| 8173664145 | Java Cookbook, 890 Pages | Darwin | 150.00 |
| 8173660557 | Java Foundation Classes in a Nutshell, 752 Pages | Flanagan | 75.00 |
| 8173662711 | Java Internationalization, 456 Pages | Deitsch | 75.00 |
| 8173663807 | Java Programming with Oracle SQLJ, 404 Pages | Price | 75.00 |
| 8173661103 | JavaScript Application Cookbook, 512 Pages | Bradenbaugh | 75.00 |
| 8173661111 | JavaScript Pocket Reference, 96 Pages | Flanagan | 25.00 |
| 8173662509 | Jini in a Nutshell, 420 Pages | Oaks | 75.00 |
| 8173662320 | Learning Java (B / CD-ROM), 732 Pages | Niemeyer | 75.00 |
| 8173660603 | Learning Perl/Tk, 380 Pages | Walsh | 75.00 |
| 8173661677 | Learning Web Design: A Beginner's Guide to HTML, Graphics & Web Environment (2 Color Book), 432 Pages | Niederst | 100.00 |
| 8173663173 | Learning WML & WMLScript, 204 Pages | Frost | 50.00 |
| 8173663149 | Learning XML, 376 Pages | Ray | 75.00 |
| 8173662193 | MCSD in a Nutshell: The Visual Basic Exams, 636 Pages | Foxall | 75.00 |
| 8173662398 | MCSE in a Nutshell: The Windows 2000 Exams, 504 Pages | Moncur | 75.00 |
| 8173662517 | MP3: The Definitive Guide, 408 Pages | Hacker | 75.00 |
| 8173660697 | Oracle PL/SQL Language Pocket Reference, 80 Pages | Feuerstein | 25.00 |
| 8173661243 | Perl/Tk Pocket Reference, 104 Pages | Lidie | 25.00 |
| 817366269X | PHP Pocket Reference, 124 Pages | Lerdorf | 25.00 |
| 8173661251 | PNG: The Definitive Guide, 344 Pages | Roelofs | 50.00 |
| 817366126X | Practical Internet Groupware, 520 Pages | Udell | 75.00 |
| 8173660751 | Practical UNIX & Internet Security, 2/ed, 1,008 Pages | Garfinkel | 150.00 |
| 8173660190 | QuarkXPress in a Nutshell, 552 Pages | O'Quinn | 50.00 |
| 8173662487 | sed & awk Pocket Reference, 60 Pages | Robbins | 25.00 |
| 8173661294 | sendmail Desktop Reference, 74 Pages | Costales | 25.00 |
| 8173662606 | Tcl/Tk Pocket Reference, 100 Pages | Raines | 25.00 |
| 8173663734 | VB .NET Language in a Nutshell, 662 Pages | Roman | 100.00 |
| 8173663475 | Web Database Applications with PHP & MySQL, 600 Pages | Williams | 75.00 |
| 8173661359 | Webmaster in a Nutshell, 2/ed, 540 Pages | Spainhour | 75.00 |
| 8173662630 | Windows 2000 Active Directory, 624 Pages | Lowe-Norris | 75.00 |
| 8173663327 | Windows 2000 Performance Guide, 650 Pages | Friedman | 75.00 |
| 8173663289 | XML in a Nutshell, 400 Pages | Harold | 100.00 |
| 8173662096 | XSLT, 486 Pages | Tidwell | 100.00 |

### PUBLISHED TITLES

| ISBN | Title | Author | Price |
|------|-------|--------|-------|
| 8173666539 | .NET and XML, 484 Pages | Bornstein | 425.00 |
| 8173669201 | .NET Compact Framework Pocket Guide, 122 Pages | Lee | 125.00 |
| 8173666547 | .NET Framework Essentials, 3/ed, 392 Pages | Thai | 325.00 |
| 8173665753 | 802.11 Security, 200 Pages | Potter | 175.00 |
| 8173664420 | 802.11 Wireless Networks: The Definitive Guide, 474 Pages | Gast | 400.00 |
| 8173664285 | Access Database Design & Programming, 3/ed, 454 Pages | Roman | 325.00 |

| ISBN | Title | Author | Price |
|------|-------|--------|-------|
| 8173667233 | ActionScript Cookbook, *904 Pages* | Lott | 675.00 |
| 8173666555 | ActionScript for Flash MX Pocket Reference, *152 Pages* | Moock | 125.00 |
| 8173665761 | ActionScript for Flash MX: The Definitive Guide, 2/ed, *904 Pages* | Colin Moock | 750.00 |
| 8173666563 | Active Directory for Windows Server 2003, 2/ed, *692 Pages* | Allen | 575.00 |
| 8173667357 | Active Directory Cookbook for Windows Server 2003 and Windows 2000, *632 Pages* | Allen | 525.00 |
| 817366725X | ADO .NET Cookbook, *636 Pages* | Hamilton | 500.00 |
| 8173665222 | ADO .NET for Visual Basic .NET 2003 in a Nutshell: A Desktop Quick Reference **(B / CD-ROM)**, *626 Pages* | Hamilton | 500.00 |
| **0596006004** | **Adobe Encore DVD: In the Studio, *336 Pages*** | **Dixon** | **1,225.00** |
| **0596007361** | **Adobe InDesign CS One-on-One (B / CD-ROM), *400 Pages*** | **McClelland** | **1,375.00** |
| **0596006187** | **Adobe Photoshop CS One-on-One (B / CD-ROM), *488 Pages*** | **McClelland** | **1,225.00** |
| **8173668205** | **AI for Game Developers, *400 Pages*** | **Bourg** | **375.00** |
| **8173669384** | **AspectJ Cookbook, *364 Pages*** | **Miles** | **350.00** |
| 8173667292 | Amazon Hacks: 100 Industrial Strength Tips & Tricks, *312 Pages* | Bausch | 250.00 |
| 8173665524 | Ant: The Definitive Guide, *296 Pages* | Tilly | 275.00 |
| 8173665133 | Apache: The Definitive Guide (Covers Apache 2.0 & 1.3) 3/ed, *594 Pages* | Laurie | 500.00 |
| 8173667446 | Apache Cookbook (Covers Apache 2.0 & 1.3), *264 Pages* | Coar | 250.00 |
| 8173662525 | Apache Pocket Reference, *112 Pages* | Ford | 75.00 |
| **8173662274** | **Apache Security, *428 Pages*** | **Ristic** | **400.00** |
| **8173666571** | **ASP .NET Cookbook (Cover ASP .NET 1.1), *846 Pages*** | **Kittel** | **700.00** |
| 8173667306 | ASP .NET in a Nutshell: A Desktop Quick Reference, 2/ed, *1,008 Pages* | Duthie | 600.00 |
| **8173667837** | **The Art of Project Management, *512 Pages*** | **Berkun** | **350.00** |
| 8173662347 | AutoCAD 2000 In a Nutshell: A Command Reference Guide, *592 Pages* | Kent | 325.00 |
| 8173663955 | Beginning Perl for Bioinformatics, *390 Pages* | Tisdall | 300.00 |
| 8173668981 | Better, Faster, Lighter Java, *270 Pages* | Tate | 250.00 |
| 817366658X | BGP, *292 Pages* | van Beijnum | 275.00 |
| 8173665125 | BLAST, *372 Pages* | Korf | 325.00 |
| **817366899X** | **BSD Hacks:100 Industrial-Strength Tips & Tools, *458 Pages*** | **Lavigne** | **375.00** |
| 8173666598 | Building Embedded Linux Systems, *422 Pages* | Yaghmour | 350.00 |
| 8173661014 | Building Internet Firewalls 2/ed, *904 Pages* | Chapman | 650.00 |
| 8173662282 | Building Java Enterprise Applications: Vol. 1 - Architecture, *324 Pages* | McLaughlin | 225.00 |
| 8173661391 | Building Linux Clusters **(B / CD-ROM)**, *360 Pages* | Spector | 350.00 |
| 8173665621 | Building Secure Servers with Linux, *454 Pages* | Bauer | 375.00 |
| 8173666601 | C Pocket Reference, *142 Pages* | Prinz | 100.00 |
| 8173664439 | C# & VB .NET Conversion Pocket Reference, *156 Pages* | Mojica | 75.00 |
| **8173665885** | **C# Cookbook, *876 Pages*** | **Teilhet** | **600.00** |
| 8173664293 | C# Essentials, 2/ed, *224 Pages* | Albahari | 175.00 |
| 8173665192 | C# Language Pocket Reference, *132 Pages* | Drayton | 100.00 |
| 8173663726 | C# in a Nutshell: A Desktop Quick Reference, *864 Pages* | Drayton | 600.00 |
| 8173666628 | C++ in a Nutshell, (Cover ISO/IEC 14882 STD) *816 Pages* | Lischner | 500.00 |
| 8173667101 | C++ Pocket Reference, *148 Pages* | Loudon | 100.00 |
| **0596001088** | **The Cathedral & The Bazaar: Musings On Linux and Open Source by an Accidental Revolutionary, Revised & Expanded, *256 Pages*** | **Raymond** | **525.00** |
| **8173669066** | **Cascading Style Sheets: The Definitive Guide (Covers CSS2 & CSS 2.1), 2/ed, *538 Pages*** | **Meyer** | **475.00** |
| 8173662266 | CDO & MAPI Programming with Visual Basic, *388 Pages* | Grundgeiger | 175.00 |
| 8173664269 | CGI Programming on the World Wide Web, *454 Pages* | Gundavaram | 300.00 |

| ISBN | Title | Author | Price |
|------|-------|--------|-------|
| 817366045X | CGI Programming with Perl 2/ed, *476 Pages* | Gundavaram | 325.00 |
| 8173667241 | Cisco Cookbook, *918 Pages* | Dooley | 700.00 |
| 8173663653 | COM & .NET Component Services, *390 Pages* | Lowy | 250.00 |
| 8173663645 | COM+ Programming with Visual Basic, *372 Pages* | Mojica | 225.00 |
| 8173660638 | Creating Effective JavaHelp, *196 Pages* | Lewis | 125.00 |
| **8173669163** | **CSS Cookbook (Cover CSS 2.1), *280 Pages*** | **Schmitt** | **275.00** |
| **8173667802** | **Database In Depth: The Relational Model for Practitioners, *250 Pgs*** | **C.J.Date** | **225.00** |
| 8173662363 | Database Nation: The Death of Privacy in the 21st Century, *336 Pages* | Garfinkel | 235.00 |
| 8173662894 | Database Programming with JDBC & Java 2/ed, *348 Pages* | Reese | 150.00 |
| 8173665664 | Designing Embedded Hardware, *324 Pages* | Catsoulis | 250.00 |
| 8173663882 | Designing Large Scale LANs, *408 Pages* | Dooley | 275.00 |
| 8173662428 | Developing Bio-informatics Computer Skills, *504 Pages* | Gibas | 225.00 |
| **0596005474** | **Digital Photography: Expert Techniques (Covers Photoshop CS), *496 Pages*** | **Milburn** | **1,375.00** |
| **0596006667** | **Digital Photography Hacks: 100 Industrial - Strength Tips & Tools, *336 Pages*** | **Story** | **800.00** |
| **0596006276** | **Digital Photography Pocket Guide, 2/ed, *128 Pages*** | **Story** | **500.00** |
| **0596005237** | **Digital Video Pocket Guide, *474 Pages*** | **Story** | **500.00** |
| 8173662983 | DNS & BIND (Covers BIND 9), 4/ed, *642 Pages* | Albitz | 500.00 |
| 8173665672 | DNS & BIND Cookbook, *248 Pages* | Liu | 250.00 |
| 8173663785 | DNS on Windows 2000, 2/ed, *376 Pages* | Larson | 275.00 |
| 8173660506 | DNS on Windows NT, *352 Pages* | Albitz | 195.00 |
| 8173662991 | Dreamweaver MX: The Missing Manual, *750 Pages* | McFarland | 600.00 |
| 8173665281 | Dynamic HTML: The Definitive Reference, 2/ed, *1,428 Pages* | Goodman | 650.00 |
| **8173669015** | **Eclipse (Coverage of 3.0), *344 Pages*** | **Holzner** | **325.00** |
| **8173669309** | **Eclipse Cookbook (Cover 3.0), *372 Pages*** | **Holzner** | **350.00** |
| 8173663017 | Effective awk Programming, 3/ed, *454 Pages* | Robbins | 325.00 |
| **8173667268** | **Enterprise JavaBeans (Covers EJB 2.1 & EJB 2.0 Includes workbook for JBoss 4.0), 4/ed, *798 Pages*** | **Monson - Haefel** | **500.00** |
| 8173668167 | Enterprise Service Architecture - O'Reilly SAP Series, *236 Pages* | Woods | 225.00 |
| **8173669317** | **Essential ActionScript 2.0, *528 Pages*** | **Moock** | **400.00** |
| **8173666784** | **Enterprise Service Bus, *284 Pages*** | **Chappell** | **300.00** |
| 8173663580 | Essential SNMP, *338 Pages* | Mauro | 300.00 |
| 817366529X | Essential System Administration, 3/ed, *1,178 Pages* | Frisch | 525.00 |
| 8173666644 | Essential System Administration Pocket Reference, *152 Pages* | Frisch | 125.00 |
| 8173660255 | Essential Windows NT System Administration, *488 Pages* | Frisch | 225.00 |
| 8173662495 | Ethernet: The Definitive Guide, *528 Pages* | Spurgeon | 300.00 |
| 8173662754 | Excel 2000 In a Nutshell: A Power User's Quick Reference, *560 Pages* | Simon | 300.00 |
| **8173669619** | **Excel 2003 Personal Trainer (B / CD-ROM), (2 Color book) *490 Pages*** | **CustomGuide** | **550.00** |
| **8173668299** | **Excel 2003 Programming: A Developer's Notebook, *330 Pages*** | **Webb** | **325.00** |
| **8173668035** | **Excel: The Missing Manual, *802 Pages*** | **MacDonald** | **550.00** |
| **8173669406** | **Excel Annoyances: How to Fix the Most Annoying Things about Your Favorite Spreadsheet , *266 Pages*** | **Frye** | **275.00** |
| **8173668612** | **Excel Hacks: 100 Industrial Strength Tips & Tools, *316 Pages*** | **David** | **275.00** |
| **8173665257** | **Exploring the JDS Linux Desktop (B/CD-ROM), *418 Pages*** | **Adelstein** | **400.00** |
| **8173667470** | **Flash Hacks: 100 Industrial Strength Tips & Tools, *504 Pages*** | **Bhangal** | **400.00** |
| 8173667314 | Flash Remoting MX: The Definitive Guide, *652 Pages* | Muck | 550.00 |
| **8173668590** | **Flash Out of the Box: A User-Centric Beginner's Guide to Flash (B / CD-ROM), *264 Pages*** | **Hoekman** | **300.00** |
| 0596002874 | Free As In Freedom: Richard Stallman's Crusade for Free Software, *243 Pages* | Williams | 750.00 |

| ISBN | Title | Author | Price |
|---|---|---|---|
| 817366708X | Google Hacks: 100 Industrial Strenght Tips & Tricks, *358 Pages* | Calishain | 300.00 |
| 8173667136 | Google Pocket Guide, *144 Pages* | Calishain | 125.00 |
| **8173669325** | **Google: The Missing Manual, *312 Pages*** | **Milstein** | **325.00** |
| 0596006624 | **Hackers & Painters: Big Ideas from the Computer Age, *272 Pages*** | Graham | 700.00 |
| 8173668256 | **Hardcore Java, *354 Pages*** | **Simmons** | **300.00** |
| 8173663424 | Hardening Cisco Routers, *196 Pages* | Akin | 150.00 |
| **8173668213** | **Hardware Hacking Projects for Geeks, *358 Pages*** | **Fullam** | **350.00** |
| **8173664668** | **Head First Design Patterns, *688 Pages*** | **Sierra** | **500.00** |
| 8173665265 | Head First EJB: Passing the Sun Certified Business Component Developer Exam, *744 Pages* | Sierra | 450.00 |
| **8173666024** | **Head First Java (Covers Java 5.0) 2/ed, *730 Pages*** | **Sierra** | **450.00** |
| **817366403X** | **Head First Servlets & JSP: Passing the Sun Certified Web Component Developer Exam, *666 Pages*** | **Sierra** | **600.00** |
| **8173669341** | **Hibernate: A Developer's Notebook, *190 Pages*** | **Elliott** | **200.00** |
| **8173669260** | **High Performance Linux Cluster with OSCAR, Rocks, OpenMosix, and MPI, *380 Pages*** | **Sloan** | **350.00** |
| **8173669023** | **High Performance MySQL, *304 Pages*** | **Zawodny** | **300.00** |
| 8173665141 | HTML & XHTML: The Definitive Guide, 5/ed, *676 Pages* | Musciano | 500.00 |
| 8173664323 | HTML Pocket Reference, 2/ed, *100 Pages* | Niederst | 70.00 |
| **8173663165** | **Home Hacking Projects for Geeks, *346 Pages*** | **Faulkner** | **325.00** |
| **8173669449** | **Home Networking Annoyances: How to Fix the Most Annoying Things About Your Home Network, *234 Pages*** | **Ivens** | **250.00** |
| 0596008597 | **Illustrations with Photoshop: A Designer's Notebook, *96 Pages*** | Rodarmor | 775.00 |
| 8173665109 | Information Architecture for the World Wide Web, 2/ed, *492 Pages* | Rosenfeld | 400.00 |
| **8173669414** | **Internet Annoyances: How to Fix the Most Annoying Things about Going Online, *266 Pages*** | **Gralla** | **250.00** |
| 8173661057 | Internet Core Protocols: The Definitive Guide (**B / CD-ROM**), *476 Pages* | Hall | 375.00 |
| 8173660158 | Internet in a Nutshell, *456 Pages* | Quercia | 215.00 |
| 8173663378 | IP Routing, *244 Pages* | Malhotra | 200.00 |
| 817366448X | IPv6 Essentials, *362 Pages* | Hagen | 300.00 |
| **8173663025** | **IPv6 Network Administration, *316 Pages*** | **Murphy** | **325.00** |
| **8173667489** | **IRC Hack: 100 Industrial-Strength Tips & Tools, *442 Pages*** | **Mutton** | **400.00** |
| 8173667373 | J2EE Design Patterns, *390 Pages* | Crawford | 325.00 |
| 8173663432 | J2ME in a Nutshell: A Desktop Quick Reference, *474 Pages* | Topley | 400.00 |
| **8173669295** | **Jakarta Commons Cookbook, *412 Pages*** | **O'Brien** | **375.00** |
| **8173669481** | **Jakarta Struts Cookbook, *536 Pages*** | **Siggelkow** | **400.00** |
| 8173667144 | Jakarta Struts Pocket Reference, *142 Pages* | Cavaness | 125.00 |
| **8173668477** | **Java 1.5 Tiger: A Developer's Notebook, *210 Pages*** | **McLaughlin** | **175.00** |
| 8173664471 | Java & SOAP, *286 Pages* | Englander | 275.00 |
| 817366367X | Java & XML, 2/ed, *534 Pages* | McLaughlin | 450.00 |
| 8173664498 | Java & XML Data Binding, *224 Pages* | McLaughlin | 225.00 |
| 8173663793 | Java & XSLT, *534 Pages* | Burke | 350.00 |
| 8173669368 | Java Cookbook (Coverage of 1.5), 2/ed, *872 Pages* | Darwin | 600.00 |
| 8173666660 | Java Database Best Practices, *304 Pages* | Eckstein | 275.00 |
| 8173666679 | Java Data Objects, *568 Pages* | Jordan | 350.00 |
| 817366577X | Java Enterprise Best Practices, *296 Pages* | Eckstein | 275.00 |
| 8173664625 | Java Enterprise in a Nutshell: A Desktop Quick Reference, 2/ed, *1,004 Pages* | Farley | 600.00 |
| 8173662843 | Java Examples in a Nutshell 2/ed, *592 Pages* | Flanagan | 225.00 |
| **8173668639** | **Java Examples in a Nutshell: A Tutorial Companion to Java in a Nutshell, 3/ed, *728 Pages*** | **Flanagan** | **400.00** |
| 8173666687 | Java Extreme Programming Cookbook, *296 Pages* | Burke | 225.00 |
| 817366434X | Java in a Nutshell: A Desktop Quick Reference, 4/ed, *1,000 Pages* | Flanagan | 600.00 |

| ISBN | Title | Author | Price |
|------|-------|--------|-------|
| 8173664404 | Java Management Extensions, *318 Pages* | Perry | 275.00 |
| 8173663211 | Java Message Service, *300 Pages* | Monson-Haefel | 225.00 |
| 817366353X | **Java Network Programming, 3/ed, 770 Pages** | **Haroid** | **500.00** |
| 8173665117 | Java NIO, *308 Pages* | Hitchens | 275.00 |
| 8173665788 | Java Performance Tuning, 2/ed, *600 Pages* | Shirazi | 450.00 |
| 8173663904 | Java Programming with Oracle JDBC, *504 Pages* | Bales | 300.00 |
| 8173663815 | Java RMI, *578 Pages* | Grosso | 400.00 |
| 8173664129 | Java Security, 2/ed, *624 Pages* | Oaks | 500.00 |
| **8173668221** | **Java Servlet & JSP Cookbook, 756 Pages** | **Perry** | **500.00** |
| 8173662851 | Java Servlet Programming 2/ed, *786 Pages* | Hunter | 500.00 |
| 8173665680 | Java Swing, 2/ed, *1,288 Pages* | Loy | 750.00 |
| 8173665923 | Java Threads (Covers J2SE 5.0), 3/ed, *368 Pages* | Oaks | 300.00 |
| 8173663440 | Java Web Services, *286 Pages* | Chappell | 250.00 |
| 8173666695 | Java Web Services in a Nutshell: A Desktop Quick Reference (Covers J2EE 1.4 & JWSDP), *696 Pages* | Topley | 500.00 |
| 8173666709 | JavaScript and DHTML Cookbook, *546 Pages* | Goodman | 475.00 |
| 8173663823 | JavaScript: The Definitive Guide (Covers JavaScript 1.5), 4/ed, *942 Pages* | Flanagan | 750.00 |
| **8173669031** | **JavaServer Faces, 614 Pages** | **Bergsten** | **450.00** |
| **8173665303** | **JavaServer Pages (Covers JSP 2.0 & JSTL 1.1), 3/ed, 762 Pages** | **Bergsten** | **500.00** |
| 8173663831 | JavaServer Pages Pocket Reference, *96 Pages* | Bergsten | 65.00 |
| 8173666717 | JDBC Pocket Reference, *160 Pages* | Bales | 100.00 |
| **8173668604** | **JUnit Pocket Guide, 100 Pages** | **Beck** | **100.00** |
| 059600768X | Just A Geek, *296 Pages* | Wheaton | 700.00 |
| 817366515X | JXTA in a Nutshell: A Desktop Quick Reference, *422 Pages* | Oaks | 225.00 |
| 8173665605 | Kerberos: The Definitive Guide, *280 Pages* | Garman | 275.00 |
| 8173666725 | LDAP System Administration, *318 Pages* | Carter | 300.00 |
| 8173665168 | Learning C#, *374 Pages* | Liberty | 325.00 |
| **8173669635** | **Learning GNU Emacs, 3/ed, 544 Pages** | **Cameron** | **450.00** |
| 8173663912 | Learning Oracle PL/SQL (Covers Oracle9i), *452 Pages* | Pribyl | 325.00 |
| 8173663718 | Learning Perl, 3/ed, *344 Pages* | Schwartz | 275.00 |
| **8173667322** | **Learning PHP 5, 378 Pages** | **Sklar** | **350.00** |
| 8173667381 | Learning Python (Covers Python 2.3), 2/ed, *630 Pages* | Lutz | 525.00 |
| **8173668051** | **Learning the Bash Shell, 3/ed, 362 Pages** | **Newham** | **350.00** |
| 8173664447 | Learning the Korn Shell, 2/ed, *438 Pages* | Rosenblett | 325.00 |
| 8173664234 | Learning the UNIX Operating System, 5/ed, *174 Pages* | Peek | 125.00 |
| 8173660611 | Learning the vi Editor 6/ed, *352 Pages* | Lamb | 250.00 |
| 8173666741 | Learning UML, *304 Pages* | Si Alhir | 150.00 |
| 817366563X | Learning Visual Basic .NET, *326 Pages* | Liberty | 250.00 |
| **8173669422** | **Learning Windows Server 2003, 682 Pages** | **Hassell** | **525.00** |
| 817366062X | lex & yacc 2/ed, *392 Pages* | Levine | 225.00 |
| **8173668442** | **Linux Cookbook, 590 Pages** | **Schroder** | **450.00** |
| **8173668493** | **Linux Device Drivers (Covers Version 2.6.10 Linux Kernel), 3/ed, 646 Pages** | **Rubini** | **450.00** |
| 8173667179 | Linux in a Nutshell, 4/ed, *994 Pages* | Siever | 500.00 |
| **8173669457** | **Linux in a Windows World, 504 Pages** | **Smith** | **450.00** |
| **8173668507** | **Linux iptables Pocket Reference, 106 Pages** | **Purdy** | **100.00** |
| 8173664544 | Linux Network Administrator's Guide, 3/ed, *372 Pages* | Kirch | 350.00 |
| 8173668647 | Linux Pocket Guide, *212 Pages* | Barrett | 150.00 |
| 8173667187 | Linux Security Cookbook, *340 Pages* | Barrett | 325.00 |
| 817366675X | Linux Server Hacks: 100 Industrial - Strength Tips & Tools, *240 Pages* | Flickenger | 225.00 |
| 8173668434 | Linux Unwired, *322 Pages* | Weeks | 300.00 |
| 817366465X | Managing & Using MySQL, 2/ed, *448 Pages* | Reese | 325.00 |

| ISBN | Title | Author | Price |
| --- | --- | --- | --- |
| 8173662746 | Managing IMAP, *412 Pages* | Mullet | 200.00 |
| 8173660271 | Managing IP Networks with Cisco Routers, *352 Pages* | Ballew | 200.00 |
| 8173663610 | Managing NFS & NIS, 2/ed, *518 Pages* | Stern | 400.00 |
| **8173669589** | **Managing Projects with GNU Make, 3/ed, *310 Pages*** | **Mecklenburg** | **300.00** |
| 8173665230 | Managing RAID on Linux, *268 Pages* | Vadala | 275.00 |
| **8173668655** | **Managing Security with Snort & IDS Tools, *296 Pages*** | **Cox Ph.D.** | **300.00** |
| 8173662800 | Managing the Windows 2000 Registry, *564 Pages* | Robicheaux | 325.00 |
| 8173661162 | Mastering Algorithms with C **(B / DISK)**, *572 Pages* | Loudon | 400.00 |
| **8173664455** | **Mastering FreeBSD and OpenBSD Security, *472 Pages*** | **Korff** | **425.00** |
| 8173664366 | Mastering Oracle SQL, (Cover Oracle9i), *348 Pages* | Mishra | 225.00 |
| **8173664617** | **Mastering Oracle SQL (Covers Oracle Database10g), 2/ed, *504 Pages*** | **Mishra** | **400.00** |
| 8173666768 | Mastering Perl for Bioinformatics, *406 Pages* | Tisdall | 300.00 |
| 8173665087 | Mastering Regular Expressions, 2/ed, *492 Pages* | Friedl | 400.00 |
| 8173665702 | Mastering Visual Studio .NET 2003, *420 Pages* | Flanders | 375.00 |
| **8173667497** | **Mono: A Developer's Notebook, *312 Pages*** | **Dumbill** | **325.00** |
| 8173665648 | MySQL Cookbook (Covers MySQL 4.0), *1,028 Pages* | DuBois | 750.00 |
| 8173666776 | MySQL Pocket Reference, *94 Pages* | Reese | 100.00 |
| 8173665249 | NetBeans: The Definitive Guide, *662 Pages* | Boudreau | 500.00 |
| **8173668809** | **Network Security Assessment, *398 Pages*** | **McNab** | **400.00** |
| **8173668396** | **Network Security Tools: Writing, Hacking, and Modifying Security Tools , *350 Pages*** | **Dhanjani** | **350.00** |
| 8173663521 | **Networking Security Hacks: 100 Industrial-Strength Tips & Tools, *328 Pages*** | **Lockhart** | **325.00** |
| 8173663688 | Network Troubleshooting Tools, *370 Pages* | Sloan | 250.00 |
| **8173667845** | **NUnit Pocket Reference, *100 Pages*** | **Hamilton** | **100.00** |
| 8173665613 | Object-Oriented Programming with Visual Basic .NET, *306 Pages* | Hamilton | 225.00 |
| **8173668264** | **Office 2003 XML, *596 Pages*** | **Lenz** | **450.00** |
| **8173667519** | **OpenOffice.org Writer (B / CD-ROM), *234 Pages*** | **Weber** | **250.00** |
| 8173667403 | Optimizing Oracle Performance, *426 Pages* | Milsap | 375.00 |
| **8173669287** | **Oracle Applications Server 10g Essentials, *292 Pages*** | **Greenwald** | **275.00** |
| 8173661170 | Oracle Built-in Packages **(B / DISK)**, *956 Pages* | Feuerstein | 475.00 |
| 8173667071 | Oracle Data Dictionary Pocket Reference, *150 Pages* | Kreines | 125.00 |
| 8173660670 | Oracle Database Administration: The Essential Reference, *552 Pages* | Kreines | 325.00 |
| 817366417X | Oracle DBA Checklist Pocket Reference, *88 Pages* | RevealNet | 65.00 |
| 8173660689 | Oracle Distributed Systems **(B / DISK)**, *552 Pages* | Dye | 325.00 |
| 8173664110 | Oracle Essentials: Oracle9i, Oracle8i & Oracle8, 2/ed, *382 Pages* | Greenwald | 250.00 |
| 817366935X | Oracle Essentials: Oracle Database 10g, 3/ed, *368 Pages* | Greenwald | 275.00 |
| 817366580X | Oracle in a Nutshell: A Desktop Quick Reference, *934 Pages* | Greenwald | 600.00 |
| **8173664560** | **Oracle Initialization Parameters Pocket Reference (Oracle Database 10g), *128 Pages*** | **Kreines** | **125.00** |
| 8173663246 | Oracle Net8 Configuration & Troubleshooting, *412 Pages* | Toledo | 250.00 |
| 8173663629 | Oracle PL/SQL Best Practices, *208 Pages* | Feuerstein | 175.00 |
| 8173661189 | Oracle PL/SQL Built-ins Pocket Reference, *78 Pages* | Feuerstein | 60.00 |
| 8173665176 | Oracle PL/SQL Programming, 3/ed, *1,024 Pages* | Feuerstein | 600.00 |
| 8173662401 | Oracle PL/SQL Programming: A Developer's Workbook, *576 Pages* | Feuerstein | 300.00 |
| 8173661197 | Oracle PL/SQL Programming: Guide to Oracle8i Features **(B / DISK)**, *264 Pages* | Feuerstein | 235.00 |
| 8173668116 | Oracle Regular Expression Pocket Reference, *74 Pages* | Burcham | 75.00 |
| 8173661200 | Oracle SAP Administration, *208 Pages* | Burleson | 175.00 |
| 8173660298 | Oracle Scripts **(B / CD-ROM)**, *208 Pages* | Lomansky | 250.00 |
| 8173660719 | Oracle Security, *448 Pages* | Theriault | 220.00 |
| 8173663637 | Oracle SQL* Loader: The Definitive Guide, *278 Pages* | Gennick | 175.00 |
| **8173669333** | **Oracle SQL*Plus Pocket Reference, 3/ed, *160 Pages*** | **Gennick** | **125.00** |

| ISBN | Title | Author | Price |
|---|---|---|---|
| 8173666067 | **Oracle SQL*Plus: The Definitive Guide, 2/ed, *592 Pages*** | **Gennick** | **400.00** |
| 8173662916 | Oracle SQL: The Essential Reference, *424 Pages* | Kreines | 200.00 |
| 8173661847 | **Oracle Utilities Pocket Reference, *136 Pages*** | **Mishra** | **100.00** |
| 8173661219 | Oracle Web Applications: PL/SQL Developer's Intro, *264 Pages* | Odewahn | 180.00 |
| 817366028X | Oracle8 Design Tips, *136 Pages* | Ensor | 120.00 |
| 8173668027 | PC Annoyances: How to Fix the Most Annoying | | |
| | Thingsabout your Personal Computer, *236 Pages* | Bass | 225.00 |
| 8173667152 | **PC Hacks: 100 Industrial-Strength Tips & Tools, *316 Pages*** | **Aspinwall** | **300.00** |
| 8173669732 | **PC Hardware Annoyances: How to Fix the Most** | | |
| | **ANNOYING Things About Your Computer Hardware, *276 Pages*** | **Bigelow** | **275.00** |
| 817366532X | PC Hardware in a Nutshell: A Desktop Quick | | |
| | Reference, 3/ed, *848 Pages* | Thompson | 325.00 |
| 8173667128 | **PDF Hacks: 100 Industrial-Strength Tips & Tools, *308 Pages*** | **Steward** | **300.00** |
| 8173664463 | Perl & XML, *224 Pages* | Ray | 175.00 |
| 8173661073 | Perl 5 Pocket Reference, 3/ed, *96 Pages* | Vromans | 70.00 |
| 8173667195 | Perl 6 Essentials, *208 Pages* | Randal | 175.00 |
| 8173667330 | Perl Cookbook, 2/ed, *976 Pages* | Christiansen | 675.00 |
| 8173668043 | Perl Template Toolkit, *600 Pages* | Chamberlain | 525.00 |
| 8173665710 | PHP Cookbook, *638 Pages* | Sklar | 550.00 |
| 0596008600 | **Photo Retouching with Photoshop: A Designer's Notebook, *96 Pages*** | **CLEC'H** | **775.00** |
| 817366871X | **Postfix: The Definitive Guide, *288 Pages*** | **Dent** | **275.00** |
| 8173669805 | **Powerpoint 2003 PersonalTrainer** | | |
| | **(B / CD-ROM), (2 Color book) *342 Pages*** | **CustomGuide** | **425.00** |
| 8173660301 | Practical C Programming 3/ed, *456 Pages* | Oualline | 225.00 |
| 8173666822 | Practical C++ Programming, 2/ed, *582 Pages* | Oualline | 225.00 |
| 817366711X | Practical mod_perl, *932 Pages* | Bekman | 675.00 |
| 8173663920 | Practical PostgreSQL **(B / CD-ROM)**, *642 Pages* | Command Prompt Inc. | 450.00 |
| 8173666733 | Practical RDF, *360 Pages* | Powers | 325.00 |
| 8173666830 | Practical Unix & Internet Security, 3/ed, *994 Pages* | Garfinkel | 650.00 |
| 8173664390 | Practical VoIP Using VOCAL, *532 Pages* | Dang | 450.00 |
| 8173665818 | Programming  .NET 1.1 Components, *488 Pages* | Lowy | 375.00 |
| 8173667209 | Programming  .NET Security, *704 Pages* | Freeman | 550.00 |
| 8173667411 | Programming  .NET Windows Applications | | |
| | (Covers .NET 1.1, & Visual Studio .NET 2003), *1316 Pages* | Liberty | 750.00 |
| 8173664382 | Programming  .NET Web Services, *500 Pages* | Ferrara | 375.00 |
| 817366742X | Programming ASP .NET (Covers .NET 1.1, & | | |
| | Visual Studio .NET 2003), 2/ed, *1026 Pages* | Liberty | 675.00 |
| 8173669651 | **Programming C# (Covers C# 2.0, .NET 2.0 &** | | |
| | **Visual Studio 2005), 4/ed, *680 Pages*** | **Liberty** | **525.00** |
| 817366076X | Programming Embedded Systems in C & C++, *198 Pages* | Barr | 150.00 |
| 8173669694 | **Programming Flash Communication Server, *842 Pages*** | **Lesser** | **600.00** |
| 8173661278 | Programming Internet E-mail, *384 Pages* | Wood | 225.00 |
| 8173668183 | **Programming Jakarta Struts 2/ed, *470 Pages*** | **Cavaness** | **400.00** |
| 8173662657 | Programming Perl 3/ed, *1,116 Pages* | Wall | 675.00 |
| 8173663114 | Programming PHP, *530 Pages* | Lerdorf | 350.00 |
| 8173667500 | **Programming Python (Covers Python 2)** | | |
| | **(B / CD-ROM), 2/ed, *1,305 Pages*** | **Lutzf** | **750.00** |
| 8173662371 | Programming the Perl DBI, *372 Pages* | Descartes | 200.00 |
| 8173667063 | Programming Visual Basic  .NET 2003, 2/ed, *564 Pages* | Liberty | 425.00 |
| 8173665737 | Programming Web Services with Perl, *492 Pages* | Ray | 400.00 |
| 8173662045 | Programming Web Services with SOAP, *268 Pages* | Snell | 200.00 |
| 817366207X | Programming Web Services with XML-RPC, *240 Pages* | St.Laurent | 175.00 |
| 8173668175 | Programming with QT (Covers Qt 3), 2/ed, *532 Pages* | Dalheimer | 450.00 |

| ISBN | Title | Author | Price |
|---|---|---|---|
| 817366479X | Python Cookbook (Covers Python 2.3 & 2.4), 2/ed, 852 Pages | Martelli | 600.00 |
| 8173669708 | Python Pocket Reference (Covers Python 2.4), 3/ed, 168 Pages | Lutz | 125.00 |
| 8173666857 | Python in a Nutshell: A Desktop Quick Reference (Cover Python 2.2), 662 Pages | Martelli | 500.00 |
| 8173668485 | qmail, 268 Pages | Levine | 275.00 |
| 817366689X | Real World Web Services, 230 Pages | Iverson | 225.00 |
| 8173667276 | Regular Expression Pocket Reference, 112 Pages | Stubblebine | 100.00 |
| 0596007191 | Revolution in the Valley, 324 Pages | Hertzfeld | 775.00 |
| 8173665206 | Running Linux, 4/ed, 702 Pages | Welsh | 425.00 |
| 8173667055 | Samba Pocket Reference, 2/ed, 146 Pages | Eckstein | 125.00 |
| 8173664226 | SAX2 (Simple API for XML), 248 Pages | Brownell | 175.00 |
| 8173667217 | Secure Coding: Principles & Practices, 200 Pages | Graff | 225.00 |
| 8173667284 | Secure Programming Cookbook for C and C++, 800 Pages | Viega | 600.00 |
| 817366840X | Security Warrior, 562 Pages | Peikari | 500.00 |
| 8173663262 | Securing Windows NT/2000 Servers for the Internet, 200 Pages | Norberg | 125.00 |
| 8173669376 | Securing Windows Server 2003, 456 Pages | Danseglio | 400.00 |
| 8173660786 | sed & awk, 2/ed, 440 Pages | Dougherty | 300.00 |
| 817366918X | SELINUX NSA's Open Source Security Enhanced Linux, 264 Pages | McCarty | 275.00 |
| 8173665834 | sendmail, 3/ed, 1,238 Pages | Costales | 850.00 |
| 817366823X | sendmail Cookbook, 418 Pages | Hunt | 400.00 |
| 8173666865 | Sequence Analysis in a Nutshell: A Guide to Common Tools and Databases (Covers EMBOSS 2.5.0), 310 Pages | Markel | 275.00 |
| 8173664161 | Server Load Balancing, 198 Pages | Bourke | 150.00 |
| 817366739X | SharePoint User's Guide, 158 Pages | IDC | 150.00 |
| 8173669503 | Snort Cookbook, 296 Pages | Orebaugh | 300.00 |
| 8173663866 | Solaris 8 Administrator's Guide, 308 Pages | Watters | 225.00 |
| 8173669198 | SpamAssassin (Covers 3.0), 232 Pages | Schwartz | 250.00 |
| 8173668191 | Spidering Hacks: 100 Industrial - Strength Tips & Tools, 436 Pages | Hemenway | 350.00 |
| 817366837X | Spring: A Developer's Notebook, 202 Pages | Tate | 200.00 |
| 8173666520 | SQL in a Nutshell (Covers SQL Server, DB2, MySQL, Oracle & PostgreSQL), 2/ed, 720 Pages | Kline | 450.00 |
| 8173667438 | SQL Pocket Reference (Cover Oracle. DB2, SQL Server & MySQL), 170 Pages | Gennick | 125.00 |
| 8173668248 | SQL Tunning (Covers Oracle, DB2 & SQL Server), 356 Pages | Tow | 325.00 |
| 8173668418 | Squid: The Definitive Guide, 472 Pages | Wessels | 450.00 |
| 8173662924 | SSH: The Secure Shell: The Definitive Guide, 564 Pages | Barrett | 325.00 |
| 8173668574 | STL Pocket Reference, 136 Pages | Lischner | 100.00 |
| 8173669511 | SWT: A Developer's Notebook, 330 Pages | Hatton | 325.00 |
| 8173663254 | T1: A Survival Guide, 312 Pages | Gast | 225.00 |
| 817366093X | Tcl/Tk in a Nutshell: A Desktop Quick Reference, 480 Pages | Raines | 240.00 |
| 8173664676 | TCP/IP Network Administration 3/ed, 756 Pages | Hunt | 500.00 |
| 8173666873 | Tomcat: The Definitive Guide (Cover Tomcat 4), 336 Pages | Brittain | 300.00 |
| 8173660352 | UML in a Nutshell: A Desktop Quick Reference, 336 Pages | Alhir | 225.00 |
| 8173667225 | UML Pocket Reference, 96 Pages | Pilone | 100.00 |
| 8173665893 | Understanding the Linux Kernel, 2/ed, 832 Pages | Bovet | 500.00 |
| 817366627X | Unit Test Frameworks (B / CD-ROM), 222 Pages | Hamill | 225.00 |
| 8173661324 | UNIX in a Nutshell: A Desktop Quick Reference for SVR4 & Solaris 7, 3/ed, 628 Pages | Robbins | 325.00 |
| 8173665656 | Unix Power Tools, 3/ed, 1,162 Pages | Powers | 750.00 |
| 8173666202 | Upgrading to PHP 5 (Covers MySQL 4.1), 358 Pages | Trachtenberg | 350.00 |
| 8173660948 | Using & Managing PPP, 464 Pages | Sun | 240.00 |
| 8173665842 | Using Samba, 2/ed, 570 Pages | Eckstein | 500.00 |
| 8173664374 | VB .NET Core Classes in a Nutshell: A Desktop Quick Reference (B / CD-ROM), 584 Pages | Kurniawan | 500.00 |

| ISBN | Title | Author | Price |
|------|-------|--------|-------|
| 817366594X | VB .NET Language Pocket Reference, *160 Pages* | Roman | 125.00 |
| 8173666881 | VBScript in a Nutshell: A Desktop Quick Reference, 2/e, *528 Pages* | Lomax | 400.00 |
| 8173663300 | VBScript Pocket Reference, *118 Pages* | Childs | 60.00 |
| **8173668582** | **Version Control With Subversion, *332 Pages*** | **Collins - Sussman** | **350.00** |
| 8173662622 | Vi Editor Pocket Reference, *76 Pages* | Robbins | 60.00 |
| 8173661340 | Virtual Private Networks, 2/ed, *228 Pages* | Scott | 150.00 |
| **8173666164** | **Visual Basic 2005: A Developer's Notebook, *272 Pages*** | **MacDonald** | **250.00** |
| **8173669740** | **Visual C# 2005: A Developer's Notebook, *250 Pages*** | **Liberty** | **225.00** |
| 8173660964 | Visual Basic Controls in a Nutshell, *512 Pages* | Dictor | 310.00 |
| **817366501X** | **Visual Studio Hacks: Tips & Tools for Turbocharging the IDE, *304 Pages*** | **Avery** | **375.00** |
| 8173668094 | Volume One: Xlib Programming Manual (Version 11), *824 Pages* | Nye | 575.00 |
| 8173668108 | Volume Two: Xlib Reference Manual (Version 11), 3/ed, *948 Pages* | Nye | 600.00 |
| 8173668086 | Volume Zero: X Protocol Reference Manual (Version X11), *468 Pages* | Nye | 350.00 |
| 8173668310 | X Windows Reference Manaul (3 Volume Set) | Nye | 1,350.00 |
| **0596007337** | **We the Media: Grassroots Journalism by the People,for the People, *320 Pages*** | **Gillmor** | **775.00** |
| **8173663092** | **WebLogic 8.1: The Definitive Guide, *860 Pages*** | **Mountjoy** | **600.00** |
| **8173669058** | **Web Database Application with PHP & MySQL (Covers PEAR, PHP 5 & MySQL 4.1), 2/ed, *828 Pages*** | **Williams** | **600.00** |
| 8173663750 | Web Design in a Nutshell: A Desktop Quick Reference, 2/ed, *656 Pages* | Niederst | 425.00 |
| 8173664412 | Web Performance Tuning, 2/ed, *488 Pages* | Killelea | 350.00 |
| 8173665214 | Web Privacy with P3P, *350 Pages* | Cranor | 300.00 |
| 8173663947 | Web Security, Privacy & Commerce, 2/ed, *768 Pages* | Garfinkel | 500.00 |
| 8173663394 | Web Services Essentials, *320 Pages* | Cerami | 200.00 |
| 8173665931 | WebLogic Server 6.1 Workbook for Enterprise JavaBeans, 3/ed, *264 Pages* | Nyberg | 200.00 |
| 8173661308 | The Whole Internet: The Next Generation, *576 Pages* | Conner/Krol | 425.00 |
| 8173661367 | Win32 API Programming with Visual Basic **(B / CD-ROM)**, *534 Pages* | Roman | 400.00 |
| 8173662789 | Windows 2000 Administration in a Nutshell: A Desktop Quick Reference, *1000 Pages* | Tulloch | 350.00 |
| 8173663319 | Windows 2000 Commands Pocket Reference, *122 Pages* | Frisch | 60.00 |
| 8173660743 | Windows 2000 Quick Fixes, *304 Pages* | Boyce | 225.00 |
| 8173660883 | Windows NT TCP/IP Network Administration, *512 Pages* | Hunt | 250.00 |
| 8173666903 | Windows Server 2003 in a Nutshell: A Desktop Quick Reference, *672 Pages* | Tulloch | 550.00 |
| **8173668833** | **Windows Server Hacks: 100 Industrial-Strength Tips & Tools , *328 Pages*** | **Tulloch** | **325.00** |
| 8173667454 | Windows XP Hacks: 100 Industrial-Strength Tips & Tools, *294 Pages* | Gralla | 350.00 |
| 8173663564 | Windows XP in a Nutshell: A Desktop Quick Reference, *640 Pages* | Karp | 375.00 |
| **8173669643** | **Windows XP Personal Trainer (B / CD-ROM), *480 Pages*** | **CustomGuide** | **550.00** |
| 8173666911 | Windows XP Pocket Reference, *196 Pages* | Karp | 125.00 |
| 8173665915 | Windows XP Unwired: A Guide for Home, Office, and the Road, *316 Pages* | Lee | 275.00 |
| 8173667462 | Wireless Hacks: 100 Industrial-Strength Tips & Tools, *424 Pages* | Flickenger | 275.00 |
| 8173662770 | Word 2000 in a Nutshell: A Power User's Quick Reference, *516 Pages* | Glenn | 225.00 |
| 817366692X | Word Pocket Guide, *160 Pages* | Glenn | 125.00 |
| 8173665354 | Writing Excel Macros with VBA, 2/ed, *580 Pages* | Roman | 450.00 |
| 8173660778 | Writing Word Macros, *416 Pages* | Roman | 275.00 |
| **8173668450** | **XML in a Nutshell (Covers XML 1.1 & XInclude), 3/ed, *724 Pages*** | **Harold** | **500.00** |
| **8173666156** | **XML Hacks: 100 Industrial-Strength Tips & Tools, *490 Pages*** | **Fitzgerald** | **425.00** |
| 8173663343 | XML Pocket Reference, 2/ed, *128 Pages* | Eckstein | 100.00 |

### FORTHCOMING TITLES

**July 2005**

| | | | |
|------|-------|--------|-------|
| 8173665729 | .NET Gotchas, *406 Pages* | Subramaniam | 300.00 |
| 8173664587 | ASP .NET 2.0: Developer's Notebook, *358 Pages* | Lee | 325.00 |

| ISBN | Title | Author | Price |
|------|-------|--------|-------|

### October 2005

| ISBN | Title | Author | Price |
|------|-------|--------|-------|
| 8173670315 | Access Annoyances: How to Avoid the Most Annoying Things About Your Favorite Database , *314 Pages* | Mitchell | 325.00 |
| 8173670323 | Access for Rookies: The Missing Manual, *314 Pages* | Palmer | 300.00 |
| 8173670331 | Asterisk: The Future of Telephony, *514 Pages* | Smith | 450.00 |
| 817367034X | Beyond Java, *170 Pages* | Tate | 175.00 |
| 8173670358 | Designing Interfaces, *384 Pages* | Tidwell | 350.00 |
| 8173670366 | Essentail PHP Security, *310 Pages* | Shiflett | 300.00 |
| 8173670374 | Excel for Rookies: The Missing Manual, *314 Pages* | MacDonald | 300.00 |
| 8173670382 | Learning SQL, *410 Pages* | Beaulieu | 350.00 |
| 8173670390 | Linux Desktop Pocket Reference, *154 Pages* | Brickner | 125.00 |
| 8173670404 | Photoshop Retouching Cookbook for Digital Photographers, *176 Pages* | Huggins | 1,400.00 |
| 8173670412 | Prefactoring, *200 Pages* | Pugh | 200.00 |
| 8173670420 | Programming Apache Axis, *410 Pages* | Haddad | 400.00 |
| 8173670439 | Programming Visual Basic 2005, *800 Pages* | Liberty | 500.00 |
| 8173670447 | Visual Basic 2005 Jumpstart Pocket Guide, *164 Pages* | Lee | 125.00 |

### November 2005

| ISBN | Title | Author | Price |
|------|-------|--------|-------|
| 8173670455 | Blackberry Hacks, *256 Pages* | Mabe | 275.00 |
| 8173670463 | Integrating Excel and Access, *514 Pages* | Schmalz | 425.00 |
| 8173670471 | Internet Forensics, *304 Pages* | Jones | 325.00 |
| 817367048X | PHP in a Nutshell, *314 Pages* | Hudson | 300.00 |
| 8173670498 | Photoshop Photo Effects Cookbook, *176 Pages* | Shelbournce | 1,400.00 |
| 8173670501 | Photoshop RAW, *266 Pages* | Aaland | 1,600.00 |
| 817367051X | Powerpoint Annoyances, *266 Pages* | Swinford | 250.00 |
| 8173670528 | Practical Development Environments, *352 Pages* | Doar | 350.00 |
| 8173670536 | Programming Avalon (B / CD - ROM), *410 Pages* | Sells | 400.00 |
| 8173670544 | Producing Free Software, *266 Pages* | Fogel | 275.00 |
| 8173670552 | Twisted Network Programming Essentials, *210 Pages* | Fettig | 225.00 |
| 8173670560 | Yahoo ! Hacks, *362 Pages* | Bausch | 325.00 |

### December 2005

| ISBN | Title | Author | Price |
|------|-------|--------|-------|
| 8173670579 | JBoss at Work: A Practical Guide, *256 Pages* | Marrs | 250.00 |
| 8173670587 | Oracle PL/SQL for DBAs, *466 Pages* | Feuerstein | 425.00 |
| 8173670595 | Programming SQL Server 2005, *362 Pages* | Wildermuth | 325.00 |

### January 2006

| ISBN | Title | Author | Price |
|------|-------|--------|-------|
| 8173670609 | Bonjour: The Definitive Guide, *256 Pages* | Steinberg | 275.00 |
| 8173670617 | C in a Nutshell, *400 Pages* | Prinz | 275.00 |
| 8173670625 | Firewall Warrior, *610 Pages* | Artymiak | 500.00 |
| 8173670633 | JUnit: The Definitive Guide, *310 Pages* | Lane | 300.00 |

- Dates & Prices of forthcoming titles are tentative and subject to change without notice.
- All Prices are in Indian Rupees except where indicated in
  ¤ (Euro Dollar) $ (US Dollar) and £ (Pound)
- TITLES RELEASED AFTER AUGUST 2004 ARE MARKED IN BOLD.